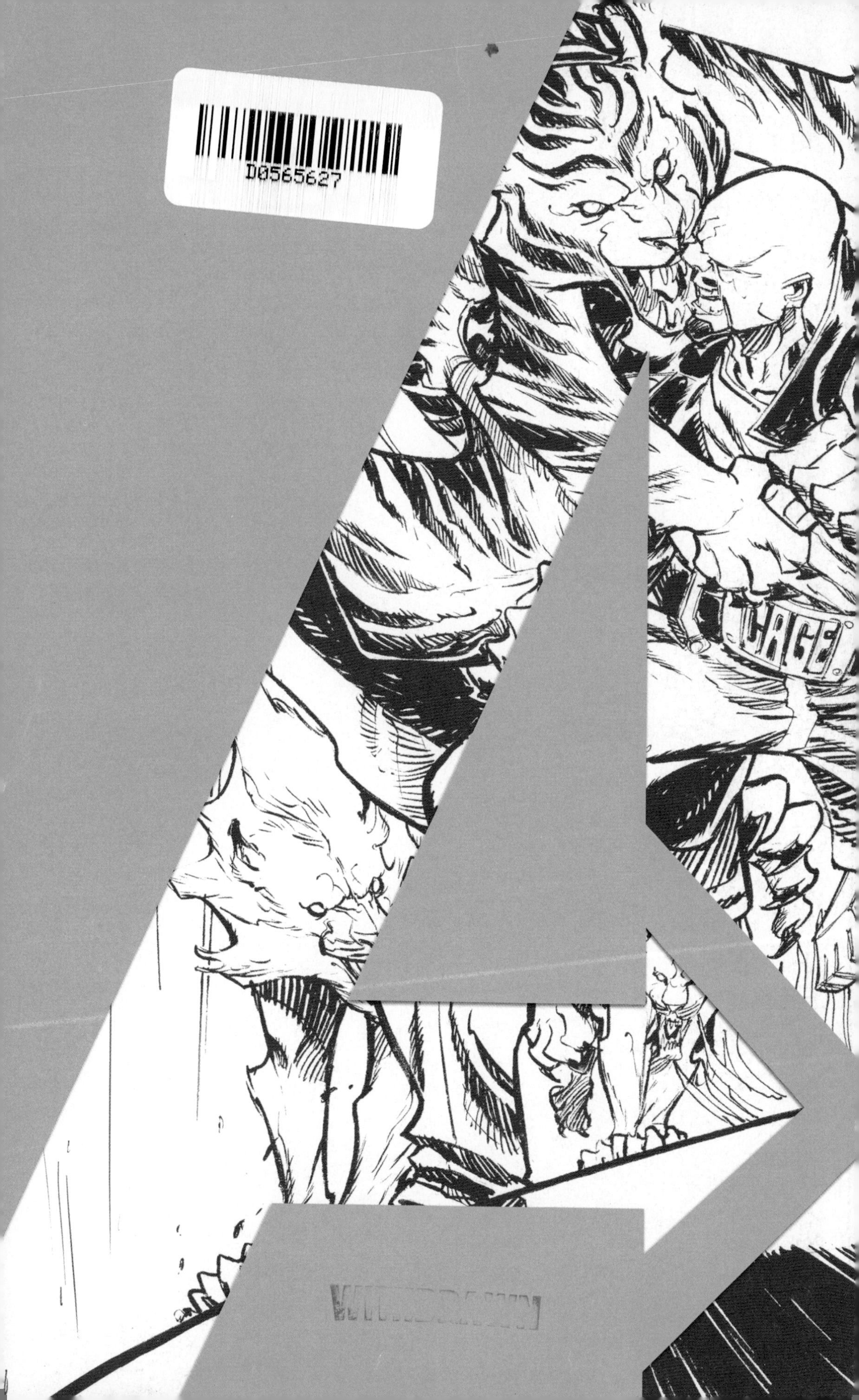

LUKE CAGE:
AVENGER

AVENGERS ORIGINS: LUKE CAGE

ADAM GLASS & MIKE BENSON
WRITERS

DALIBOR TALAJIĆ
ARTIST

JEAN-FRANCOIS BEAULIEU
COLORIST

DAVE LANPHEAR
LETTERER

MARKO DJURDJEVIC
COVER ART

NEW AVENGERS: LUKE CAGE

JOHN ARCUDI
WRITERS

ERIC CANETE WITH **PEPE LARRAZ** [#2-3]
ARTIST

CHRIS CHUCKRY WITH **ANDRES MOSSA** [#2-3]
COLORIST

VC's JOE SABINO
LETTERER

ERIC CANETE
COVER ART

NEW AVENGERS #22 & #49

BRIAN MICHAEL BENDIS
WRITER

LEINIL FRANCIS YU [#22], **BILLY TAN & BATT** [#49]
ARTISTS

DAVE McCAIG [#22], **PAUL MOUNTS** [#49]
COLORIST

RICHARD STARKINGS & COMICRAFT's ALBERT DESCHESNE
LETTERER

LEINIL FRANCIS YU & DAVE McCAIG [#22],
BILLY TAN, BATT & JASON KEITH [#49]
COVER ART

MARVEL TEAM-UP ANNUAL #4

FRANK MILLER
WRITERS

HERB TRIMPE
PENCILER

MICHAEL ESPOSITO
INKER

GEORGE ROUSSOS
COLORIST

DIANA ALBERS
LETTERER

FRANK MILLER & JOSEF RUBINSTEIN
COVER ART

JOHN DENNING, MOLLY LAZER & AUBREY SITTERSON
ASSISTANT EDITORS

JEANINE SCHAEFER
ASSOCIATE EDITOR (*NEW AVENGERS #49*)

LAUREN SANKOVITCH, TOM BRENNAN & TOM DEFALCO
EDITORS

STEPHEN WACKER
SUPERVISING EDITOR (*NEW AVENGERS: LUKE CAGE*)

TOM BREVOORT
EXECUTIVE EDITOR

STUART IMMONEN, WADE VON GRAWBADGER & LAURA MARTIN
FRONT COVER ARTISTS

LEINIL FRANCIS YU & DAVE McCAIG
BACK COVER ARTISTS

MARK D. BEAZLEY
COLLECTION EDITOR

SARAH BRUNSTAD
ASSOCIATE EDITOR

JOE HOCHSTEIN
ASSOCIATE MANAGER, DIGITAL ASSETS

ALEX STARBUCK
ASSOCIATE MANAGING EDITOR

JENNIFER GRÜNWALD
EDITOR, SPECIAL PROJECTS

JEFF YOUNGQUIST
VP, PRODUCTION & SPECIAL PROJECTS

JEPH YORK
RESEARCH & LAYOUT

COLORTEK & JOE FRONTIRRE
PRODUCTION

ADAM DEL RE
BOOK DESIGNER

DAVID GABRIEL
SVP PRINT, SALES & MARKETING

AXEL ALONSO
EDITOR IN CHIEF

JOE QUESADA
CHIEF CREATIVE OFFICER

DAN BUCKLEY
PUBLISHER

ALAN FINE
EXECUTIVE PRODUCER

LUKE CAGE: AVENGER. Contains material originally published in magazine form as AVENGERS ORIGINS: L CAGE, NEW AVENGERS #22 and #49, NEW AVENGERS: LUKE CAGE #1-3, and MARVEL TEAM-UP ANNUAL #4. F printing 2016. ISBN# 978-1-302-90194-3. Published by MARVEL WORLDWIDE, INC., a subsidiary of MAR ENTERTAINMENT, LLC. OFFICE OF PUBLICATION: 135 West 50th Street, New York, NY 10020. Copyright © 2 MARVEL No similarity between any of the names, characters, persons, and/or institutions in this magazine v those of any living or dead person or institution is intended, and any such similarity which may exist is pu coincidental. **Printed in the U.S.A.** ALAN FINE, President, Marvel Entertainment; DAN BUCKLEY, President, Publishing & Brand Management; JOE QUESADA, Chief Creative Officer; TOM BREVOORT, SVP of Publishing; DA BOGART, SVP of Business Affairs & Operations, Publishing & Partnership; C.B. CEBULSKI, VP of Brand Managem & Development, Asia; DAVID GABRIEL, SVP of Sales & Marketing, Publishing; JEFF YOUNGQUIST, VP of Produc & Special Projects; DAN CARR, Executive Director of Publishing Technology; ALEX MORALES, Director of Publish Operations; SUSAN CRESPI, Production Manager; STAN LEE, Chairman Emeritus. For information regard advertising in Marvel Comics or on Marvel.com, please contact Vit DeBellis, Integrated Sales Manager, at vdebell marvel.com. For Marvel subscription inquiries, please call 888-511-5480. **Manufactured between 5/20/2016** 7/4/2016 by R.R. Donnelley, INC., SALEM, VA, USA.

10 9 8 7 6 5 4 3 2 1

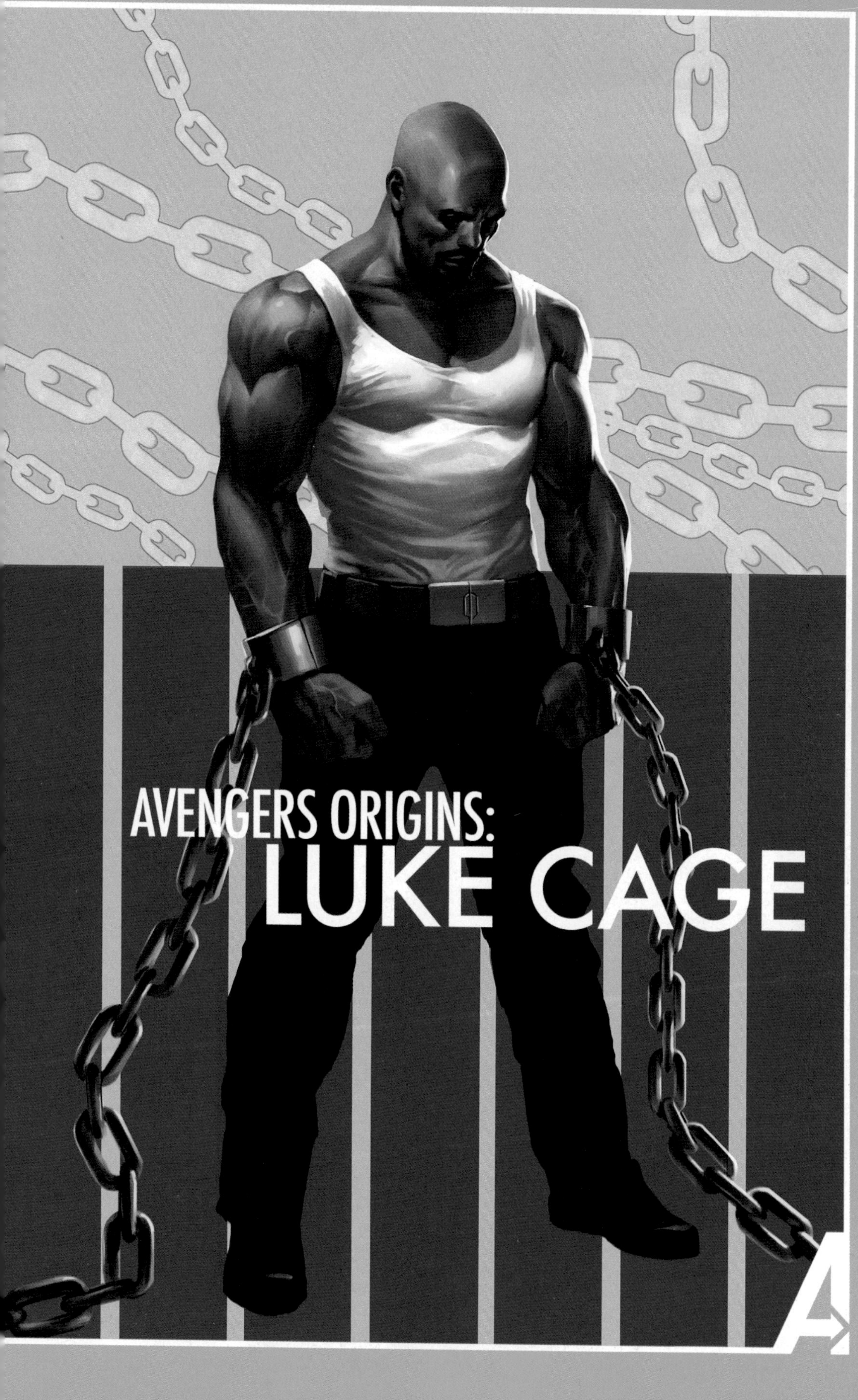
AVENGERS ORIGINS:
LUKE CAGE

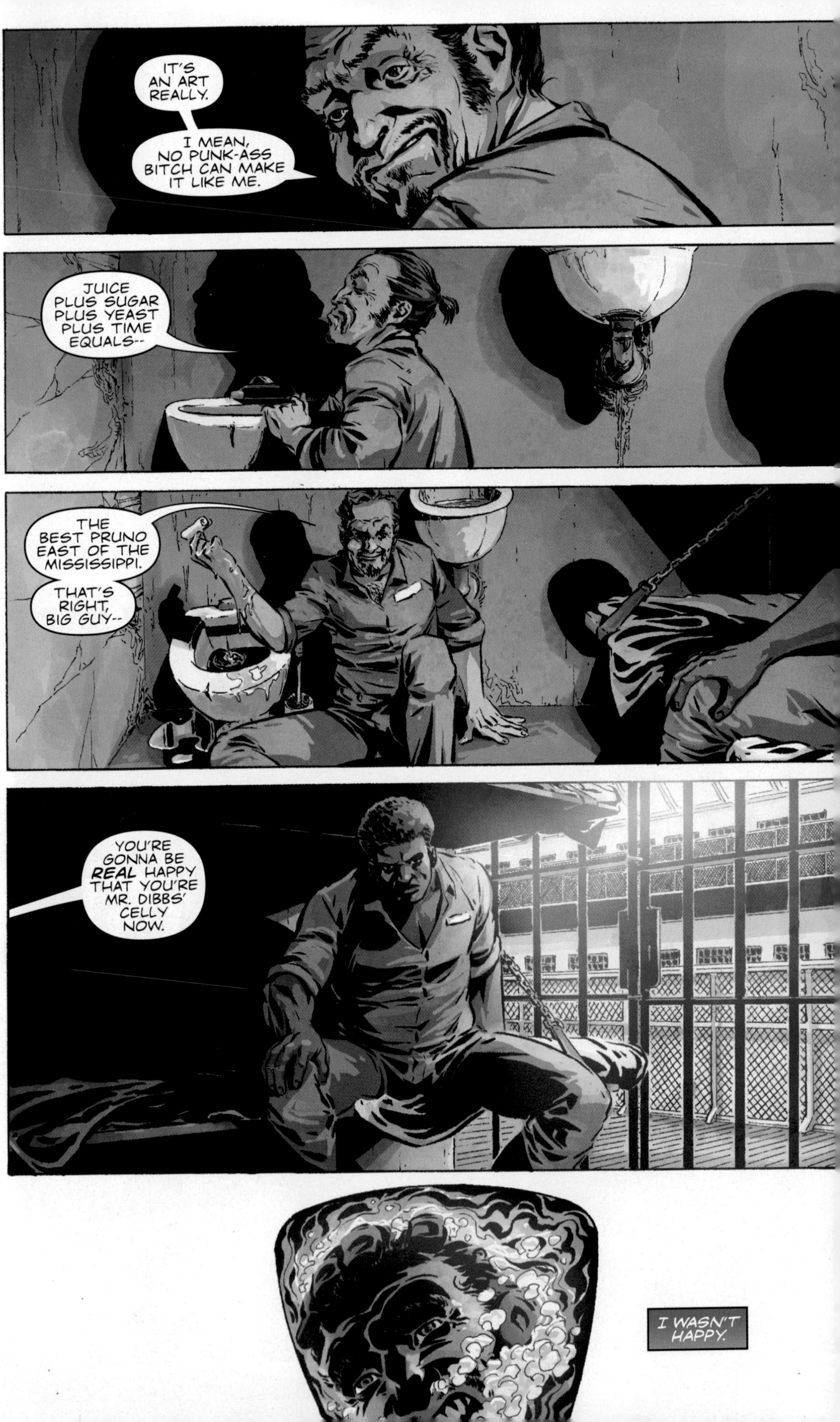
IT'S AN ART REALLY.
I MEAN, NO PUNK-ASS BITCH CAN MAKE IT LIKE ME.
JUICE PLUS SUGAR PLUS YEAST PLUS TIME EQUALS--
THE BEST PRUNO EAST OF THE MISSISSIPPI.
THAT'S RIGHT, BIG GUY--
YOU'RE GONNA BE REAL HAPPY THAT YOU'RE MR. DIBBS' CELLY NOW.
I WASN'T HAPPY.

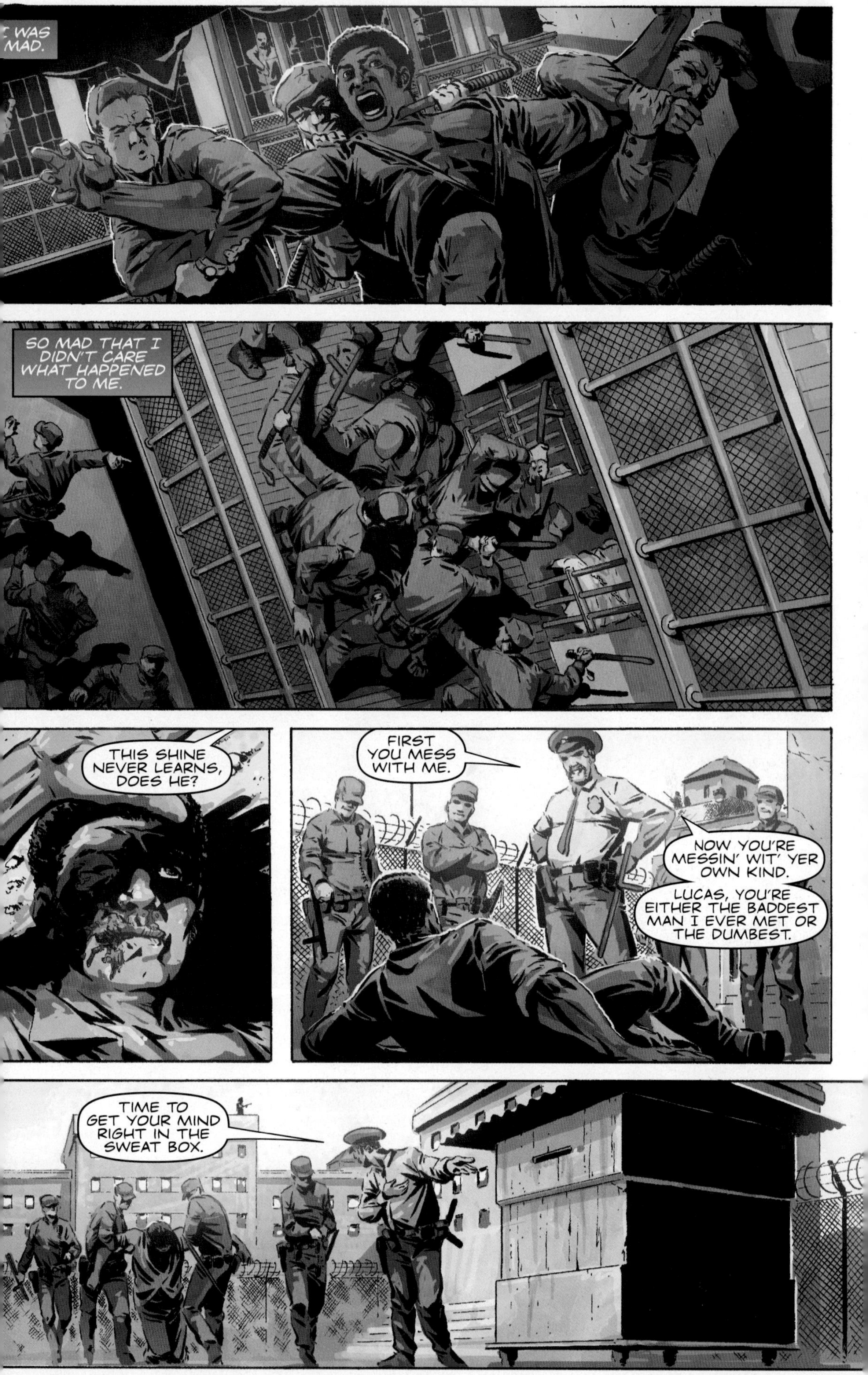

I WAS MAD.
SO MAD THAT I DIDN'T CARE WHAT HAPPENED TO ME.
THIS SHINE NEVER LEARNS, DOES HE?
FIRST YOU MESS WITH ME.
NOW YOU'RE MESSIN' WIT' YER OWN KIND.
LUCAS, YOU'RE EITHER THE BADDEST MAN I EVER MET OR THE DUMBEST.
TIME TO GET YOUR MIND RIGHT IN THE SWEAT BOX.

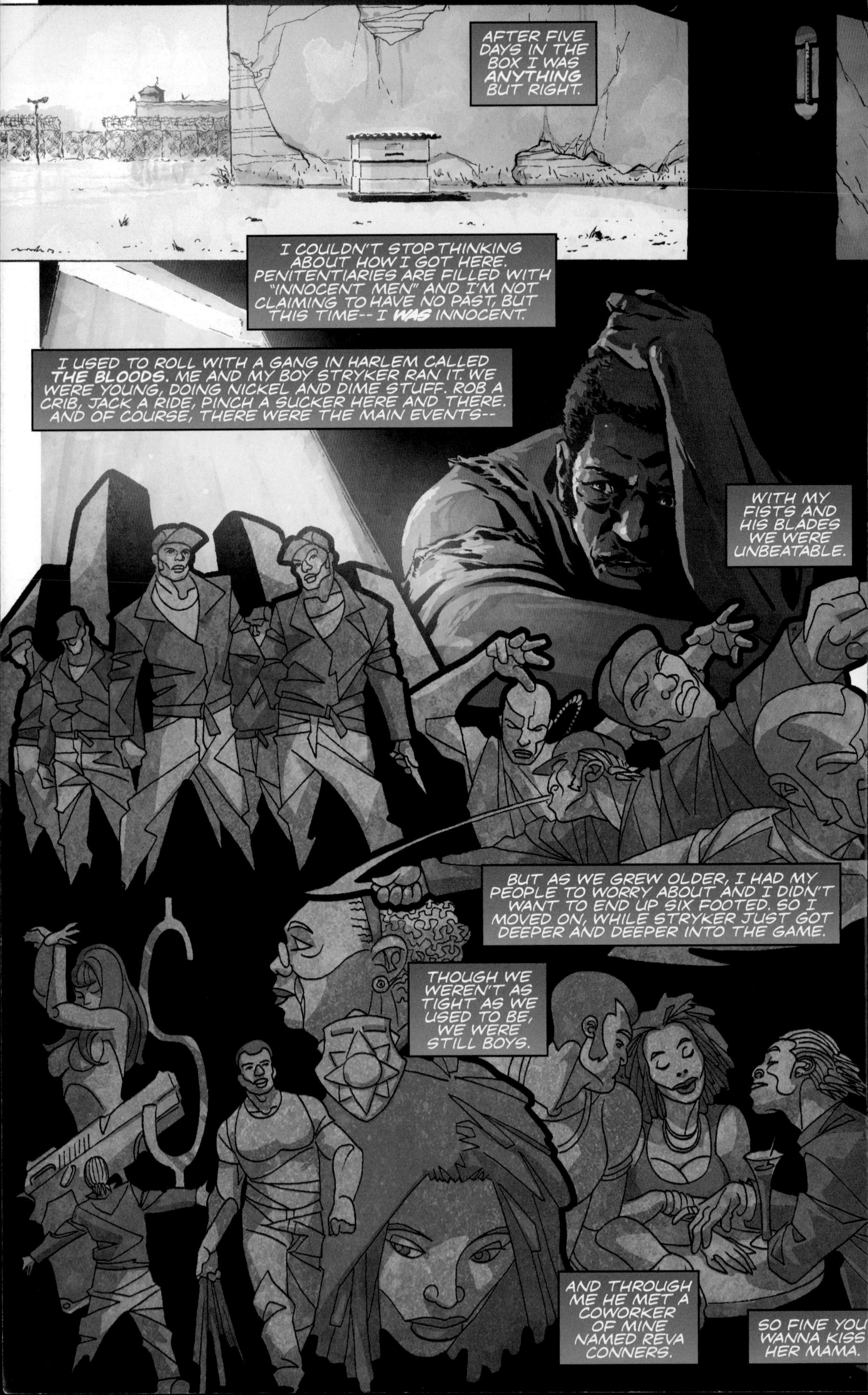
AFTER FIVE DAYS IN THE BOX I WAS ANYTHING BUT RIGHT.
I COULDN'T STOP THINKING ABOUT HOW I GOT HERE. PENITENTIARIES ARE FILLED WITH "INNOCENT MEN" AND I'M NOT CLAIMING TO HAVE NO PAST, BUT THIS TIME-- I WAS INNOCENT.
I USED TO ROLL WITH A GANG IN HARLEM CALLED THE BLOODS. ME AND MY BOY STRYKER RAN IT. WE WERE YOUNG, DOING NICKEL AND DIME STUFF. ROB A CRIB, JACK A RIDE, PINCH A SUCKER HERE AND THERE. AND OF COURSE, THERE WERE THE MAIN EVENTS--
WITH MY FISTS AND HIS BLADES WE WERE UNBEATABLE.
BUT AS WE GREW OLDER, I HAD MY PEOPLE TO WORRY ABOUT AND I DIDN'T WANT TO END UP SIX FOOTED. SO I MOVED ON, WHILE STRYKER JUST GOT DEEPER AND DEEPER INTO THE GAME.
THOUGH WE WEREN'T AS TIGHT AS WE USED TO BE, WE WERE STILL BOYS.
AND THROUGH ME HE MET A COWORKER OF MINE NAMED REVA CONNERS.
SO FINE YOU WANNA KISS HER MAMA.

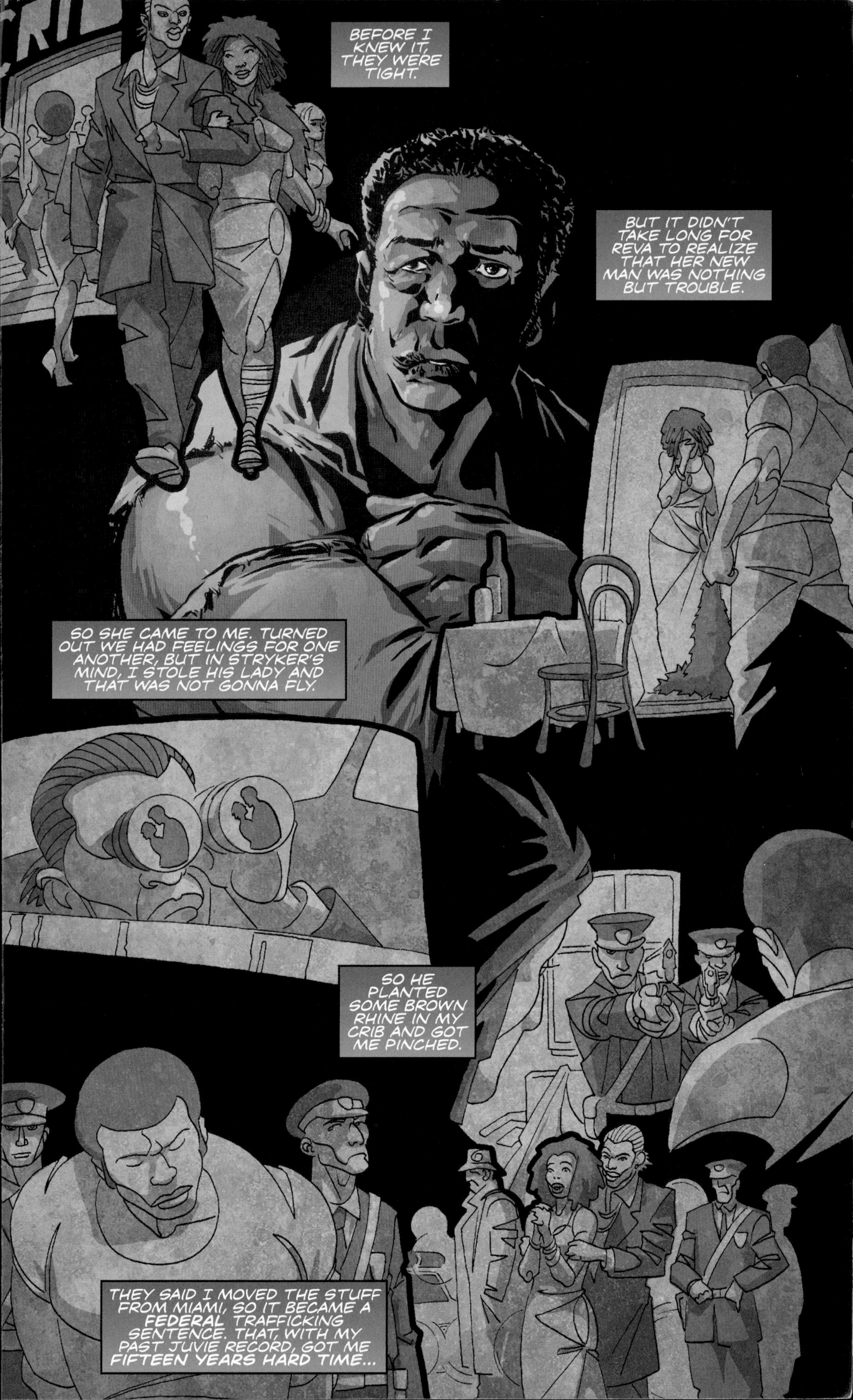
BEFORE I KNEW IT, THEY WERE TIGHT.
BUT IT DIDN'T TAKE LONG FOR REVA TO REALIZE THAT HER NEW MAN WAS NOTHING BUT TROUBLE.
SO SHE CAME TO ME. TURNED OUT WE HAD FEELINGS FOR ONE ANOTHER, BUT IN STRYKER'S MIND, I STOLE HIS LADY AND THAT WAS NOT GONNA FLY.
SO HE PLANTED SOME BROWN RHINE IN MY CRIB AND GOT ME PINCHED.
THEY SAID I MOVED THE STUFF FROM MIAMI, SO IT BECAME A FEDERAL TRAFFICKING SENTENCE. THAT, WITH MY PAST JUVIE RECORD, GOT ME FIFTEEN YEARS HARD TIME...

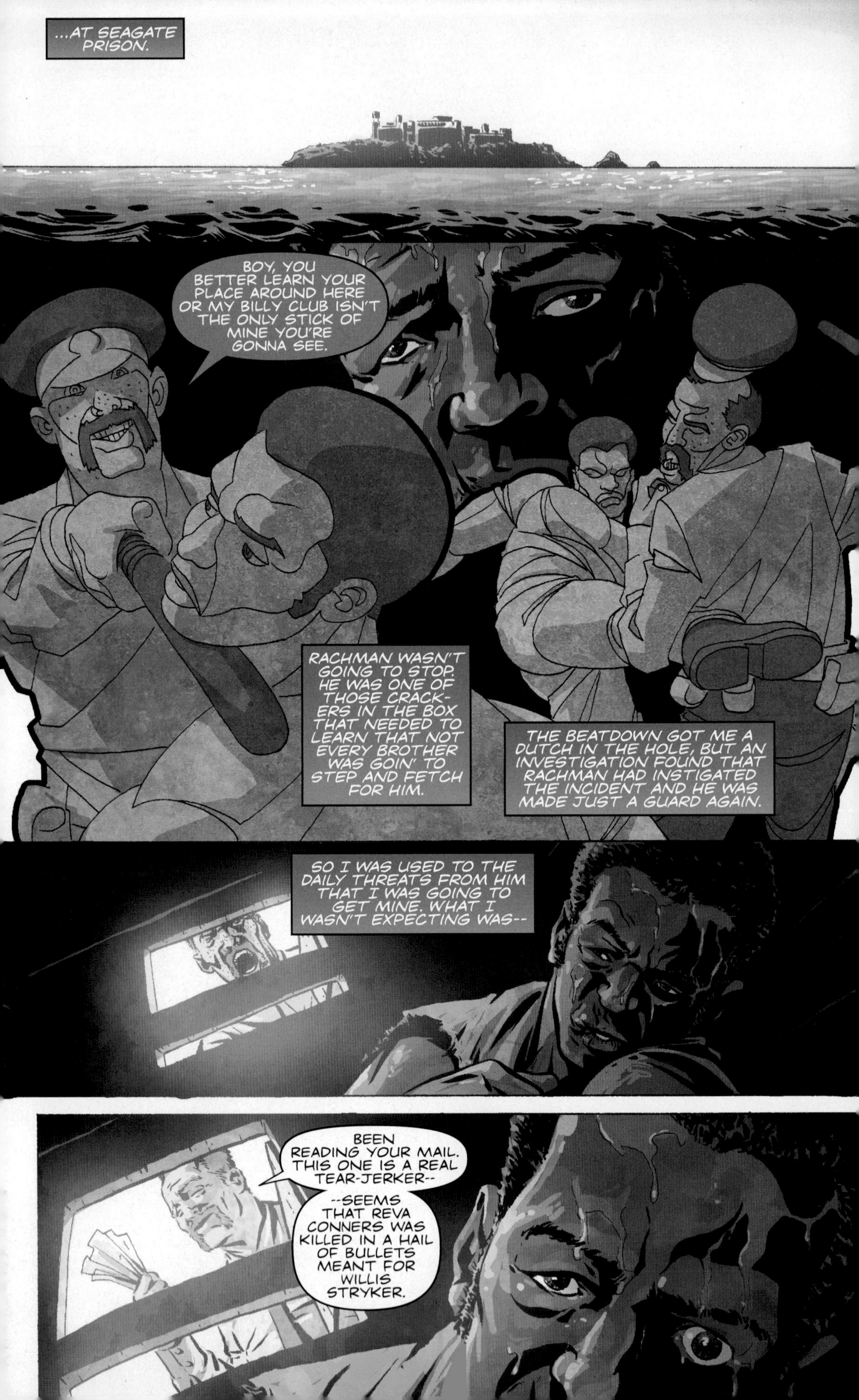
...AT SEAGATE PRISON.
BOY, YOU BETTER LEARN YOUR PLACE AROUND HERE OR MY BILLY CLUB ISN'T THE ONLY STICK OF MINE YOU'RE GONNA SEE.
RACHMAN WASN'T GOING TO STOP. HE WAS ONE OF THOSE CRACKERS IN THE BOX THAT NEEDED TO LEARN THAT NOT EVERY BROTHER WAS GOIN' TO STEP AND FETCH FOR HIM.
THE BEATDOWN GOT ME A DUTCH IN THE HOLE, BUT AN INVESTIGATION FOUND THAT RACHMAN HAD INSTIGATED THE INCIDENT AND HE WAS MADE JUST A GUARD AGAIN.
SO I WAS USED TO THE DAILY THREATS FROM HIM THAT I WAS GOING TO GET MINE. WHAT I WASN'T EXPECTING WAS--
BEEN READING YOUR MAIL. THIS ONE IS A REAL TEAR-JERKER--
--SEEMS THAT REVA CONNERS WAS KILLED IN A HAIL OF BULLETS MEANT FOR WILLIS STRYKER.

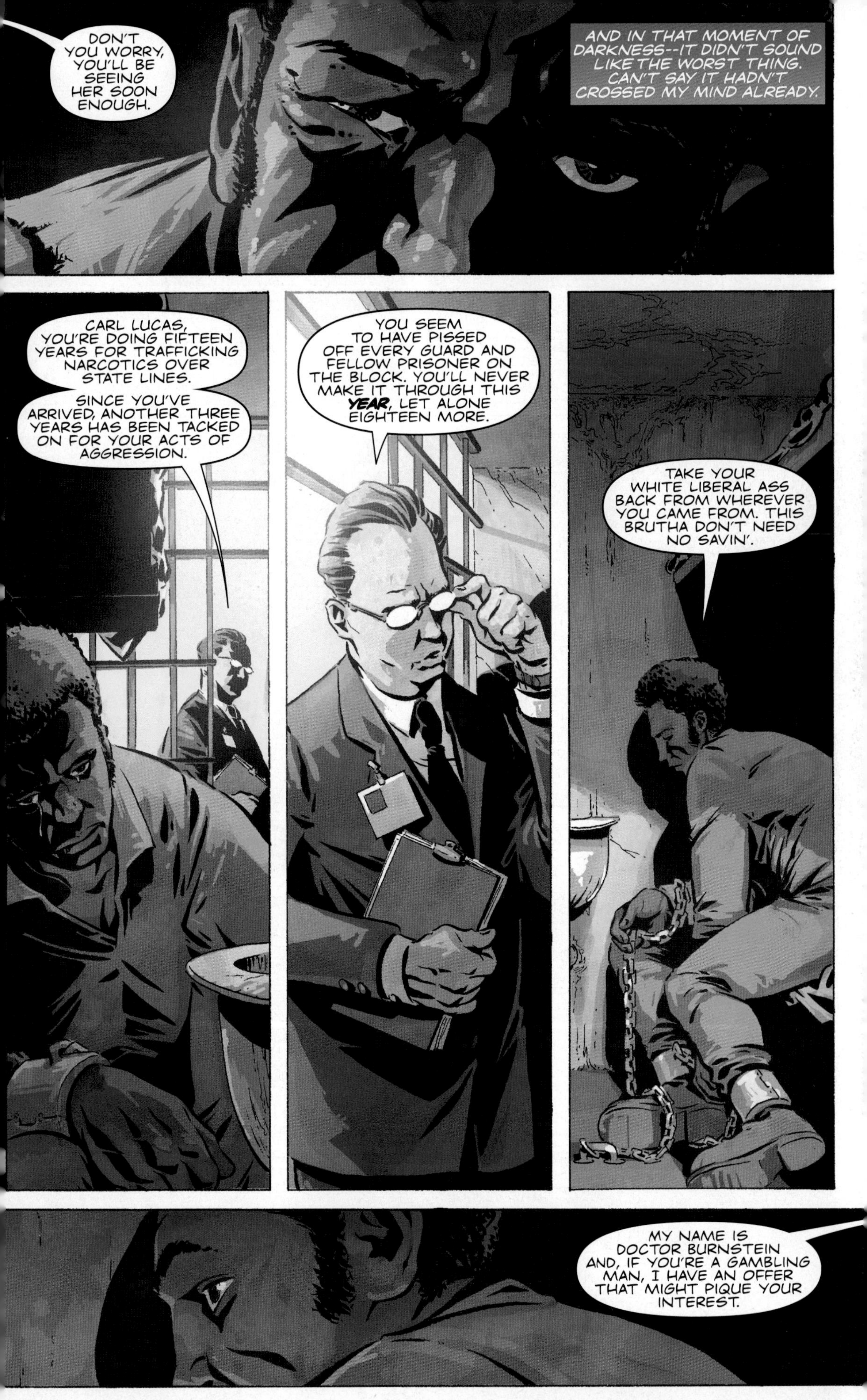
DON'T YOU WORRY, YOU'LL BE SEEING HER SOON ENOUGH.
AND IN THAT MOMENT OF DARKNESS--IT DIDN'T SOUND LIKE THE WORST THING. CAN'T SAY IT HADN'T CROSSED MY MIND ALREADY.
CARL LUCAS, YOU'RE DOING FIFTEEN YEARS FOR TRAFFICKING NARCOTICS OVER STATE LINES.
SINCE YOU'VE ARRIVED, ANOTHER THREE YEARS HAS BEEN TACKED ON FOR YOUR ACTS OF AGGRESSION.
YOU SEEM TO HAVE PISSED OFF EVERY GUARD AND FELLOW PRISONER ON THE BLOCK. YOU'LL NEVER MAKE IT THROUGH THIS YEAR, LET ALONE EIGHTEEN MORE.
TAKE YOUR WHITE LIBERAL ASS BACK FROM WHEREVER YOU CAME FROM. THIS BRUTHA DON'T NEED NO SAVIN'.
MY NAME IS DOCTOR BURNSTEIN AND, IF YOU'RE A GAMBLING MAN, I HAVE AN OFFER THAT MIGHT PIQUE YOUR INTEREST.

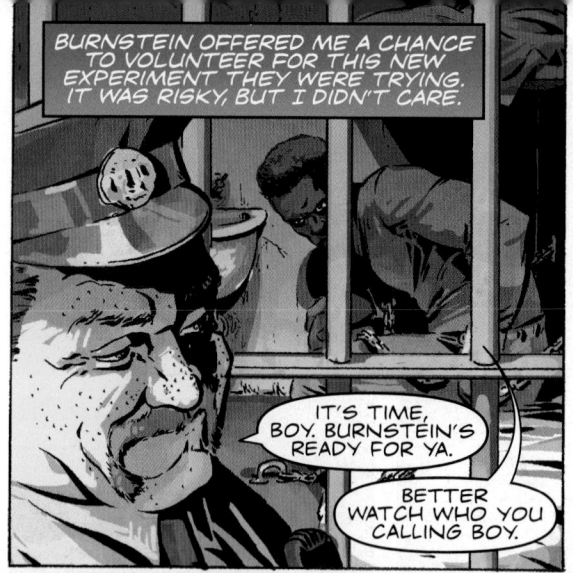

BURNSTEIN OFFERED ME A CHANCE TO VOLUNTEER FOR THIS NEW EXPERIMENT THEY WERE TRYING. IT WAS RISKY, BUT I DIDN'T CARE.

IT'S TIME, BOY. BURNSTEIN'S READY FOR YA.

BETTER WATCH WHO YOU CALLING BOY.

IF IT WORKED, I GOT A CHANCE AT PAROLE. IF IT DIDN'T, I WOULDN'T KNOW ANY BETTER.

IT'S AN ELECTRO-BIOCHEMICAL SYSTEM FOR STIMULATING HUMAN CELL REGENERATION.

IF SUCCESSFUL, IT COULD COUNTER THE DAMAGES OF ALMOST ANY DISEASE--EVEN AGING.

JUST TELL ME WHAT YOU NEED ME TO DO, DOC.

WE'RE GOING TO START SLOW AND BUILD YOUR TOLERANCE.

THIS STUFF SMELLS FUNKY. I DON'T EVEN WANT TO KNOW WHAT I'M SITTIN' IN.

YOU'RE RIGHT, YOU DON'T. NOW TRY AND RELAX, MR. LUCAS, WHILE I GO CHECK THE SENSORY UNITS.

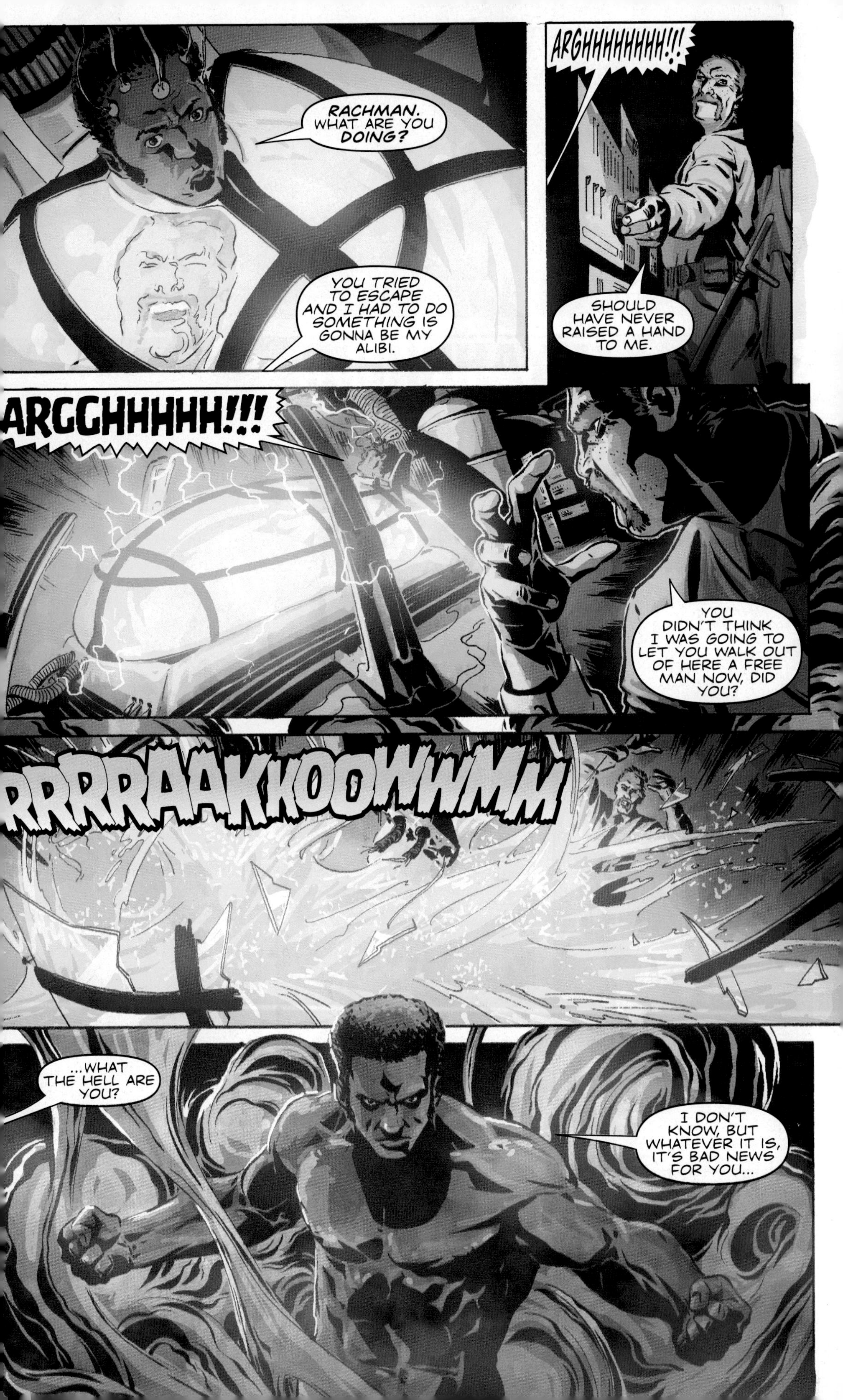
RACHMAN. WHAT ARE YOU DOING?
YOU TRIED TO ESCAPE AND I HAD TO DO SOMETHING IS GONNA BE MY ALIBI.
ARGHHHHHHHH!!!
SHOULD HAVE NEVER RAISED A HAND TO ME.
ARGGHHHHH!!!
YOU DIDN'T THINK I WAS GOING TO LET YOU WALK OUT OF HERE A FREE MAN NOW, DID YOU?
RRRRAAKKOOWWMM
...WHAT THE HELL ARE YOU?
I DON'T KNOW, BUT WHATEVER IT IS, IT'S BAD NEWS FOR YOU...

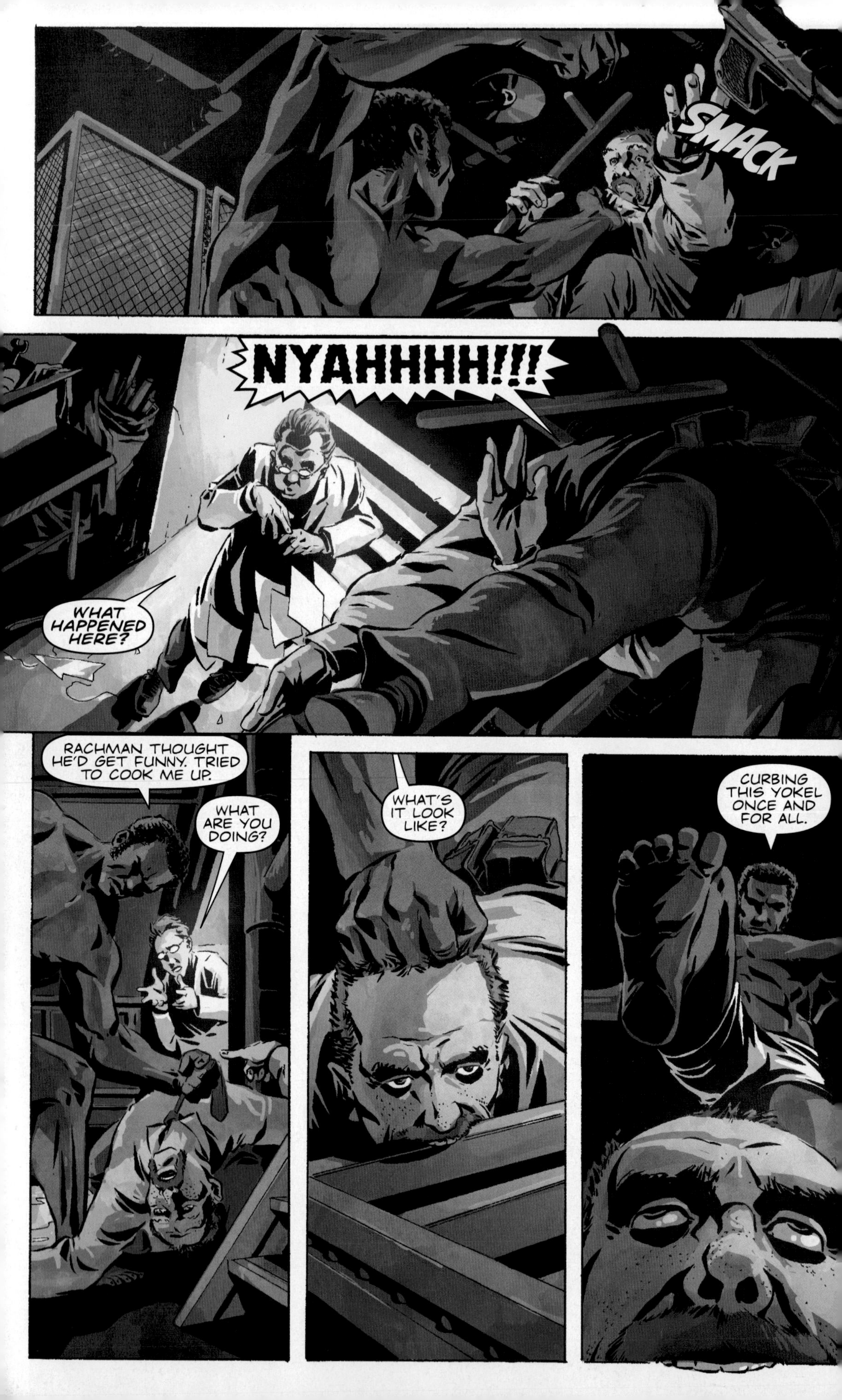
SMACK
NYAHHHH!!!
WHAT HAPPENED HERE?
RACHMAN THOUGHT HE'D GET FUNNY. TRIED TO COOK ME UP.
WHAT ARE YOU DOING?
WHAT'S IT LOOK LIKE?
CURBING THIS YOKEL ONCE AND FOR ALL.

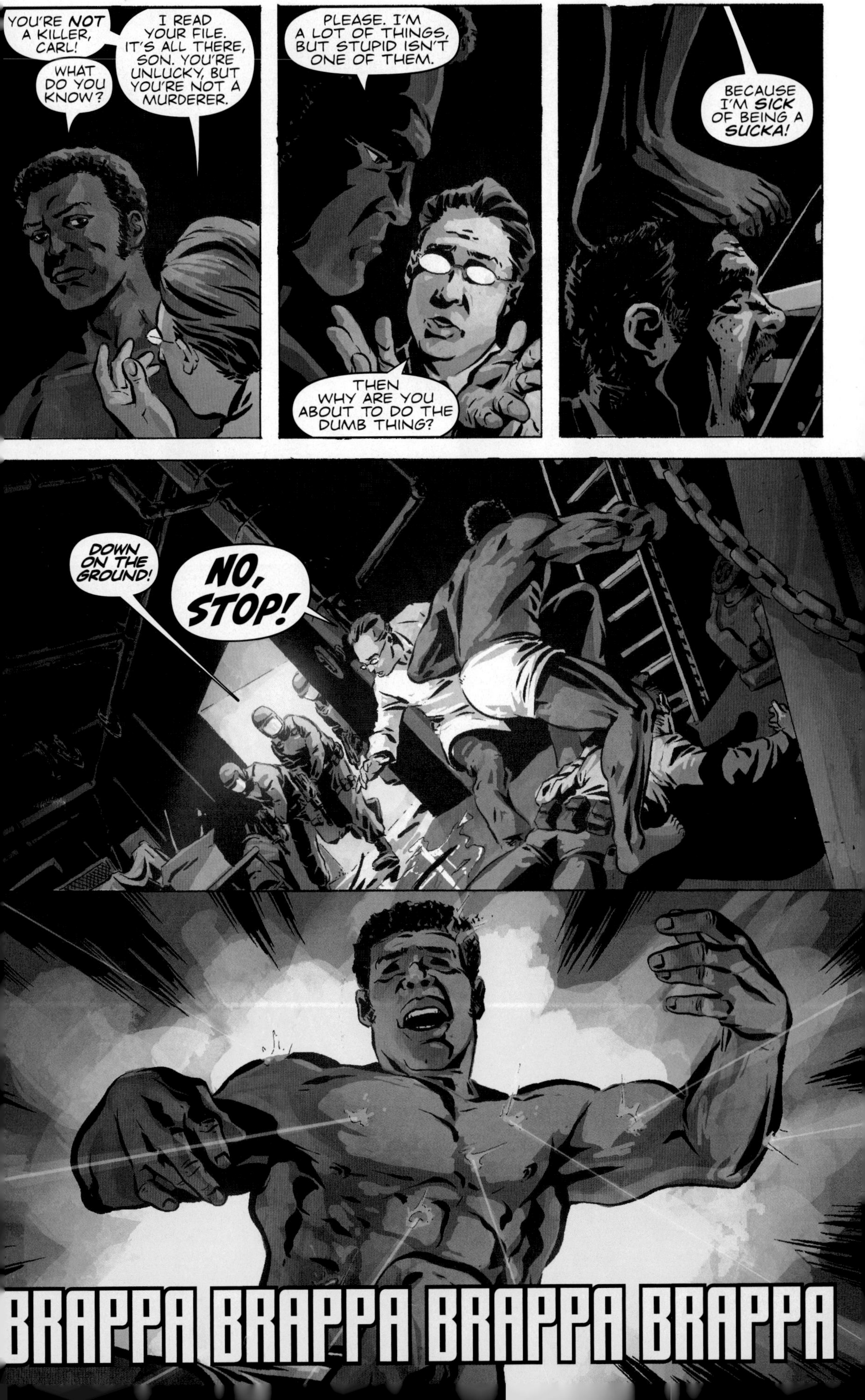

YOU'RE **NOT** A KILLER, CARL!
WHAT DO YOU KNOW?
I READ YOUR FILE. IT'S ALL THERE, SON. YOU'RE UNLUCKY, BUT YOU'RE NOT A MURDERER.
PLEASE. I'M A LOT OF THINGS, BUT STUPID ISN'T ONE OF THEM.
THEN WHY ARE YOU ABOUT TO DO THE DUMB THING?
BECAUSE I'M **SICK** OF BEING A **SUCKA!**
DOWN ON THE GROUND!
NO, STOP!
BRAPPA BRAPPA BRAPPA BRAPPA

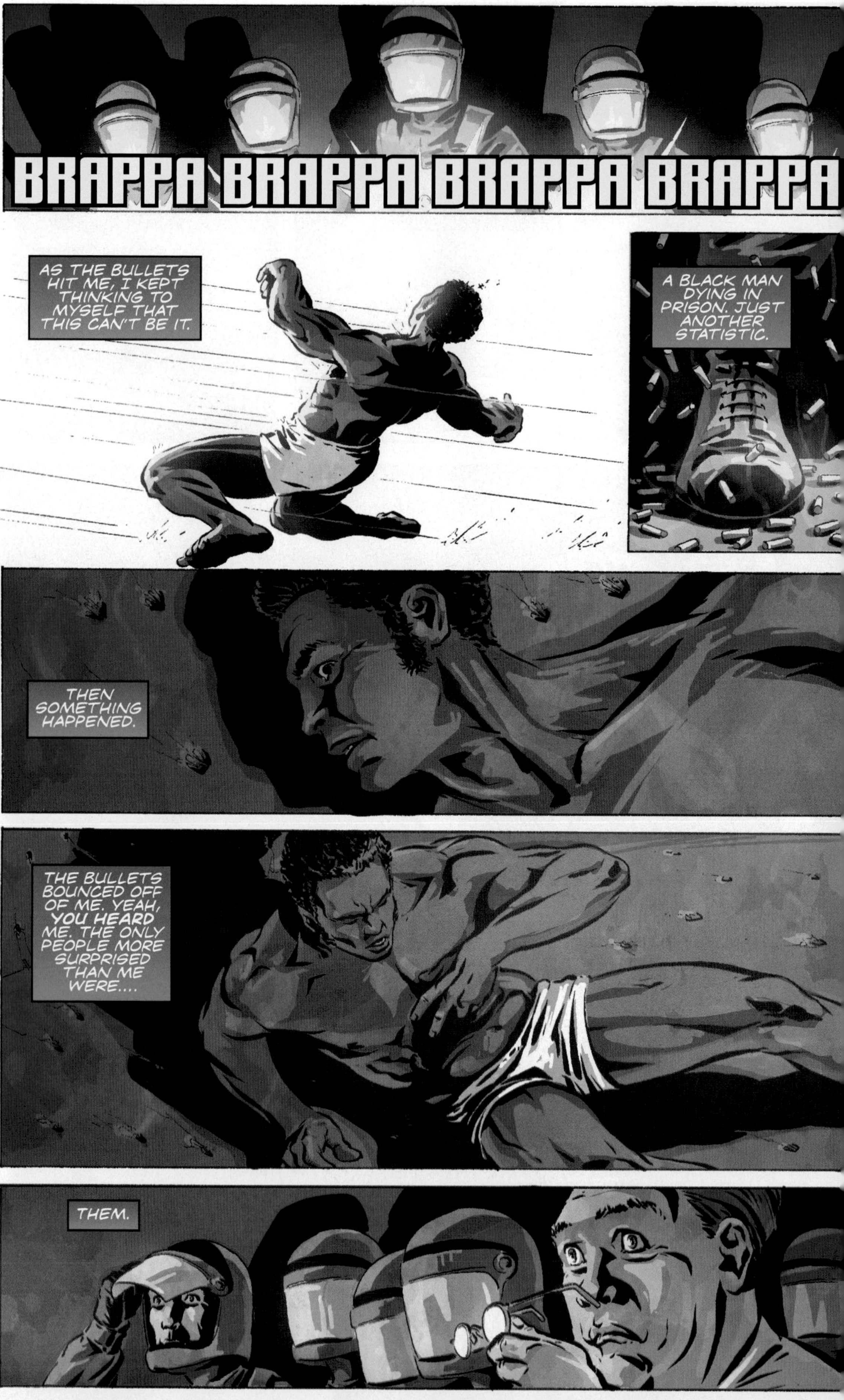
BRAPPA BRAPPA BRAPPA BRAPPA
AS THE BULLETS HIT ME, I KEPT THINKING TO MYSELF THAT THIS CAN'T BE IT.
A BLACK MAN DYING IN PRISON. JUST ANOTHER STATISTIC.
THEN SOMETHING HAPPENED.
THE BULLETS BOUNCED OFF OF ME. YEAH, **YOU HEARD** ME. THE ONLY PEOPLE MORE SURPRISED THAN ME WERE....
THEM.

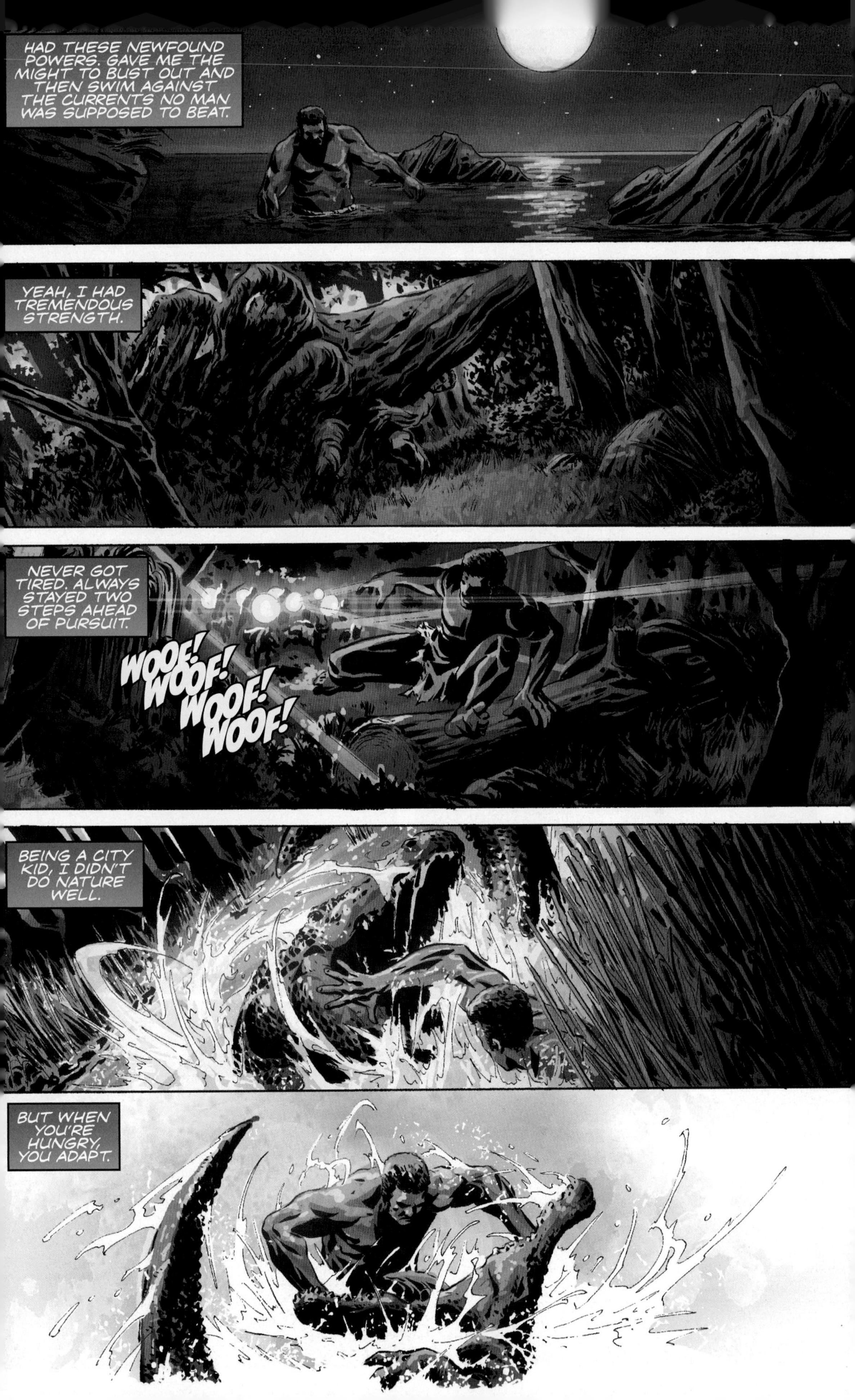
HAD THESE NEWFOUND POWERS. GAVE ME THE MIGHT TO BUST OUT AND THEN SWIM AGAINST THE CURRENTS NO MAN WAS SUPPOSED TO BEAT.
YEAH, I HAD TREMENDOUS STRENGTH.
NEVER GOT TIRED. ALWAYS STAYED TWO STEPS AHEAD OF PURSUIT.
WOOF! WOOF! WOOF! WOOF!
BEING A CITY KID, I DIDN'T DO NATURE WELL.
BUT WHEN YOU'RE HUNGRY, YOU ADAPT.

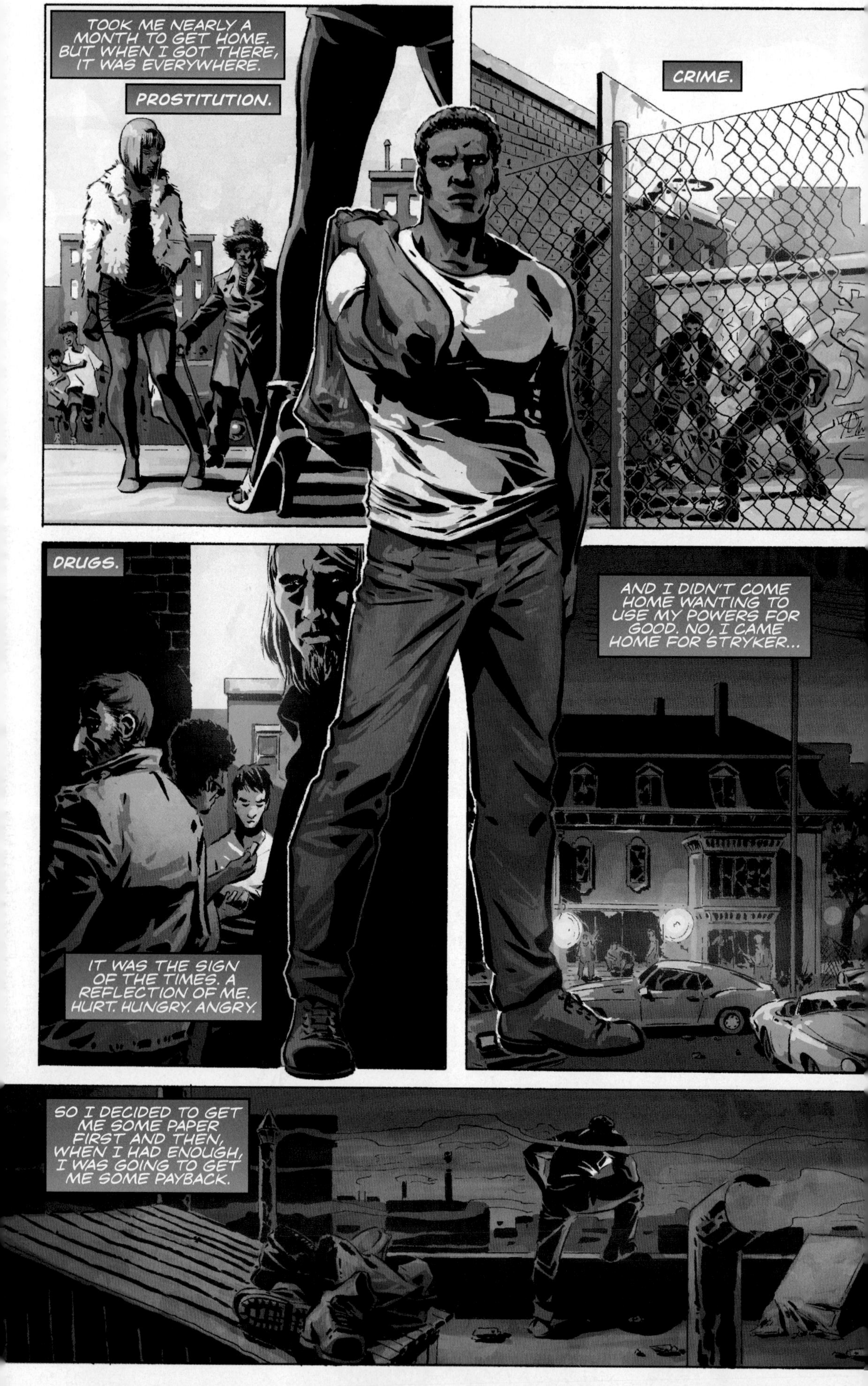

TOOK ME NEARLY A MONTH TO GET HOME. BUT WHEN I GOT THERE, IT WAS EVERYWHERE.
PROSTITUTION.
CRIME.
DRUGS.
IT WAS THE SIGN OF THE TIMES. A REFLECTION OF ME. HURT. HUNGRY. ANGRY.
AND I DIDN'T COME HOME WANTING TO USE MY POWERS FOR GOOD. NO, I CAME HOME FOR STRYKER...
SO I DECIDED TO GET ME SOME PAPER FIRST AND THEN, WHEN I HAD ENOUGH, I WAS GOING TO GET ME SOME PAYBACK.

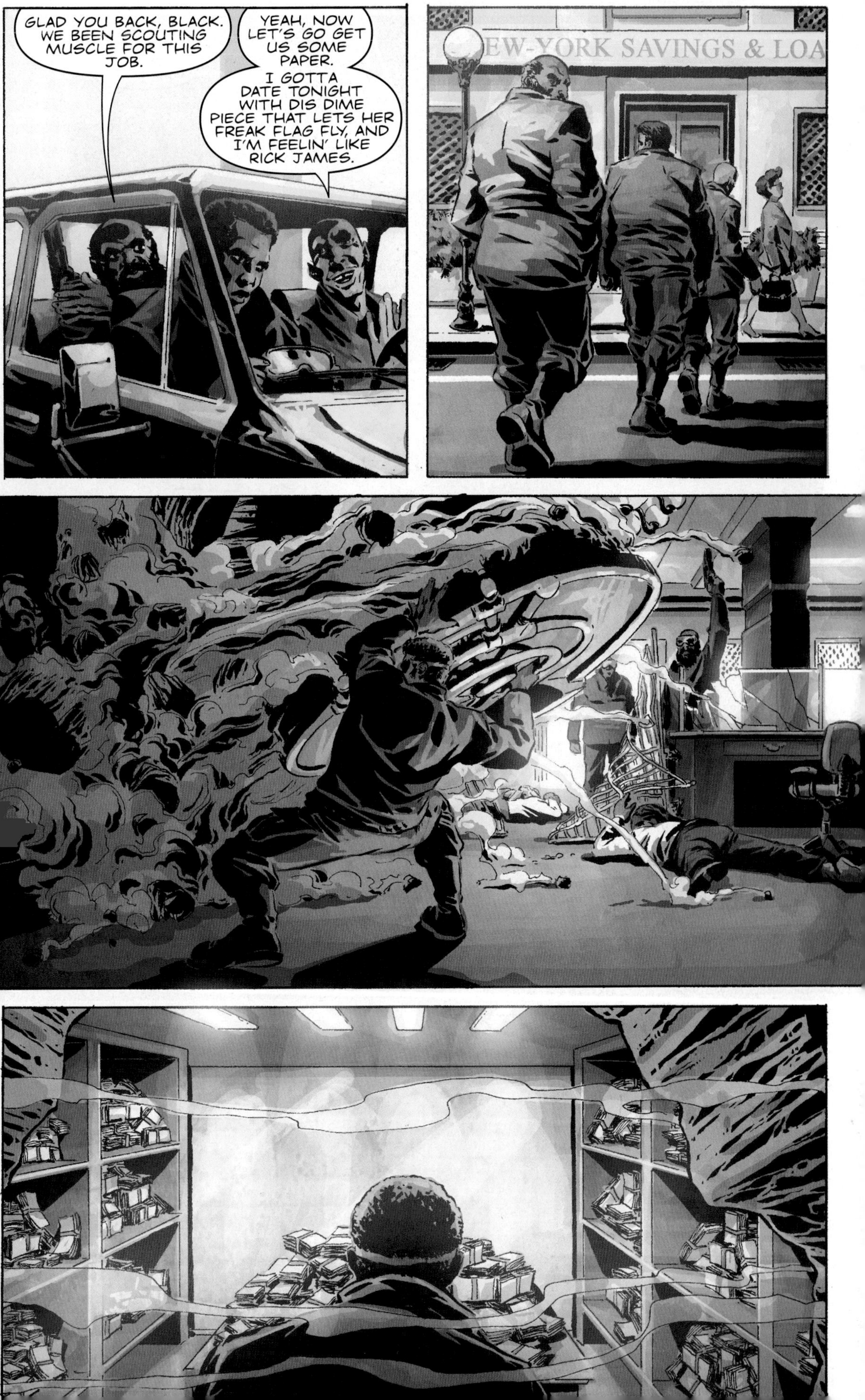
GLAD YOU BACK, BLACK. WE BEEN SCOUTING MUSCLE FOR THIS JOB.
YEAH, NOW LET'S GO GET US SOME PAPER.
I GOTTA DATE TONIGHT WITH DIS DIME PIECE THAT LETS HER FREAK FLAG FLY, AND I'M FEELIN' LIKE RICK JAMES.
EW-YORK SAVINGS & LOA

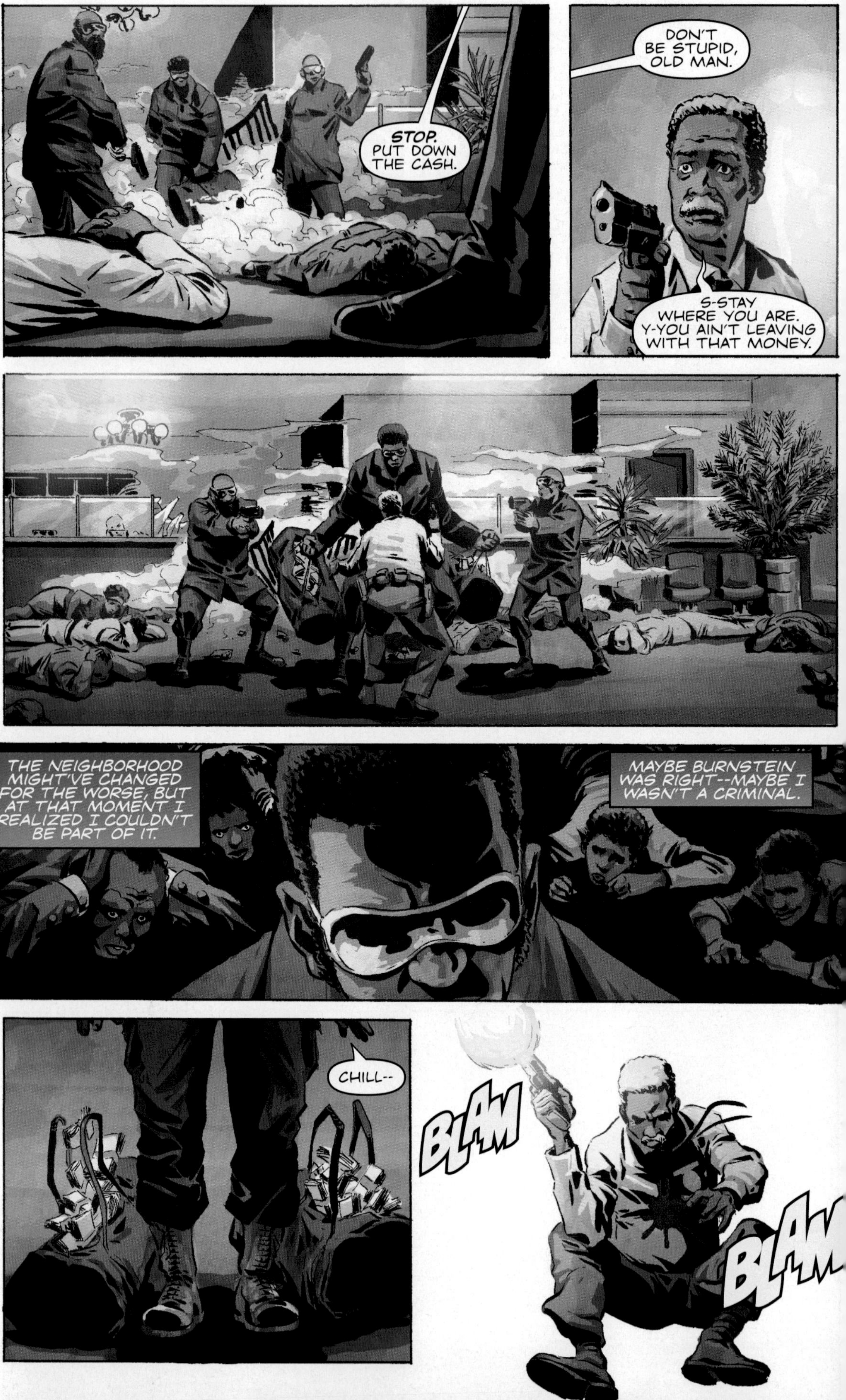
STOP. PUT DOWN THE CASH.
DON'T BE STUPID, OLD MAN.
S-STAY WHERE YOU ARE. Y-YOU AIN'T LEAVING WITH THAT MONEY.
THE NEIGHBORHOOD MIGHT'VE CHANGED FOR THE WORSE, BUT AT THAT MOMENT I REALIZED I COULDN'T BE PART OF IT.
MAYBE BURNSTEIN WAS RIGHT--MAYBE I WASN'T A CRIMINAL.
CHILL--
BLAM
BLAM

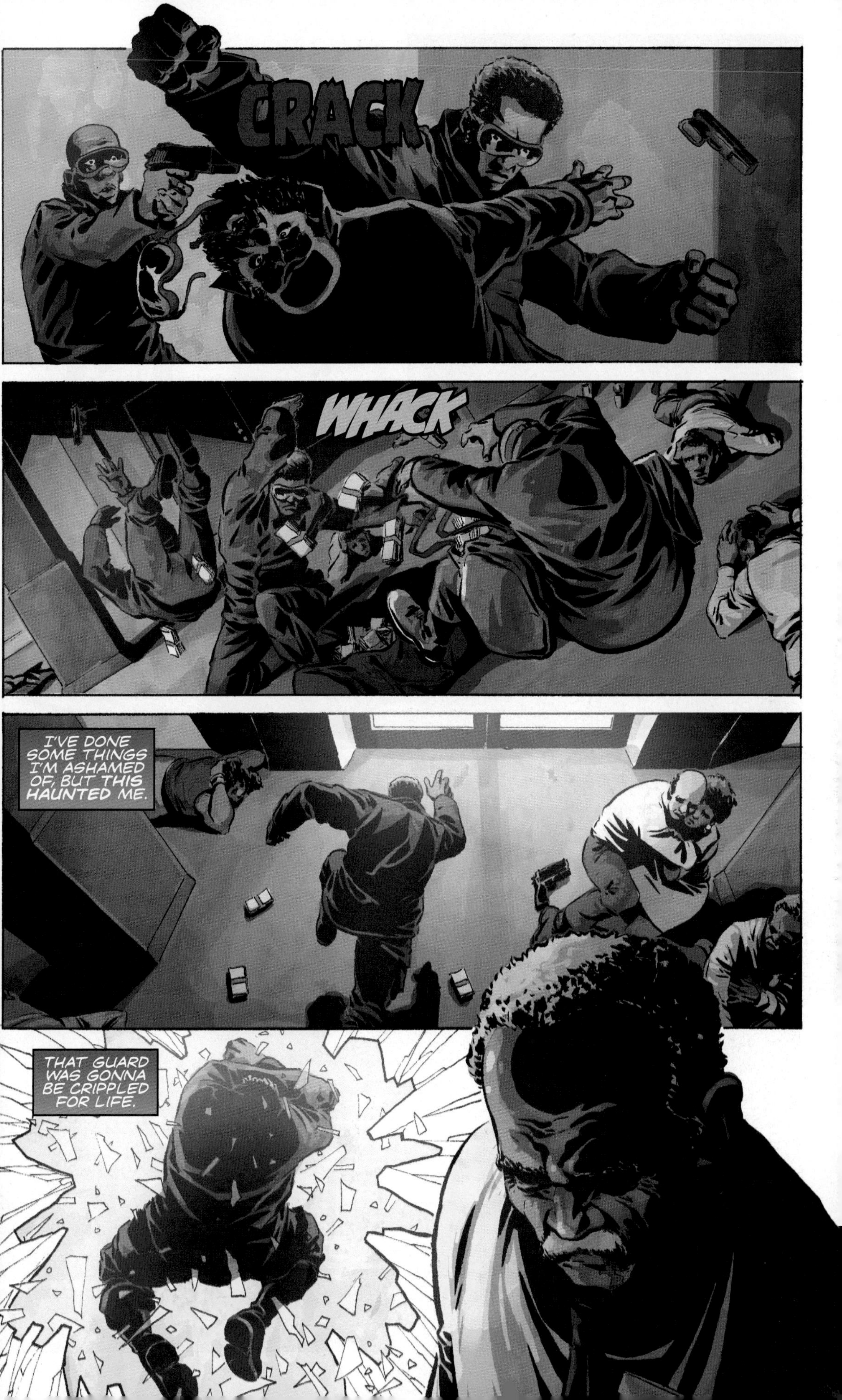
CRACK
WHACK
I'VE DONE SOME THINGS I'M ASHAMED OF, BUT THIS HAUNTED ME.
THAT GUARD WAS GONNA BE CRIPPLED FOR LIFE.

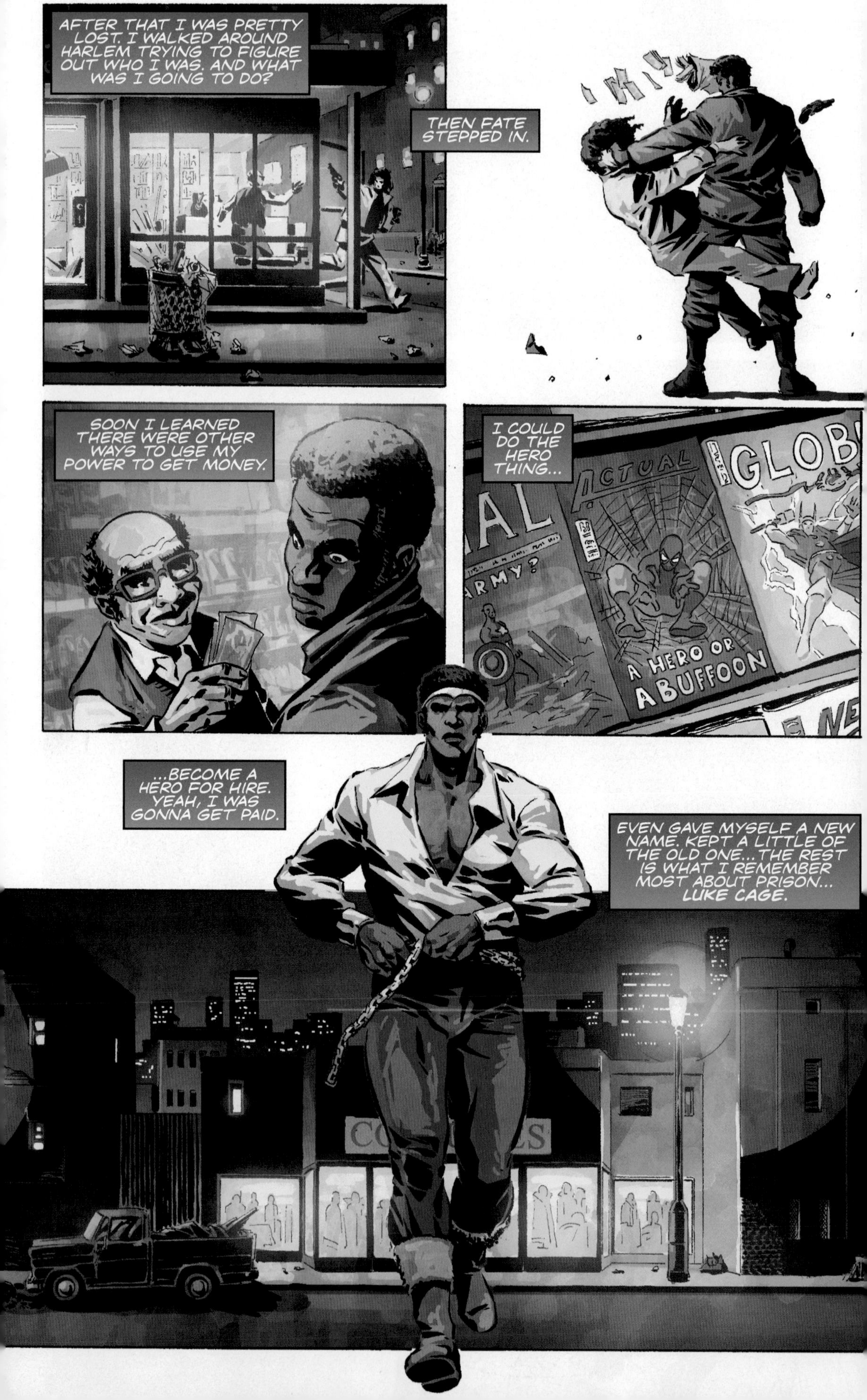
AFTER THAT I WAS PRETTY LOST. I WALKED AROUND HARLEM TRYING TO FIGURE OUT WHO I WAS. AND WHAT WAS I GOING TO DO?
THEN FATE STEPPED IN.
SOON I LEARNED THERE WERE OTHER WAYS TO USE MY POWER TO GET MONEY.
I COULD DO THE HERO THING...
ARMY?
ACTUAL
A HERO OR A BUFFOON
...BECOME A HERO FOR HIRE. YEAH, I WAS GONNA GET PAID.
EVEN GAVE MYSELF A NEW NAME. KEPT A LITTLE OF THE OLD ONE...THE REST IS WHAT I REMEMBER MOST ABOUT PRISON... LUKE CAGE.

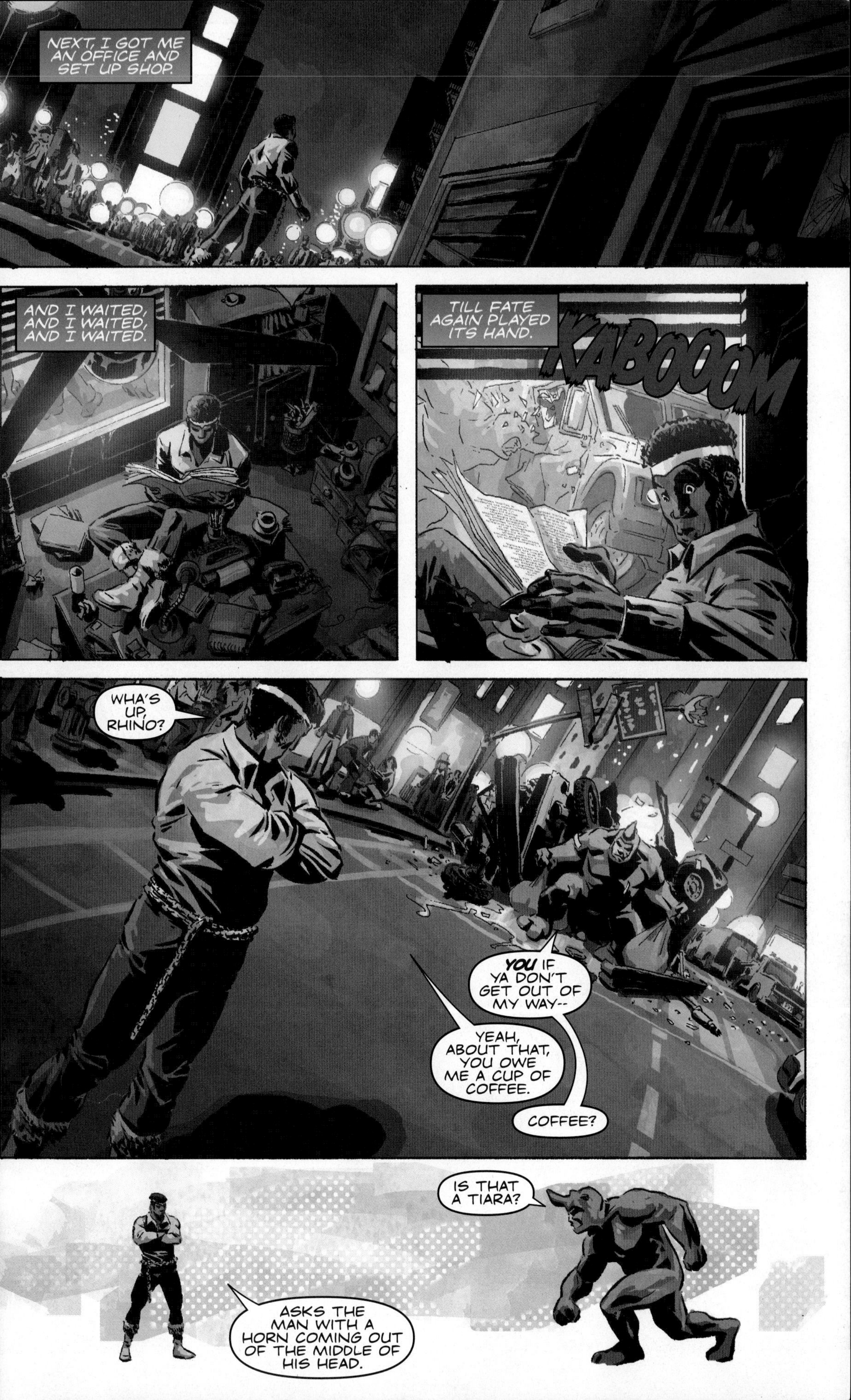

NEXT, I GOT ME AN OFFICE AND SET UP SHOP.
AND I WAITED, AND I WAITED, AND I WAITED.
TILL FATE AGAIN PLAYED ITS HAND.
KABOOOM
WHA'S UP, RHINO?
YOU IF YA DON'T GET OUT OF MY WAY--
YEAH, ABOUT THAT, YOU OWE ME A CUP OF COFFEE.
COFFEE?
IS THAT A TIARA?
ASKS THE MAN WITH A HORN COMING OUT OF THE MIDDLE OF HIS HEAD.

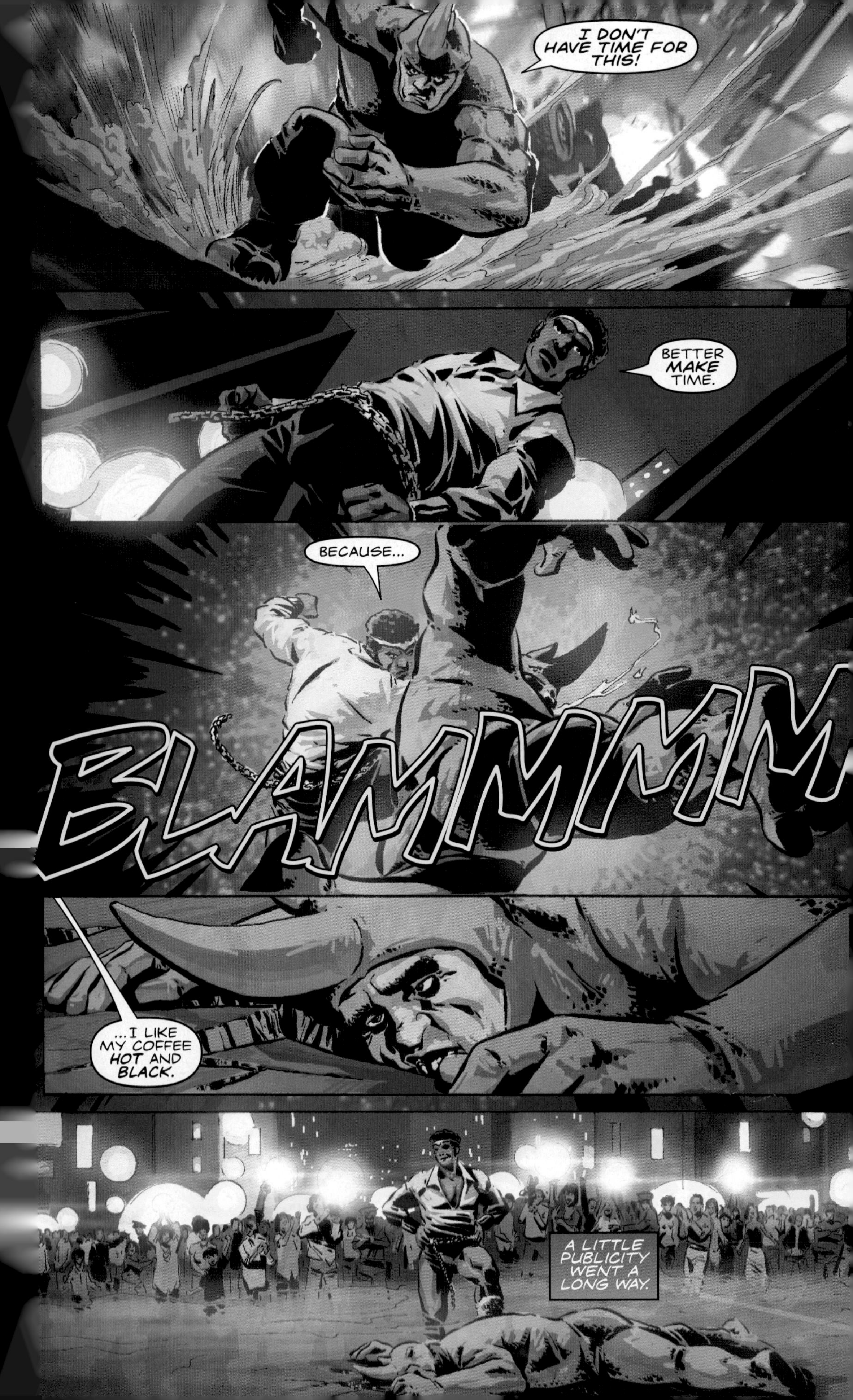
I DON'T HAVE TIME FOR THIS!
BETTER MAKE TIME.
BECAUSE...
BLAMMMM
...I LIKE MY COFFEE HOT AND BLACK.
A LITTLE PUBLICITY WENT A LONG WAY.

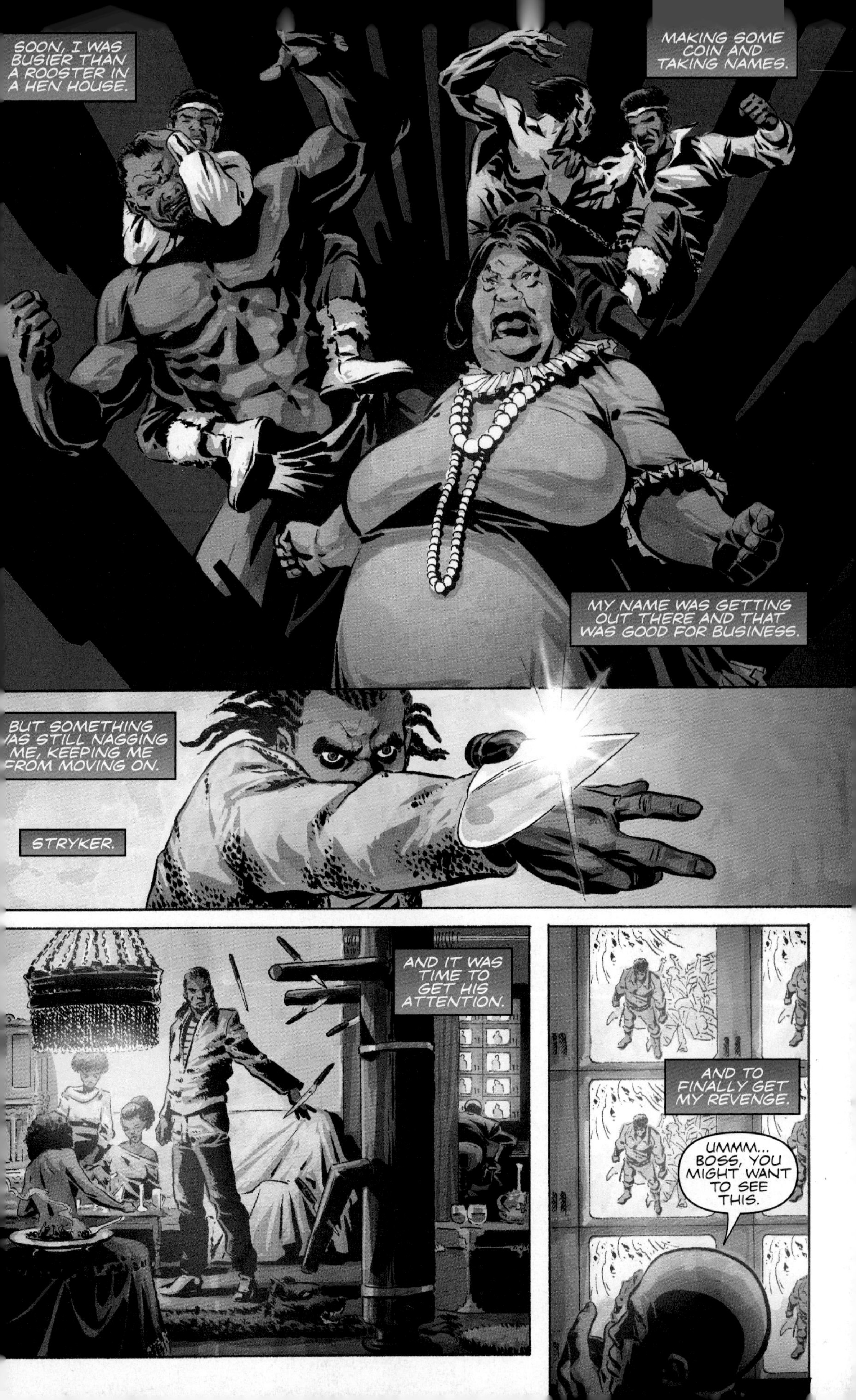
SOON, I WAS BUSIER THAN A ROOSTER IN A HEN HOUSE.
MAKING SOME COIN AND TAKING NAMES.
MY NAME WAS GETTING OUT THERE AND THAT WAS GOOD FOR BUSINESS.
BUT SOMETHING WAS STILL NAGGING ME, KEEPING ME FROM MOVING ON.
STRYKER.
AND IT WAS TIME TO GET HIS ATTENTION.
AND TO FINALLY GET MY REVENGE.
UMMM... BOSS, YOU MIGHT WANT TO SEE THIS.

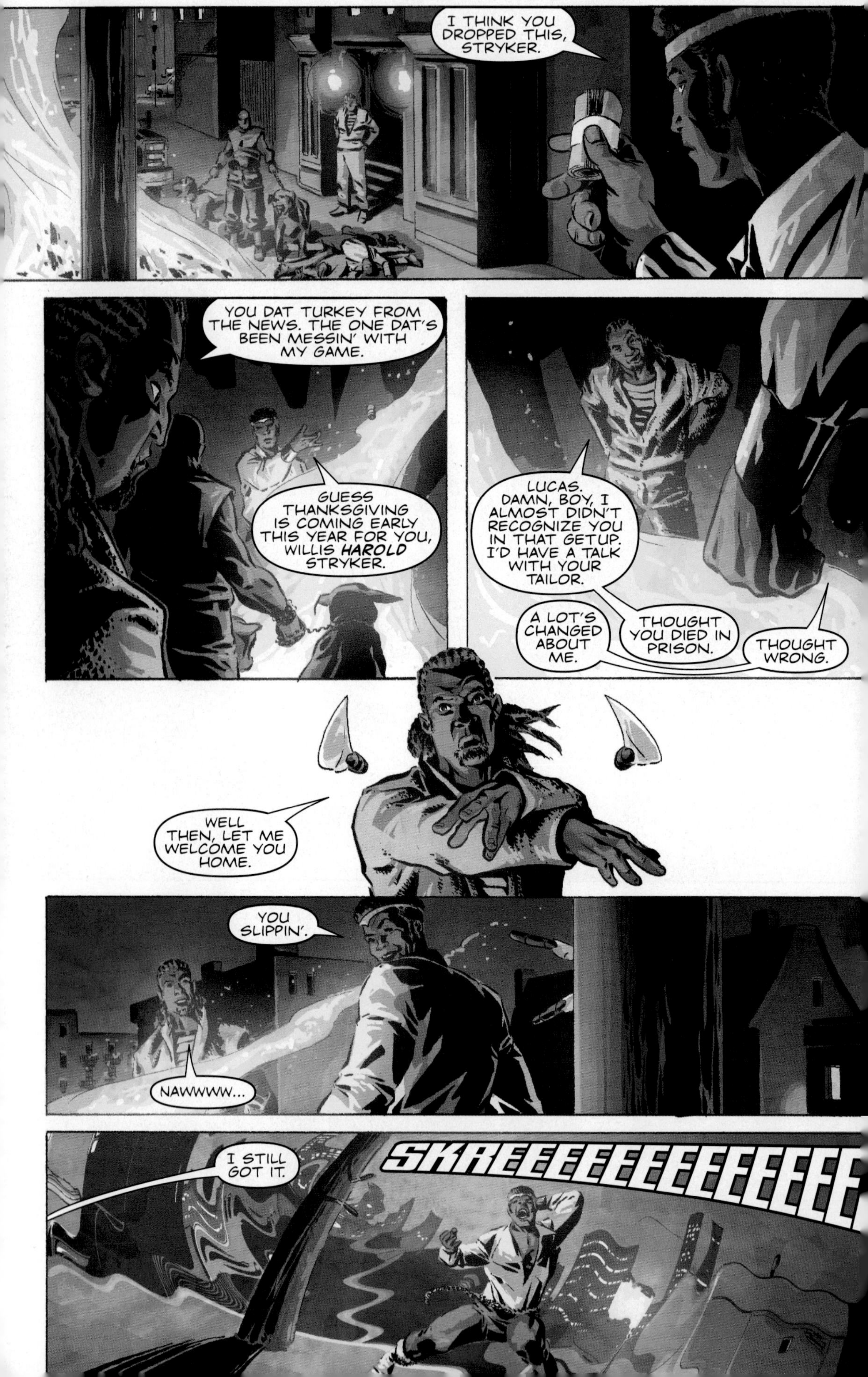

I THINK YOU DROPPED THIS, STRYKER.
YOU DAT TURKEY FROM THE NEWS. THE ONE DAT'S BEEN MESSIN' WITH MY GAME.
GUESS THANKSGIVING IS COMING EARLY THIS YEAR FOR YOU, WILLIS HAROLD STRYKER.
LUCAS. DAMN, BOY, I ALMOST DIDN'T RECOGNIZE YOU IN THAT GETUP. I'D HAVE A TALK WITH YOUR TAILOR.
THOUGHT YOU DIED IN PRISON.
A LOT'S CHANGED ABOUT ME.
THOUGHT WRONG.
WELL THEN, LET ME WELCOME YOU HOME.
YOU SLIPPIN'.
NAWWWW...
I STILL GOT IT.
SKREEEEEEEEEEEEEE

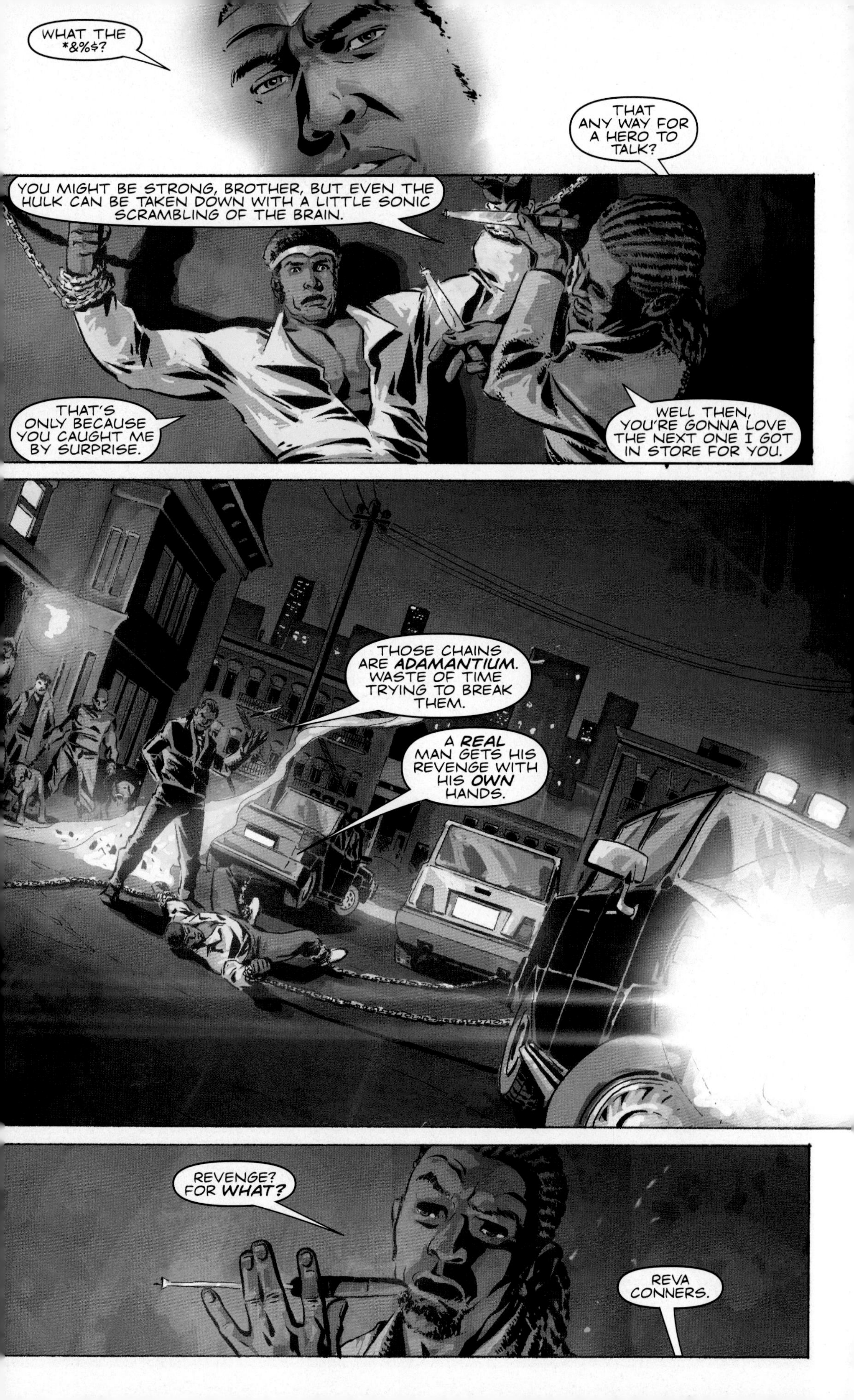
WHAT THE *&%$?
THAT ANY WAY FOR A HERO TO TALK?
YOU MIGHT BE STRONG, BROTHER, BUT EVEN THE HULK CAN BE TAKEN DOWN WITH A LITTLE SONIC SCRAMBLING OF THE BRAIN.
THAT'S ONLY BECAUSE YOU CAUGHT ME BY SURPRISE.
WELL THEN, YOU'RE GONNA LOVE THE NEXT ONE I GOT IN STORE FOR YOU.
THOSE CHAINS ARE ADAMANTIUM. WASTE OF TIME TRYING TO BREAK THEM.
A REAL MAN GETS HIS REVENGE WITH HIS OWN HANDS.
REVENGE? FOR WHAT?
REVA CONNERS.

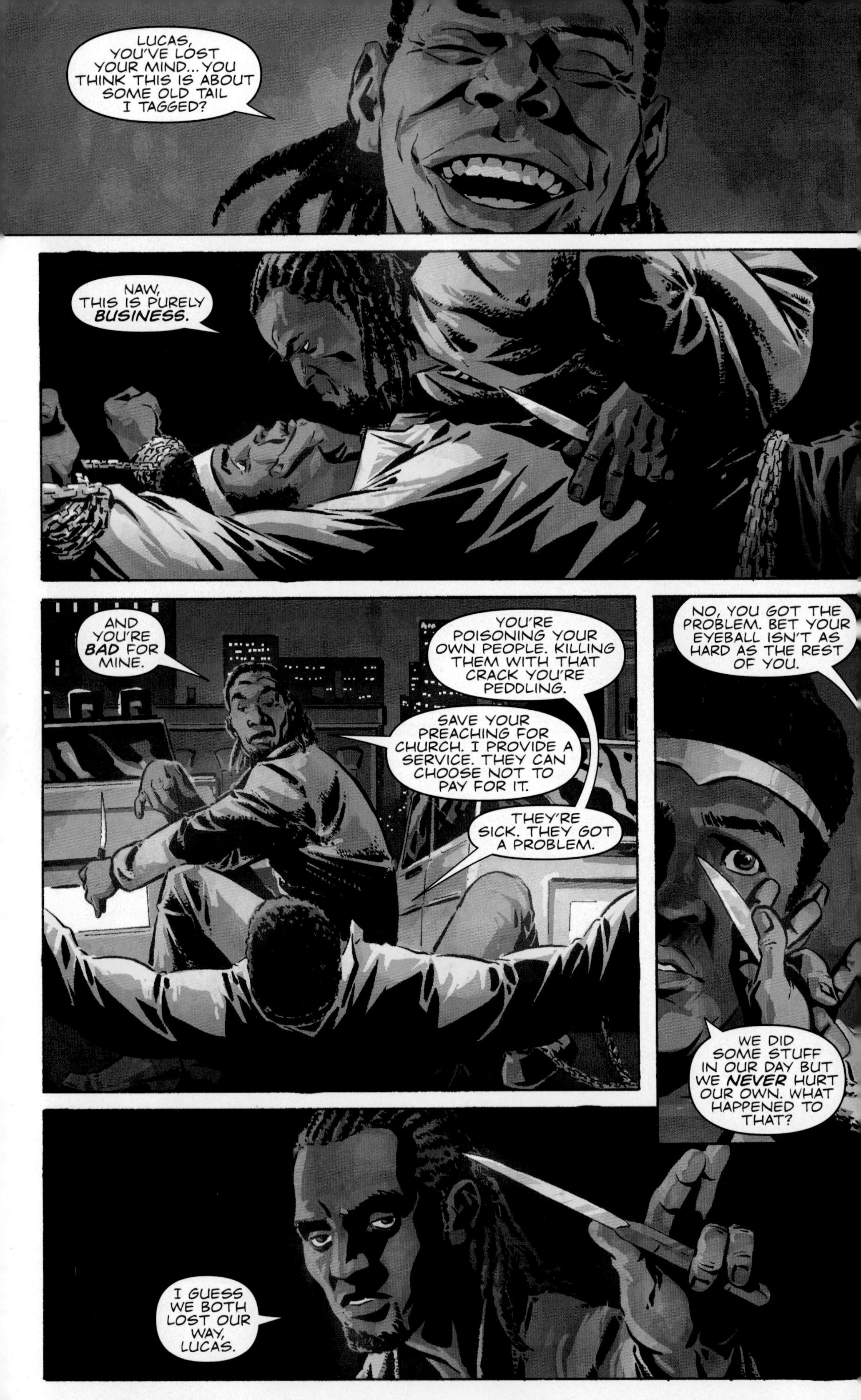
LUCAS, YOU'VE LOST YOUR MIND... YOU THINK THIS IS ABOUT SOME OLD TAIL I TAGGED?
NAW, THIS IS PURELY **BUSINESS.**
AND YOU'RE **BAD** FOR MINE.
YOU'RE POISONING YOUR OWN PEOPLE. KILLING THEM WITH THAT CRACK YOU'RE PEDDLING.
SAVE YOUR PREACHING FOR CHURCH. I PROVIDE A SERVICE. THEY CAN CHOOSE NOT TO PAY FOR IT.
THEY'RE SICK. THEY GOT A PROBLEM.
NO, YOU GOT THE PROBLEM. BET YOUR EYEBALL ISN'T AS HARD AS THE REST OF YOU.
WE DID SOME STUFF IN OUR DAY BUT WE **NEVER** HURT OUR OWN. WHAT HAPPENED TO THAT?
I GUESS WE BOTH LOST OUR WAY, LUCAS.

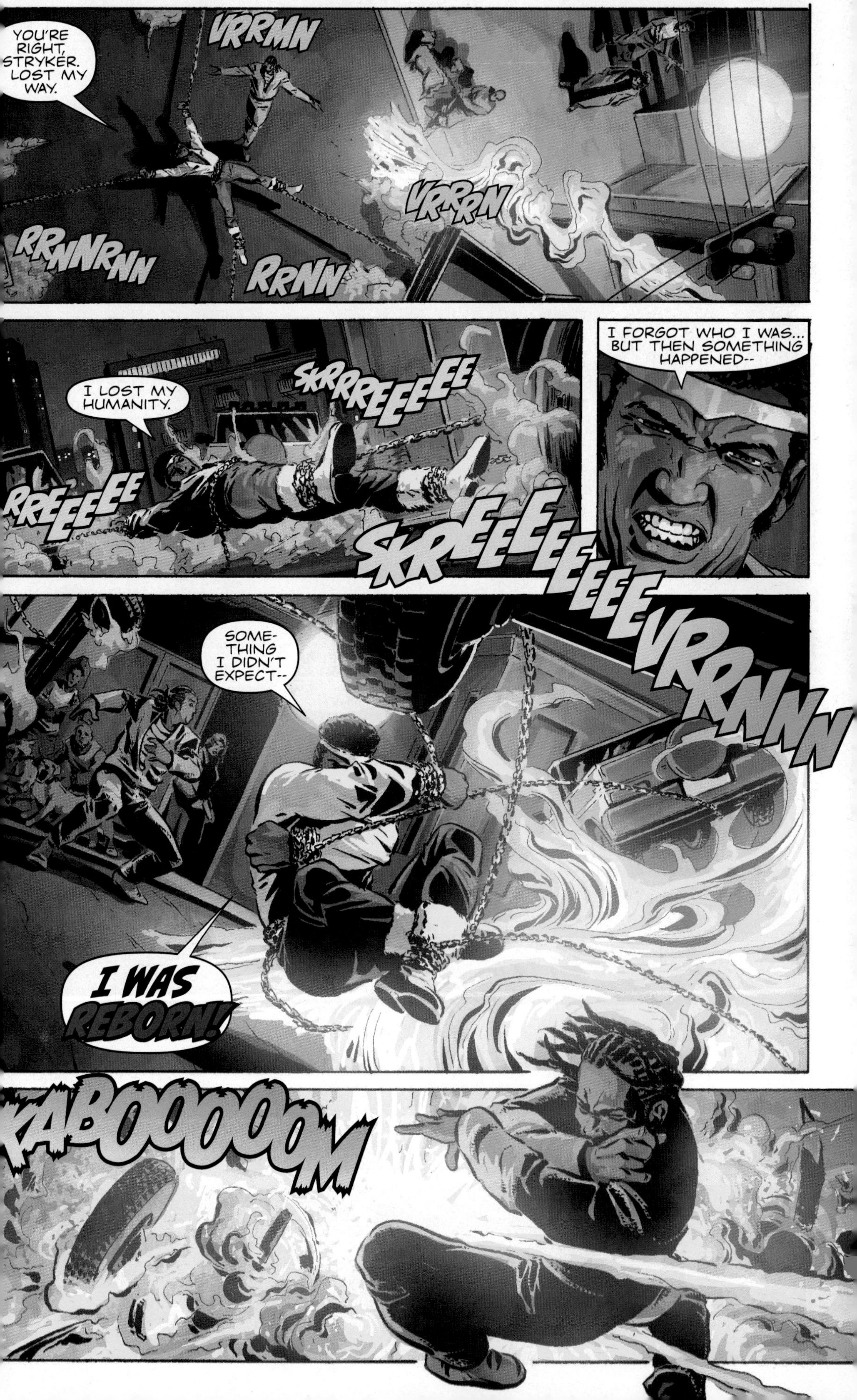

YOU'RE RIGHT, STRYKER. LOST MY WAY.
VRRMN
VRRRN
RRNNRNN
RRNN
I LOST MY HUMANITY.
SKRRREEEEEE
RREEEEE
I FORGOT WHO I WAS... BUT THEN SOMETHING HAPPENED--
SKREEEEEEEEEVRRNNN
SOME-THING I DIDN'T EXPECT--
I WAS REBORN!
KABOOOOOOM

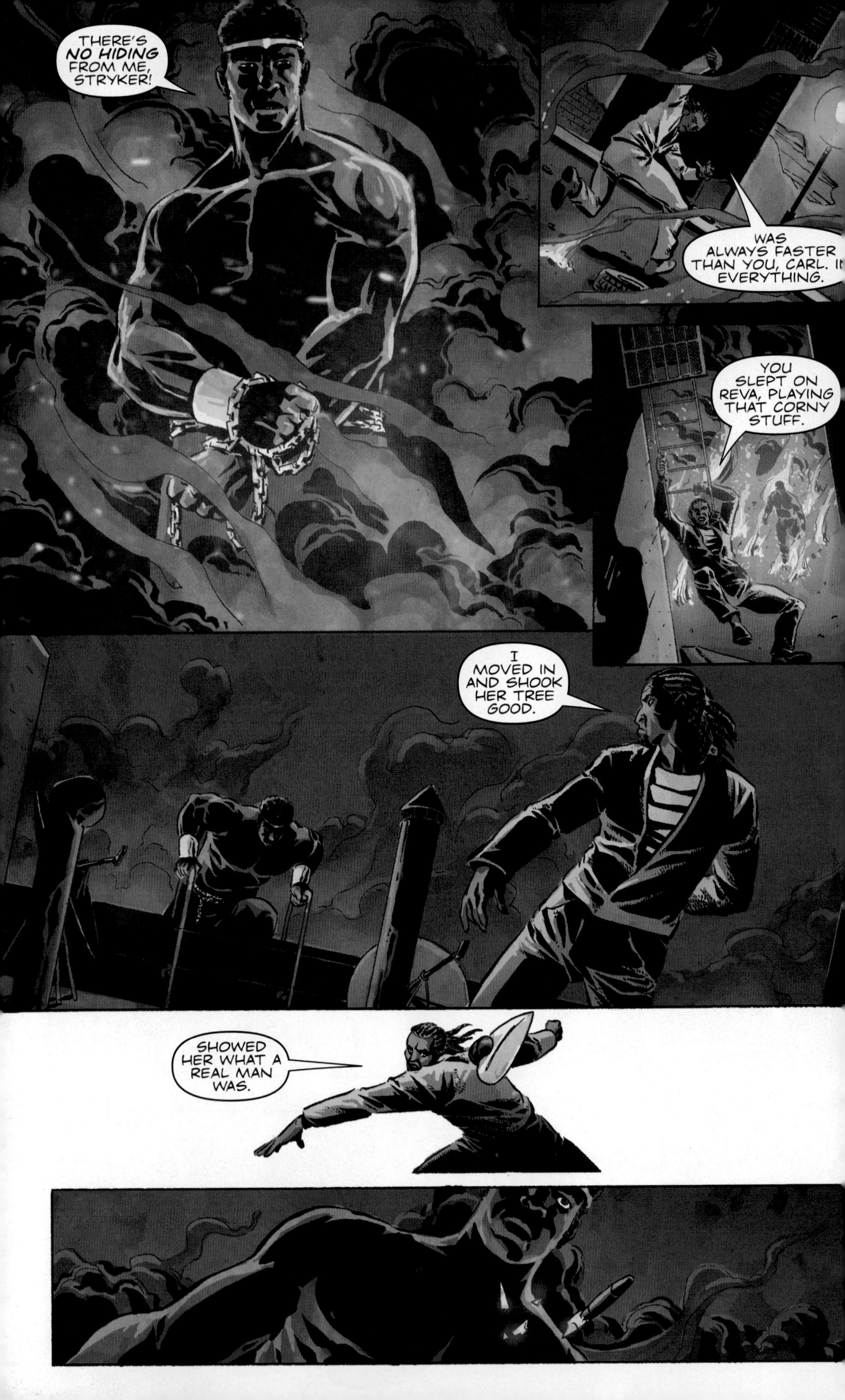
THERE'S NO HIDING FROM ME, STRYKER!
WAS ALWAYS FASTER THAN YOU, CARL. IN EVERYTHING.
YOU SLEPT ON REVA, PLAYING THAT CORNY STUFF.
I MOVED IN AND SHOOK HER TREE GOOD.
SHOWED HER WHAT A REAL MAN WAS.

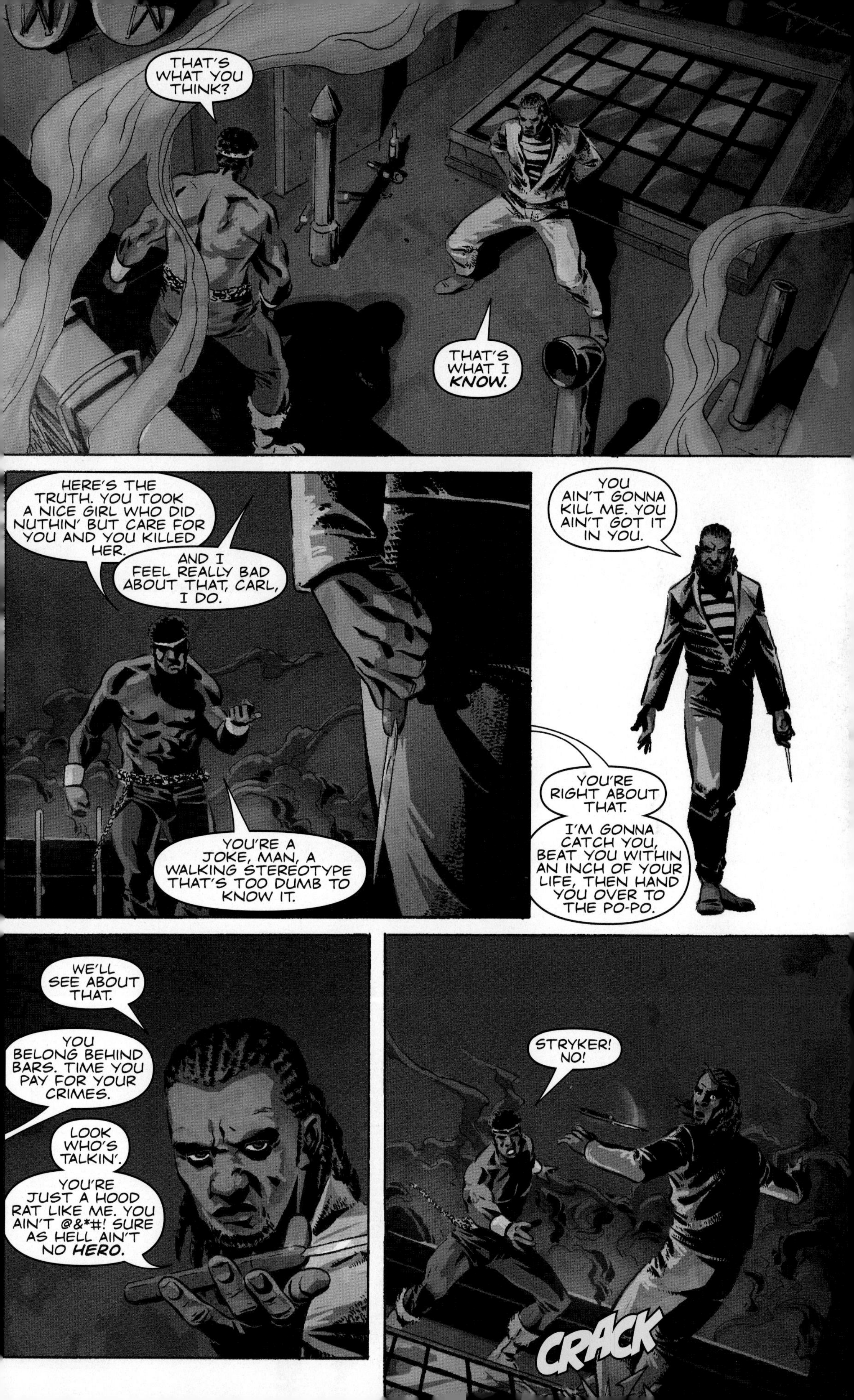
THAT'S WHAT YOU THINK?
THAT'S WHAT I *KNOW.*
HERE'S THE TRUTH. YOU TOOK A NICE GIRL WHO DID NUTHIN' BUT CARE FOR YOU AND YOU KILLED HER.
AND I FEEL REALLY BAD ABOUT THAT, CARL, I DO.
YOU'RE A JOKE, MAN, A WALKING STEREOTYPE THAT'S TOO DUMB TO KNOW IT.
YOU AIN'T GONNA KILL ME. YOU AIN'T GOT IT IN YOU.
YOU'RE RIGHT ABOUT THAT.
I'M GONNA CATCH YOU, BEAT YOU WITHIN AN INCH OF YOUR LIFE, THEN HAND YOU OVER TO THE PO-PO.
WE'LL SEE ABOUT THAT.
YOU BELONG BEHIND BARS. TIME YOU PAY FOR YOUR CRIMES.
LOOK WHO'S TALKIN'.
YOU'RE JUST A HOOD RAT LIKE ME. YOU AIN'T @&*#! SURE AS HELL AIN'T NO *HERO.*
STRYKER! NO!
CRACK

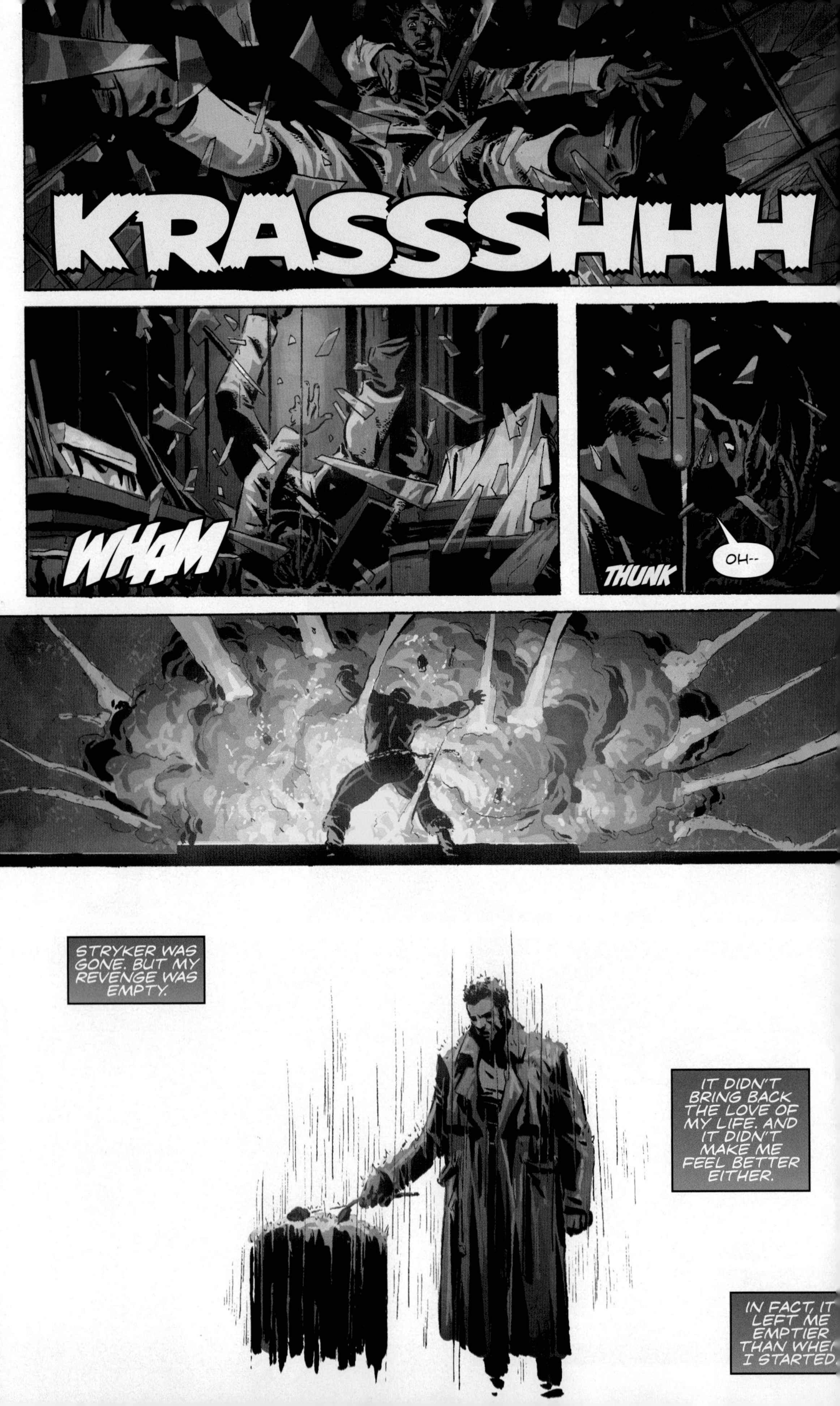
KRASSSHHH
WHAM
THUNK
OH--
STRYKER WAS GONE. BUT MY REVENGE WAS EMPTY.
IT DIDN'T BRING BACK THE LOVE OF MY LIFE. AND IT DIDN'T MAKE ME FEEL BETTER EITHER.
IN FACT, IT LEFT ME EMPTIER THAN WHEN I STARTED.

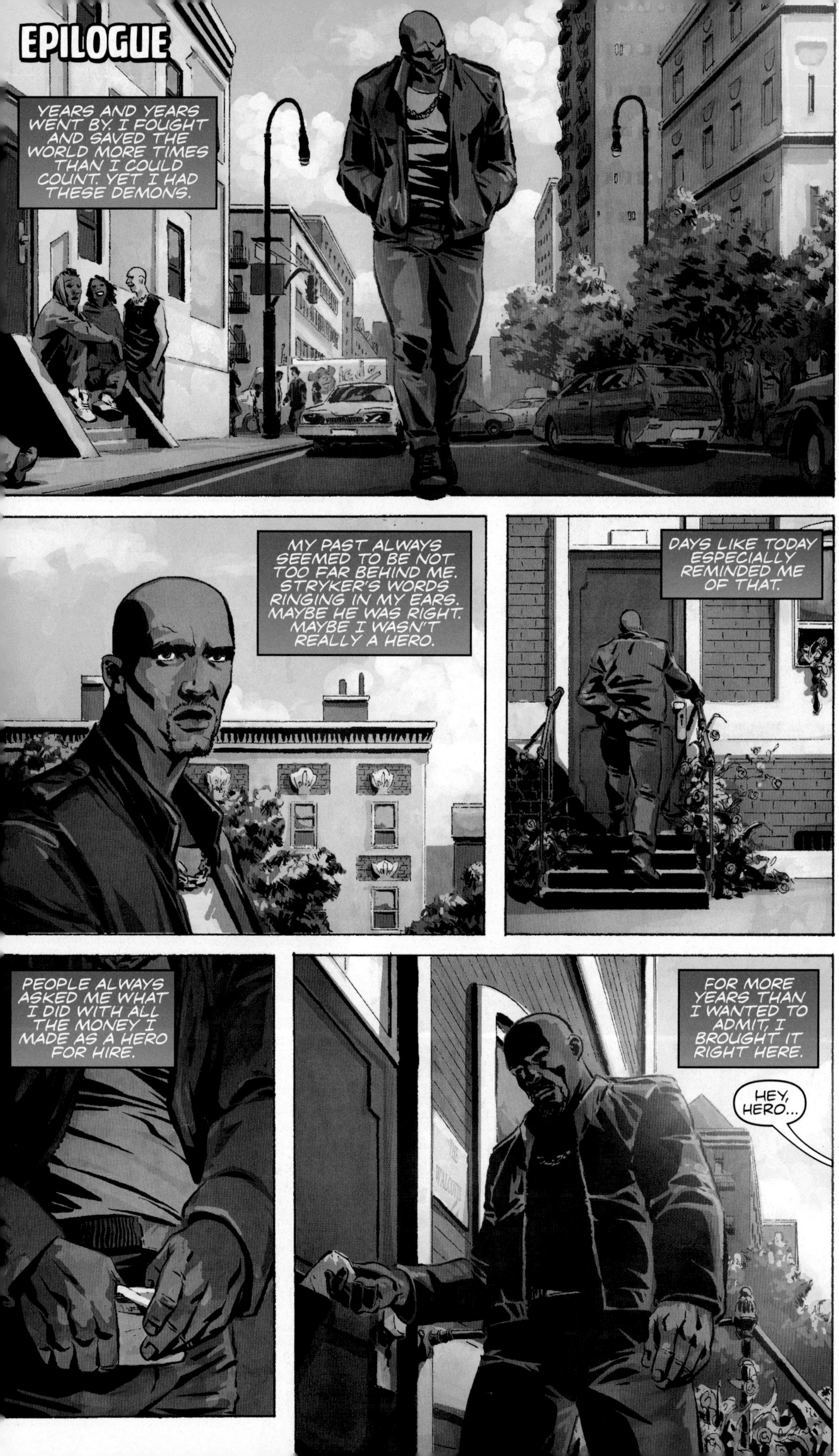
EPILOGUE
YEARS AND YEARS WENT BY. I FOUGHT AND SAVED THE WORLD MORE TIMES THAN I COULD COUNT. YET I HAD THESE DEMONS.
MY PAST ALWAYS SEEMED TO BE NOT TOO FAR BEHIND ME. STRYKER'S WORDS RINGING IN MY EARS. MAYBE HE WAS RIGHT. MAYBE I WASN'T REALLY A HERO.
DAYS LIKE TODAY ESPECIALLY REMINDED ME OF THAT.
PEOPLE ALWAYS ASKED ME WHAT I DID WITH ALL THE MONEY I MADE AS A HERO FOR HIRE.
FOR MORE YEARS THAN I WANTED TO ADMIT, I BROUGHT IT RIGHT HERE.
HEY, HERO...

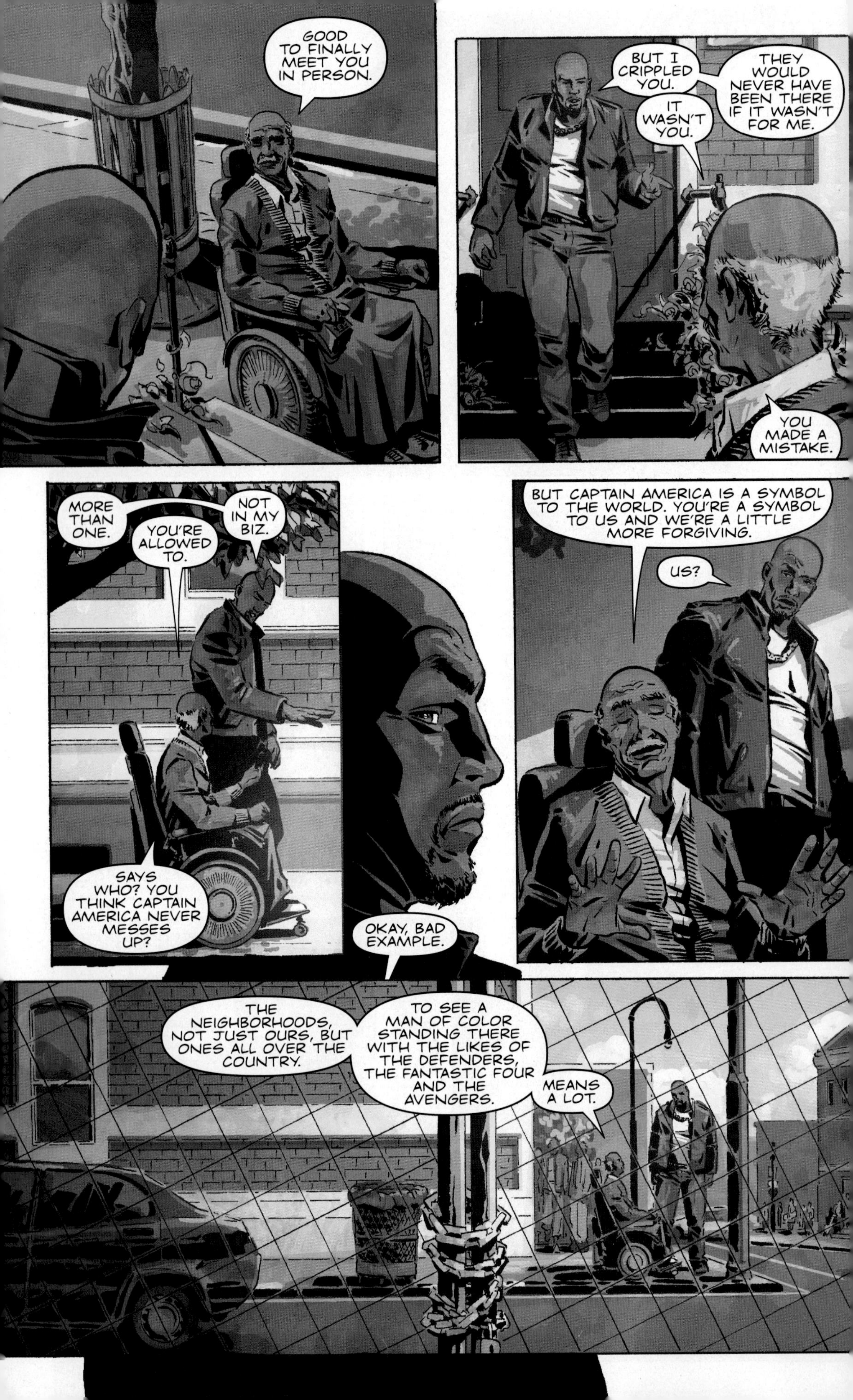
GOOD TO FINALLY MEET YOU IN PERSON.
BUT I CRIPPLED YOU.
IT WASN'T YOU.
THEY WOULD NEVER HAVE BEEN THERE IF IT WASN'T FOR ME.
YOU MADE A MISTAKE.
MORE THAN ONE.
NOT IN MY BIZ.
YOU'RE ALLOWED TO.
SAYS WHO? YOU THINK CAPTAIN AMERICA NEVER MESSES UP?
OKAY, BAD EXAMPLE.
BUT CAPTAIN AMERICA IS A SYMBOL TO THE WORLD. YOU'RE A SYMBOL TO US AND WE'RE A LITTLE MORE FORGIVING.
US?
THE NEIGHBORHOODS, NOT JUST OURS, BUT ONES ALL OVER THE COUNTRY.
TO SEE A MAN OF COLOR STANDING THERE WITH THE LIKES OF THE DEFENDERS, THE FANTASTIC FOUR AND THE AVENGERS.
MEANS A LOT.

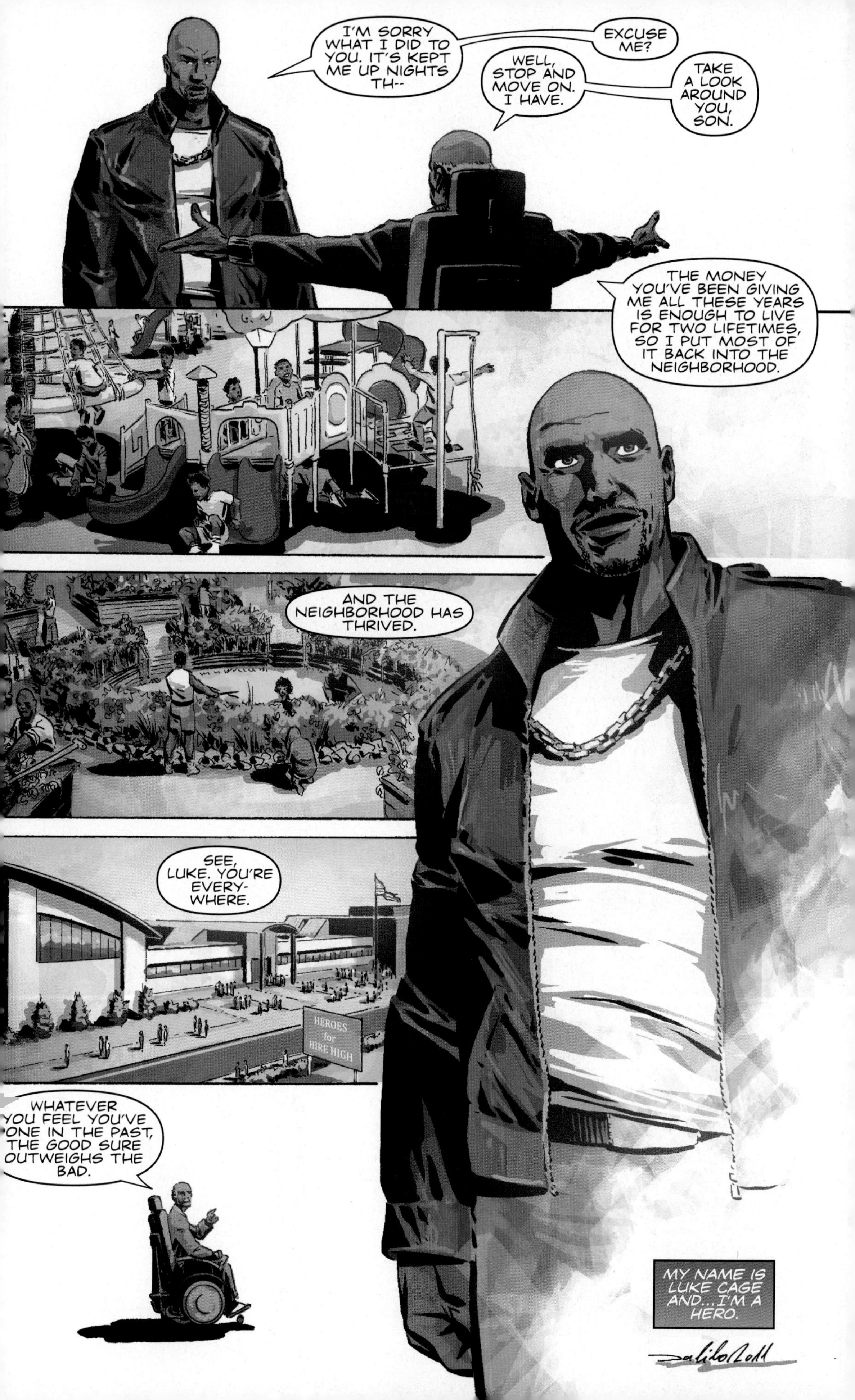
I'M SORRY WHAT I DID TO YOU. IT'S KEPT ME UP NIGHTS TH--
EXCUSE ME?
WELL, STOP AND MOVE ON. I HAVE.
TAKE A LOOK AROUND YOU, SON.
THE MONEY YOU'VE BEEN GIVING ME ALL THESE YEARS IS ENOUGH TO LIVE FOR TWO LIFETIMES, SO I PUT MOST OF IT BACK INTO THE NEIGHBORHOOD.
AND THE NEIGHBORHOOD HAS THRIVED.
SEE, LUKE. YOU'RE EVERY-WHERE.
HEROES for HIRE HIGH
WHATEVER YOU FEEL YOU'VE ONE IN THE PAST, THE GOOD SURE OUTWEIGHS THE BAD.
MY NAME IS LUKE CAGE AND... I'M A HERO.

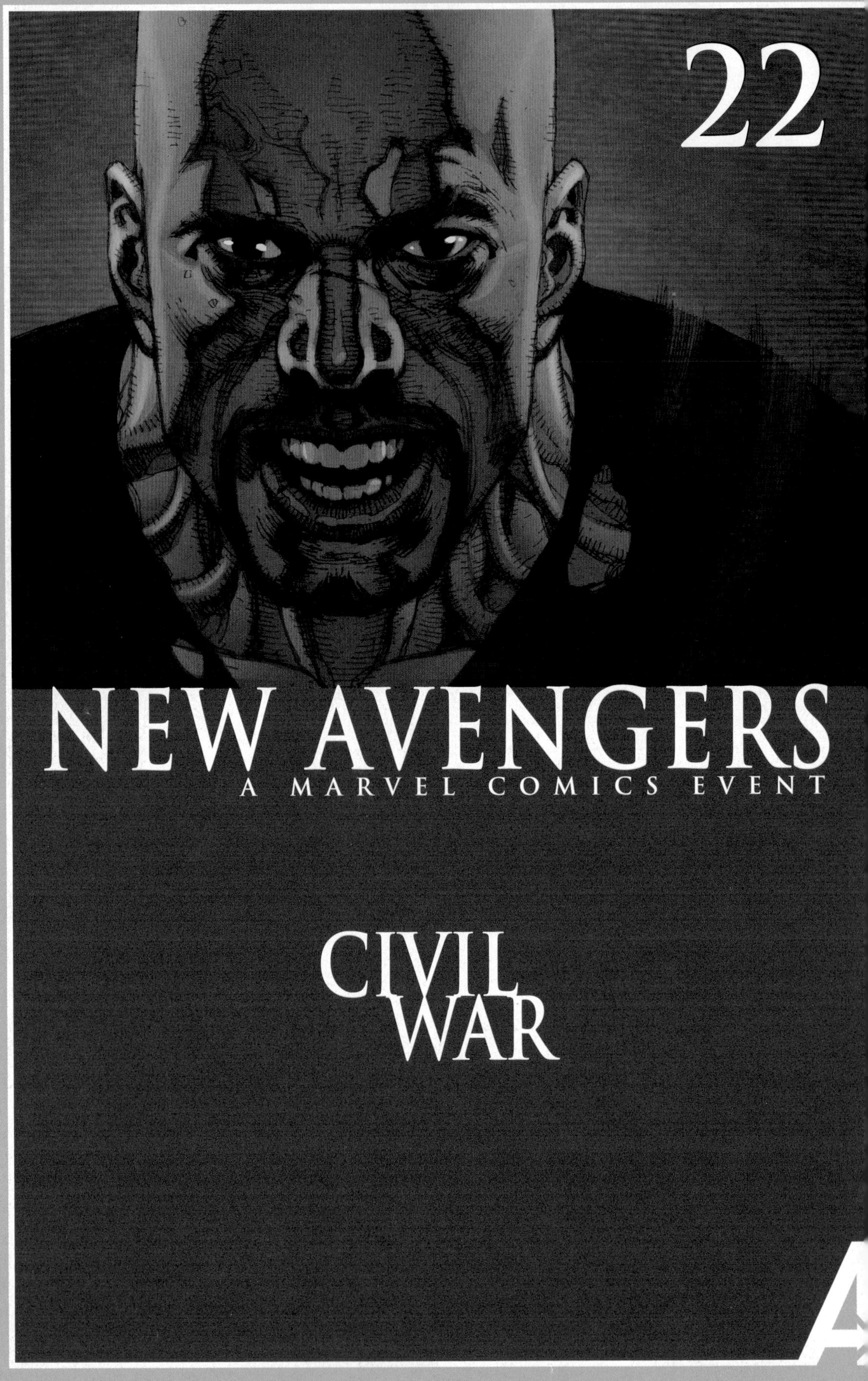
22
NEW AVENGERS
A MARVEL COMICS EVENT
CIVIL WAR

THE NEW AVENGERS

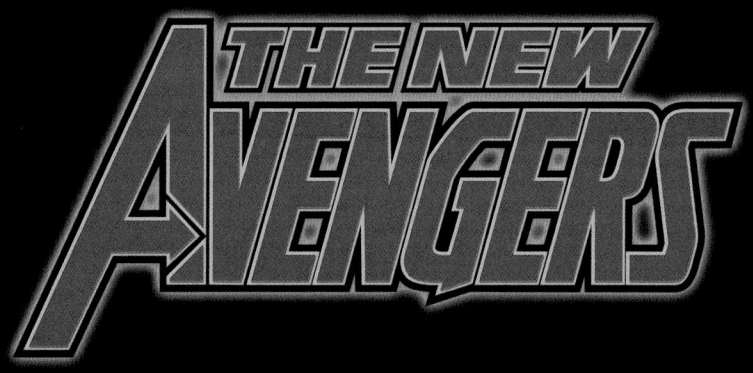

NEW AVENGERS: DISASSEMBLED
PART TWO

PREVIOUSLY IN CIVIL WAR...

After a fight between a quartet of dangerous villains and the New Warriors accidentally causes the destruction of Stamford, Connecticut and the deaths of hundreds of bystanders, public sentiment turns against super heroes. Advocates call for reform, and, as a result, a Superhuman Registration Act is debated, which would require all those possessing paranormal abilities to register with the government, divulging their true identities to the authorities and submitting to training and sanctioning in the manner of federal agents.

Some heroes, such as Iron Man, see this as a natural evolution of the role of superhumans in society, and a reasonable request. Others take umbrage at this assault on their civil liberties. After being called upon to hunt down his fellow heroes who are in defiance of the Registration Act, Captain America goes underground and, with the help of his former partner, the Falcon, begins to form a resistance movement.

MIDNIGHT:
REGISTRATION ACT BECOMES LAW
SONY
REGISTRATION ACT BECOMES LAW REGISTRATION

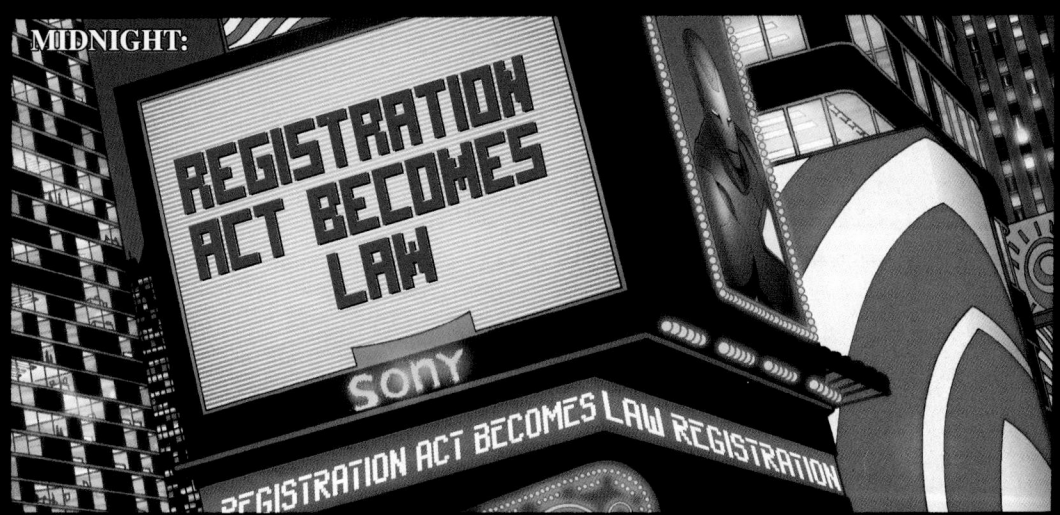

Today, the Act has been passed—the law goes into effect at midnight. Any person possessing superhuman powers who doesn't register will be considered a criminal.

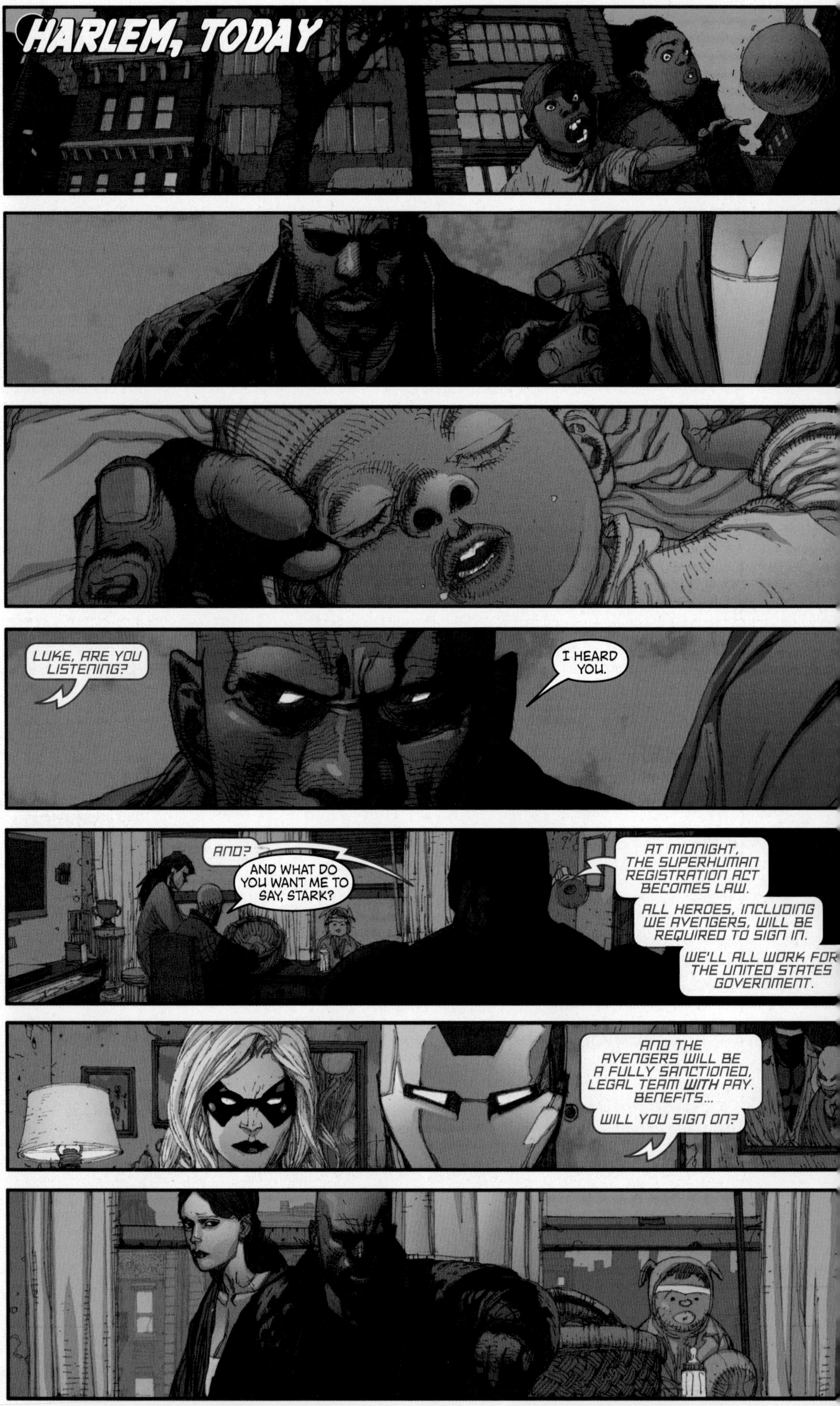
HARLEM, TODAY
LUKE, ARE YOU LISTENING?
I HEARD YOU.
AND?
AND WHAT DO YOU WANT ME TO SAY, STARK?
AT MIDNIGHT, THE SUPERHUMAN REGISTRATION ACT BECOMES LAW.
ALL HEROES, INCLUDING WE AVENGERS, WILL BE REQUIRED TO SIGN IN.
WE'LL ALL WORK FOR THE UNITED STATES GOVERNMENT.
AND THE AVENGERS WILL BE A FULLY SANCTIONED, LEGAL TEAM WITH PAY. BENEFITS...
WILL YOU SIGN ON?

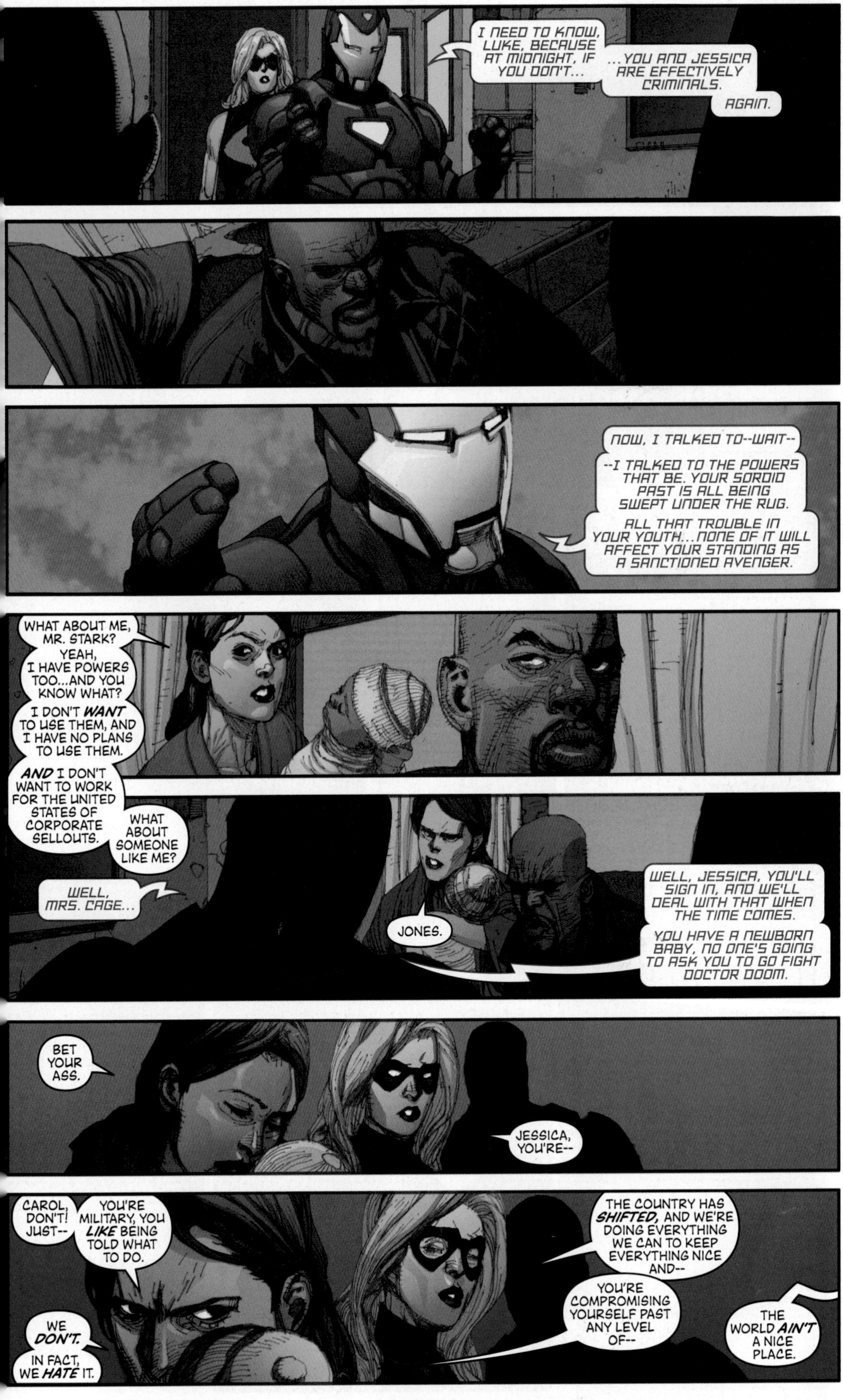

I NEED TO KNOW, LUKE, BECAUSE AT MIDNIGHT, IF YOU DON'T...
...YOU AND JESSICA ARE EFFECTIVELY CRIMINALS.
AGAIN.
NOW, I TALKED TO--WAIT--
--I TALKED TO THE POWERS THAT BE. YOUR SORDID PAST IS ALL BEING SWEPT UNDER THE RUG.
ALL THAT TROUBLE IN YOUR YOUTH...NONE OF IT WILL AFFECT YOUR STANDING AS A SANCTIONED AVENGER.
WHAT ABOUT ME, MR. STARK?
YEAH, I HAVE POWERS TOO...AND YOU KNOW WHAT?
I DON'T WANT TO USE THEM, AND I HAVE NO PLANS TO USE THEM.
AND I DON'T WANT TO WORK FOR THE UNITED STATES OF CORPORATE SELLOUTS.
WHAT ABOUT SOMEONE LIKE ME?
WELL, MRS. CAGE...
JONES.
WELL, JESSICA, YOU'LL SIGN IN, AND WE'LL DEAL WITH THAT WHEN THE TIME COMES.
YOU HAVE A NEWBORN BABY, NO ONE'S GOING TO ASK YOU TO GO FIGHT DOCTOR DOOM.
BET YOUR ASS.
JESSICA, YOU'RE--
CAROL, DON'T! JUST--
YOU'RE MILITARY, YOU LIKE BEING TOLD WHAT TO DO.
WE DON'T.
IN FACT, WE HATE IT.
THE COUNTRY HAS SHIFTED, AND WE'RE DOING EVERYTHING WE CAN TO KEEP EVERYTHING NICE AND--
YOU'RE COMPROMISING YOURSELF PAST ANY LEVEL OF--
THE WORLD AIN'T A NICE PLACE.

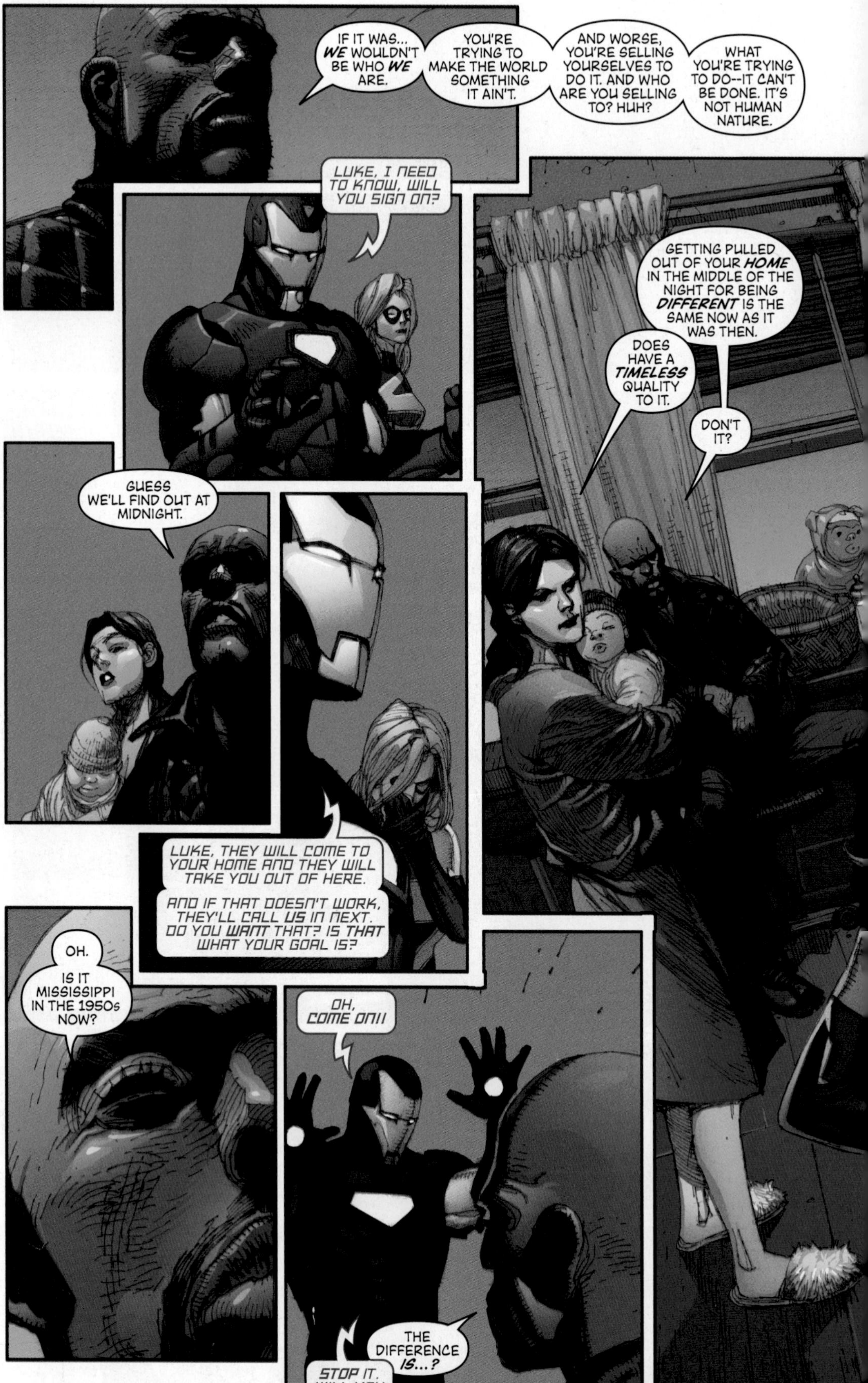
IF IT WAS... WE WOULDN'T BE WHO WE ARE.
YOU'RE TRYING TO MAKE THE WORLD SOMETHING IT AIN'T.
AND WORSE, YOU'RE SELLING YOURSELVES TO DO IT. AND WHO ARE YOU SELLING TO? HUH?
WHAT YOU'RE TRYING TO DO--IT CAN'T BE DONE. IT'S NOT HUMAN NATURE.
LUKE, I NEED TO KNOW, WILL YOU SIGN ON?
GETTING PULLED OUT OF YOUR HOME IN THE MIDDLE OF THE NIGHT FOR BEING DIFFERENT IS THE SAME NOW AS IT WAS THEN.
DOES HAVE A TIMELESS QUALITY TO IT.
DON'T IT?
GUESS WE'LL FIND OUT AT MIDNIGHT.
LUKE, THEY WILL COME TO YOUR HOME AND THEY WILL TAKE YOU OUT OF HERE.
AND IF THAT DOESN'T WORK, THEY'LL CALL US IN NEXT. DO YOU WANT THAT? IS THAT WHAT YOUR GOAL IS?
OH.
IS IT MISSISSIPPI IN THE 1950s NOW?
OH, COME ON!!
THE DIFFERENCE IS...?
STOP IT. WILL YOU STOP?

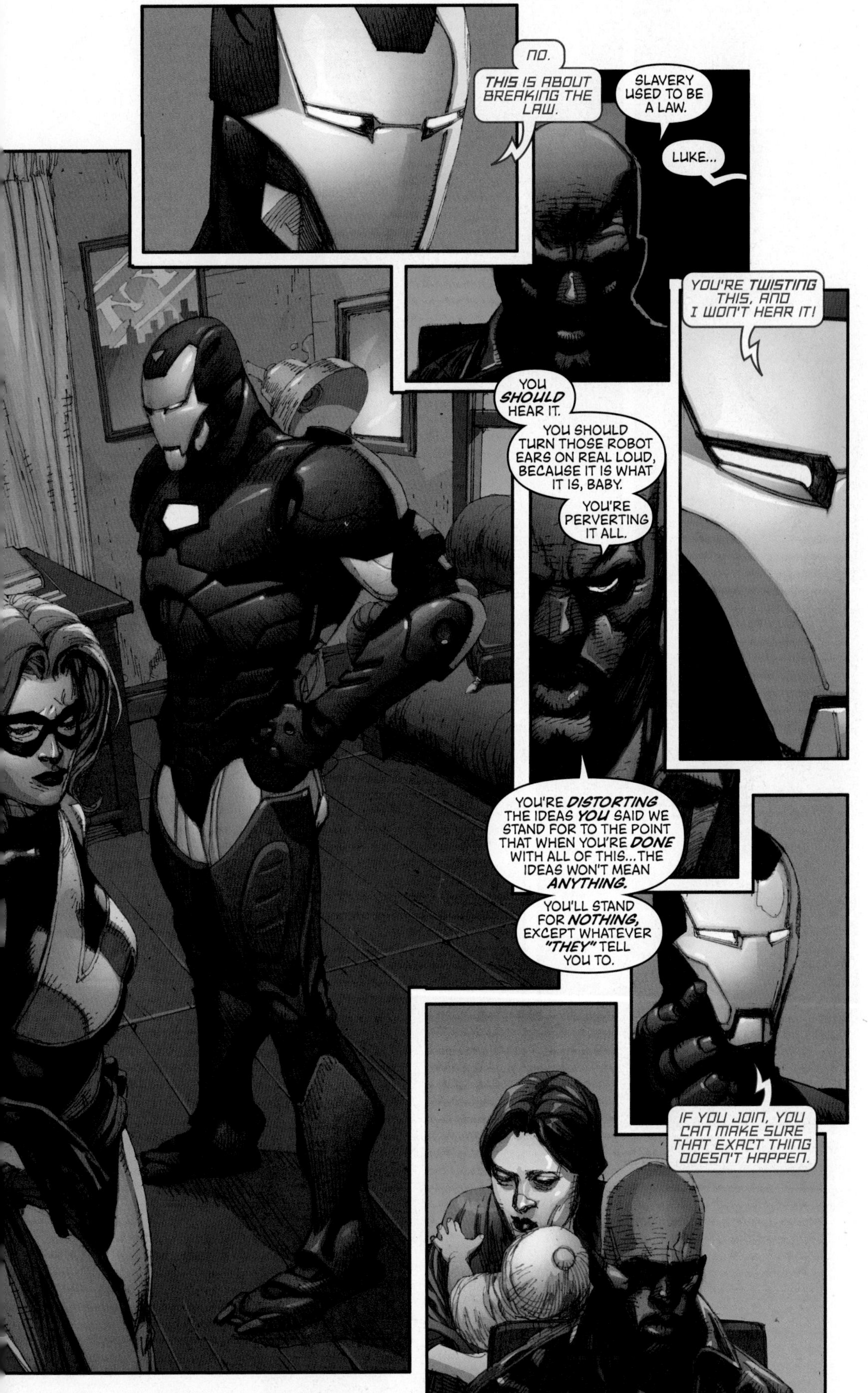

NO.
THIS IS ABOUT BREAKING THE LAW.
SLAVERY USED TO BE A LAW.
LUKE...
YOU'RE TWISTING THIS, AND I WON'T HEAR IT!
YOU SHOULD HEAR IT.
YOU SHOULD TURN THOSE ROBOT EARS ON REAL LOUD, BECAUSE IT IS WHAT IT IS, BABY.
YOU'RE PERVERTING IT ALL.
YOU'RE DISTORTING THE IDEAS YOU SAID WE STAND FOR TO THE POINT THAT WHEN YOU'RE DONE WITH ALL OF THIS...THE IDEAS WON'T MEAN ANYTHING.
YOU'LL STAND FOR NOTHING, EXCEPT WHATEVER "THEY" TELL YOU TO.
IF YOU JOIN, YOU CAN MAKE SURE THAT EXACT THING DOESN'T HAPPEN.

SO YOU'RE NOT SIGNING.

I'M GOING TO RAISE MY KID RIGHT.

WHAT DOES *THAT* MEAN?

IT'S TOO BAD YOU DON'T KNOW.

FINE.

JESSICA, I'M YOUR BEST FRIEND.

CAN'T YOU *TRUST* ME ON THIS? JUST *TRUST* ME?

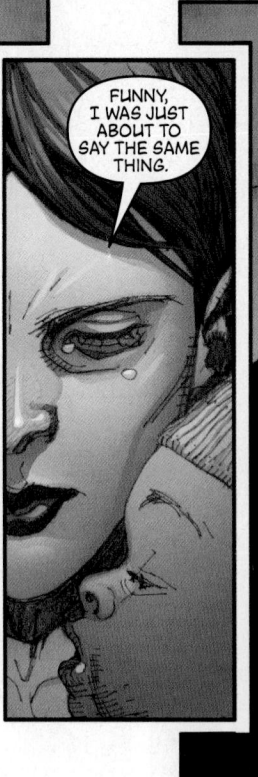

FUNNY, I WAS JUST ABOUT TO SAY THE SAME THING.

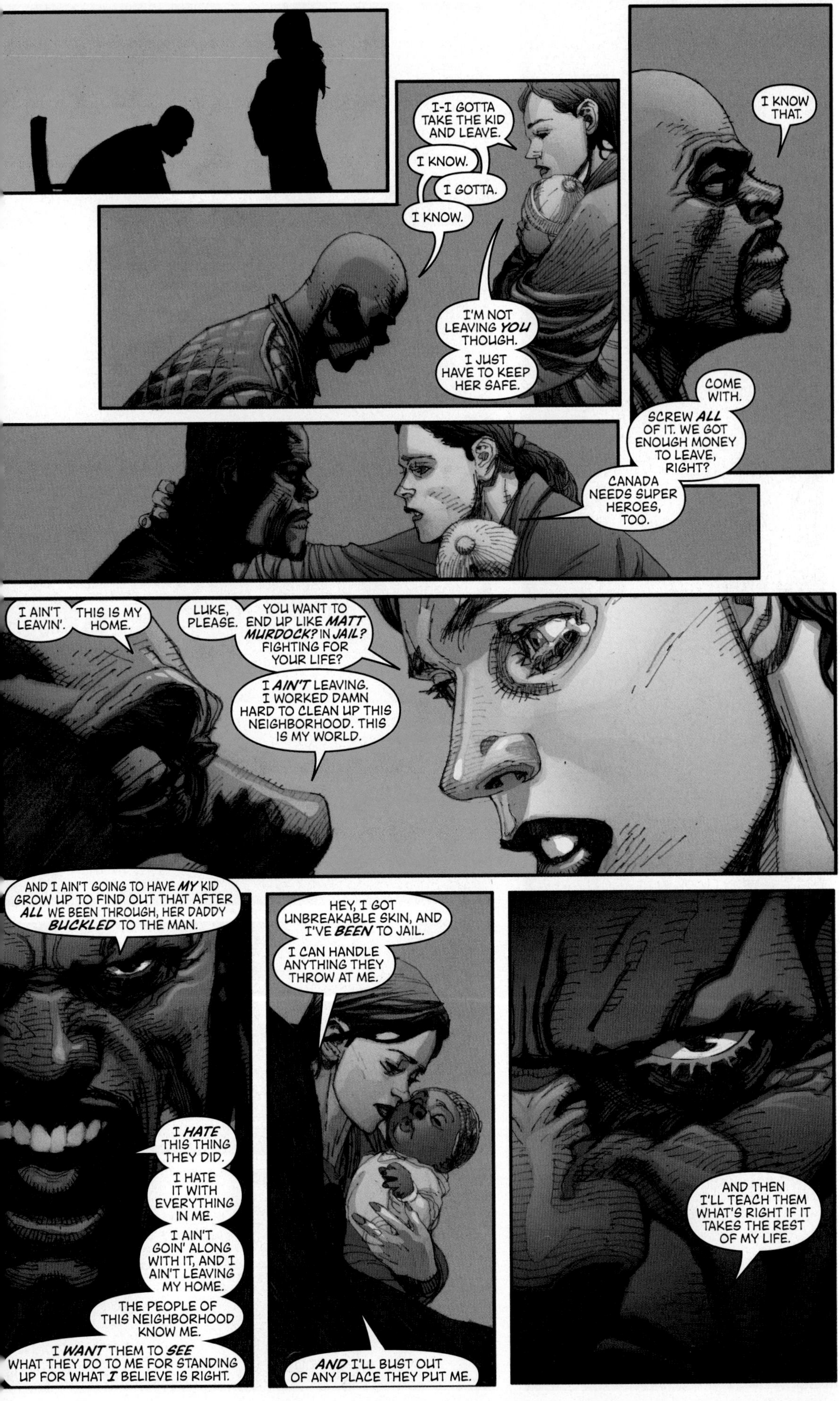
I-I GOTTA TAKE THE KID AND LEAVE.
I KNOW.
I GOTTA.
I KNOW.
I'M NOT LEAVING YOU THOUGH.
I JUST HAVE TO KEEP HER SAFE.
I KNOW THAT.
COME WITH.
SCREW ALL OF IT. WE GOT ENOUGH MONEY TO LEAVE, RIGHT?
CANADA NEEDS SUPER HEROES, TOO.
I AIN'T LEAVIN'.
THIS IS MY HOME.
LUKE, PLEASE.
YOU WANT TO END UP LIKE MATT MURDOCK? IN JAIL? FIGHTING FOR YOUR LIFE?
I AIN'T LEAVING. I WORKED DAMN HARD TO CLEAN UP THIS NEIGHBORHOOD. THIS IS MY WORLD.
AND I AIN'T GOING TO HAVE MY KID GROW UP TO FIND OUT THAT AFTER ALL WE BEEN THROUGH, HER DADDY BUCKLED TO THE MAN.
I HATE THIS THING THEY DID.
I HATE IT WITH EVERYTHING IN ME.
I AIN'T GOIN' ALONG WITH IT, AND I AIN'T LEAVING MY HOME.
THE PEOPLE OF THIS NEIGHBORHOOD KNOW ME.
I WANT THEM TO SEE WHAT THEY DO TO ME FOR STANDING UP FOR WHAT I BELIEVE IS RIGHT.
HEY, I GOT UNBREAKABLE SKIN, AND I'VE BEEN TO JAIL.
I CAN HANDLE ANYTHING THEY THROW AT ME.
AND I'LL BUST OUT OF ANY PLACE THEY PUT ME.
AND THEN I'LL TEACH THEM WHAT'S RIGHT IF IT TAKES THE REST OF MY LIFE.

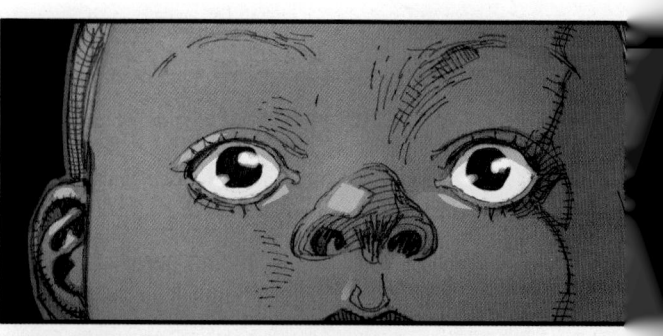

SHE WON'T LOOK AT ME.

DON'T WORRY ABOUT IT. HEY, BABY... LOOK AT ME.

DON'T TAKE NO $%#@ OFF OF NOBODY.

SHE'S THREE MONTHS OLD. HOW MUCH $%#@ YOU THINK SHE'LL BE TAKING?

I MEAN, IN GENERAL. IN LIFE.

GIVE HER OVER. I HAVE TO STRAP HER IN.

THIS IS-- THIS IS HARD.

THEN GET IN THE CAR, LUKE. WE'LL ALL BE IN TORONTO IN--

STOP.

I CAN'T.

NEITHER CAN I.

MAKE ME A PROMISE--

NO.

DON'T TURN THE TV ON.

WHEREVE YOU ARE, J THIS WEEK, WATCH I ON TV.

OH, MAN...

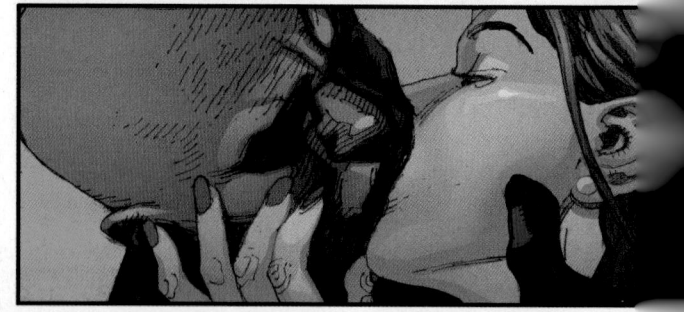

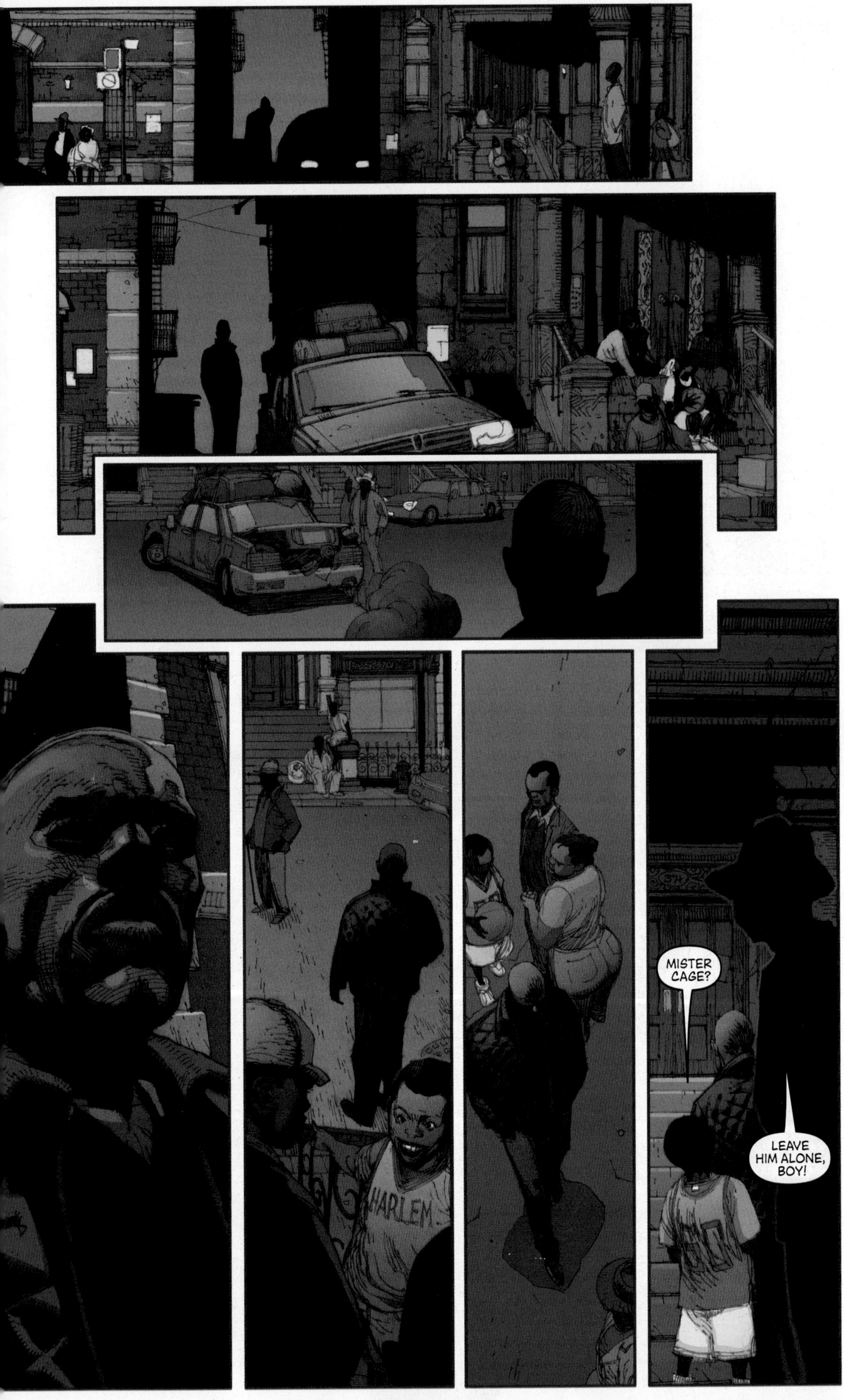
MISTER CAGE?
LEAVE HIM ALONE, BOY!

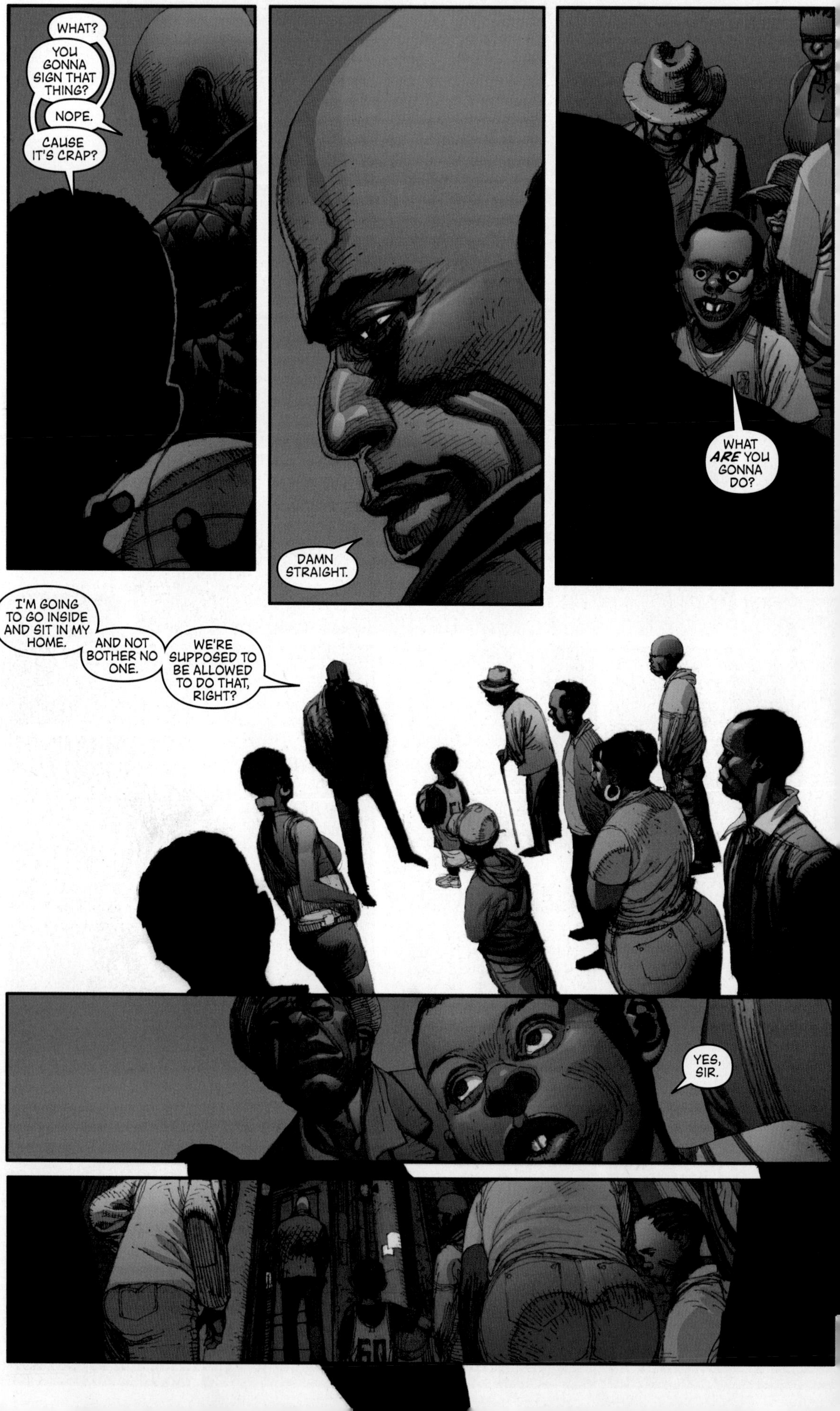
WHAT?
YOU GONNA SIGN THAT THING?
NOPE.
CAUSE IT'S CRAP?
DAMN STRAIGHT.
WHAT *ARE* YOU GONNA DO?
I'M GOING TO GO INSIDE AND SIT IN MY HOME.
AND NOT BOTHER NO ONE.
WE'RE SUPPOSED TO BE ALLOWED TO DO THAT, RIGHT?
YES, SIR.

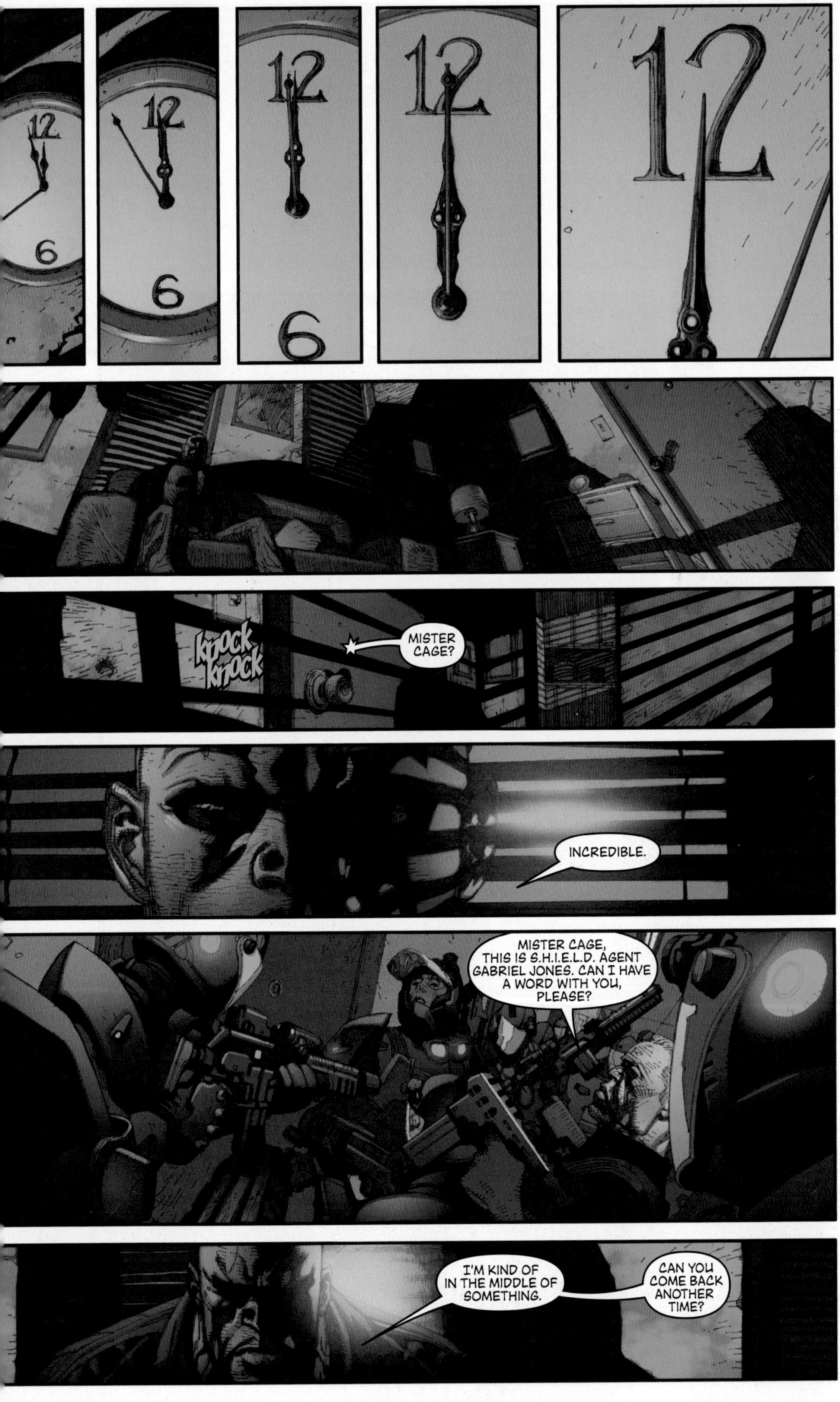

KNOCK KNOCK
MISTER CAGE?
INCREDIBLE.
MISTER CAGE, THIS IS S.H.I.E.L.D. AGENT GABRIEL JONES. CAN I HAVE A WORD WITH YOU, PLEASE?
I'M KIND OF IN THE MIDDLE OF SOMETHING.
CAN YOU COME BACK ANOTHER TIME?

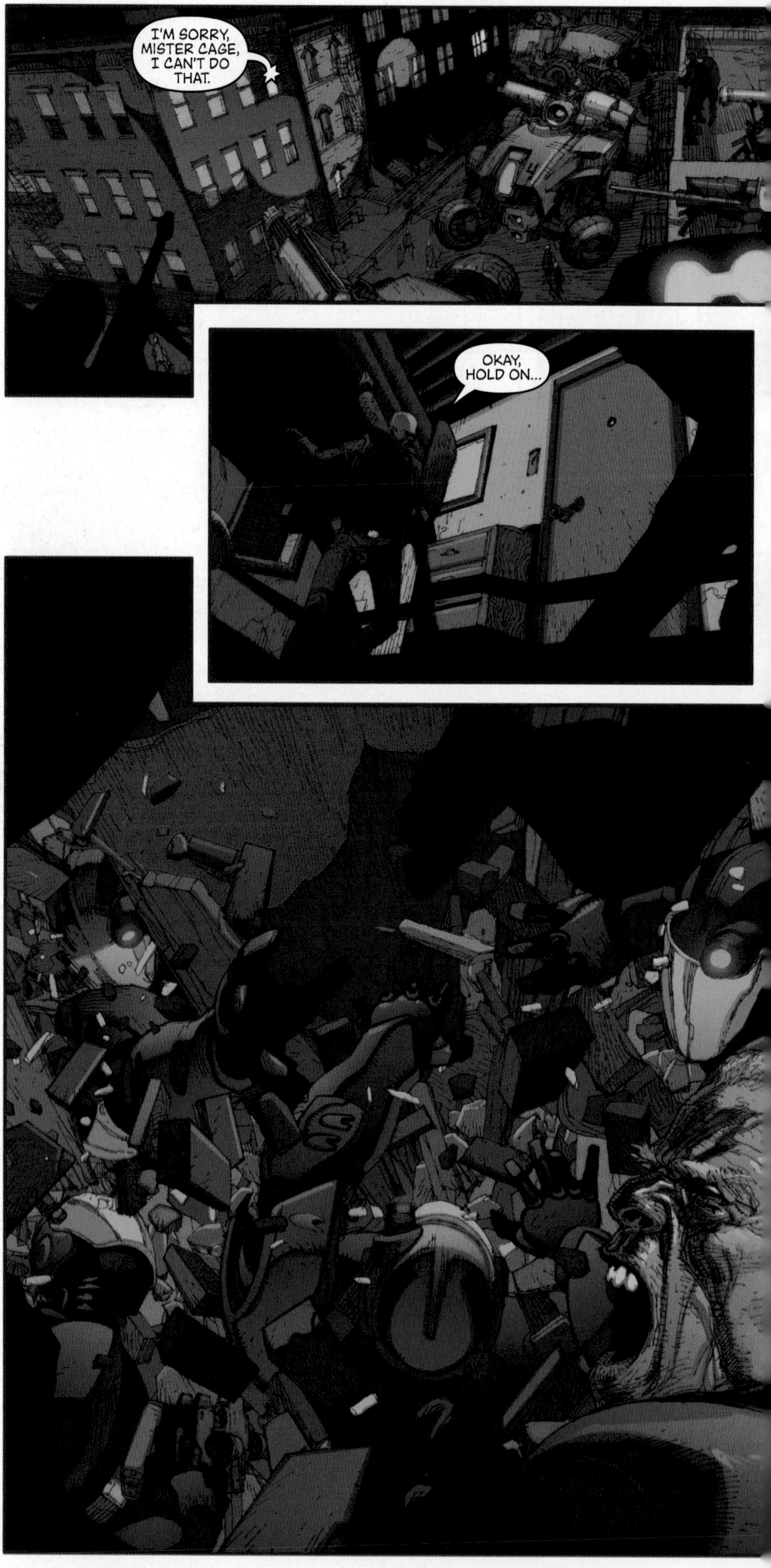
I'M SORRY, MISTER CAGE, I CAN'T DO THAT.
OKAY, HOLD ON...

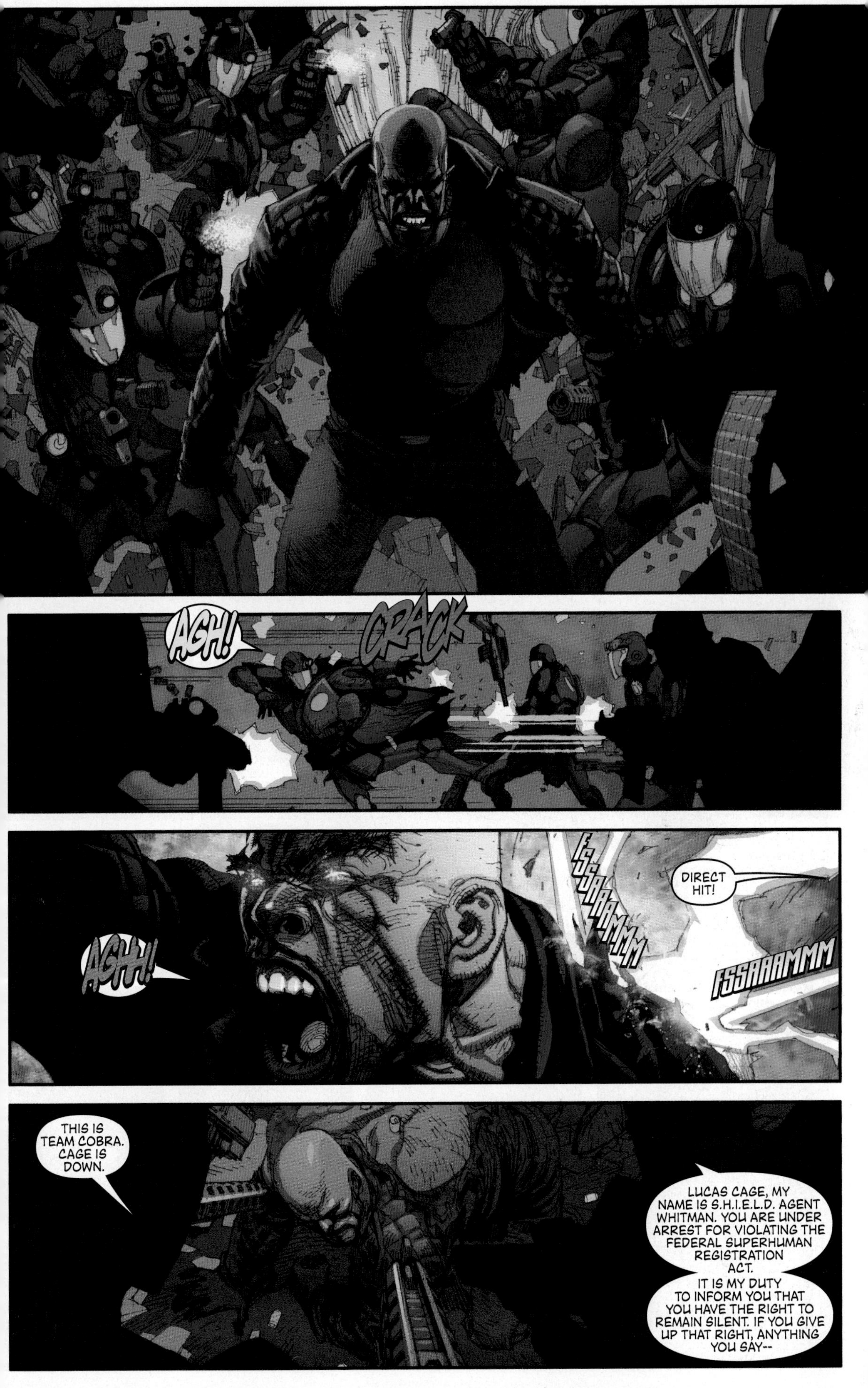
AGH!
CRACK
DIRECT HIT!
FSSAAAMMM
AGHH!
FSSAAAMMM
THIS IS TEAM COBRA. CAGE IS DOWN.
LUCAS CAGE, MY NAME IS S.H.I.E.L.D. AGENT WHITMAN. YOU ARE UNDER ARREST FOR VIOLATING THE FEDERAL SUPERHUMAN REGISTRATION ACT.
IT IS MY DUTY TO INFORM YOU THAT YOU HAVE THE RIGHT TO REMAIN SILENT. IF YOU GIVE UP THAT RIGHT, ANYTHING YOU SAY--

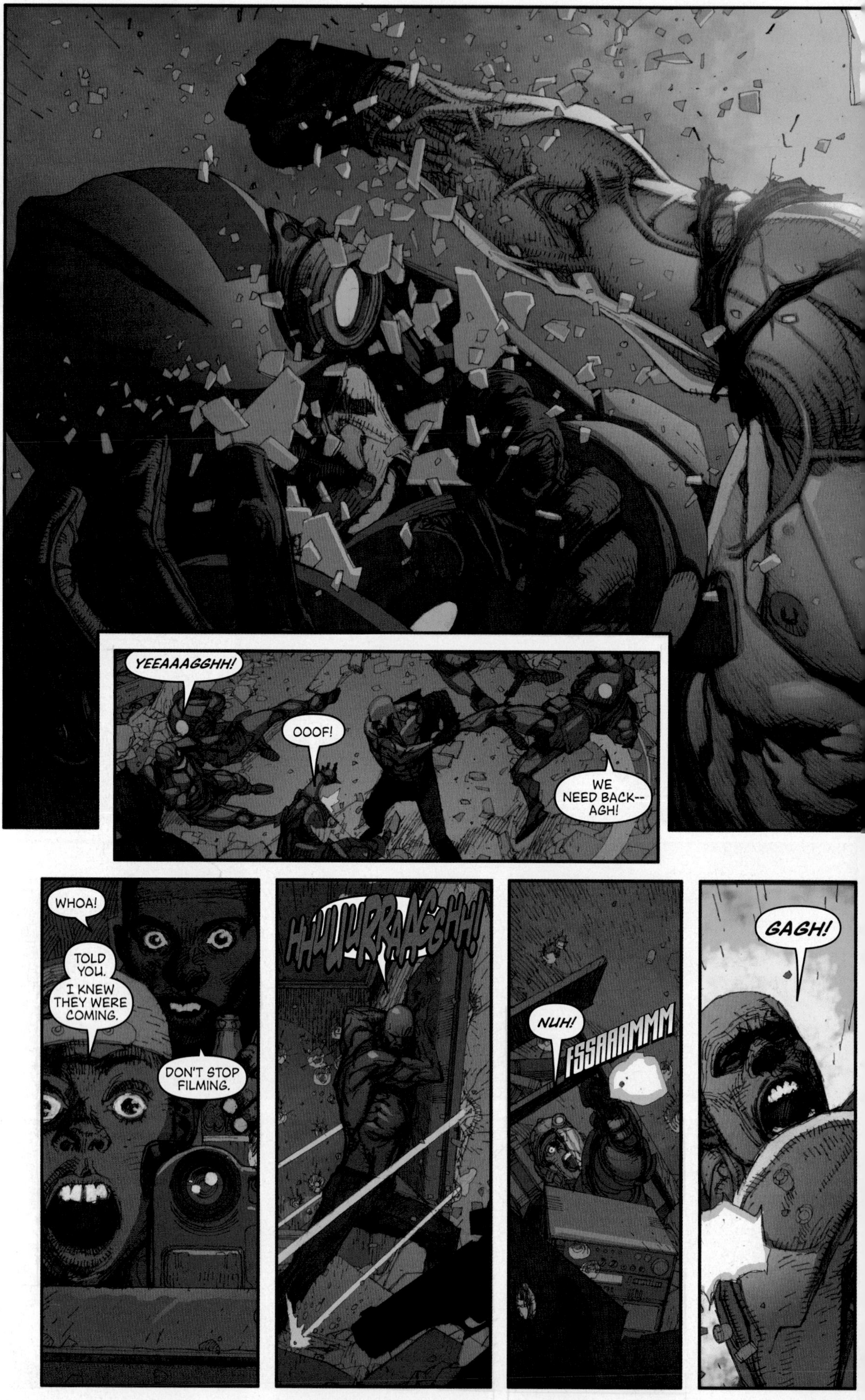
YEEAAAGGHH!
OOOF!
WE NEED BACK-- AGH!
WHOA!
TOLD YOU. I KNEW THEY WERE COMING.
DON'T STOP FILMING.
HHUURRAAGGHH!
NUH!
FSSRRRMMM
GAGH!

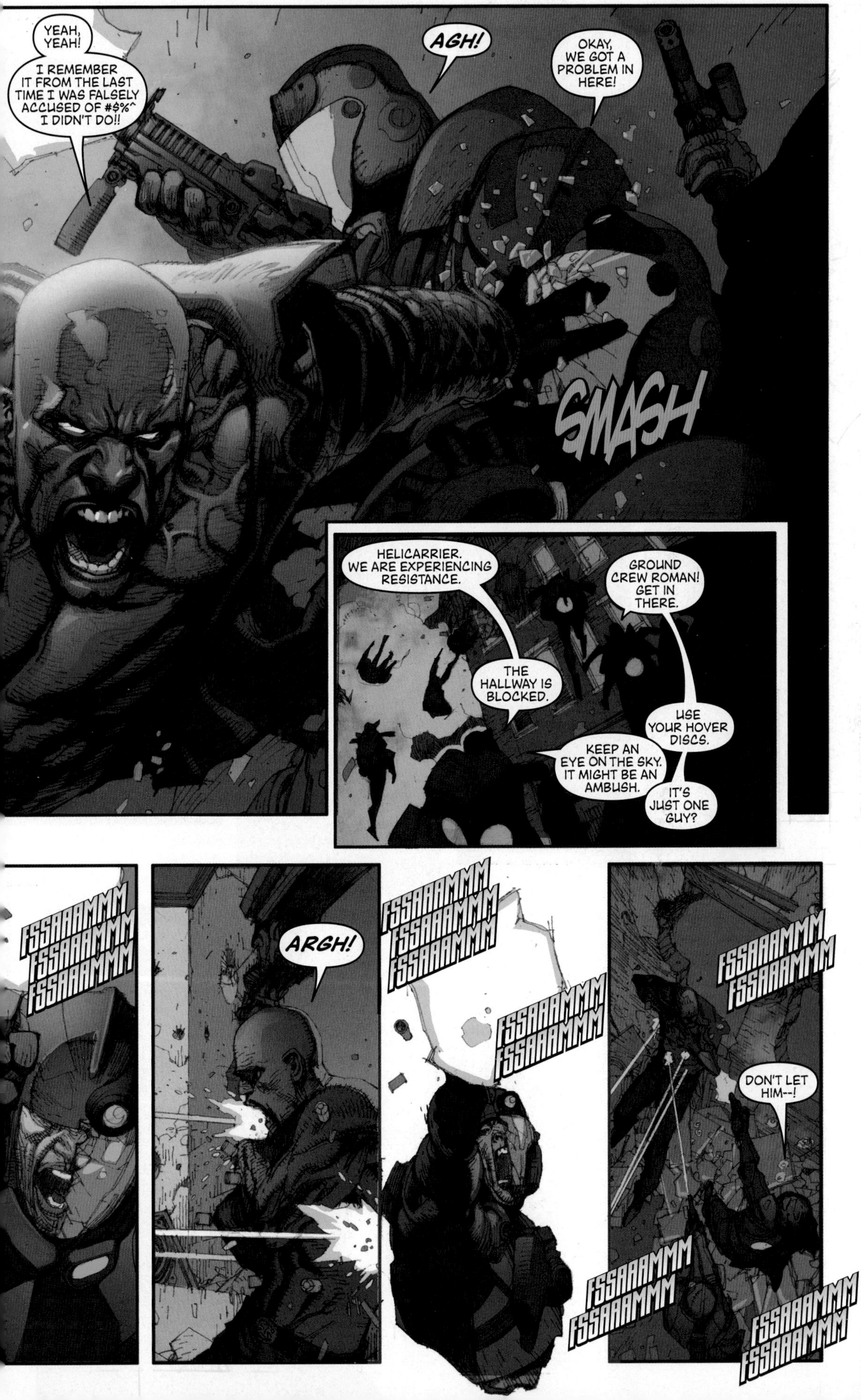
YEAH, YEAH!
I REMEMBER IT FROM THE LAST TIME I WAS FALSELY ACCUSED OF #$%^ I DIDN'T DO!!
AGH!
OKAY, WE GOT A PROBLEM IN HERE!
SMASH
HELICARRIER. WE ARE EXPERIENCING RESISTANCE.
THE HALLWAY IS BLOCKED.
GROUND CREW ROMAN! GET IN THERE.
USE YOUR HOVER DISCS.
KEEP AN EYE ON THE SKY. IT MIGHT BE AN AMBUSH.
IT'S JUST ONE GUY?
FSSAAAMMM FSSAAAMMM FSSAAAMMM
ARGH!
FSSAAAMMM FSSAAAMMM FSSAAAMMM
FSSAAAMMM FSSAAAMMM
FSSAAAMMM FSSAAAMMM
DON'T LET HIM--!
FSSAAAMMM FSSAAAMMM
FSSAAAMMM FSSAAAMMM

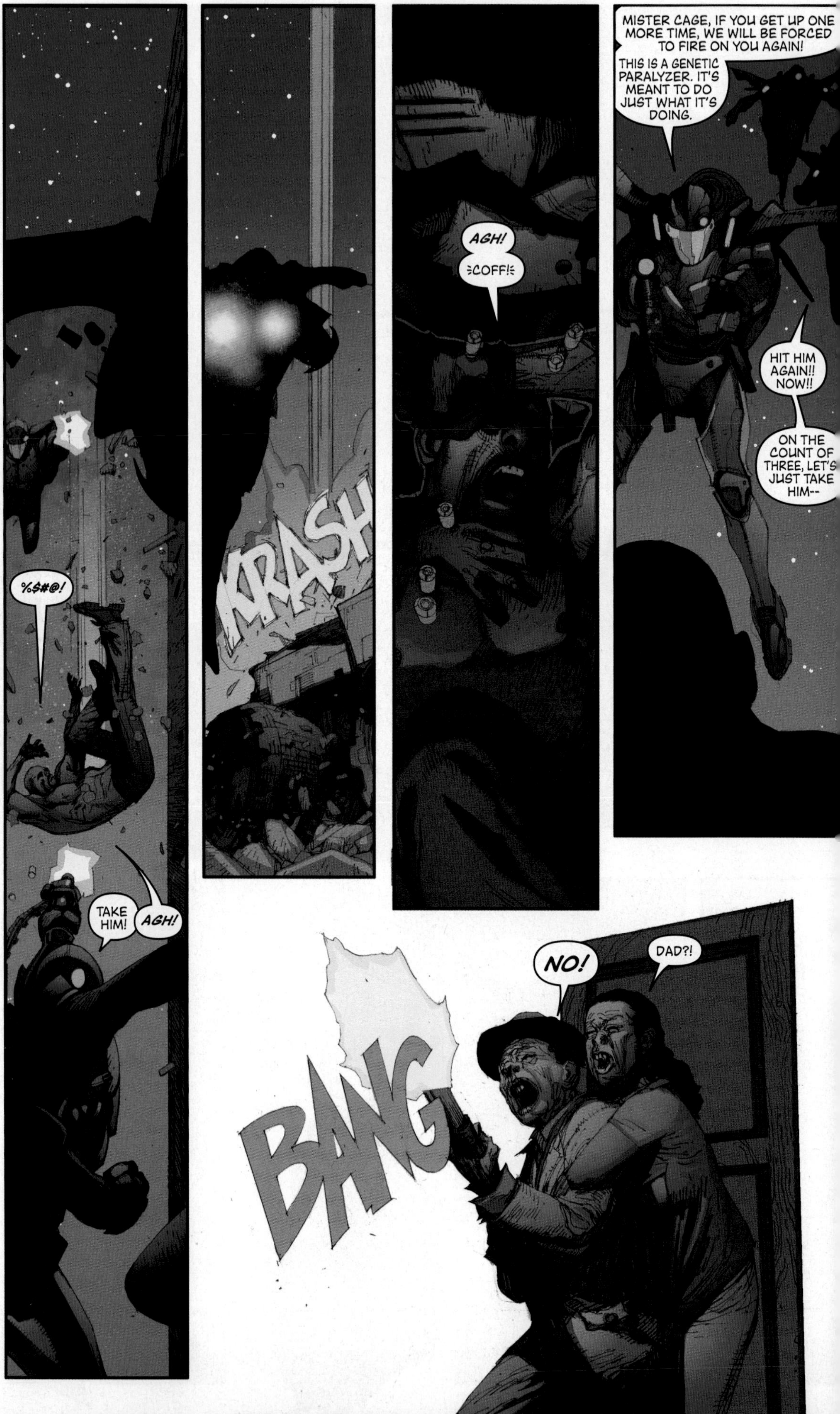
%$#@!
TAKE HIM!
AGH!
KRASH
AGH!
COFF!
MISTER CAGE, IF YOU GET UP ONE MORE TIME, WE WILL BE FORCED TO FIRE ON YOU AGAIN!
THIS IS A GENETIC PARALYZER. IT'S MEANT TO DO JUST WHAT IT'S DOING.
HIT HIM AGAIN!! NOW!!
ON THE COUNT OF THREE, LET'S JUST TAKE HIM--
BANG
NO!
DAD?!

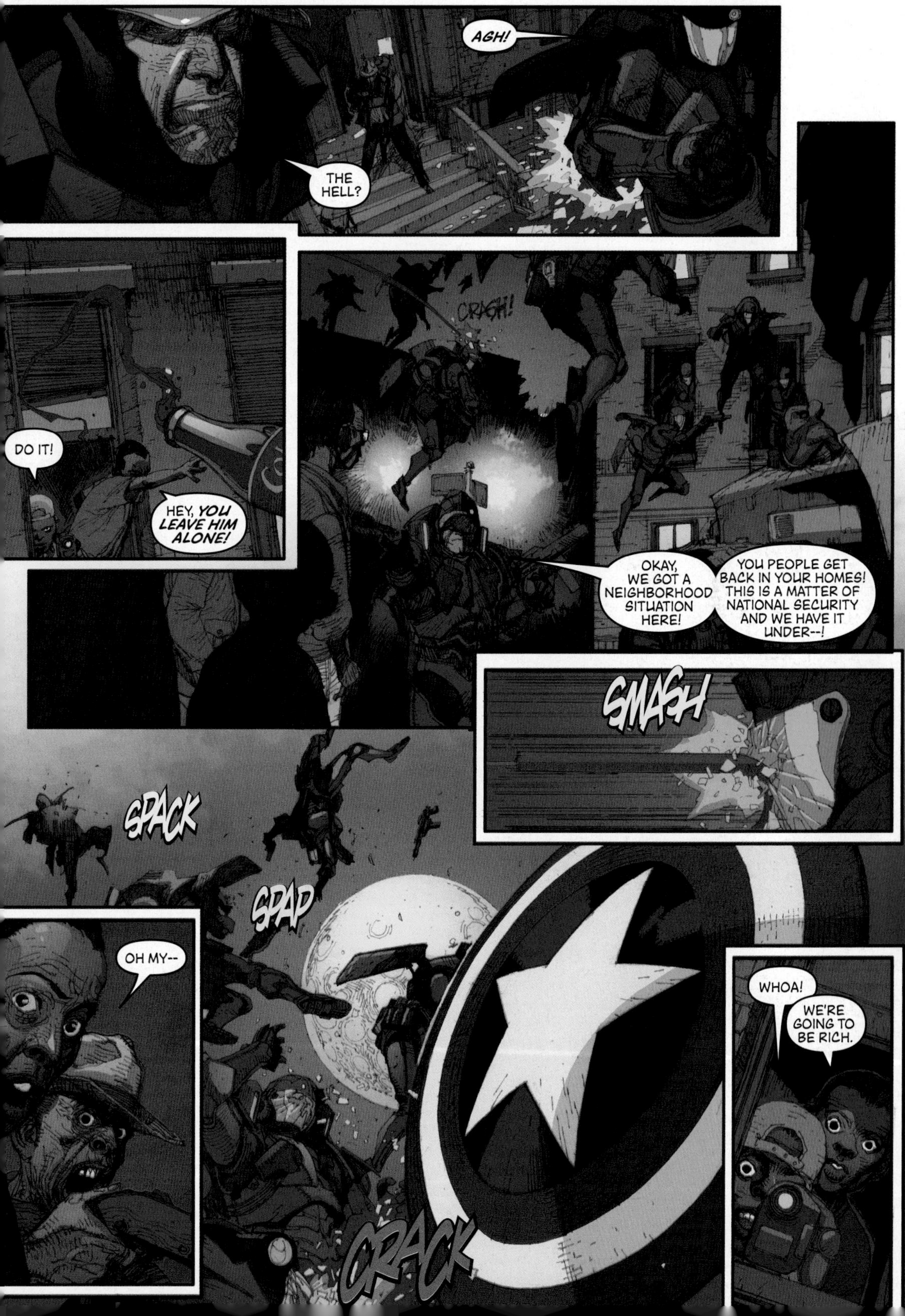
AGH!
THE HELL?
DO IT!
HEY, YOU LEAVE HIM ALONE!
CRASH!
OKAY, WE GOT A NEIGHBORHOOD SITUATION HERE!
YOU PEOPLE GET BACK IN YOUR HOMES! THIS IS A MATTER OF NATIONAL SECURITY AND WE HAVE IT UNDER--!
SMASH
SPACK
SPAP
OH MY--
CRACK
WHOA!
WE'RE GOING TO BE RICH.

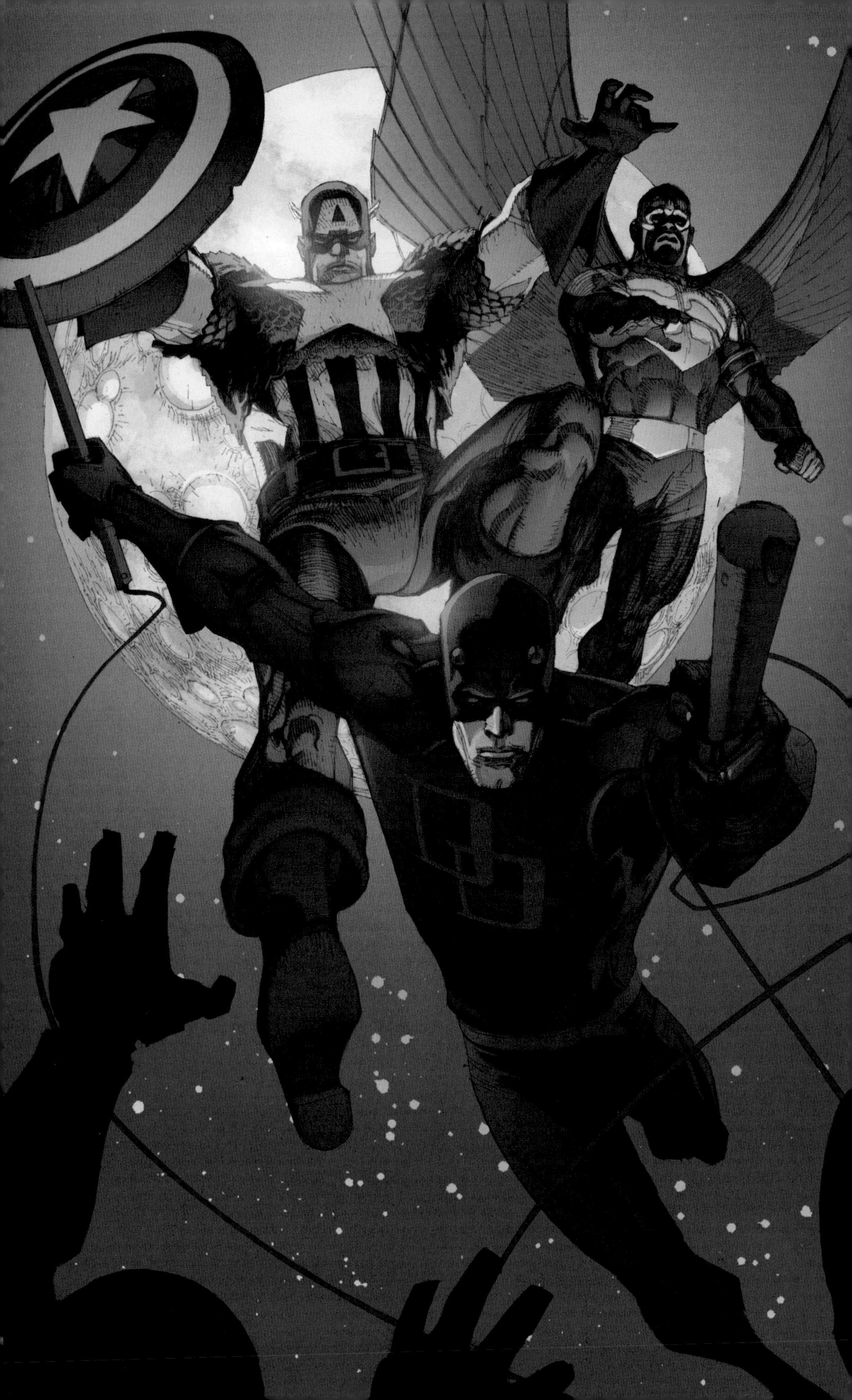

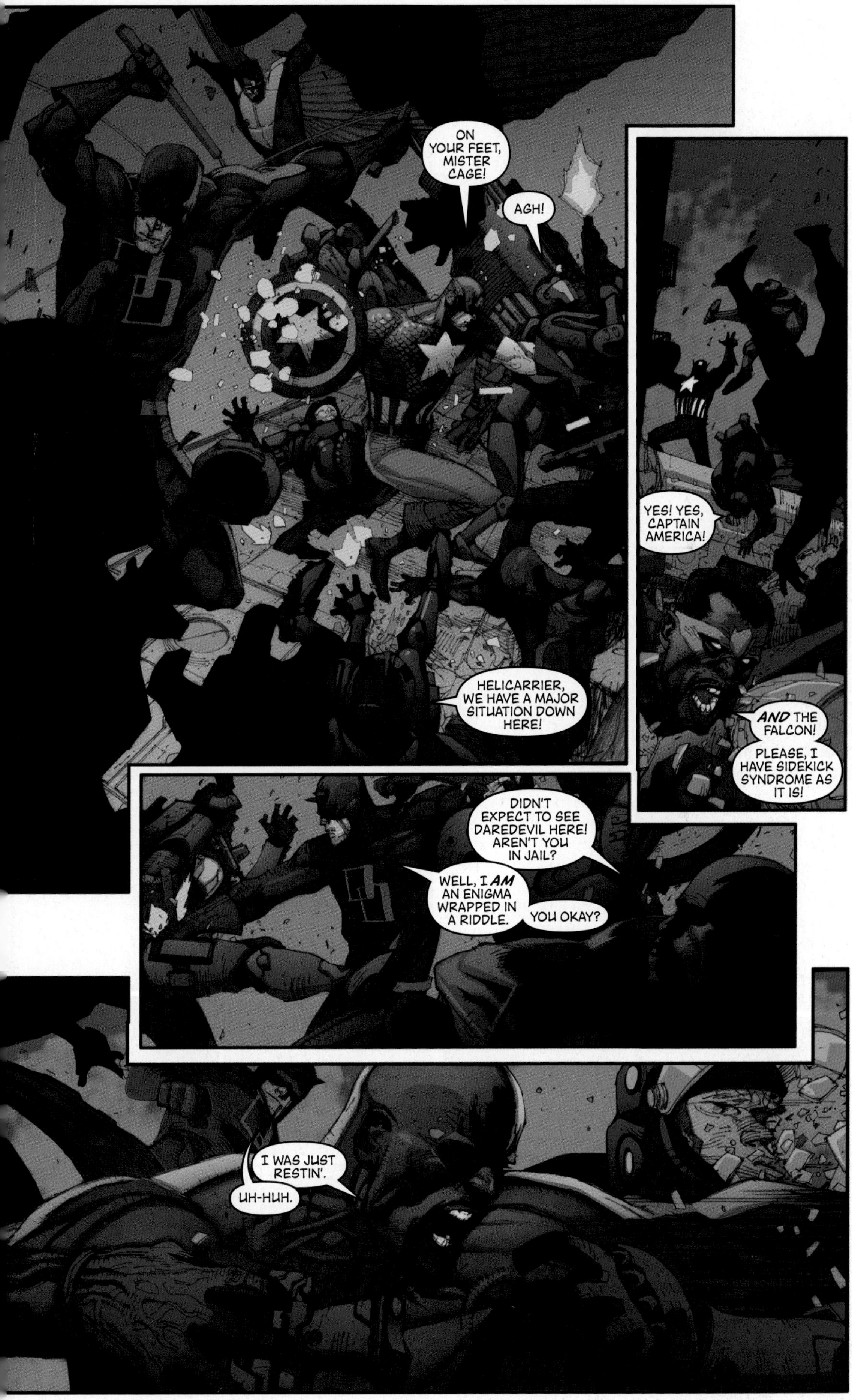
ON YOUR FEET, MISTER CAGE!
AGH!
HELICARRIER, WE HAVE A MAJOR SITUATION DOWN HERE!
YES! YES, CAPTAIN AMERICA!
AND THE FALCON!
PLEASE, I HAVE SIDEKICK SYNDROME AS IT IS!
DIDN'T EXPECT TO SEE DAREDEVIL HERE! AREN'T YOU IN JAIL?
WELL, I AM AN ENIGMA WRAPPED IN A RIDDLE.
YOU OKAY?
I WAS JUST RESTIN'.
UH-HUH.

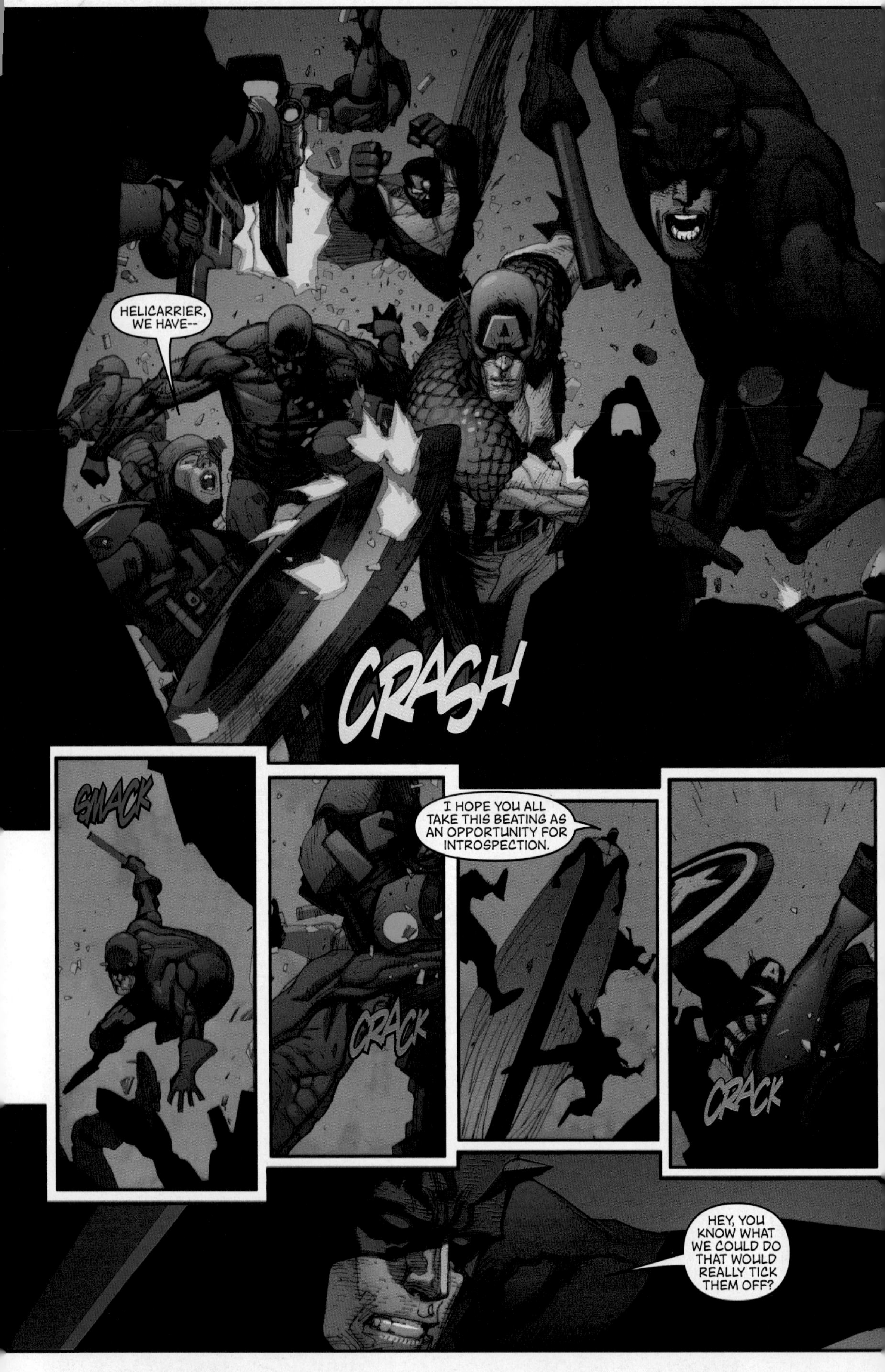
HELICARRIER, WE HAVE--
CRASH
SMACK
CRACK
I HOPE YOU ALL TAKE THIS BEATING AS AN OPPORTUNITY FOR INTROSPECTION.
CRACK
HEY, YOU KNOW WHAT WE COULD DO THAT WOULD REALLY TICK THEM OFF?

SCREEEEEEEEEEEEEEEEEEEEEEL

HELICARRIER ONE, THEY ARE FLEEING. WE DON'T HAVE CLEARANCE FOR A STREET PURSUIT, OVER?

THEY WHO?

YO! HELICARRIER, THIS IS LUKE CAGE, HOW Y'ALL DOIN' TONIGHT?

FANCY.

CAGE, THIS IS MARIA HILL, YOU'RE JUST MAKING IT WORSE FOR YOURSELF!

WE CAN TRACK THAT VEHICLE ANYWHERE YOU GO WITH IT.

YEAH, KINDA FIGURED, BUT... WE JUST WANTED Y'ALL TO KNOW. THE REVOLUTION IS COMING.

BZZT

REVOLUTION?

YEAH, I DIDN'T KNOW WHAT ELSE TO SAY.

JESSICA AND THE BABY? SENT THEM TO TORONTO.

GOOD DIM SUM THERE.

GOOD.

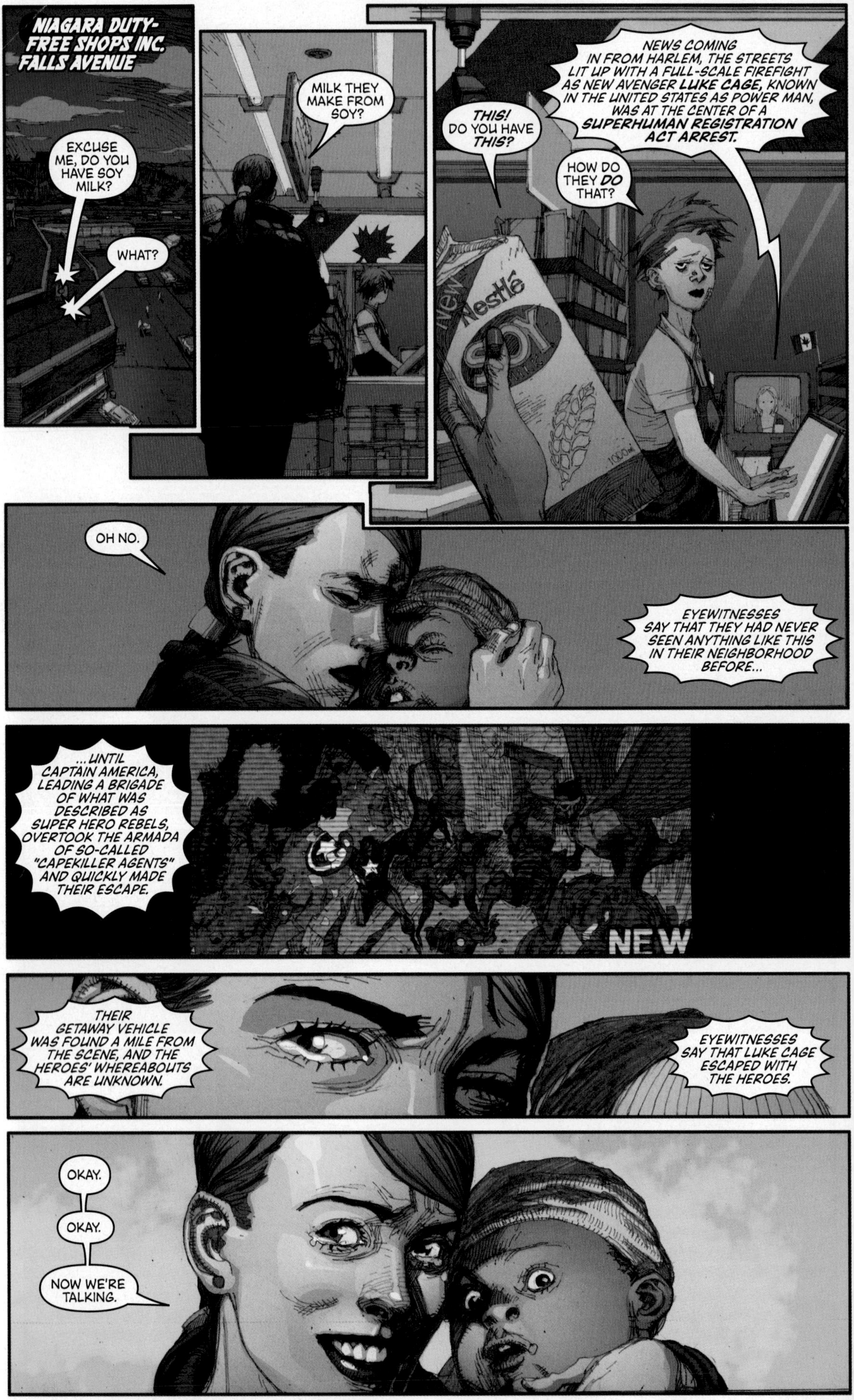
NIAGARA DUTY-FREE SHOPS INC. FALLS AVENUE
EXCUSE ME, DO YOU HAVE SOY MILK?
WHAT?
MILK THEY MAKE FROM SOY?
THIS! DO YOU HAVE THIS?
NEWS COMING IN FROM HARLEM, THE STREETS LIT UP WITH A FULL-SCALE FIREFIGHT AS NEW AVENGER LUKE CAGE, KNOWN IN THE UNITED STATES AS POWER MAN, WAS AT THE CENTER OF A SUPERHUMAN REGISTRATION ACT ARREST.
HOW DO THEY DO THAT?
New Nestlé SOY
OH NO.
EYEWITNESSES SAY THAT THEY HAD NEVER SEEN ANYTHING LIKE THIS IN THEIR NEIGHBORHOOD BEFORE...
...UNTIL CAPTAIN AMERICA, LEADING A BRIGADE OF WHAT WAS DESCRIBED AS SUPER HERO REBELS, OVERTOOK THE ARMADA OF SO-CALLED "CAPEKILLER AGENTS" AND QUICKLY MADE THEIR ESCAPE.
NEW
THEIR GETAWAY VEHICLE WAS FOUND A MILE FROM THE SCENE, AND THE HEROES' WHEREABOUTS ARE UNKNOWN.
EYEWITNESSES SAY THAT LUKE CAGE ESCAPED WITH THE HEROES.
OKAY.
OKAY.
NOW WE'RE TALKING.

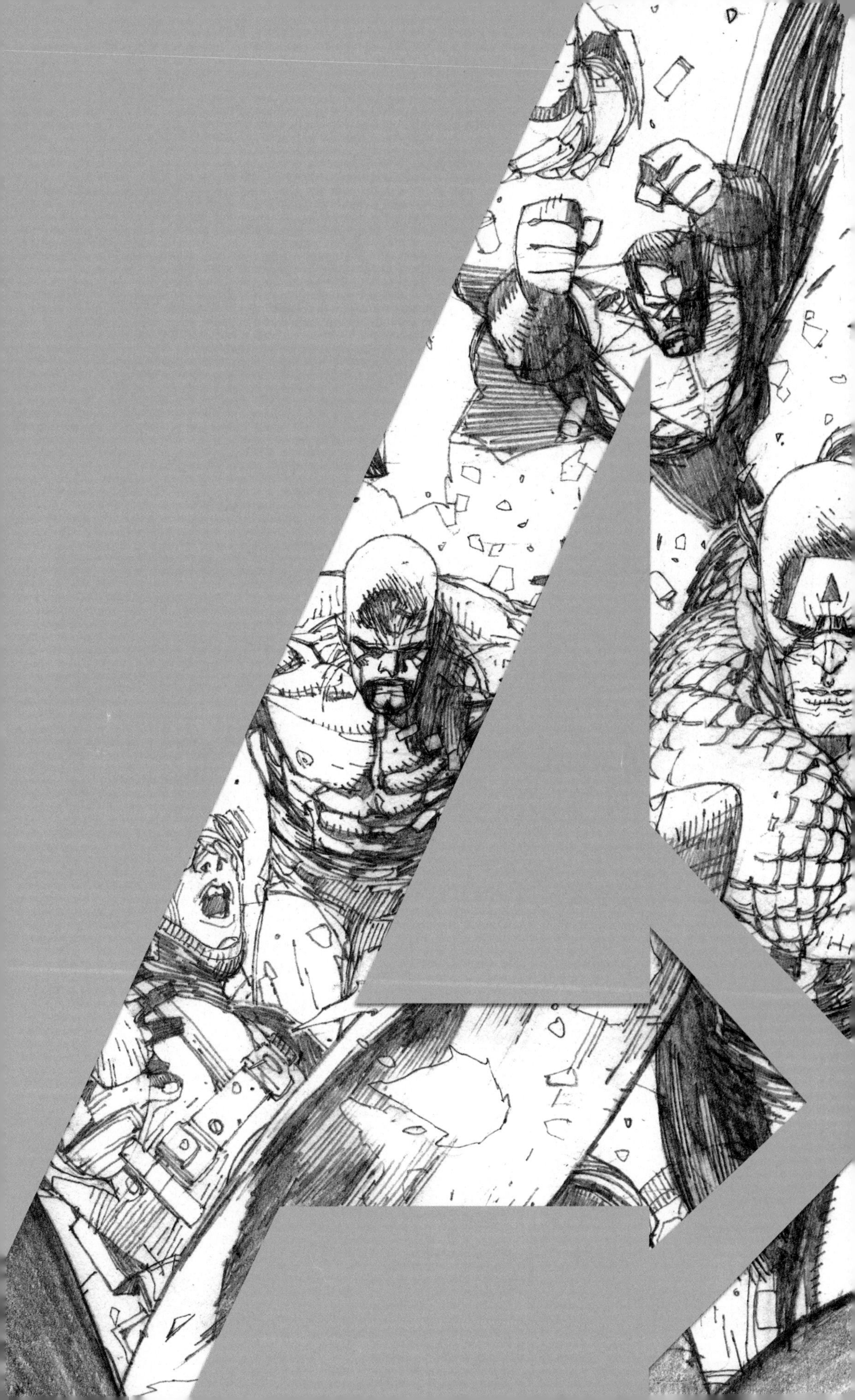

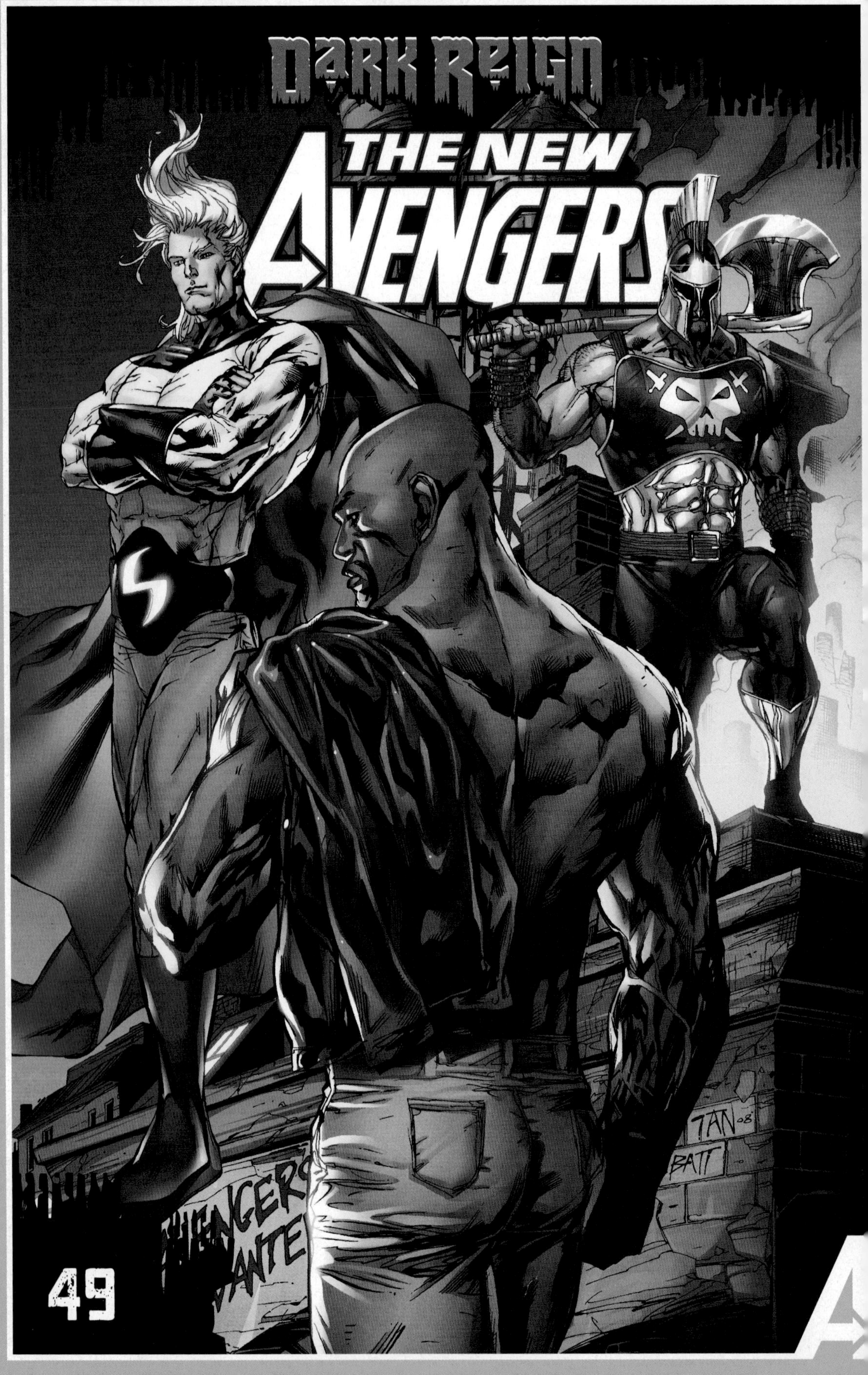
DARK REIGN
THE NEW AVENGERS
49
TAN 08
BATT

AND THERE CAME A DAY, A DAY UNLIKE ANY OTHER, WHEN EARTH'S MIGHTIEST HEROES FOUND THEMSELVES UNITED AGAINST A COMMON THREAT! ON THAT DAY, THE AVENGERS WERE BORN, TO FIGHT THE FOES NO SINGLE SUPER HERO COULD WITHSTAND!

PREVIOUSLY IN NEW AVENGERS

THE SHAPE-SHIFTING ALIEN RACE KNOWN AS THE SKRULLS HAS FAILED AT THEIR ATTEMPTED INVASION OF EARTH. BUT THE DAMAGE HAS BEEN DONE.

TONY STARK TOOK THE BLAME FOR THE INVASION AND HAS BEEN STRIPPED OF HIS ROLES AS BOTH LEADER OF THE AVENGERS AND DIRECTOR OF A NOW DEFUNCT S.H.I.E.L.D., WHILE THUNDERBOLTS LEADER (AND ONE-TIME SUPER-VILLAIN GREEN GOBLIN) NORMAN OSBORN HAS RISEN TO POWER AND BEEN APPOINTED TO REPLACE STARK.

STILL, NONE OF THEM, NOT EVEN THE AVENGERS, CAN EVEN KNOW THE FULL EXTENT OF THE INVASION OR WHICH OF THEM WAS -- OR COULD STILL BE -- A SKRULL AGENT.

DURING THE INVASION, THE GROWING PARANOIA CREATED A RIFT IN THE MARRIAGE OF AVENGER LUKE CAGE AND JESSICA JONES. WORRIED FOR THE SAFETY OF THEIR CHILD, JESSICA SOUGHT SHELTER AT AVENGERS TOWER, UNDER THE WATCHFUL EYE OF STARK'S BUTLER, JARVIS, TO WAIT OUT THE WORST OF IT.

BUT WHEN THE INVASION'S FINAL BATTLE HIT ITS ZENITH, JESSICA JONES MADE THE SELFLESS DECISION TO LEAVE HER CHILD WITH JARVIS, AND FIGHT ALONGSIDE HER HUSBAND. LITTLE DID SHE KNOW, JARVIS WAS ONE OF THE SKRULL AGENTS EMBEDDED WITHIN THE AVENGERS.

BY THE TIME JESSICA FIGURED IT OUT, JARVIS, AND THE BABY, WERE GONE.

THE NEW AVENGERS HAVE GATHERED UNDER CAPTAIN AMERICA'S ROOF, BUT TRY AS THEY MIGHT THEY CANNOT FIND THE MISSING BABY. SO LUKE CAGE TURNS TO THE ONE MAN WITH THE POWER AND INFLUENCE TO HELP HIM... NORMAN OSBORN.

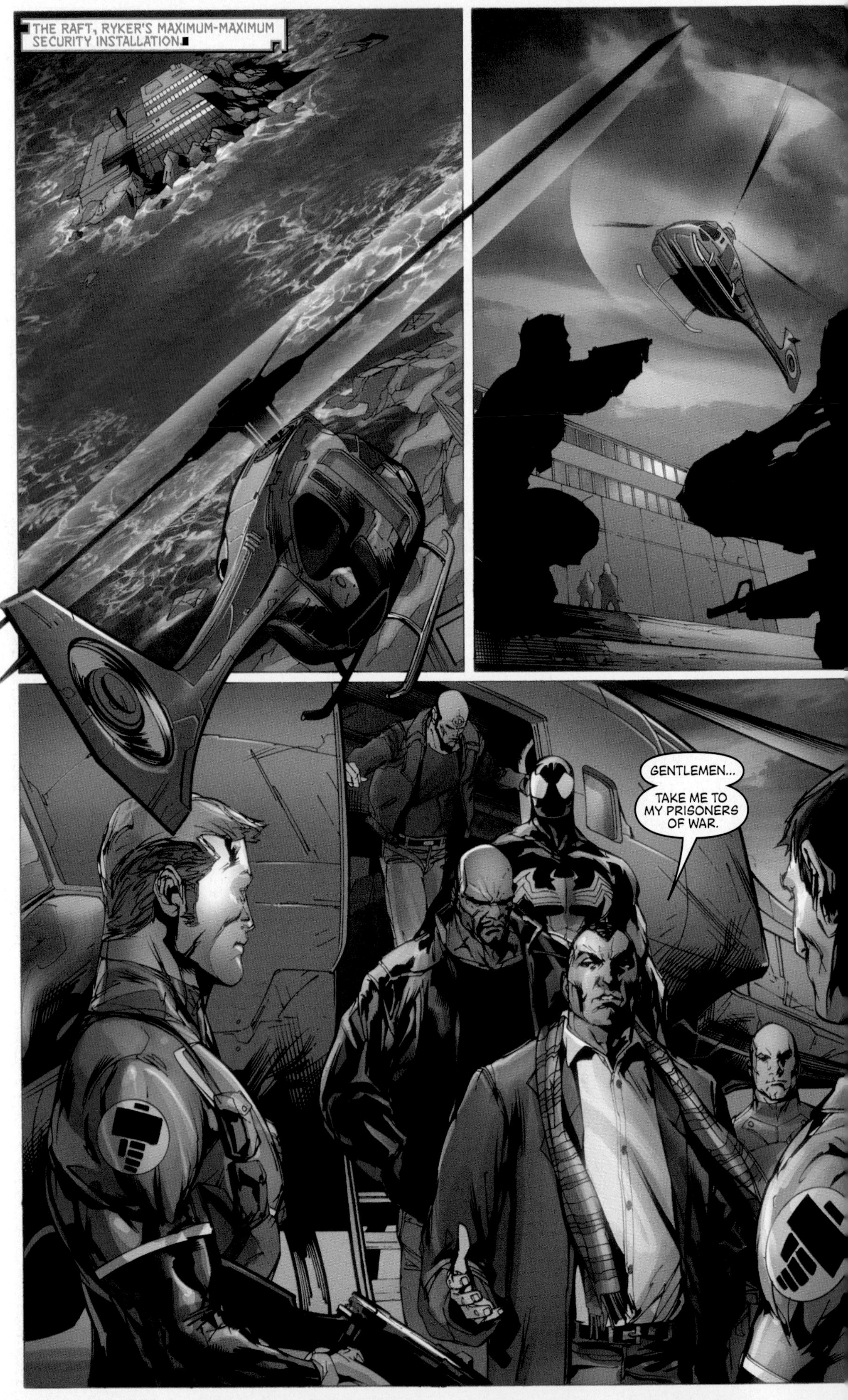
THE RAFT, RYKER'S MAXIMUM-MAXIMUM SECURITY INSTALLATION.
GENTLEMEN...
TAKE ME TO MY PRISONERS OF WAR.

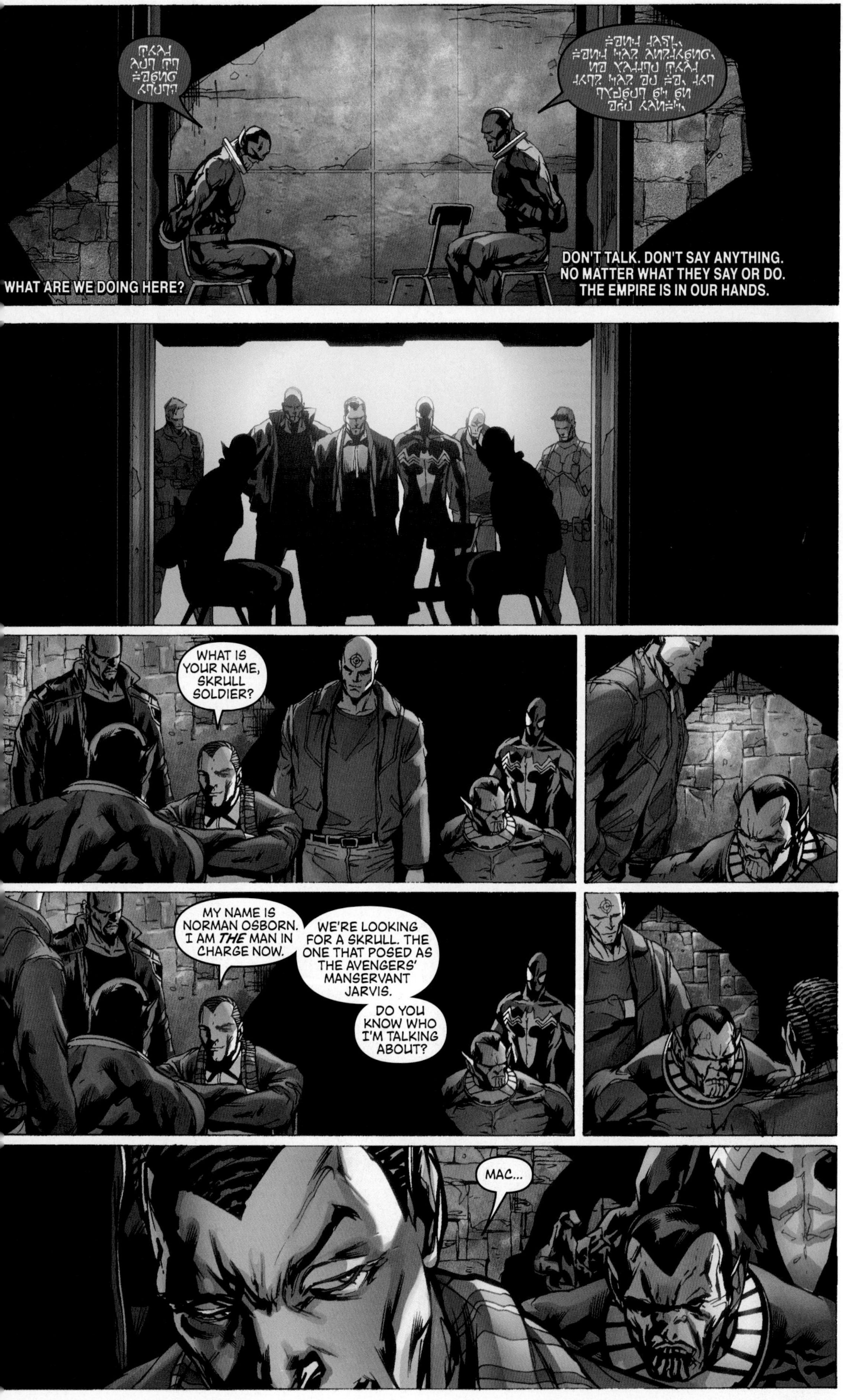
WHAT ARE WE DOING HERE?
DON'T TALK. DON'T SAY ANYTHING. NO MATTER WHAT THEY SAY OR DO. THE EMPIRE IS IN OUR HANDS.
WHAT IS YOUR NAME, SKRULL SOLDIER?
MY NAME IS NORMAN OSBORN. I AM *THE* MAN IN CHARGE NOW.
WE'RE LOOKING FOR A SKRULL. THE ONE THAT POSED AS THE AVENGERS' MANSERVANT JARVIS.
DO YOU KNOW WHO I'M TALKING ABOUT?
MAC...

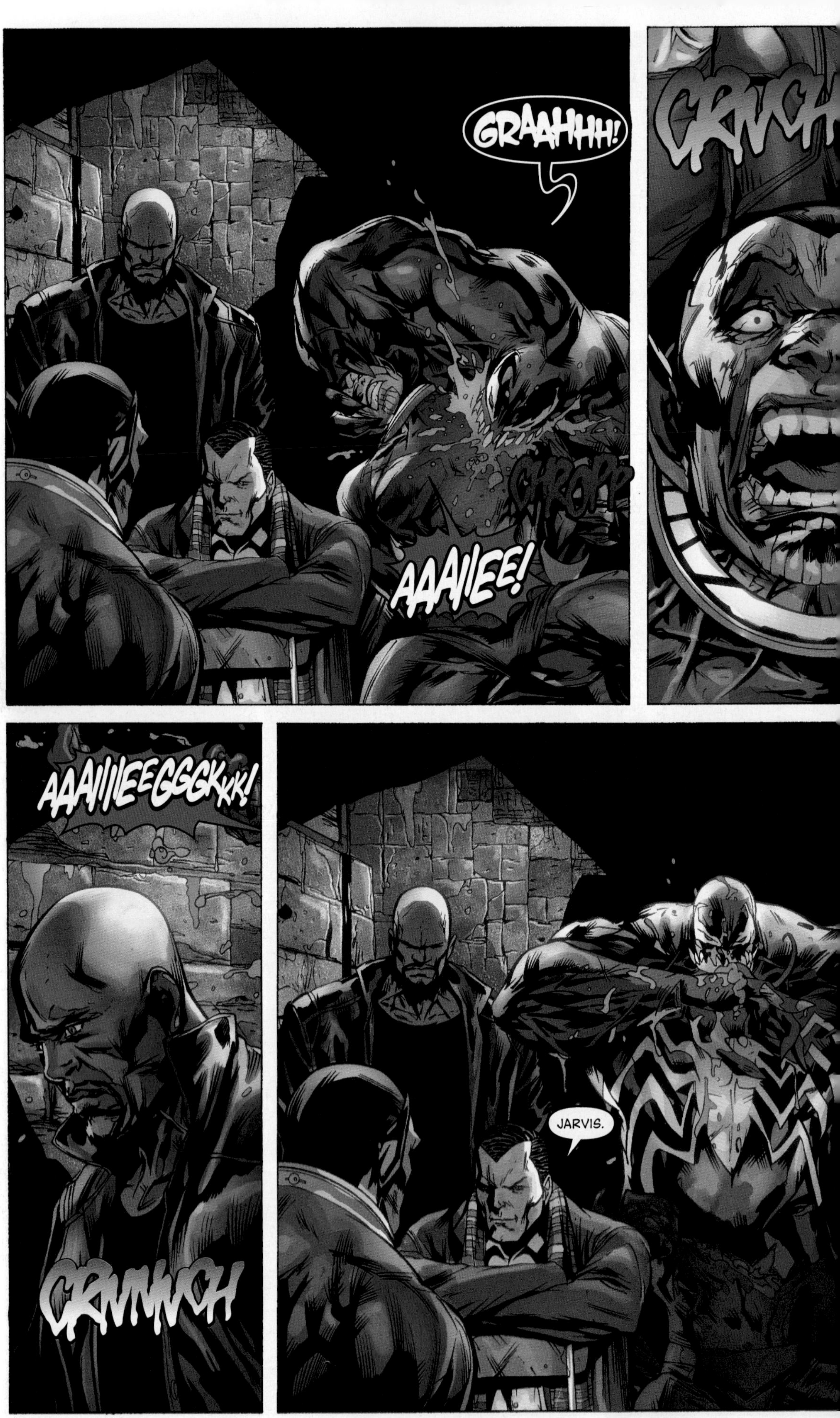
GRAAHHH!
CHROPP
AAAIIEE!
AAAIIIEEGGGKKK!
CRUNNCH
JARVIS.

I-I-I DON'T KNOW.

WE DIDN'T ALL KNOW EACH OTHER.

MAC, STILL HUNGRY?

ALWAYS.

WHERE, OH WHERE, WOULD JARVIS SKRULL BE?

I DIDN'T KNOW HIM.

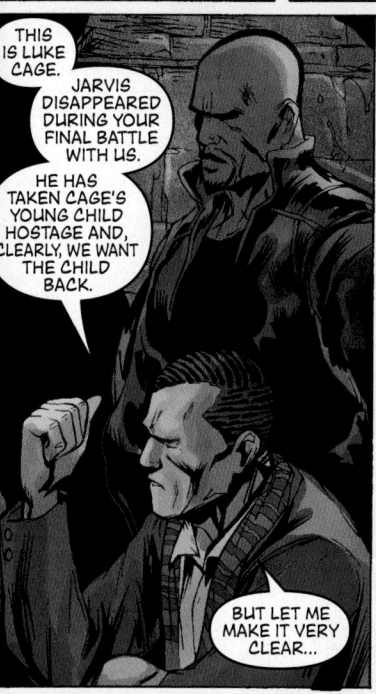

THIS IS LUKE CAGE.

JARVIS DISAPPEARED DURING YOUR FINAL BATTLE WITH US.

HE HAS TAKEN CAGE'S YOUNG CHILD HOSTAGE AND, CLEARLY, WE WANT THE CHILD BACK.

BUT LET ME MAKE IT VERY CLEAR...

WE HAVE 74 MORE SKRULLS IN CUSTODY.

TELL US SOMETHING OF VALUE OR WE'RE GOING TO MOVE ON TO THE NEXT ONE.

THERE-- THERE IS A MEETING PLACE.

WHERE?!

IN THE CITY?

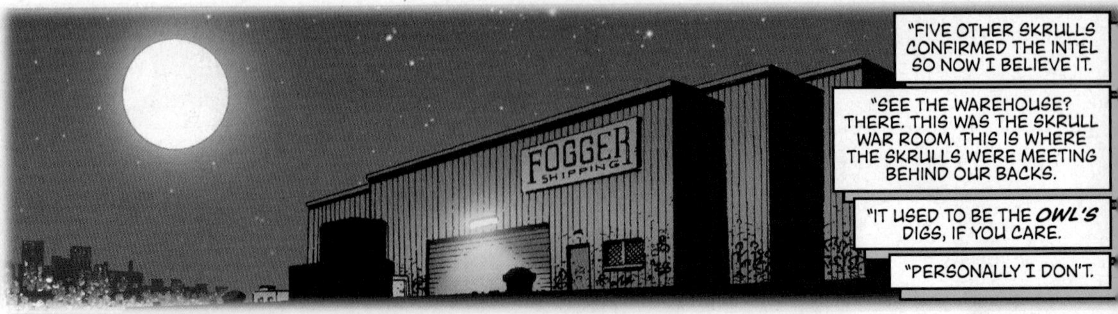
"FIVE OTHER SKRULLS CONFIRMED THE INTEL SO NOW I BELIEVE IT.
"SEE THE WAREHOUSE? THERE. THIS WAS THE SKRULL WAR ROOM. THIS IS WHERE THE SKRULLS WERE MEETING BEHIND OUR BACKS.
"IT USED TO BE THE *OWL'S* DIGS, IF YOU CARE.
"PERSONALLY I DON'T.
FOGGER SHIPPING

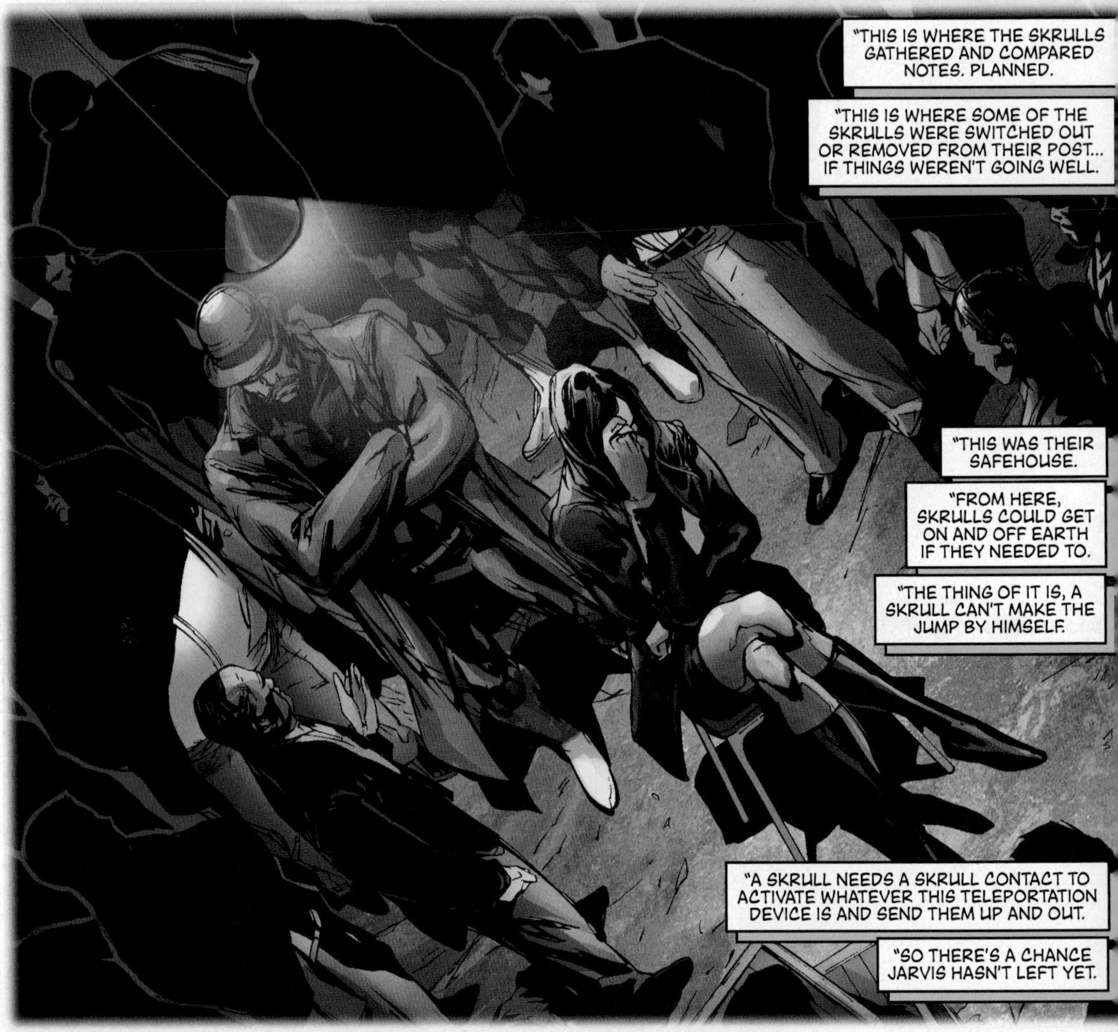
"THIS IS WHERE THE SKRULLS GATHERED AND COMPARED NOTES. PLANNED.
"THIS IS WHERE SOME OF THE SKRULLS WERE SWITCHED OUT OR REMOVED FROM THEIR POST... IF THINGS WEREN'T GOING WELL.
"THIS WAS THEIR SAFEHOUSE.
"FROM HERE, SKRULLS COULD GET ON AND OFF EARTH IF THEY NEEDED TO.
"THE THING OF IT IS, A SKRULL CAN'T MAKE THE JUMP BY HIMSELF.
"A SKRULL NEEDS A SKRULL CONTACT TO ACTIVATE WHATEVER THIS TELEPORTATION DEVICE IS AND SEND THEM UP AND OUT.
"SO THERE'S A CHANCE JARVIS HASN'T LEFT YET.

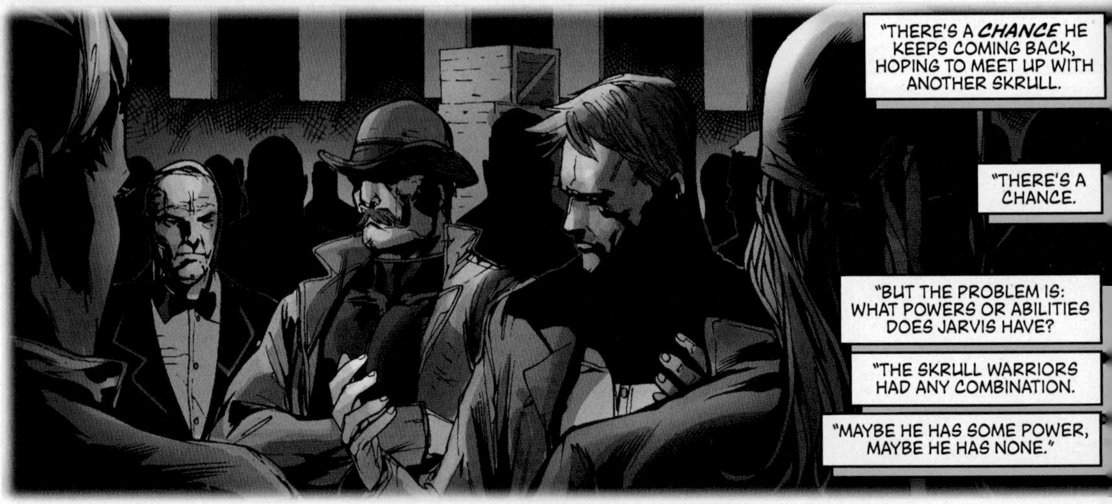
"THERE'S A *CHANCE* HE KEEPS COMING BACK, HOPING TO MEET UP WITH ANOTHER SKRULL.
"THERE'S A CHANCE.
"BUT THE PROBLEM IS: WHAT POWERS OR ABILITIES DOES JARVIS HAVE?
"THE SKRULL WARRIORS HAD ANY COMBINATION.
"MAYBE HE HAS SOME POWER, MAYBE HE HAS NONE."

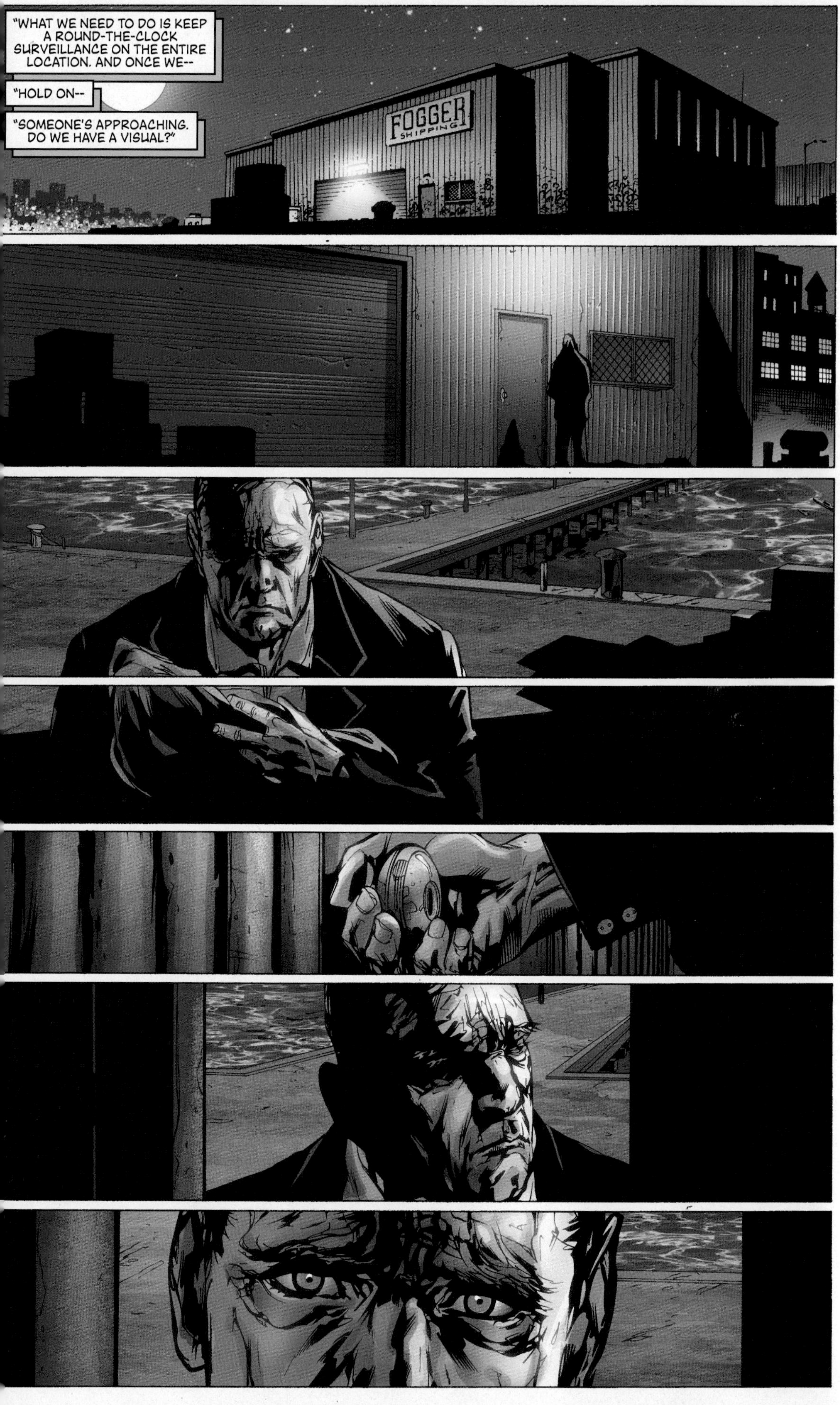
"WHAT WE NEED TO DO IS KEEP A ROUND-THE-CLOCK SURVEILLANCE ON THE ENTIRE LOCATION. AND ONCE WE--
"HOLD ON--
"SOMEONE'S APPROACHING. DO WE HAVE A VISUAL?"
FOGGER SHIPPING

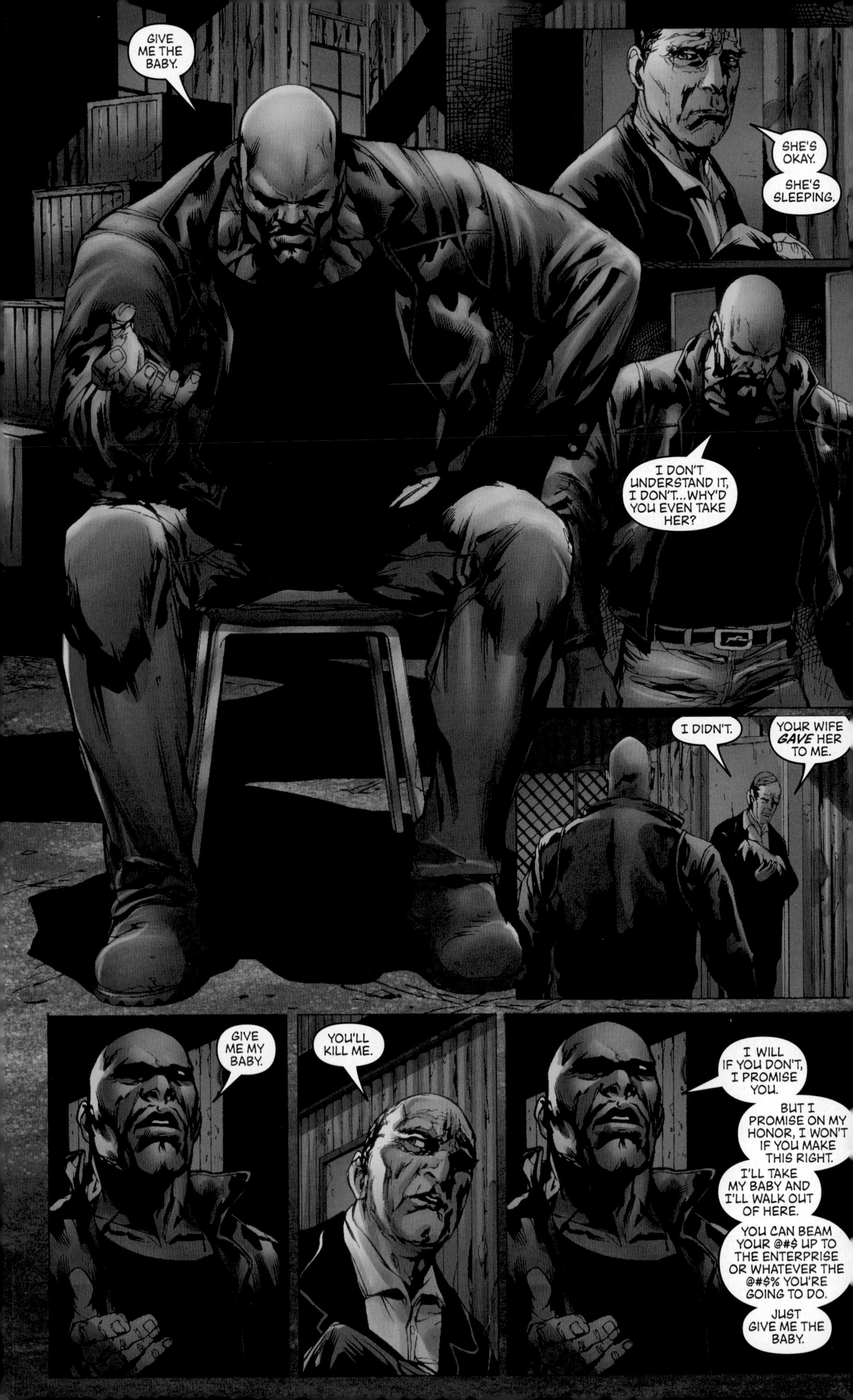
GIVE ME THE BABY.
SHE'S OKAY.
SHE'S SLEEPING.
I DON'T UNDERSTAND IT, I DON'T...WHY'D YOU EVEN TAKE HER?
I DIDN'T.
YOUR WIFE *GAVE* HER TO ME.
GIVE ME MY BABY.
YOU'LL KILL ME.
I WILL IF YOU DON'T, I PROMISE YOU.
BUT I PROMISE ON MY HONOR, I WON'T IF YOU MAKE THIS RIGHT.
I'LL TAKE MY BABY AND I'LL WALK OUT OF HERE.
YOU CAN BEAM YOUR @#$ UP TO THE ENTERPRISE OR WHATEVER THE @#$% YOU'RE GOING TO DO.
JUST GIVE ME THE BABY.

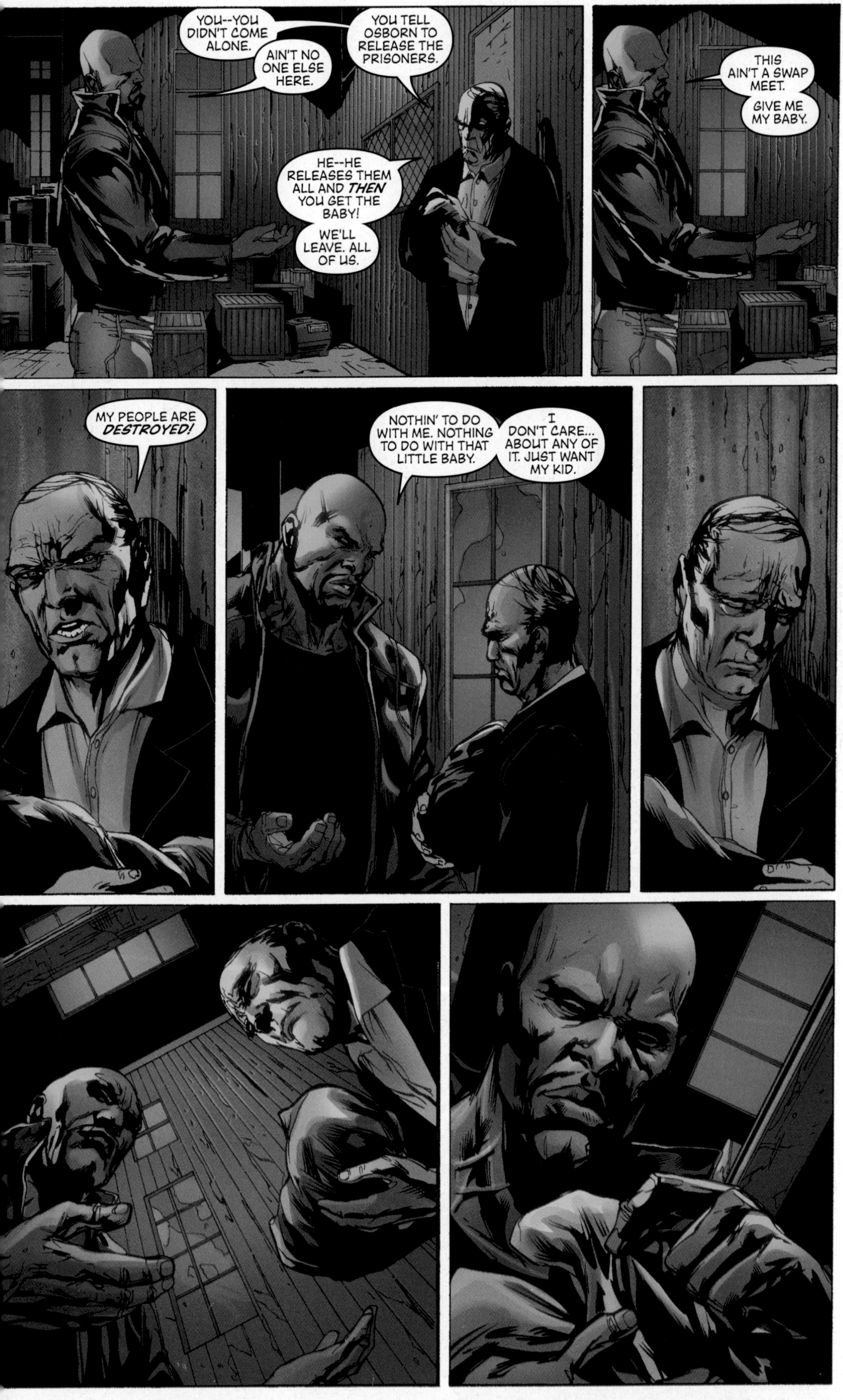
YOU--YOU DIDN'T COME ALONE.
AIN'T NO ONE ELSE HERE.
YOU TELL OSBORN TO RELEASE THE PRISONERS.
HE--HE RELEASES THEM ALL AND *THEN* YOU GET THE BABY!
WE'LL LEAVE. ALL OF US.
THIS AIN'T A SWAP MEET.
GIVE ME MY BABY.
MY PEOPLE ARE *DESTROYED!*
NOTHIN' TO DO WITH ME. NOTHING TO DO WITH THAT LITTLE BABY.
I DON'T CARE... ABOUT ANY OF IT. JUST WANT MY KID.

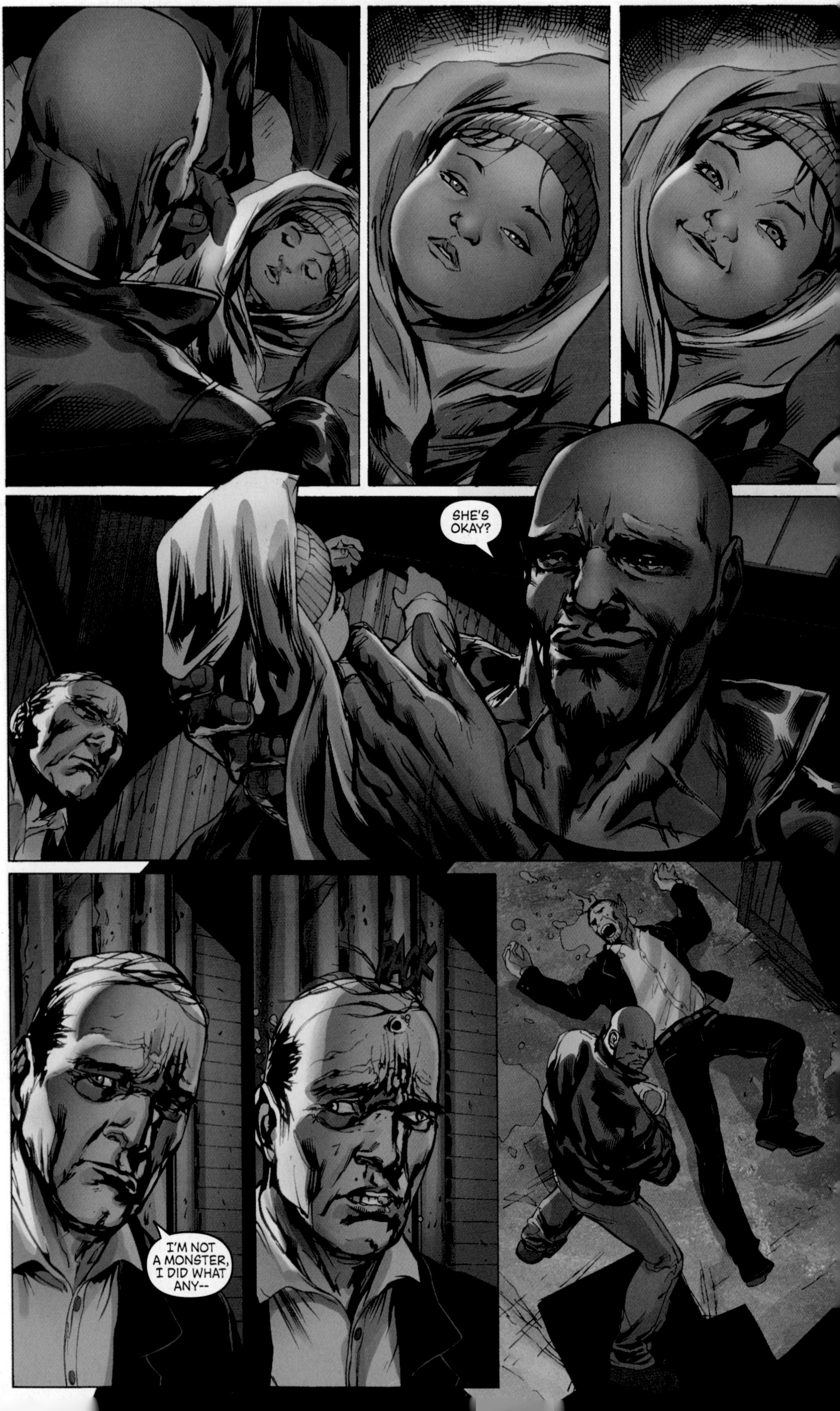
SHE'S OKAY?
I'M NOT A MONSTER, I DID WHAT ANY--
PACK

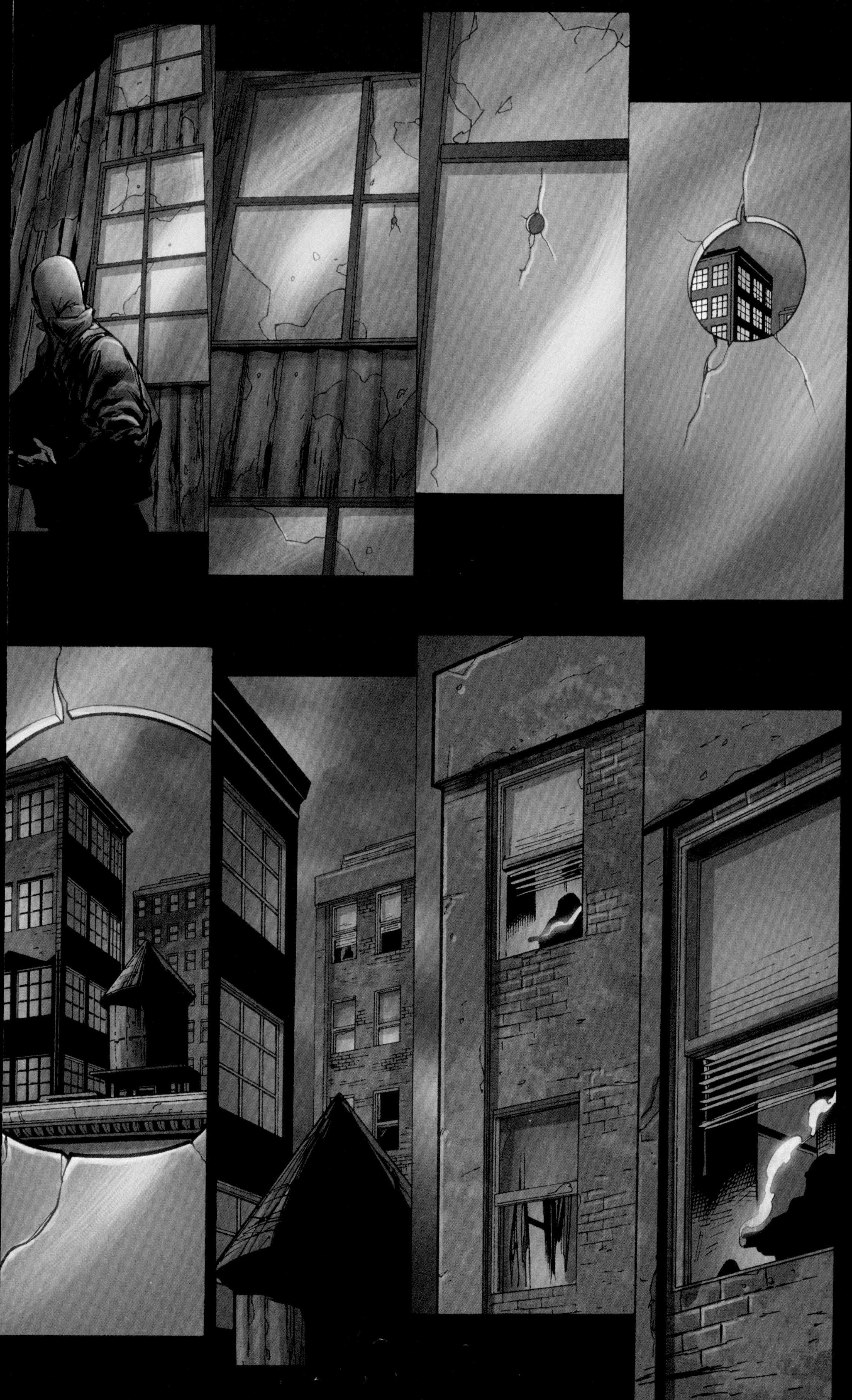

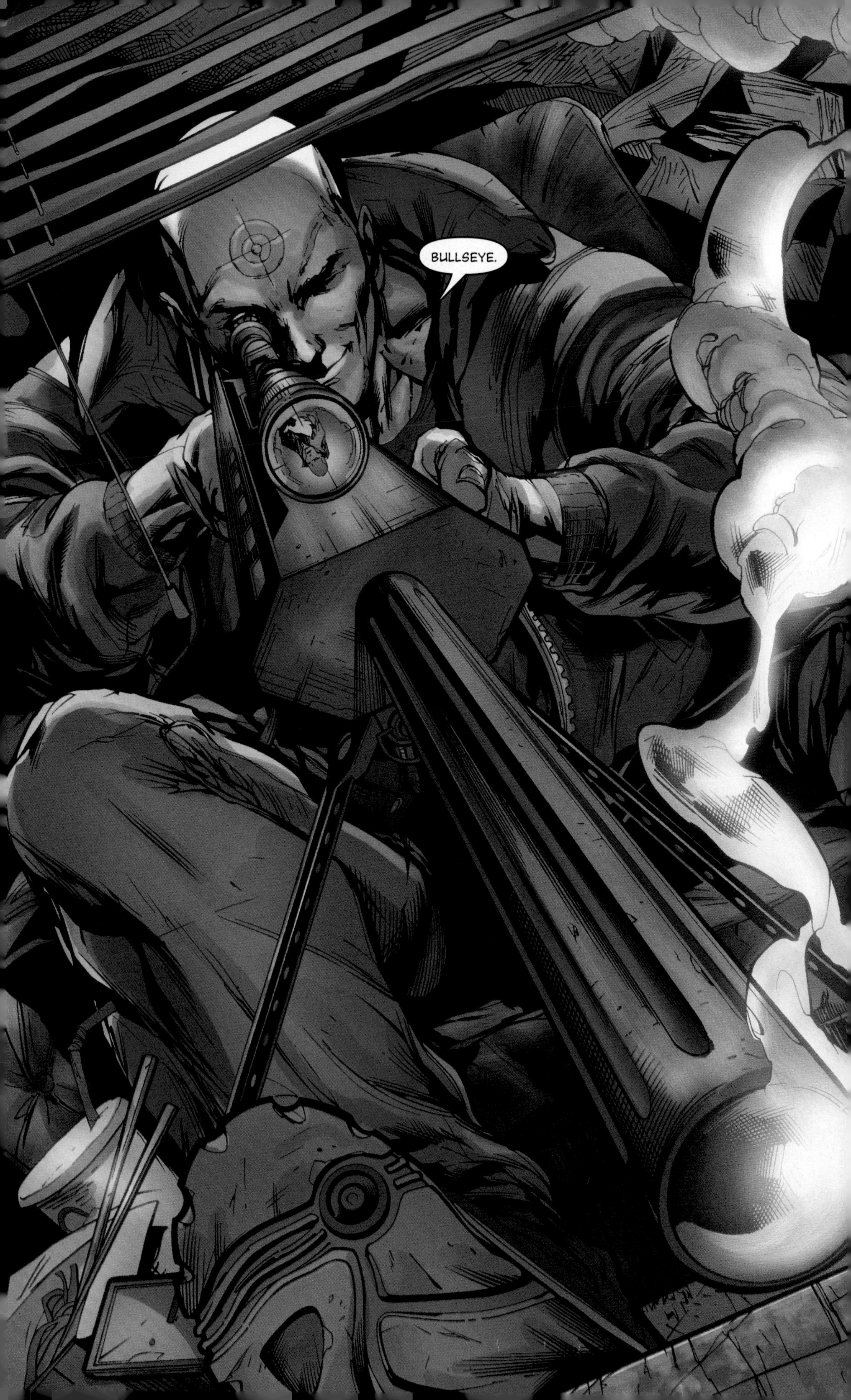
BULLSEYE.

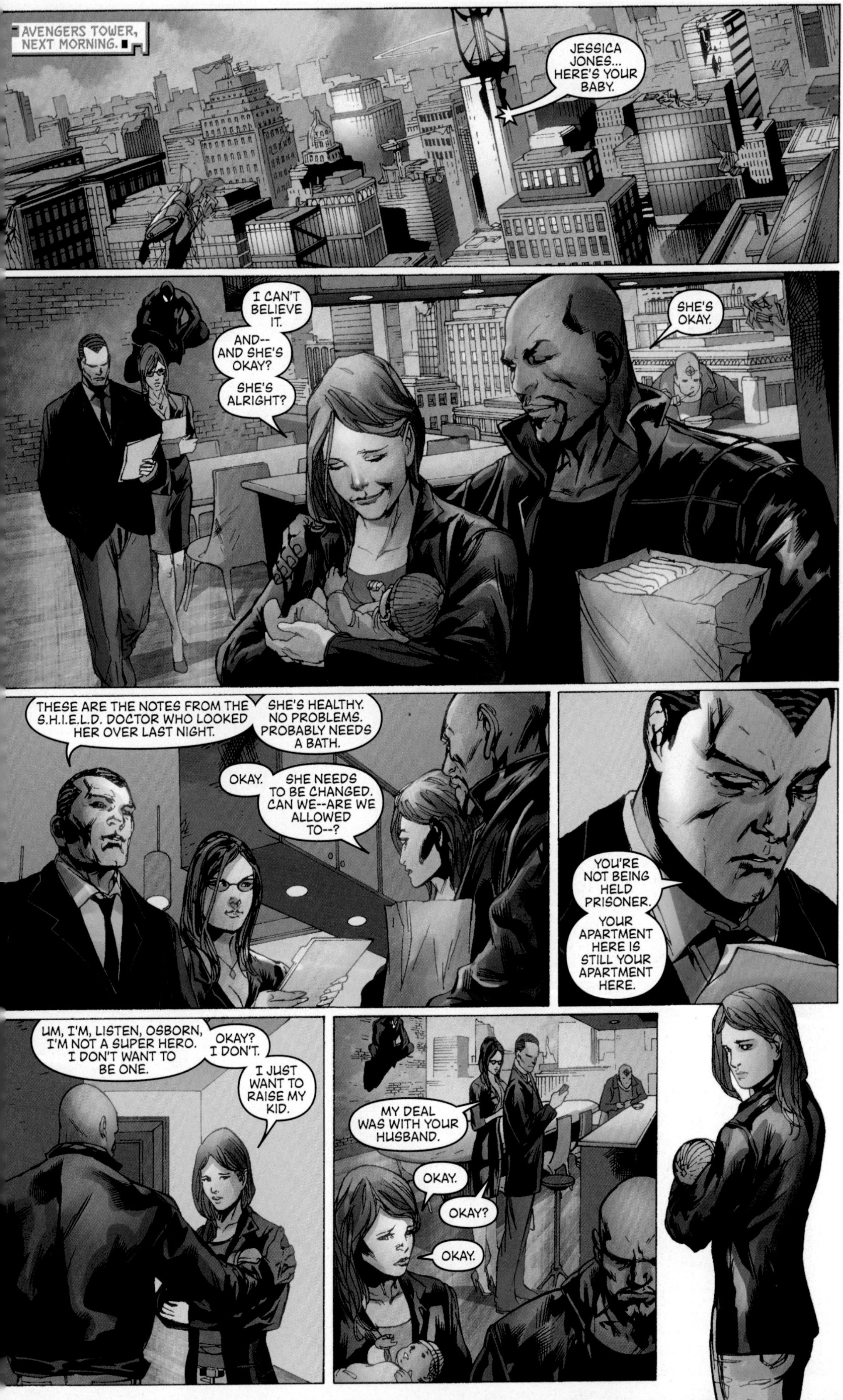

AVENGERS TOWER, NEXT MORNING.
JESSICA JONES... HERE'S YOUR BABY.
I CAN'T BELIEVE IT.
AND-- AND SHE'S OKAY?
SHE'S ALRIGHT?
SHE'S OKAY.
THESE ARE THE NOTES FROM THE S.H.I.E.L.D. DOCTOR WHO LOOKED HER OVER LAST NIGHT.
SHE'S HEALTHY. NO PROBLEMS. PROBABLY NEEDS A BATH.
OKAY.
SHE NEEDS TO BE CHANGED. CAN WE--ARE WE ALLOWED TO--?
YOU'RE NOT BEING HELD PRISONER.
YOUR APARTMENT HERE IS STILL YOUR APARTMENT HERE.
UM, I'M, LISTEN, OSBORN, I'M NOT A SUPER HERO. I DON'T WANT TO BE ONE.
OKAY? I DON'T.
I JUST WANT TO RAISE MY KID.
MY DEAL WAS WITH YOUR HUSBAND.
OKAY.
OKAY?
OKAY.

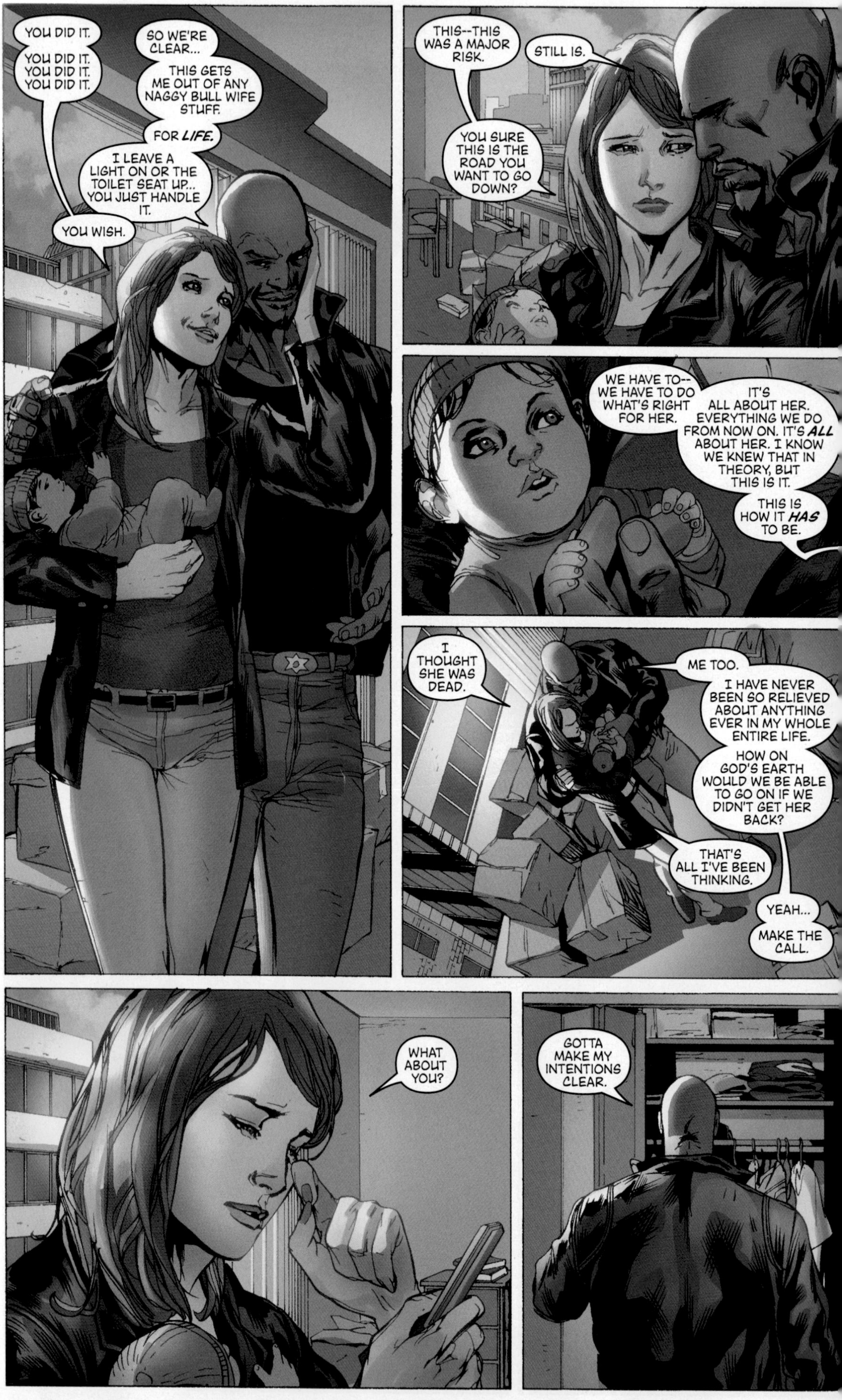

YOU DID IT.
YOU DID IT. YOU DID IT. YOU DID IT.
SO WE'RE CLEAR...
THIS GETS ME OUT OF ANY NAGGY BULL WIFE STUFF.
FOR *LIFE.*
I LEAVE A LIGHT ON OR THE TOILET SEAT UP... YOU JUST HANDLE IT.
YOU WISH.
THIS--THIS WAS A MAJOR RISK.
STILL IS.
YOU SURE THIS IS THE ROAD YOU WANT TO GO DOWN?
WE HAVE TO-- WE HAVE TO DO WHAT'S RIGHT FOR HER.
IT'S ALL ABOUT HER. EVERYTHING WE DO FROM NOW ON. IT'S *ALL* ABOUT HER. I KNOW WE KNEW THAT IN THEORY, BUT THIS IS IT.
THIS IS HOW IT *HAS* TO BE.
I THOUGHT SHE WAS DEAD.
ME TOO.
I HAVE NEVER BEEN SO RELIEVED ABOUT ANYTHING EVER IN MY WHOLE ENTIRE LIFE.
HOW ON GOD'S EARTH WOULD WE BE ABLE TO GO ON IF WE DIDN'T GET HER BACK?
THAT'S ALL I'VE BEEN THINKING.
YEAH...
MAKE THE CALL.
WHAT ABOUT YOU?
GOTTA MAKE MY INTENTIONS CLEAR.

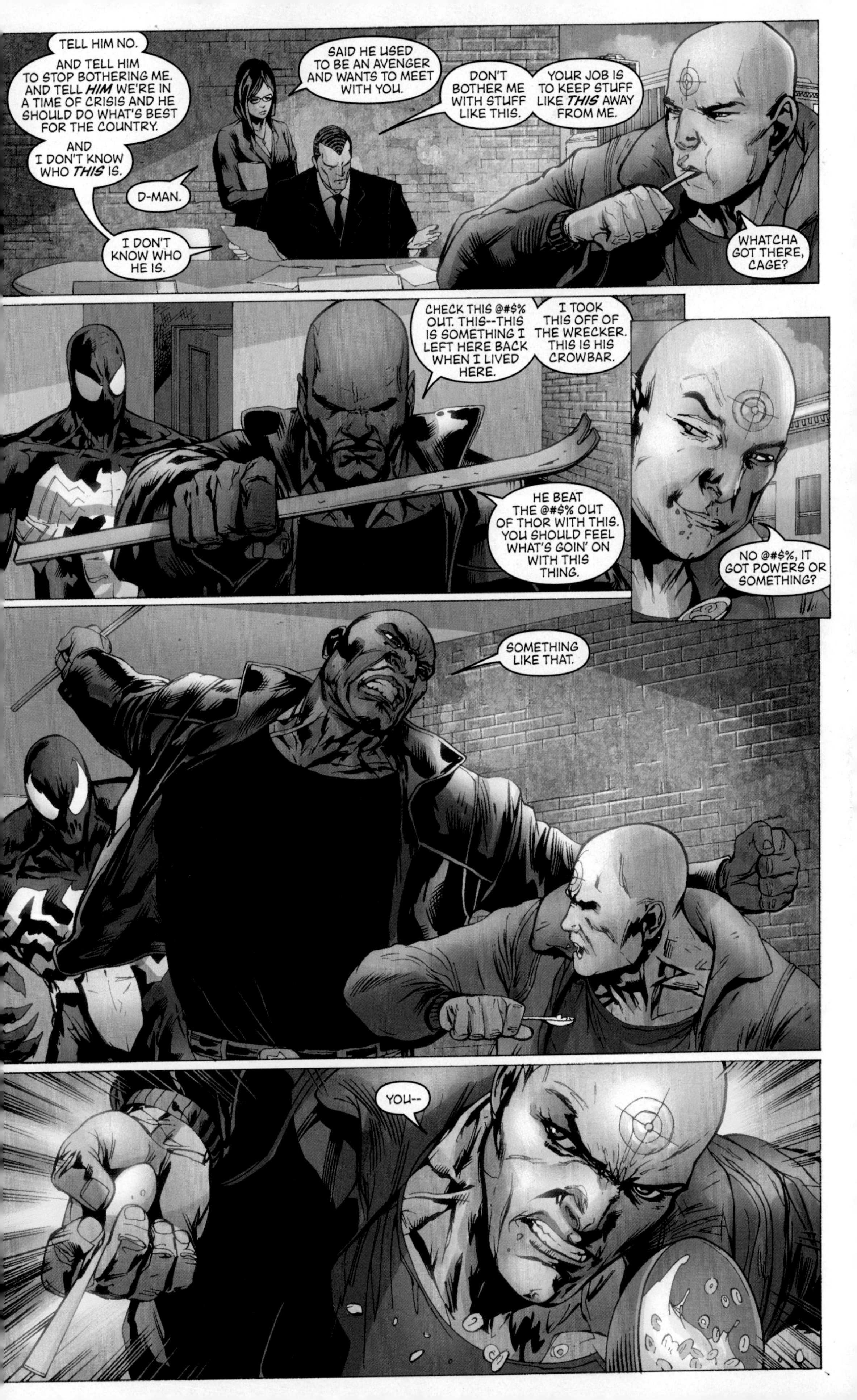
TELL HIM NO.
AND TELL HIM TO STOP BOTHERING ME. AND TELL HIM WE'RE IN A TIME OF CRISIS AND HE SHOULD DO WHAT'S BEST FOR THE COUNTRY.
AND I DON'T KNOW WHO THIS IS.
SAID HE USED TO BE AN AVENGER AND WANTS TO MEET WITH YOU.
D-MAN.
I DON'T KNOW WHO HE IS.
DON'T BOTHER ME WITH STUFF LIKE THIS.
YOUR JOB IS TO KEEP STUFF LIKE THIS AWAY FROM ME.
WHATCHA GOT THERE, CAGE?
CHECK THIS @#$% OUT. THIS--THIS IS SOMETHING I LEFT HERE BACK WHEN I LIVED HERE.
I TOOK THIS OFF OF THE WRECKER. THIS IS HIS CROWBAR.
HE BEAT THE @#$% OUT OF THOR WITH THIS. YOU SHOULD FEEL WHAT'S GOIN' ON WITH THIS THING.
NO @#$%, IT GOT POWERS OR SOMETHING?
SOMETHING LIKE THAT.
YOU--

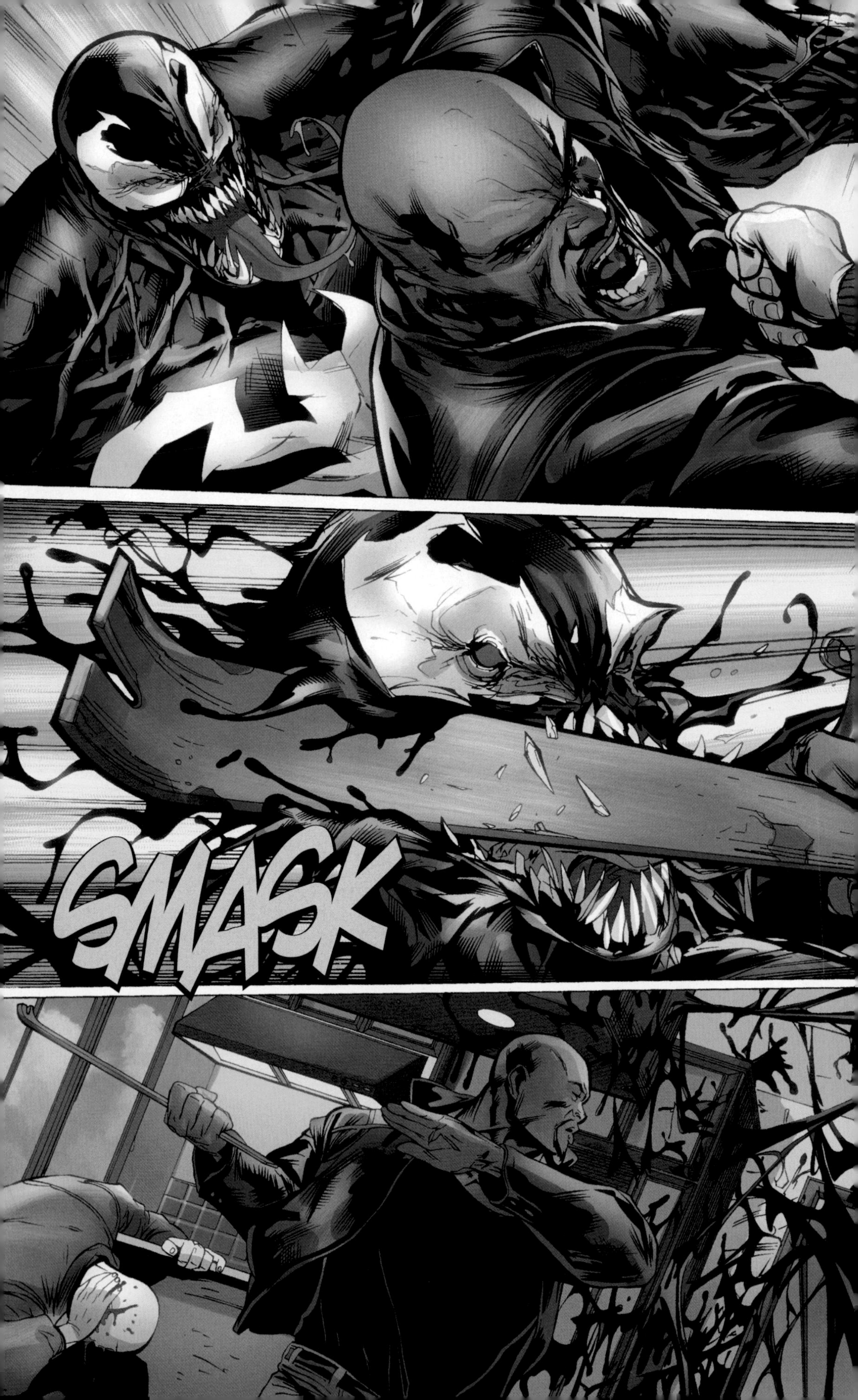
SMASK

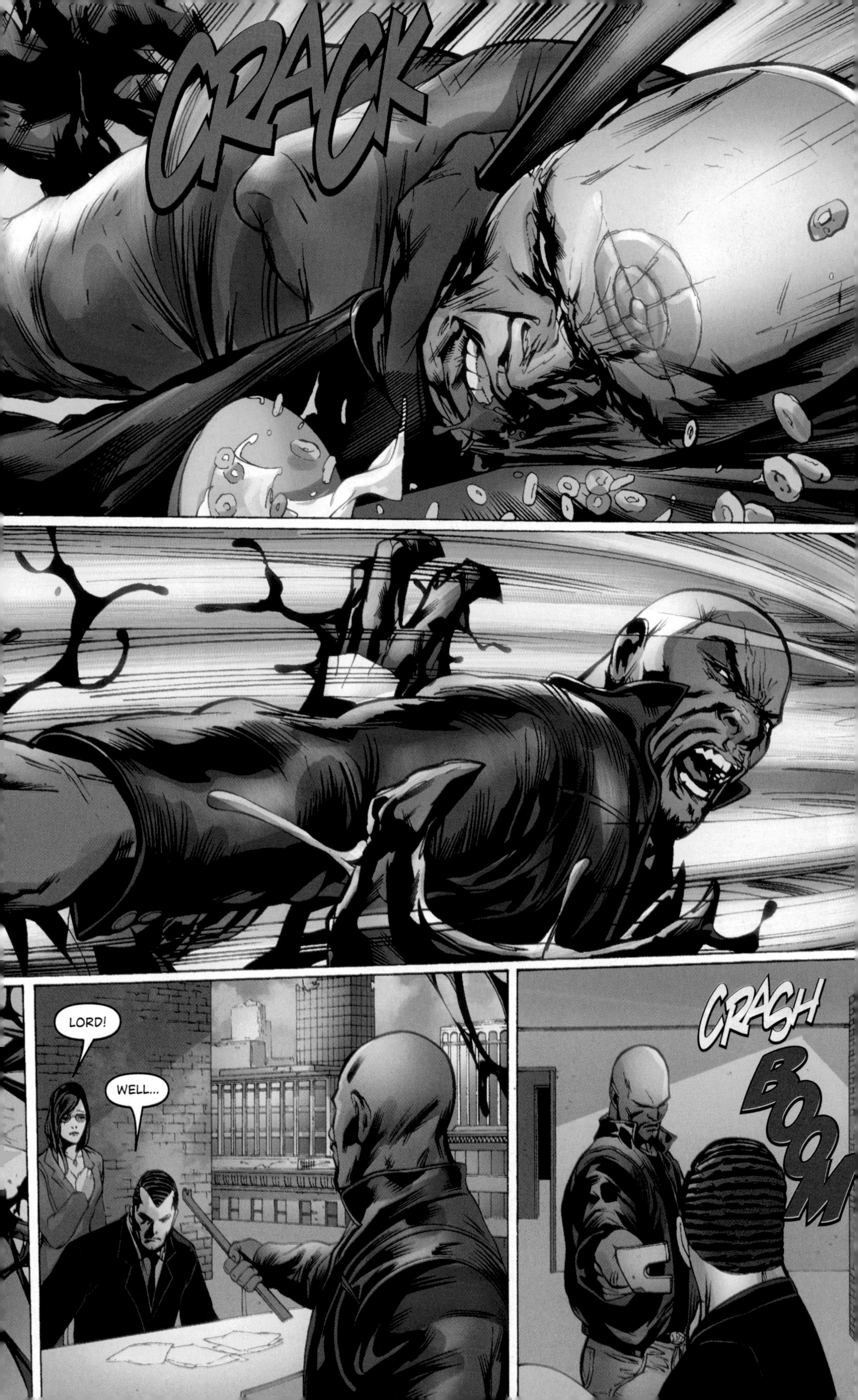
CRACK
LORD!
WELL...
CRASH
BOOM

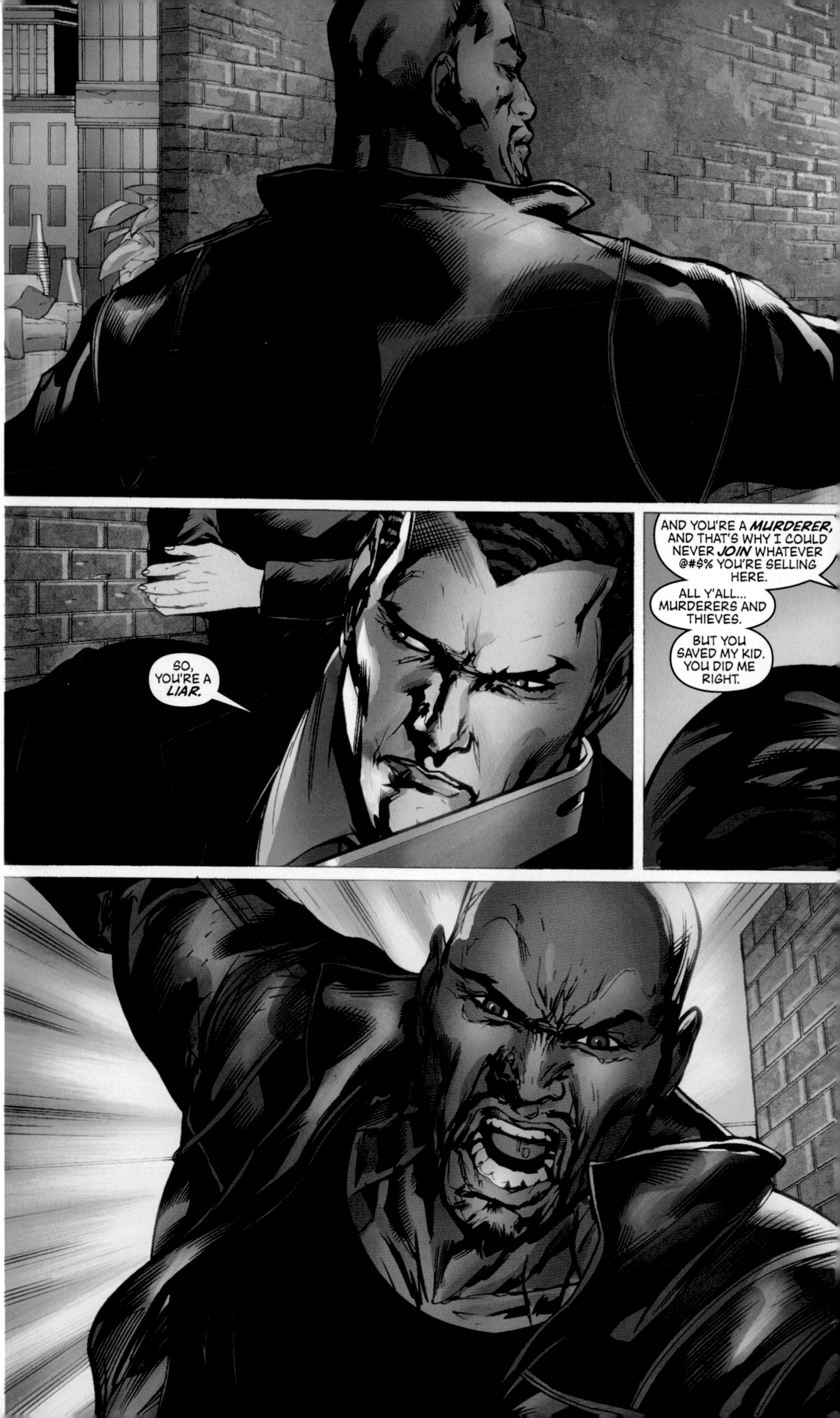
SO, YOU'RE A LIAR.
AND YOU'RE A MURDERER, AND THAT'S WHY I COULD NEVER JOIN WHATEVER @#$% YOU'RE SELLING HERE.
ALL Y'ALL... MURDERERS AND THIEVES.
BUT YOU SAVED MY KID. YOU DID ME RIGHT.

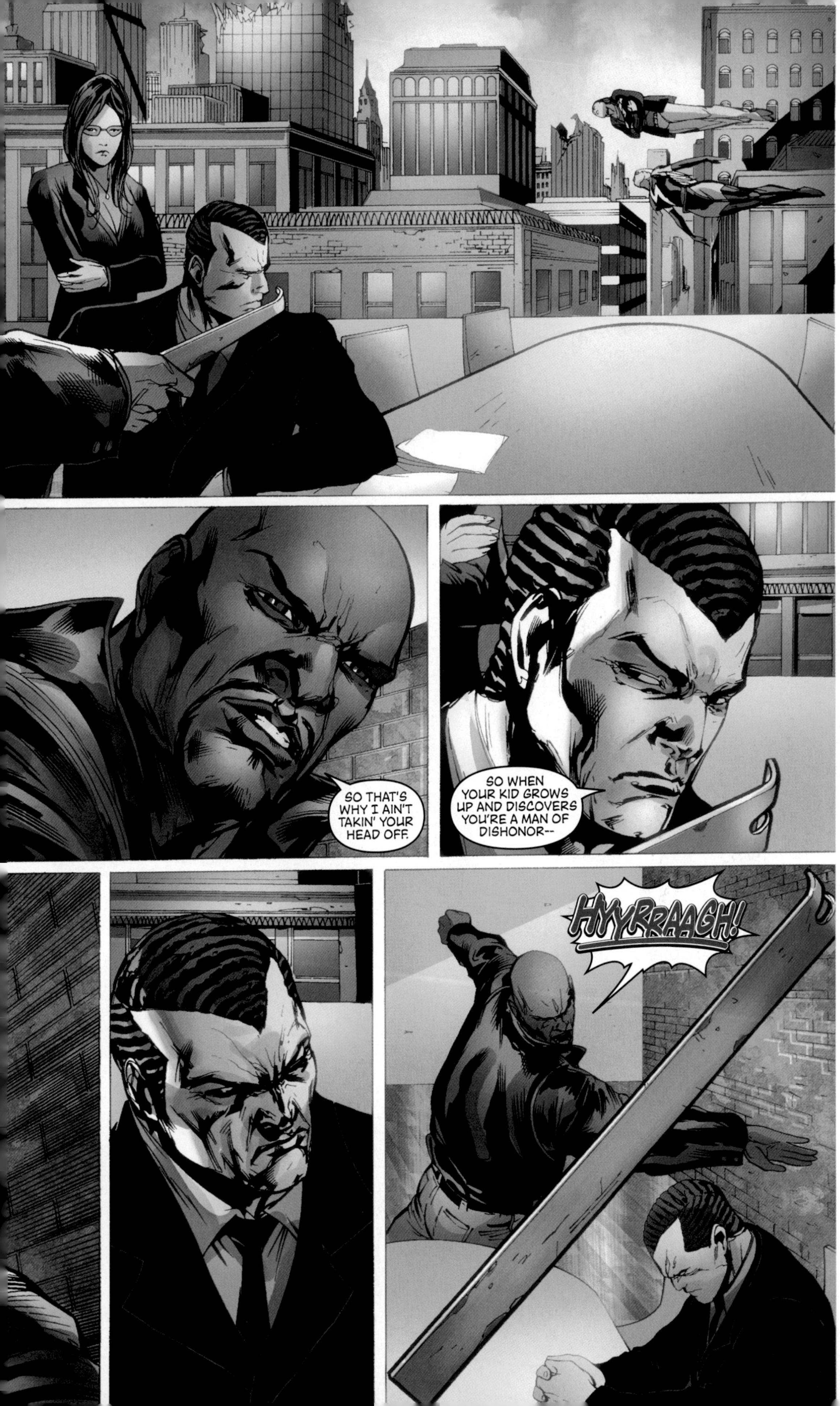
SO THAT'S WHY I AIN'T TAKIN' YOUR HEAD OFF.
SO WHEN YOUR KID GROWS UP AND DISCOVERS YOU'RE A MAN OF DISHONOR--
HYYRRAAGH!

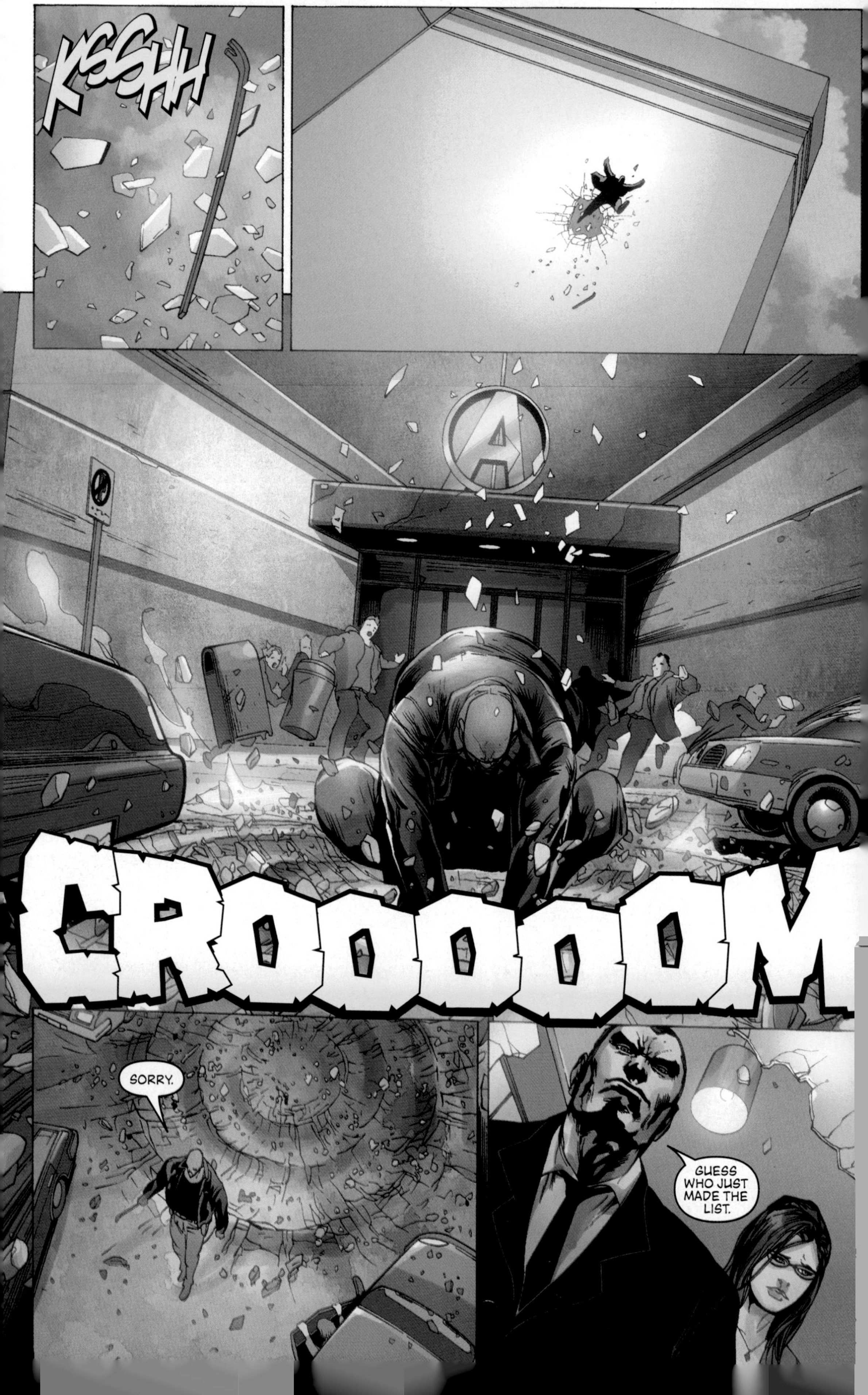
KSSHH
CROOOOOM
SORRY.
GUESS WHO JUST MADE THE LIST.

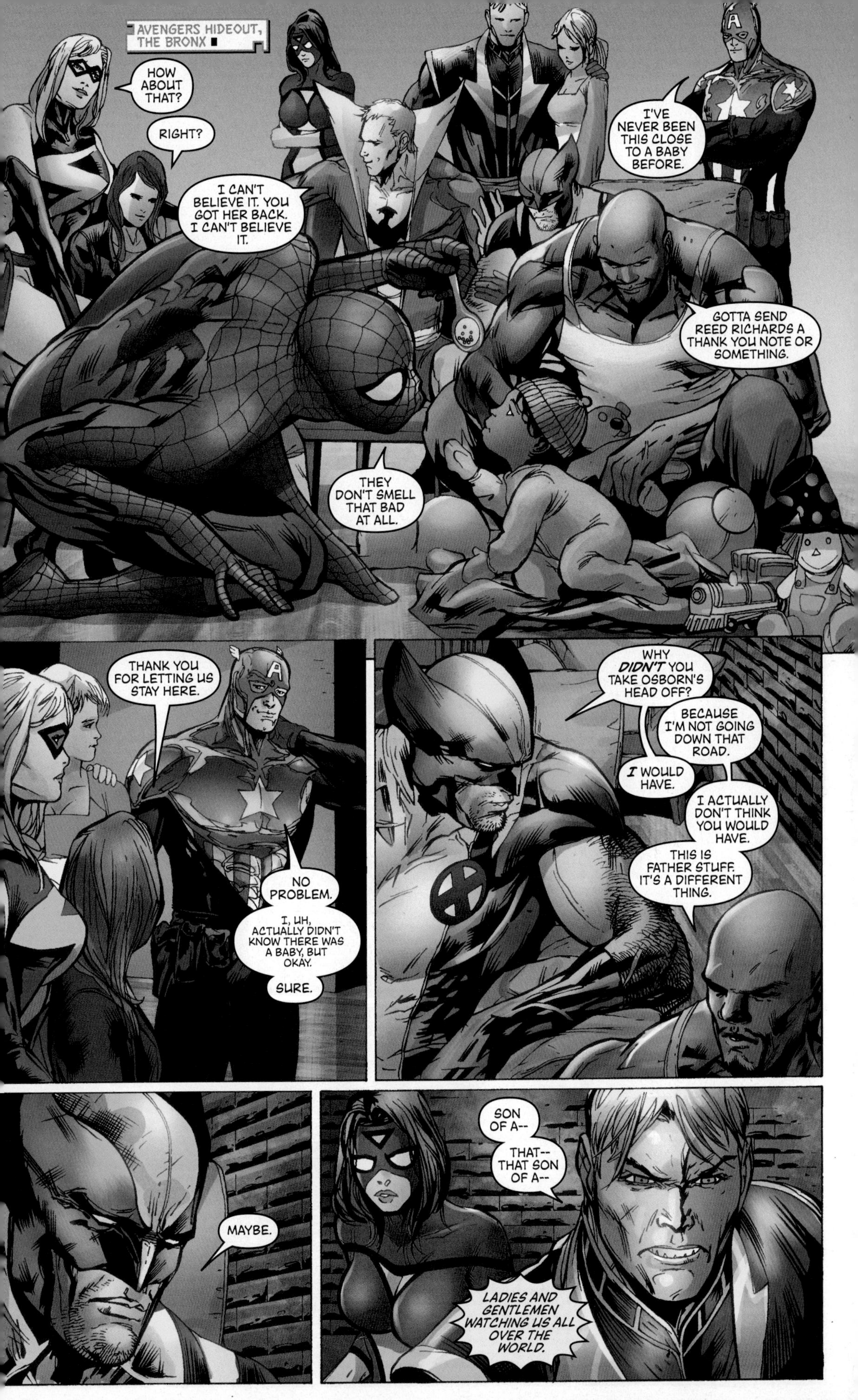
AVENGERS HIDEOUT, THE BRONX
HOW ABOUT THAT?
RIGHT?
I CAN'T BELIEVE IT. YOU GOT HER BACK. I CAN'T BELIEVE IT.
I'VE NEVER BEEN THIS CLOSE TO A BABY BEFORE.
GOTTA SEND REED RICHARDS A THANK YOU NOTE OR SOMETHING.
THEY DON'T SMELL THAT BAD AT ALL.
THANK YOU FOR LETTING US STAY HERE.
NO PROBLEM.
I, UH, ACTUALLY DIDN'T KNOW THERE WAS A BABY, BUT OKAY.
SURE.
WHY DIDN'T YOU TAKE OSBORN'S HEAD OFF?
BECAUSE I'M NOT GOING DOWN THAT ROAD.
I WOULD HAVE.
I ACTUALLY DON'T THINK YOU WOULD HAVE.
THIS IS FATHER STUFF. IT'S A DIFFERENT THING.
MAYBE.
SON OF A--
THAT-- THAT SON OF A--
LADIES AND GENTLEMEN WATCHING US ALL OVER THE WORLD.

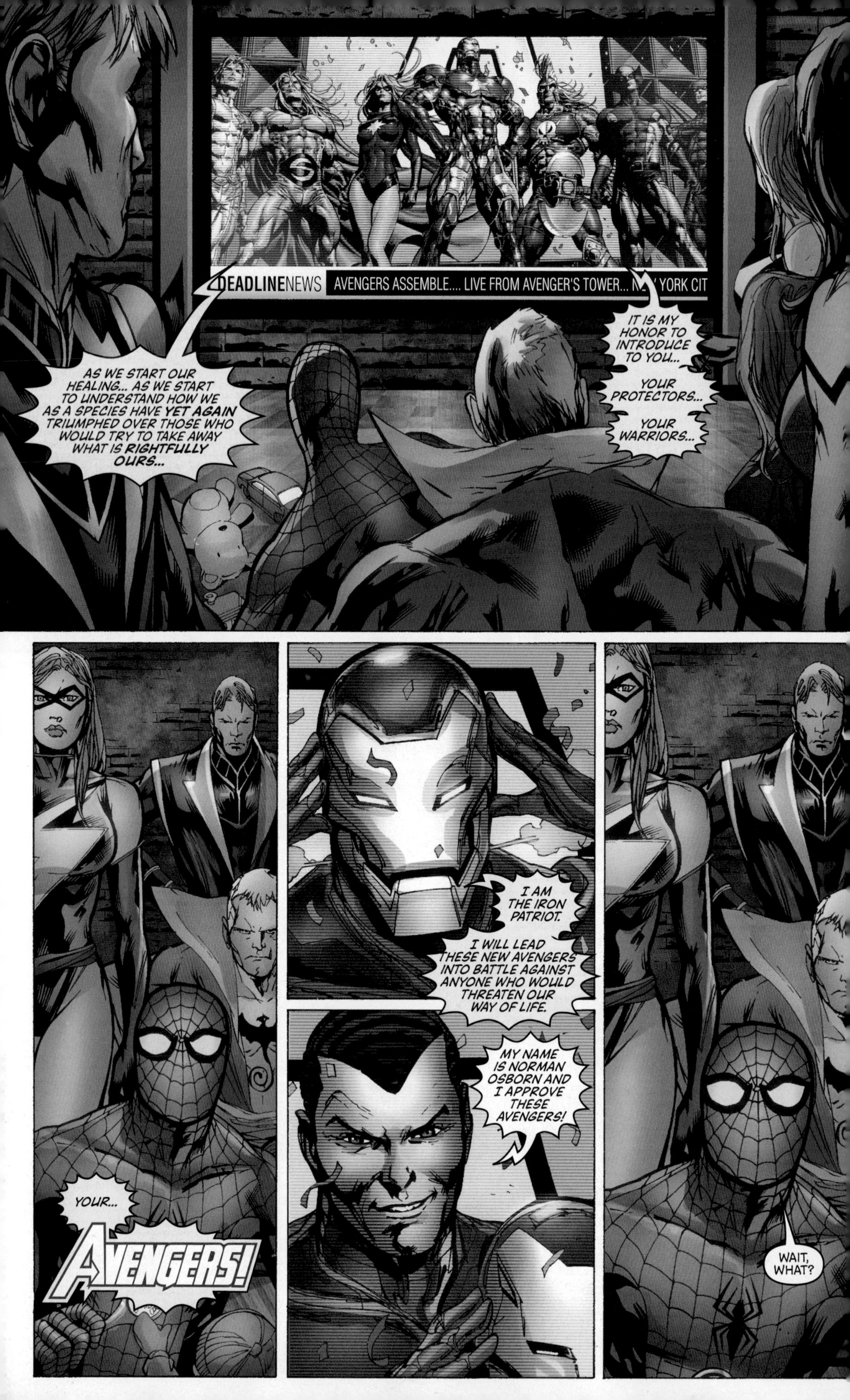
DEADLINENEWS
AVENGERS ASSEMBLE.... LIVE FROM AVENGER'S TOWER... N YORK CIT
AS WE START OUR HEALING... AS WE START TO UNDERSTAND HOW WE AS A SPECIES HAVE YET AGAIN TRIUMPHED OVER THOSE WHO WOULD TRY TO TAKE AWAY WHAT IS RIGHTFULLY OURS...
IT IS MY HONOR TO INTRODUCE TO YOU...
YOUR PROTECTORS...
YOUR WARRIORS...
YOUR...
AVENGERS!
I AM THE IRON PATRIOT.
I WILL LEAD THESE NEW AVENGERS INTO BATTLE AGAINST ANYONE WHO WOULD THREATEN OUR WAY OF LIFE.
MY NAME IS NORMAN OSBORN AND I APPROVE THESE AVENGERS!
WAIT, WHAT?

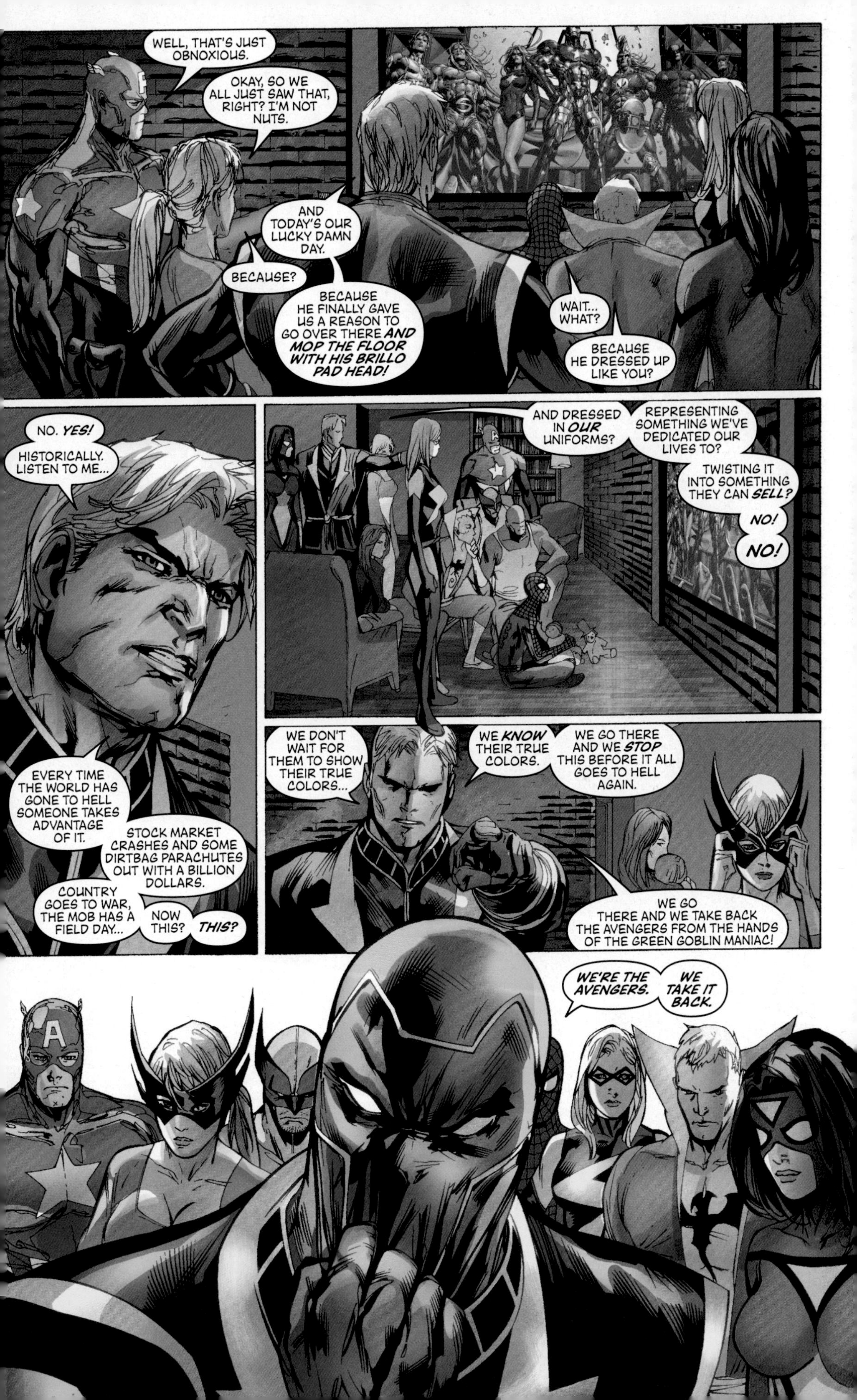
WELL, THAT'S JUST OBNOXIOUS.
OKAY, SO WE ALL JUST SAW THAT, RIGHT? I'M NOT NUTS.
AND TODAY'S OUR LUCKY DAMN DAY.
BECAUSE?
BECAUSE HE FINALLY GAVE US A REASON TO GO OVER THERE AND MOP THE FLOOR WITH HIS BRILLO PAD HEAD!
WAIT... WHAT?
BECAUSE HE DRESSED UP LIKE YOU?
NO. YES!
HISTORICALLY. LISTEN TO ME...
AND DRESSED IN OUR UNIFORMS?
REPRESENTING SOMETHING WE'VE DEDICATED OUR LIVES TO?
TWISTING IT INTO SOMETHING THEY CAN SELL?
NO!
NO!
EVERY TIME THE WORLD HAS GONE TO HELL SOMEONE TAKES ADVANTAGE OF IT.
STOCK MARKET CRASHES AND SOME DIRTBAG PARACHUTES OUT WITH A BILLION DOLLARS.
COUNTRY GOES TO WAR, THE MOB HAS A FIELD DAY...
NOW THIS?
THIS?
WE DON'T WAIT FOR THEM TO SHOW THEIR TRUE COLORS...
WE KNOW THEIR TRUE COLORS.
WE GO THERE AND WE STOP THIS BEFORE IT ALL GOES TO HELL AGAIN.
WE GO THERE AND WE TAKE BACK THE AVENGERS FROM THE HANDS OF THE GREEN GOBLIN MANIAC!
WE'RE THE AVENGERS.
WE TAKE IT BACK.

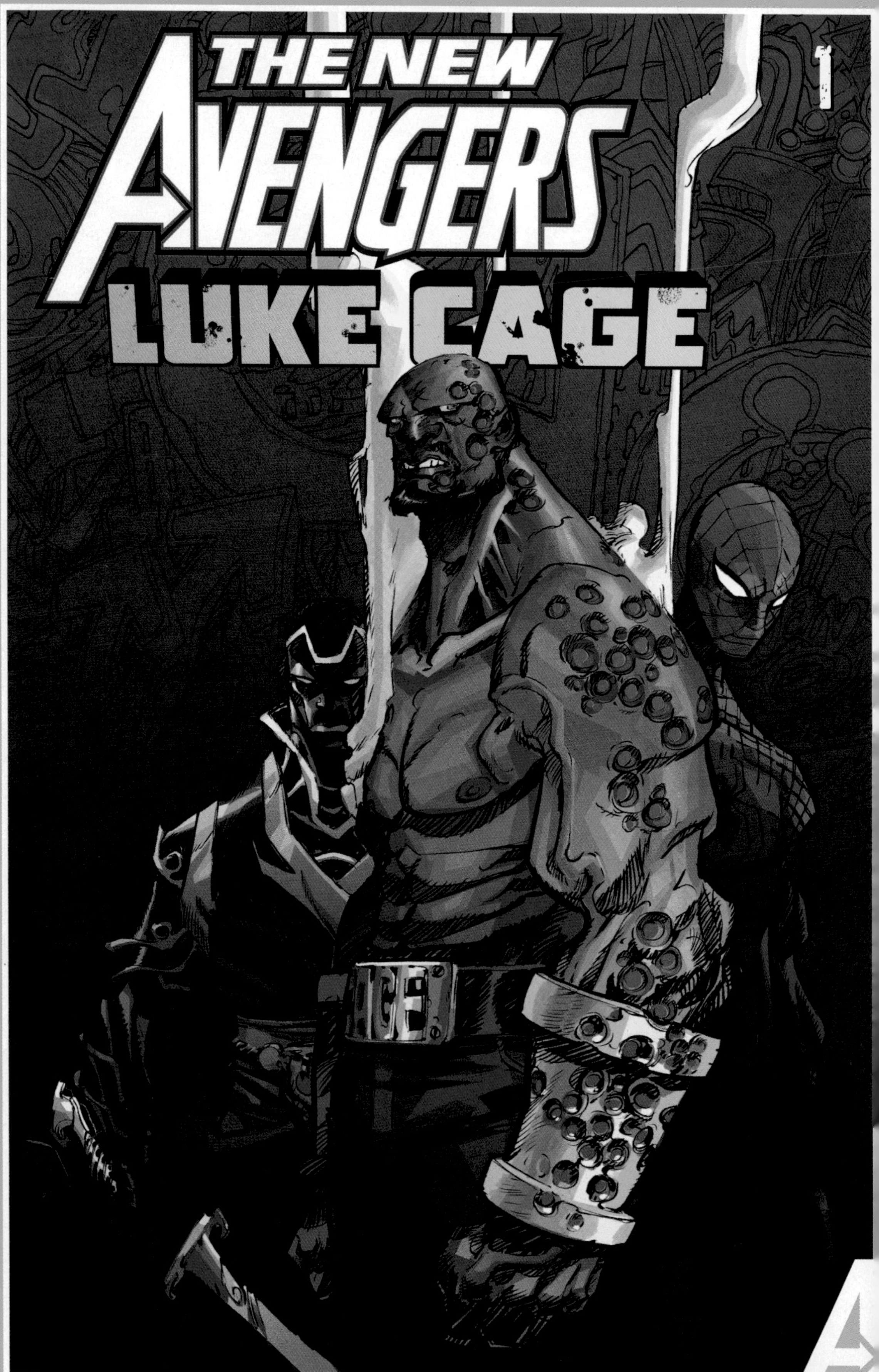
THE NEW
AVENGERS
1
LUKE CAGE

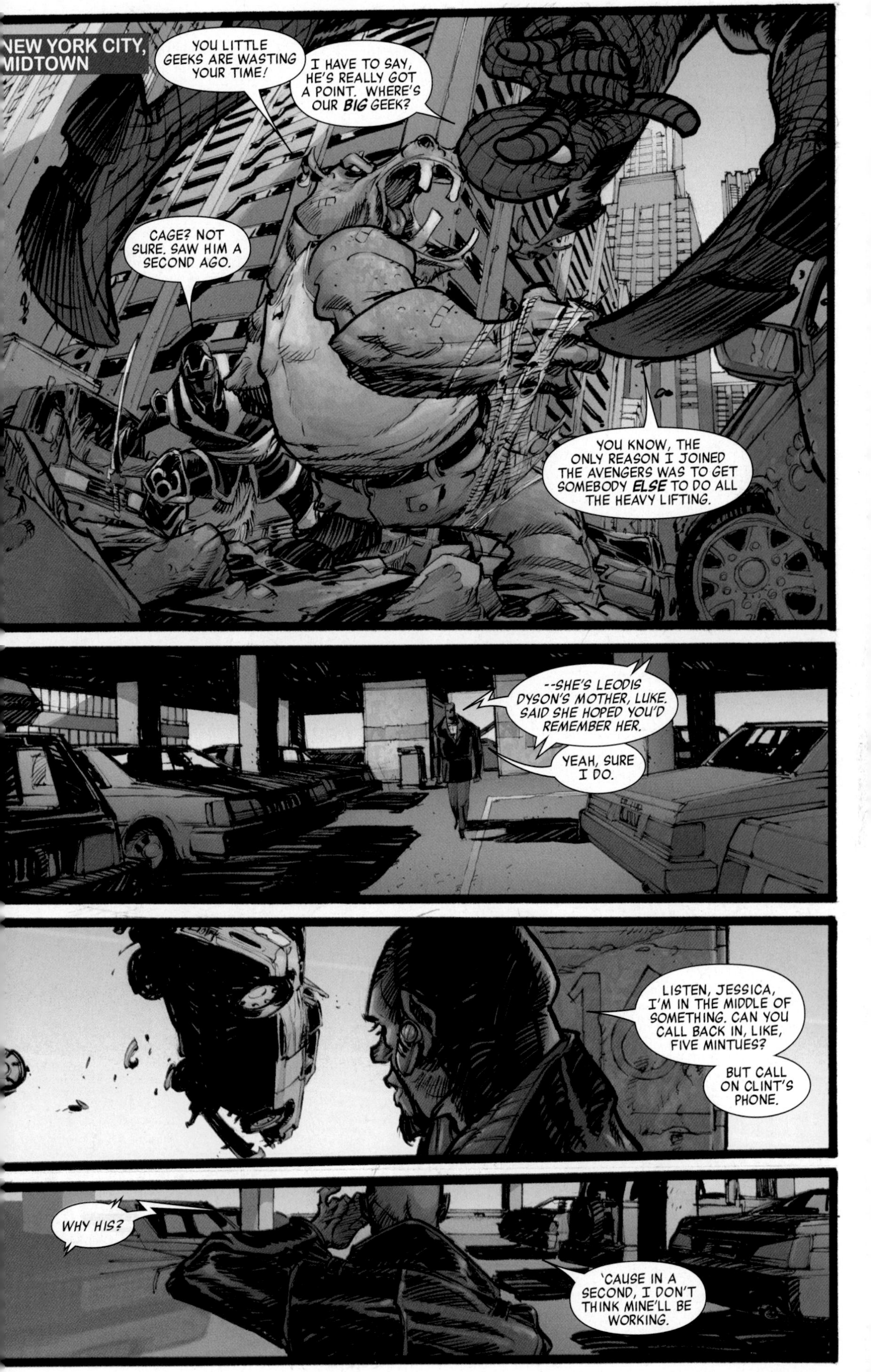

NEW YORK CITY, MIDTOWN
YOU LITTLE GEEKS ARE WASTING YOUR TIME!
I HAVE TO SAY, HE'S REALLY GOT A POINT. WHERE'S OUR BIG GEEK?
CAGE? NOT SURE. SAW HIM A SECOND AGO.
YOU KNOW, THE ONLY REASON I JOINED THE AVENGERS WAS TO GET SOMEBODY ELSE TO DO ALL THE HEAVY LIFTING.
--SHE'S LEODIS DYSON'S MOTHER, LUKE. SAID SHE HOPED YOU'D REMEMBER HER.
YEAH, SURE I DO.
LISTEN, JESSICA, I'M IN THE MIDDLE OF SOMETHING. CAN YOU CALL BACK IN, LIKE, FIVE MINTUES?
BUT CALL ON CLINT'S PHONE.
WHY HIS?
'CAUSE IN A SECOND, I DON'T THINK MINE'LL BE WORKING.

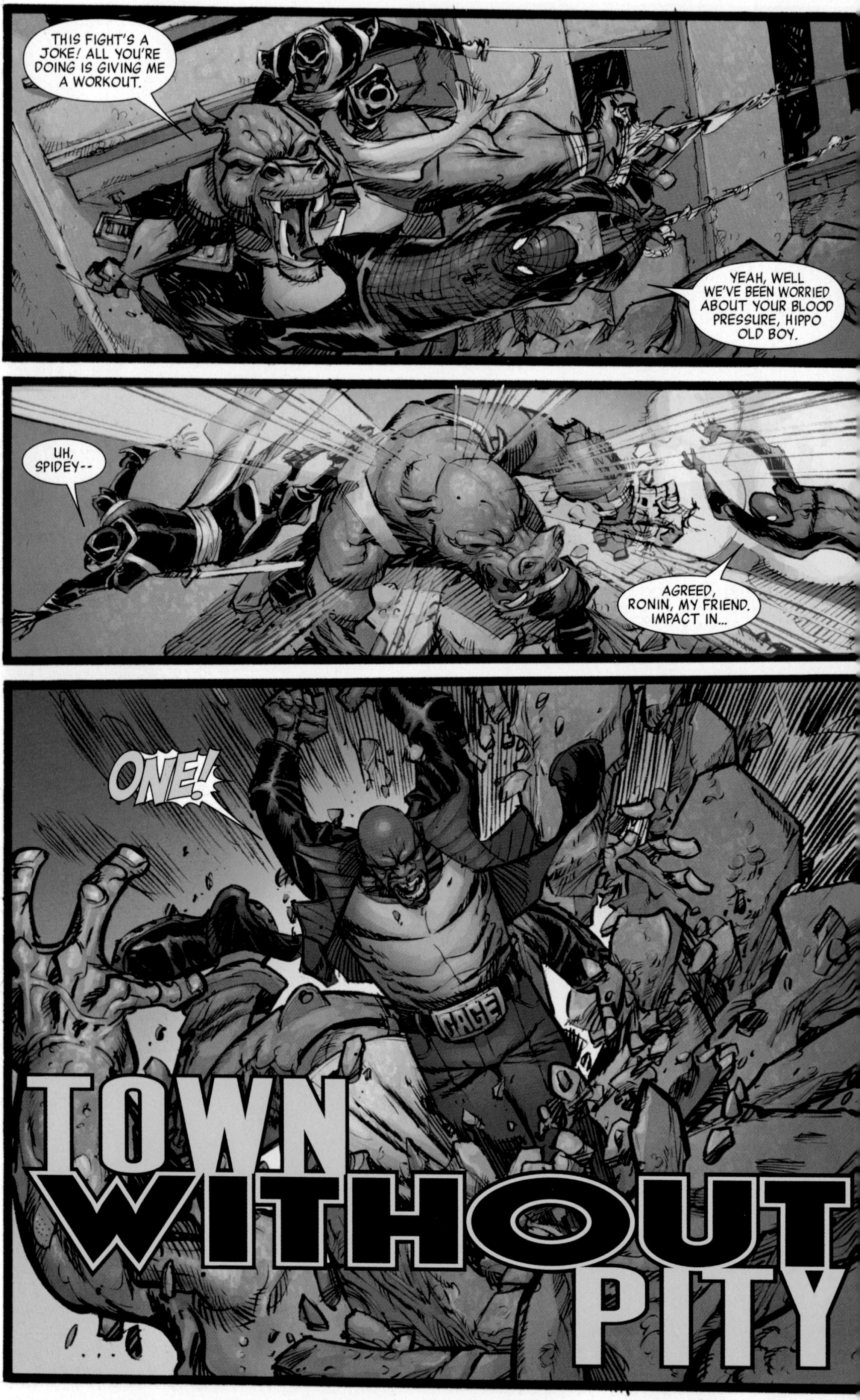
THIS FIGHT'S A JOKE! ALL YOU'RE DOING IS GIVING ME A WORKOUT.
YEAH, WELL WE'VE BEEN WORRIED ABOUT YOUR BLOOD PRESSURE, HIPPO OLD BOY.
UH, SPIDEY--
AGREED, RONIN, MY FRIEND. IMPACT IN...
ONE!
CAGE
TOWN WITHOUT PITY
...

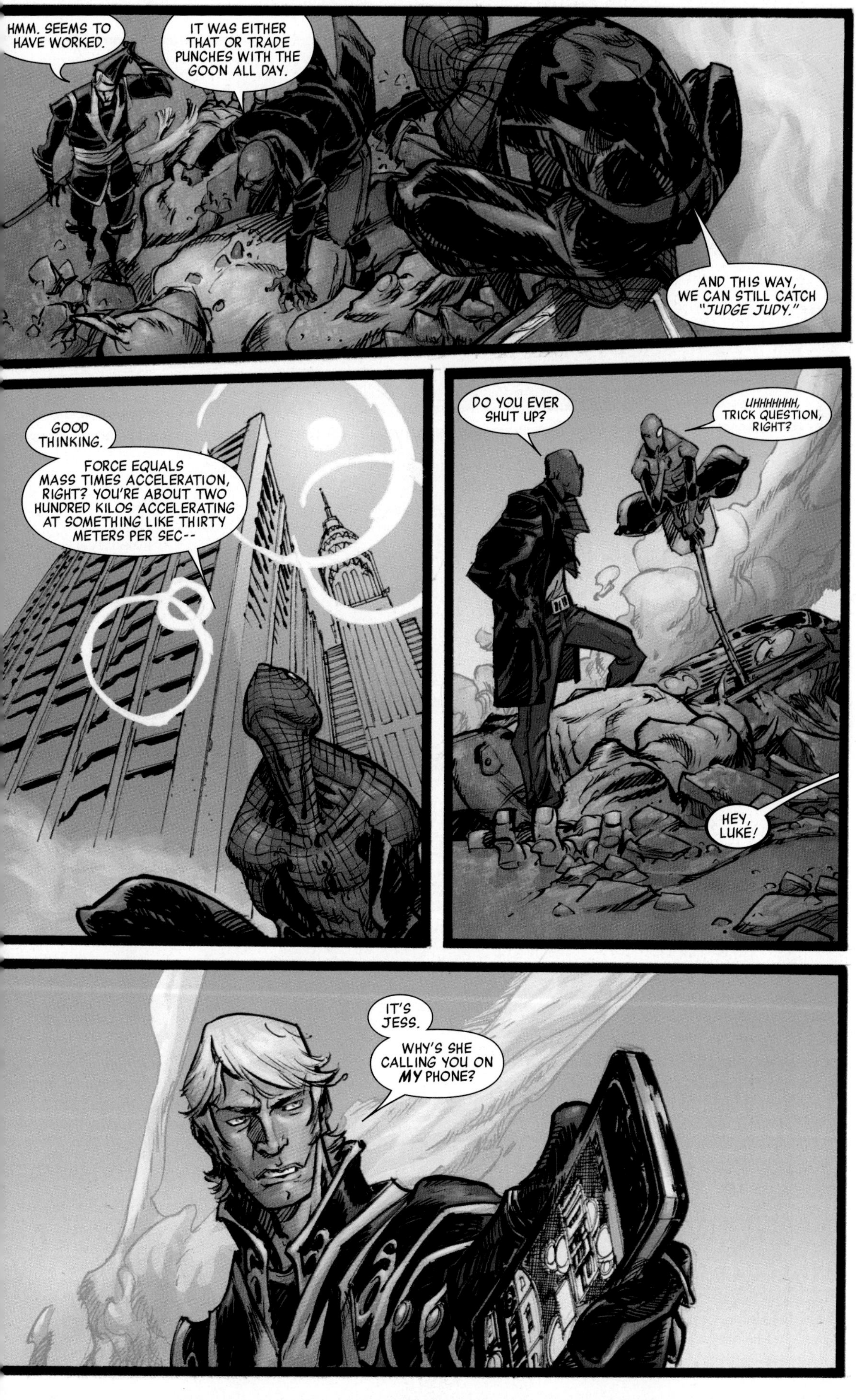
HMM. SEEMS TO HAVE WORKED.
IT WAS EITHER THAT OR TRADE PUNCHES WITH THE GOON ALL DAY.
AND THIS WAY, WE CAN STILL CATCH "JUDGE JUDY."
GOOD THINKING.
FORCE EQUALS MASS TIMES ACCELERATION, RIGHT? YOU'RE ABOUT TWO HUNDRED KILOS ACCELERATING AT SOMETHING LIKE THIRTY METERS PER SEC--
DO YOU EVER SHUT UP?
UHHHHHHH, TRICK QUESTION, RIGHT?
HEY, LUKE!
IT'S JESS.
WHY'S SHE CALLING YOU ON MY PHONE?

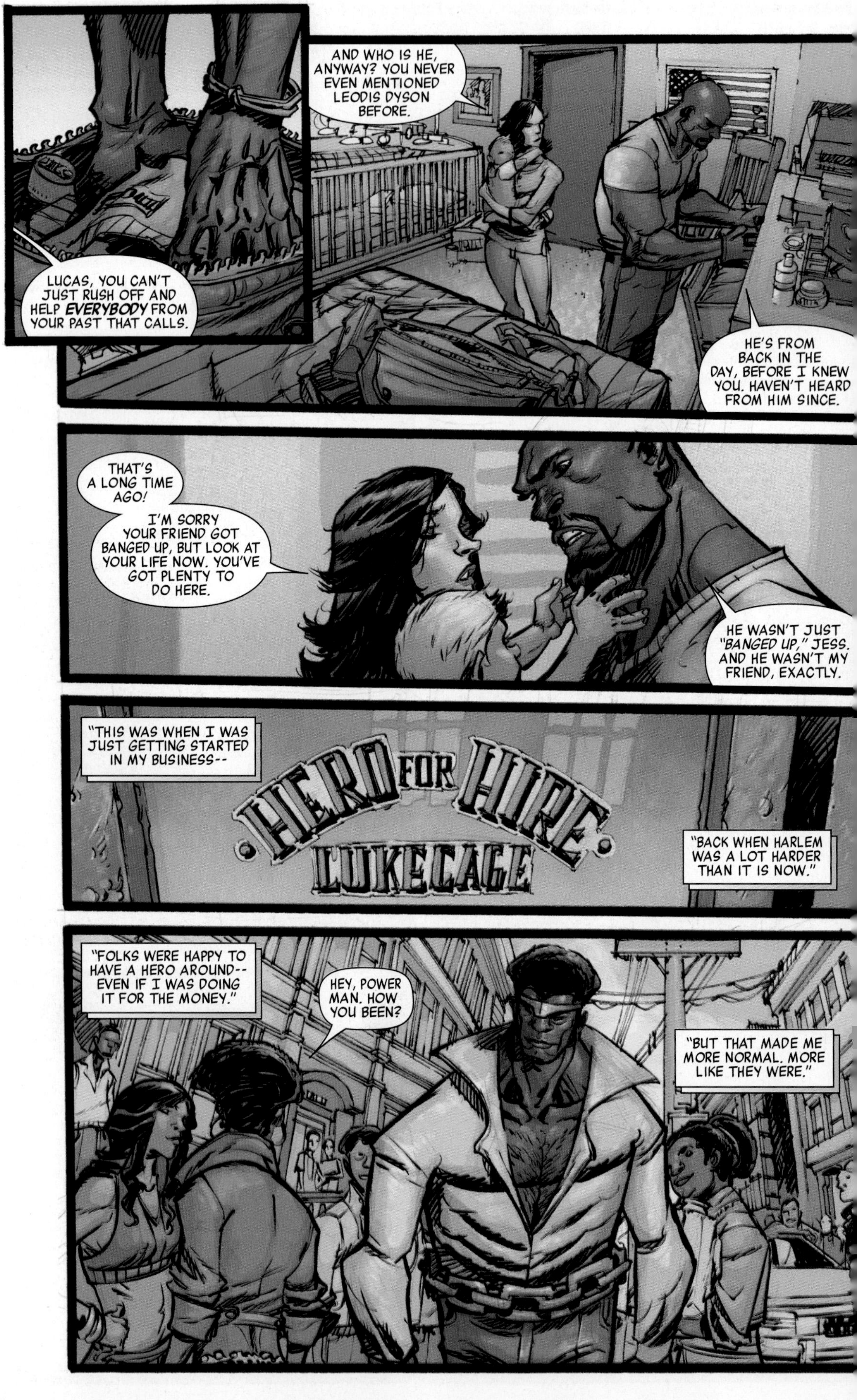
LUCAS, YOU CAN'T JUST RUSH OFF AND HELP EVERYBODY FROM YOUR PAST THAT CALLS.
AND WHO IS HE, ANYWAY? YOU NEVER EVEN MENTIONED LEODIS DYSON BEFORE.
HE'S FROM BACK IN THE DAY, BEFORE I KNEW YOU. HAVEN'T HEARD FROM HIM SINCE.
THAT'S A LONG TIME AGO!
I'M SORRY YOUR FRIEND GOT BANGED UP, BUT LOOK AT YOUR LIFE NOW. YOU'VE GOT PLENTY TO DO HERE.
HE WASN'T JUST "BANGED UP," JESS. AND HE WASN'T MY FRIEND, EXACTLY.
"THIS WAS WHEN I WAS JUST GETTING STARTED IN MY BUSINESS--
HERO FOR HIRE
LUKE CAGE
"BACK WHEN HARLEM WAS A LOT HARDER THAN IT IS NOW."
"FOLKS WERE HAPPY TO HAVE A HERO AROUND-- EVEN IF I WAS DOING IT FOR THE MONEY."
HEY, POWER MAN. HOW YOU BEEN?
"BUT THAT MADE ME MORE NORMAL. MORE LIKE THEY WERE."

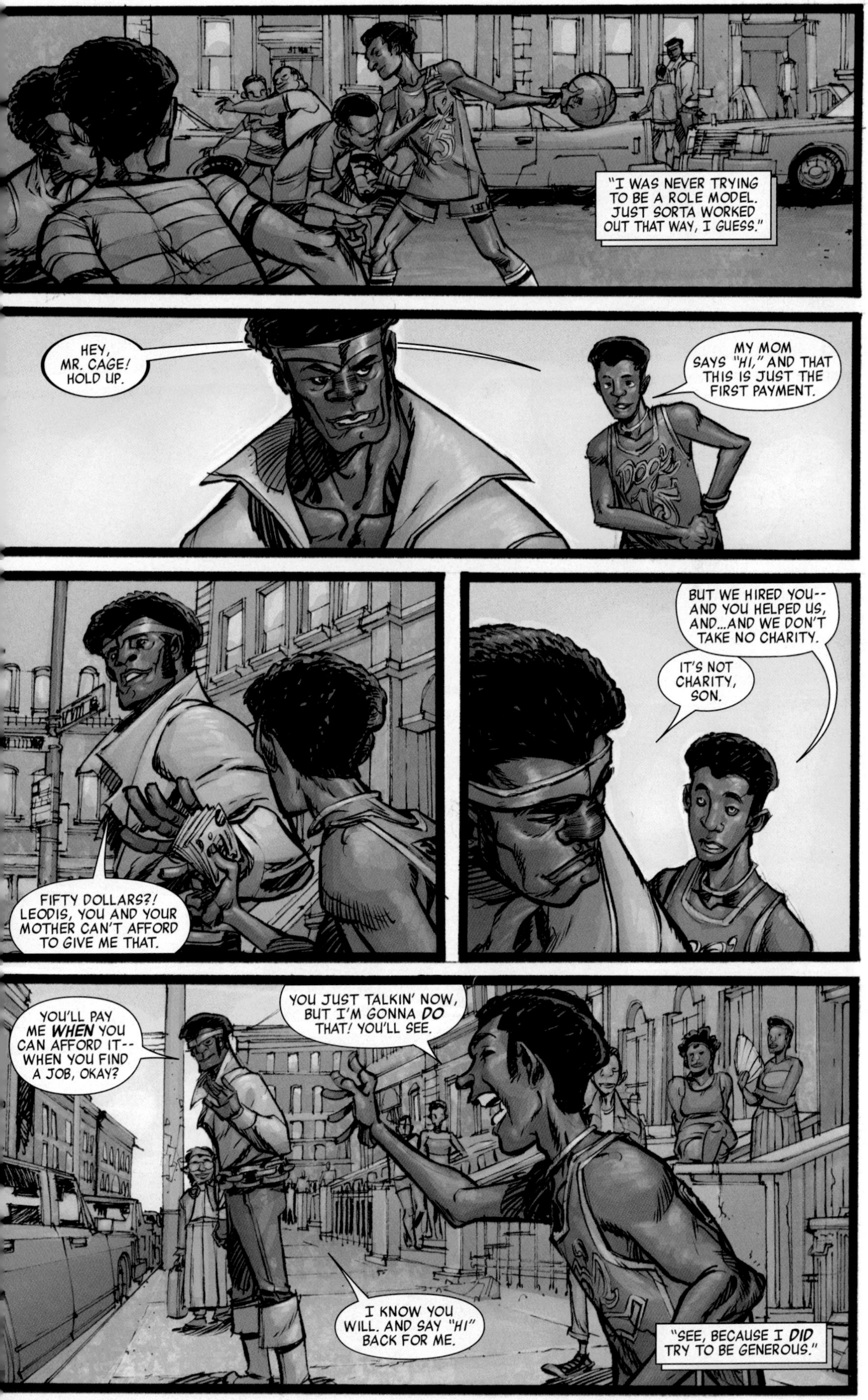
"I WAS NEVER TRYING TO BE A ROLE MODEL. JUST SORTA WORKED OUT THAT WAY, I GUESS."
HEY, MR. CAGE! HOLD UP.
MY MOM SAYS "HI," AND THAT THIS IS JUST THE FIRST PAYMENT.
FIFTY DOLLARS?! LEODIS, YOU AND YOUR MOTHER CAN'T AFFORD TO GIVE ME THAT.
BUT WE HIRED YOU-- AND YOU HELPED US, AND...AND WE DON'T TAKE NO CHARITY.
IT'S NOT CHARITY, SON.
YOU'LL PAY ME WHEN YOU CAN AFFORD IT-- WHEN YOU FIND A JOB, OKAY?
YOU JUST TALKIN' NOW, BUT I'M GONNA DO THAT! YOU'LL SEE.
I KNOW YOU WILL. AND SAY "HI" BACK FOR ME.
"SEE, BECAUSE I DID TRY TO BE GENEROUS."

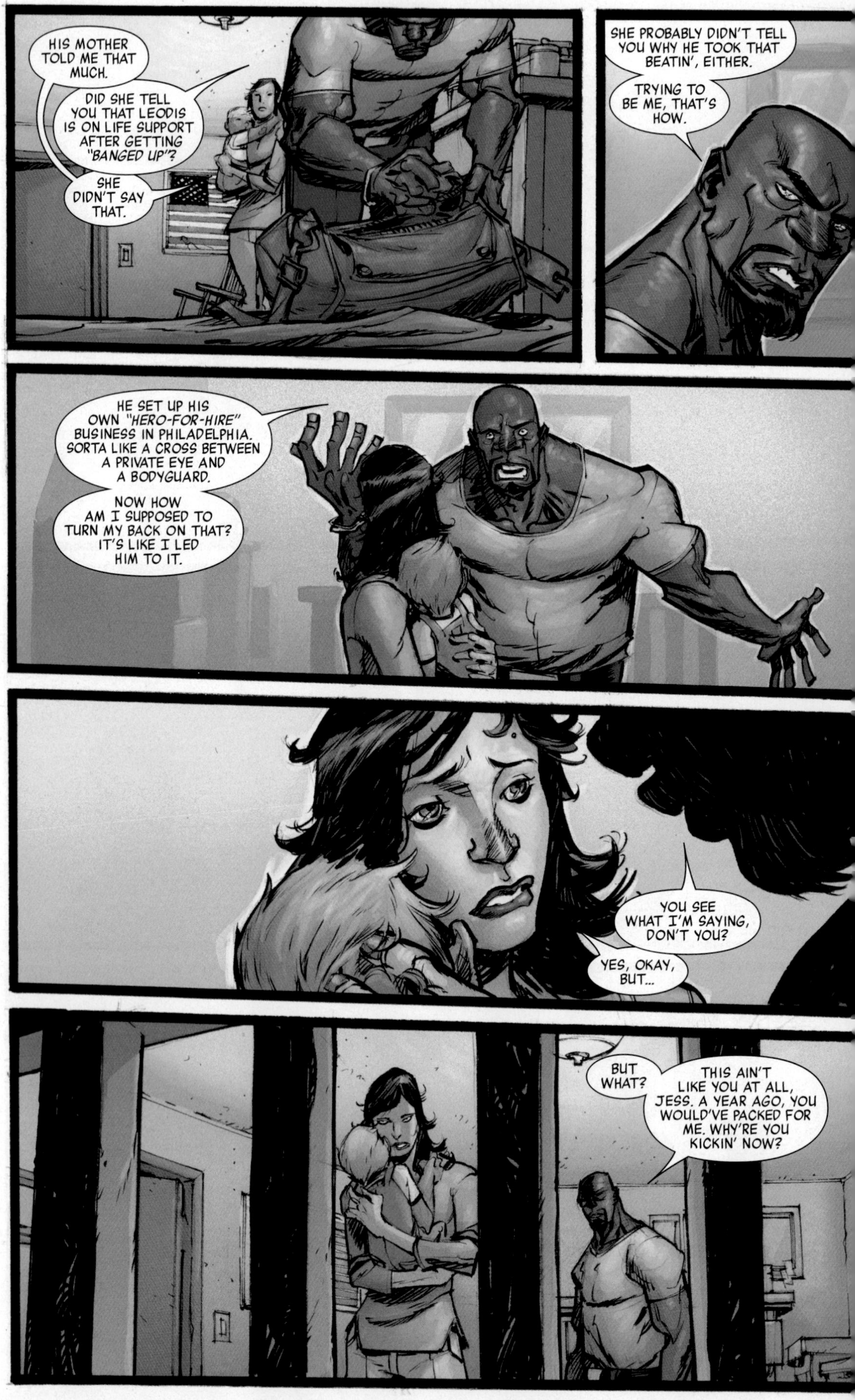
HIS MOTHER TOLD ME THAT MUCH.
DID SHE TELL YOU THAT LEODIS IS ON LIFE SUPPORT AFTER GETTING "BANGED UP"?
SHE DIDN'T SAY THAT.
SHE PROBABLY DIDN'T TELL YOU WHY HE TOOK THAT BEATIN', EITHER.
TRYING TO BE ME, THAT'S HOW.
HE SET UP HIS OWN "HERO-FOR-HIRE" BUSINESS IN PHILADELPHIA. SORTA LIKE A CROSS BETWEEN A PRIVATE EYE AND A BODYGUARD.
NOW HOW AM I SUPPOSED TO TURN MY BACK ON THAT? IT'S LIKE I LED HIM TO IT.
YOU SEE WHAT I'M SAYING, DON'T YOU?
YES, OKAY, BUT...
BUT WHAT?
THIS AIN'T LIKE YOU AT ALL, JESS. A YEAR AGO, YOU WOULD'VE PACKED FOR ME. WHY'RE YOU KICKIN' NOW?

EVERYTHING WE'VE BEEN THROUGH THESE LAST MONTHS. THE TIME WE'VE SPENT APART, THE WAR, THIS OSBORN BUSINESS...

SOMETIMES, IT'S...TOO MUCH, LUCAS.

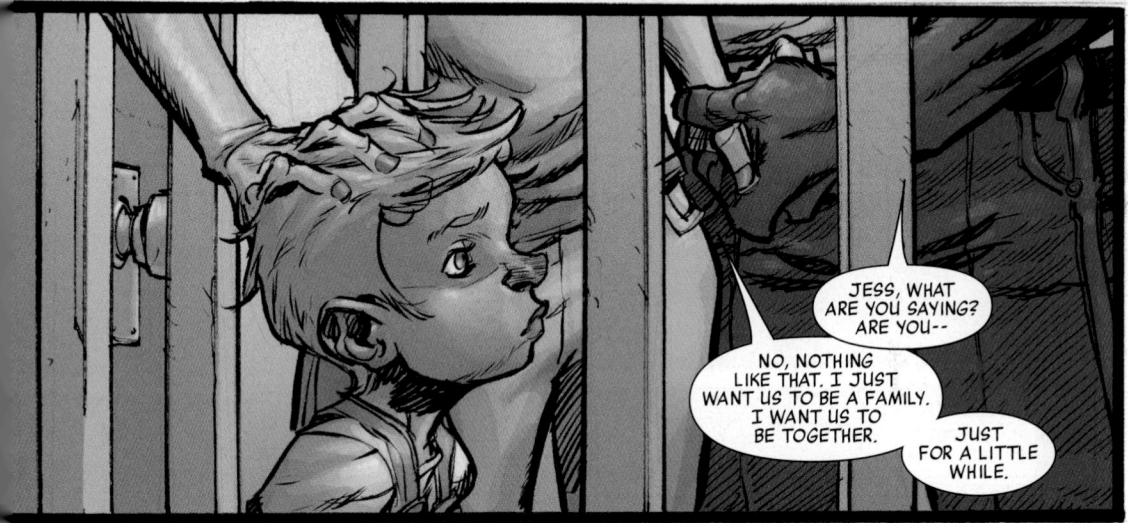

JESS, WHAT ARE YOU SAYING? ARE YOU--

NO, NOTHING LIKE THAT. I JUST WANT US TO BE A FAMILY. I WANT US TO BE TOGETHER.

JUST FOR A LITTLE WHILE.

OKAY, BABY. OKAY, I GET IT.

BUT IT'S ONLY PHILLY--NOT PAKISTAN.

I'VE BEEN TO AN EAGLE'S GAME. PHILLY'S WORSE.

JUST LET ME GO FOR A COUPLE DAYS, FIND OUT WHAT HAPPENED. AND THEN, I PROMISE, YOU WON'T BE ABLE TO GET RID OF ME.

ALL RIGHT.

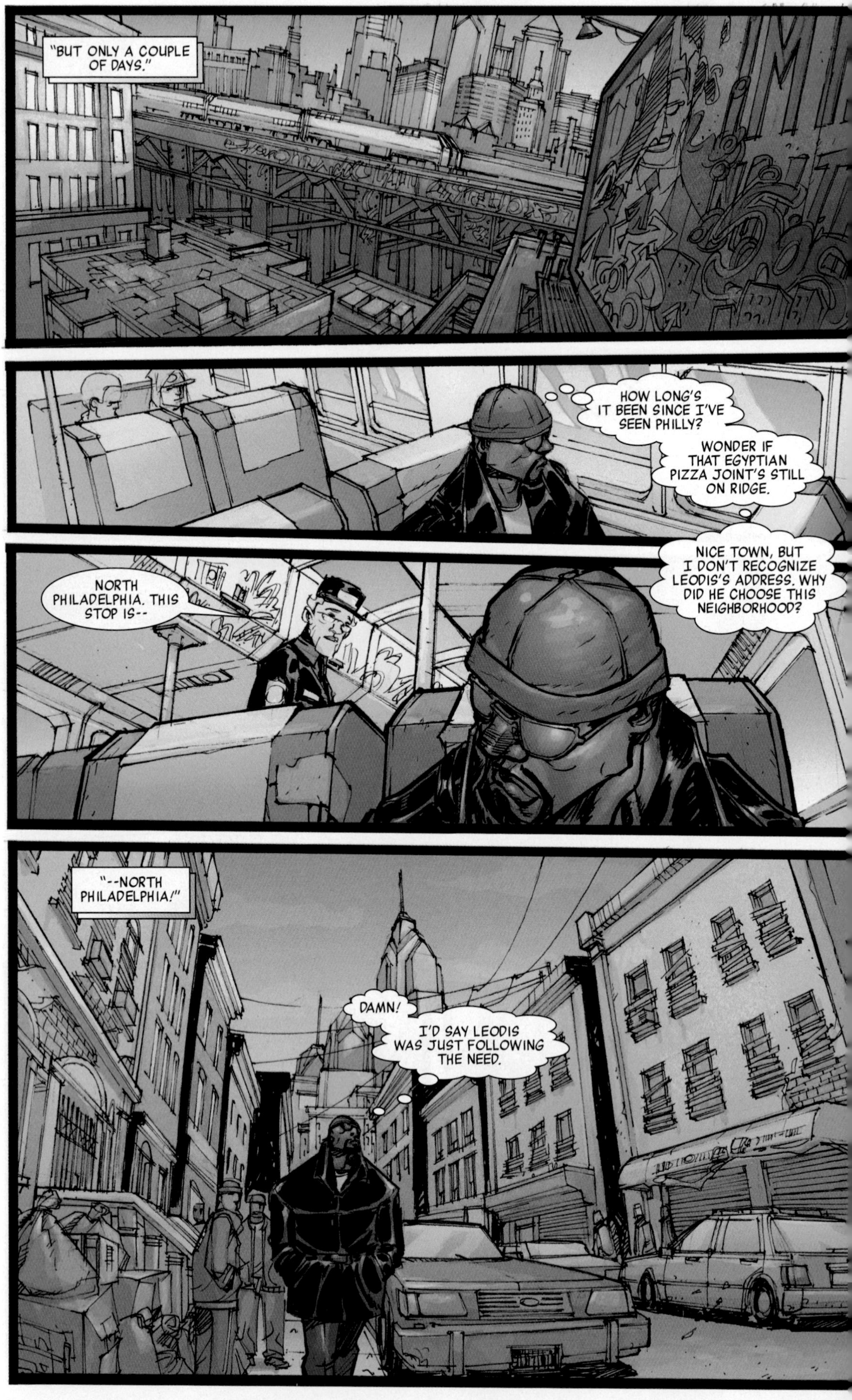
"BUT ONLY A COUPLE OF DAYS."
HOW LONG'S IT BEEN SINCE I'VE SEEN PHILLY?
WONDER IF THAT EGYPTIAN PIZZA JOINT'S STILL ON RIDGE.
NORTH PHILADELPHIA. THIS STOP IS--
NICE TOWN, BUT I DON'T RECOGNIZE LEODIS'S ADDRESS. WHY DID HE CHOOSE THIS NEIGHBORHOOD?
"--NORTH PHILADELPHIA!"
DAMN!
I'D SAY LEODIS WAS JUST FOLLOWING THE NEED.

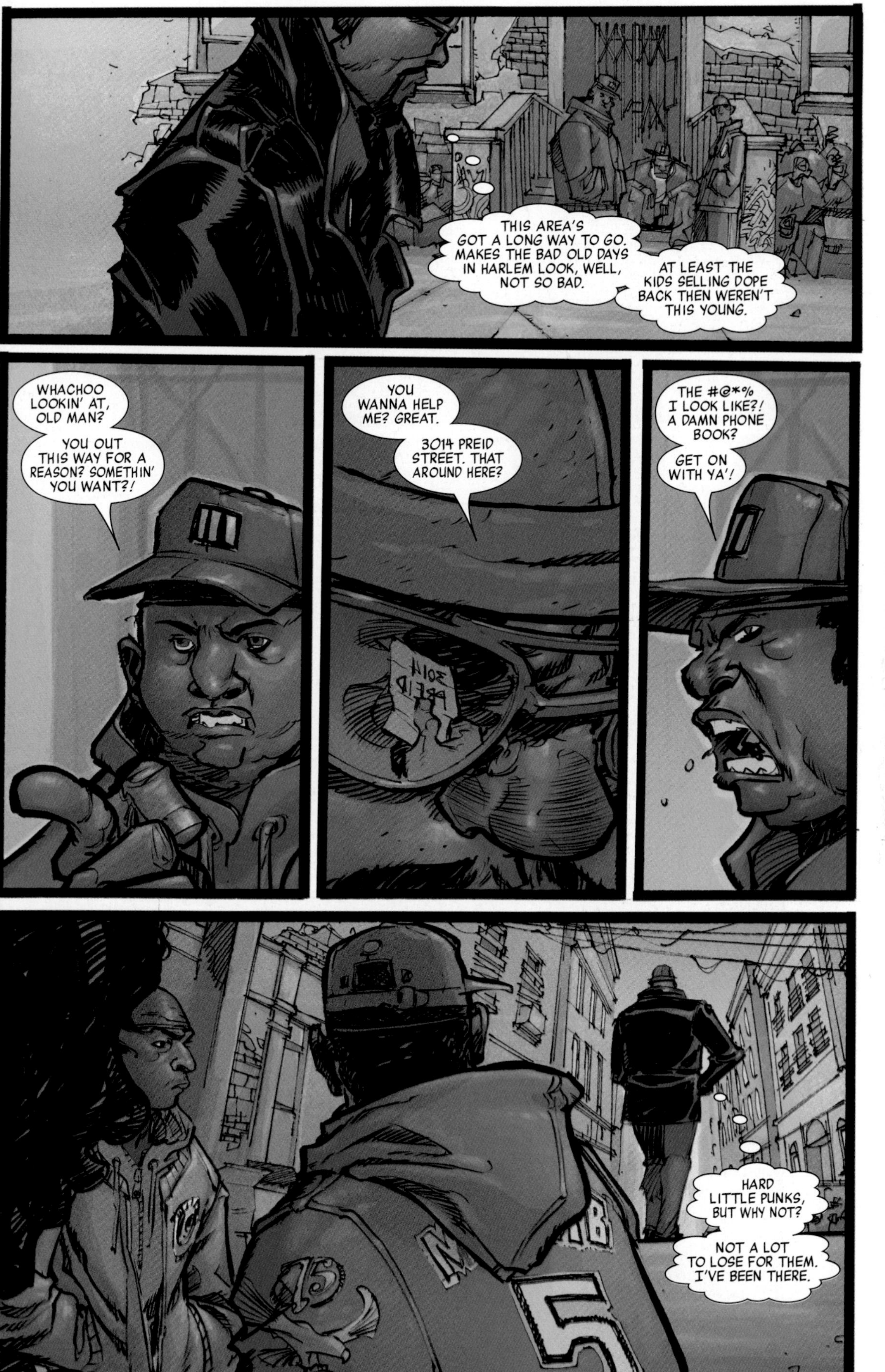
THIS AREA'S GOT A LONG WAY TO GO. MAKES THE BAD OLD DAYS IN HARLEM LOOK, WELL, NOT SO BAD.
AT LEAST THE KIDS SELLING DOPE BACK THEN WEREN'T THIS YOUNG.
WHACHOO LOOKIN' AT, OLD MAN?
YOU OUT THIS WAY FOR A REASON? SOMETHIN' YOU WANT?!
YOU WANNA HELP ME? GREAT.
3014 PREID STREET. THAT AROUND HERE?
THE #@*% I LOOK LIKE?! A DAMN PHONE BOOK?
GET ON WITH YA'!
HARD LITTLE PUNKS, BUT WHY NOT?
NOT A LOT TO LOSE FOR THEM. I'VE BEEN THERE.

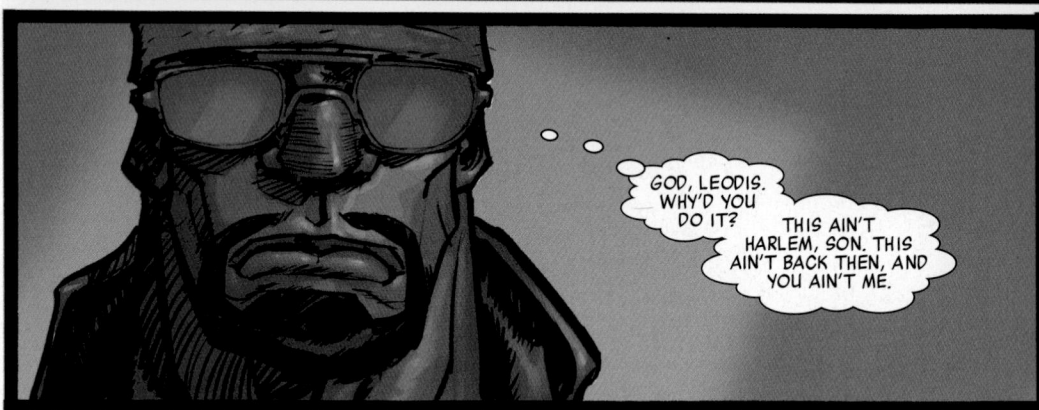

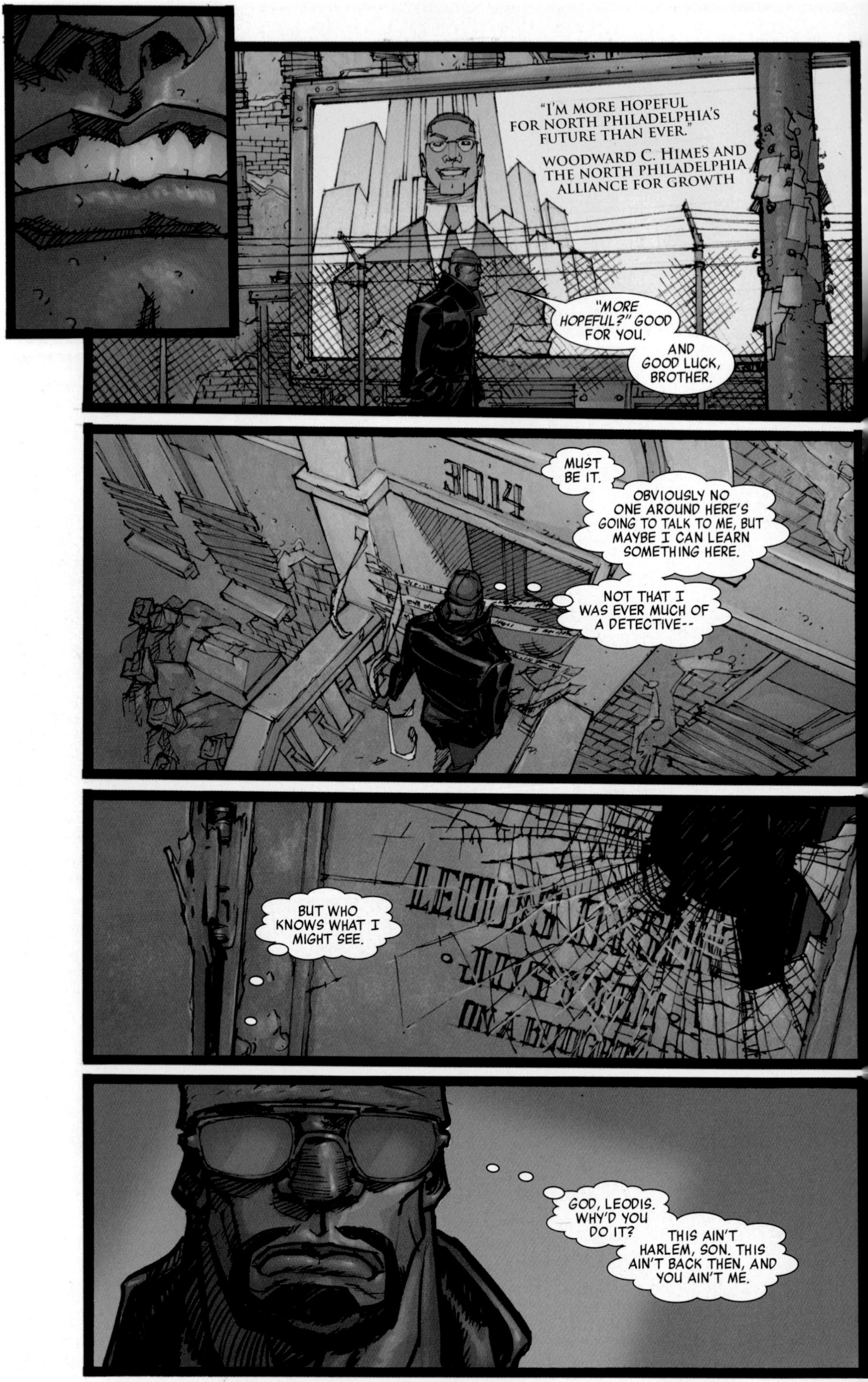
"I'M MORE HOPEFUL FOR NORTH PHILADELPHIA'S FUTURE THAN EVER."
WOODWARD C. HIMES AND THE NORTH PHILADELPHIA ALLIANCE FOR GROWTH
"MORE HOPEFUL?" GOOD FOR YOU.
AND GOOD LUCK, BROTHER.
3014
MUST BE IT.
OBVIOUSLY NO ONE AROUND HERE'S GOING TO TALK TO ME, BUT MAYBE I CAN LEARN SOMETHING HERE.
NOT THAT I WAS EVER MUCH OF A DETECTIVE--
BUT WHO KNOWS WHAT I MIGHT SEE.
GOD, LEODIS. WHY'D YOU DO IT?
THIS AIN'T HARLEM, SON. THIS AIN'T BACK THEN, AND YOU AIN'T ME.

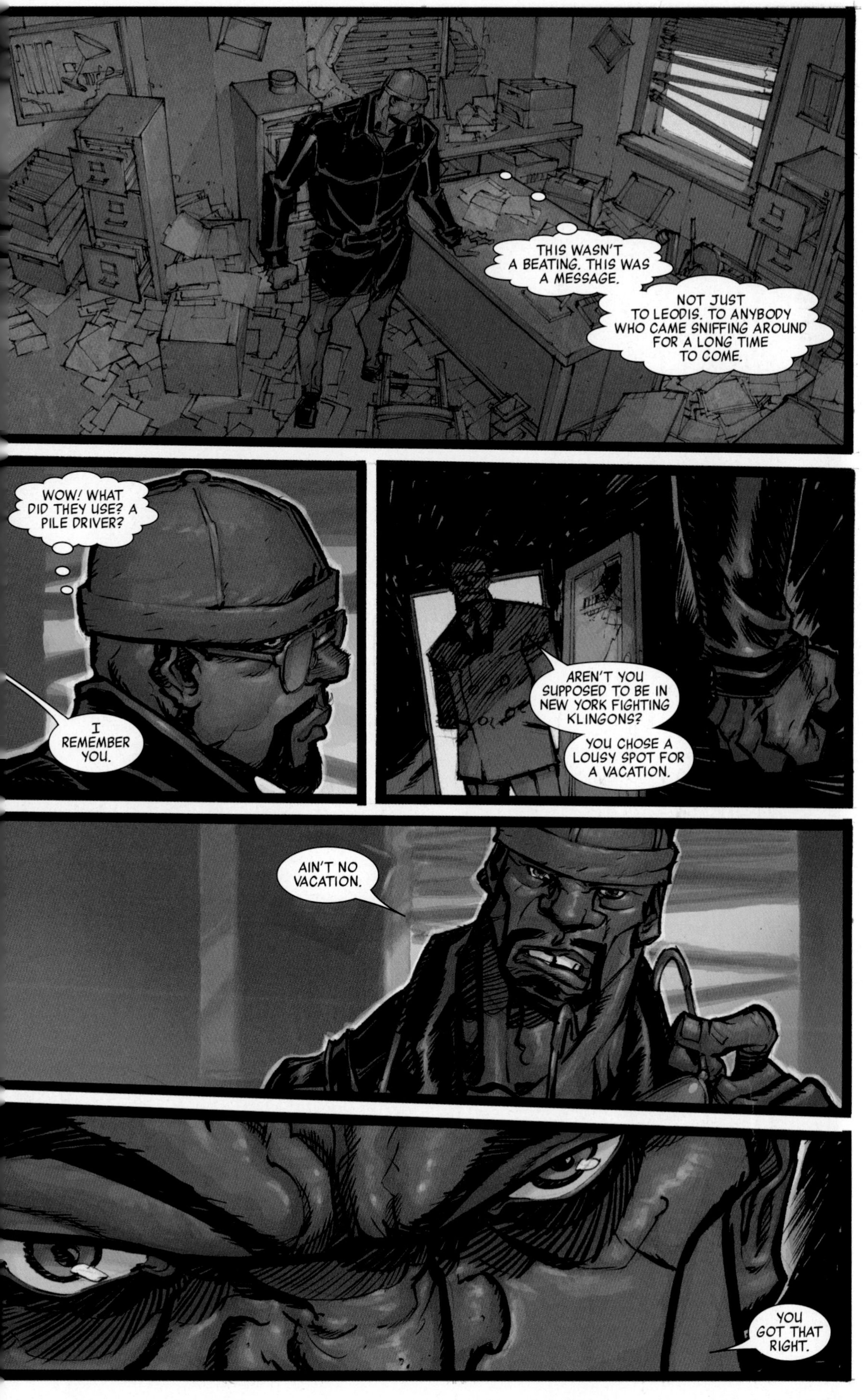
THIS WASN'T A BEATING. THIS WAS A MESSAGE.
NOT JUST TO LEODIS. TO ANYBODY WHO CAME SNIFFING AROUND FOR A LONG TIME TO COME.
WOW! WHAT DID THEY USE? A PILE DRIVER?
I REMEMBER YOU.
AREN'T YOU SUPPOSED TO BE IN NEW YORK FIGHTING KLINGONS?
YOU CHOSE A LOUSY SPOT FOR A VACATION.
AIN'T NO VACATION.
YOU GOT THAT RIGHT.

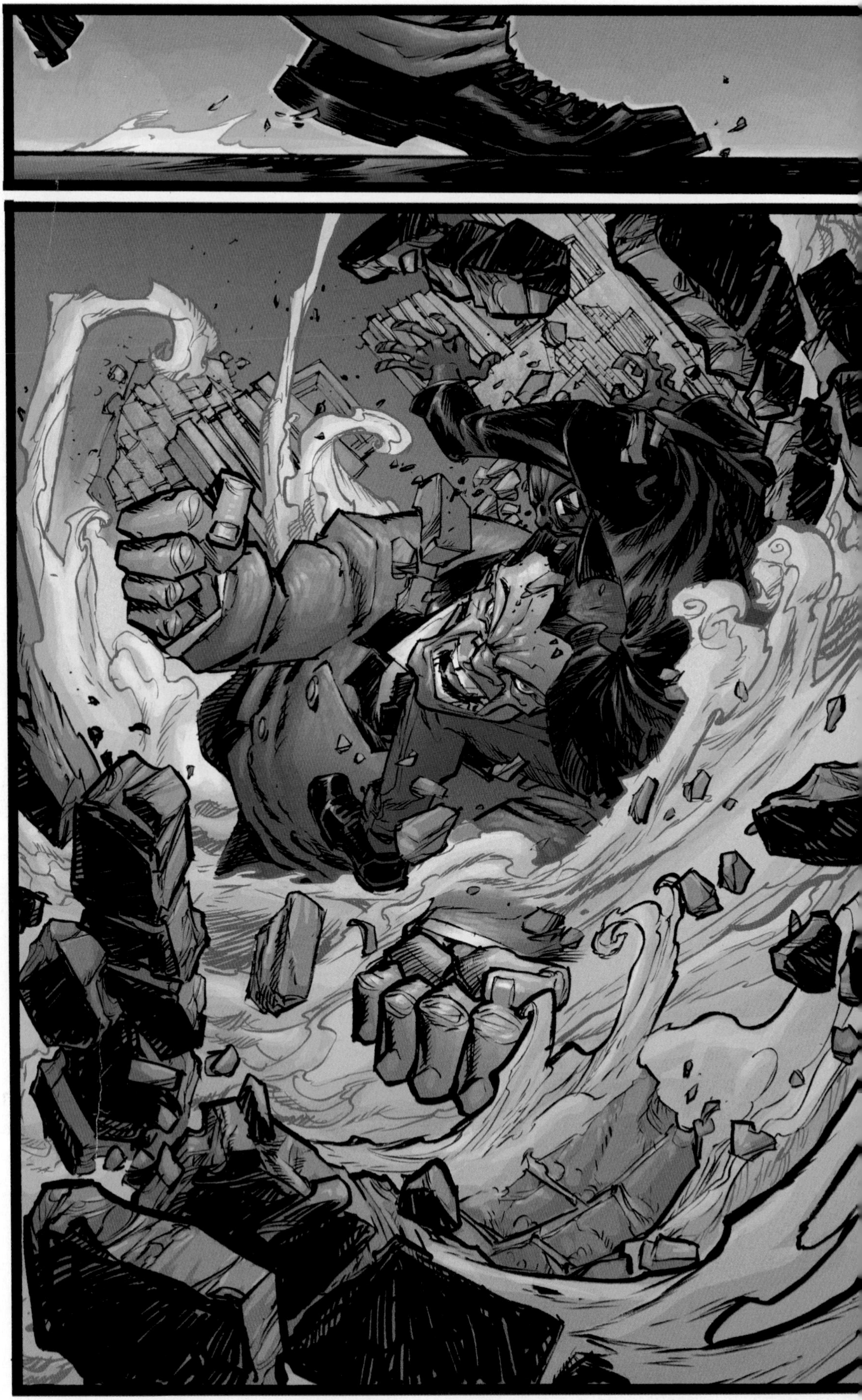

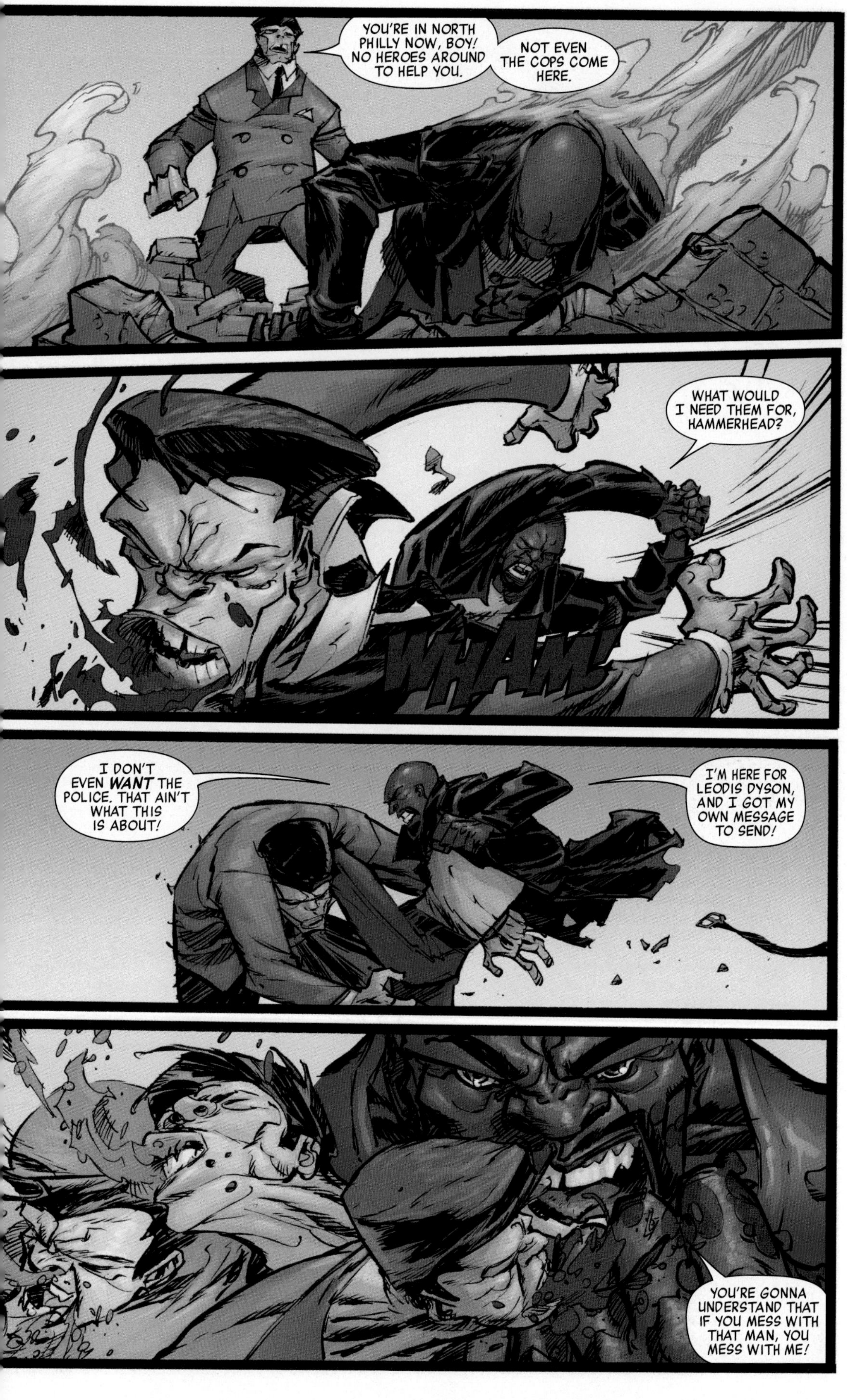
YOU'RE IN NORTH PHILLY NOW, BOY! NO HEROES AROUND TO HELP YOU.
NOT EVEN THE COPS COME HERE.
WHAT WOULD I NEED THEM FOR, HAMMERHEAD?
WHAM!
I DON'T EVEN WANT THE POLICE. THAT AIN'T WHAT THIS IS ABOUT!
I'M HERE FOR LEODIS DYSON, AND I GOT MY OWN MESSAGE TO SEND!
YOU'RE GONNA UNDERSTAND THAT IF YOU MESS WITH THAT MAN, YOU MESS WITH ME!

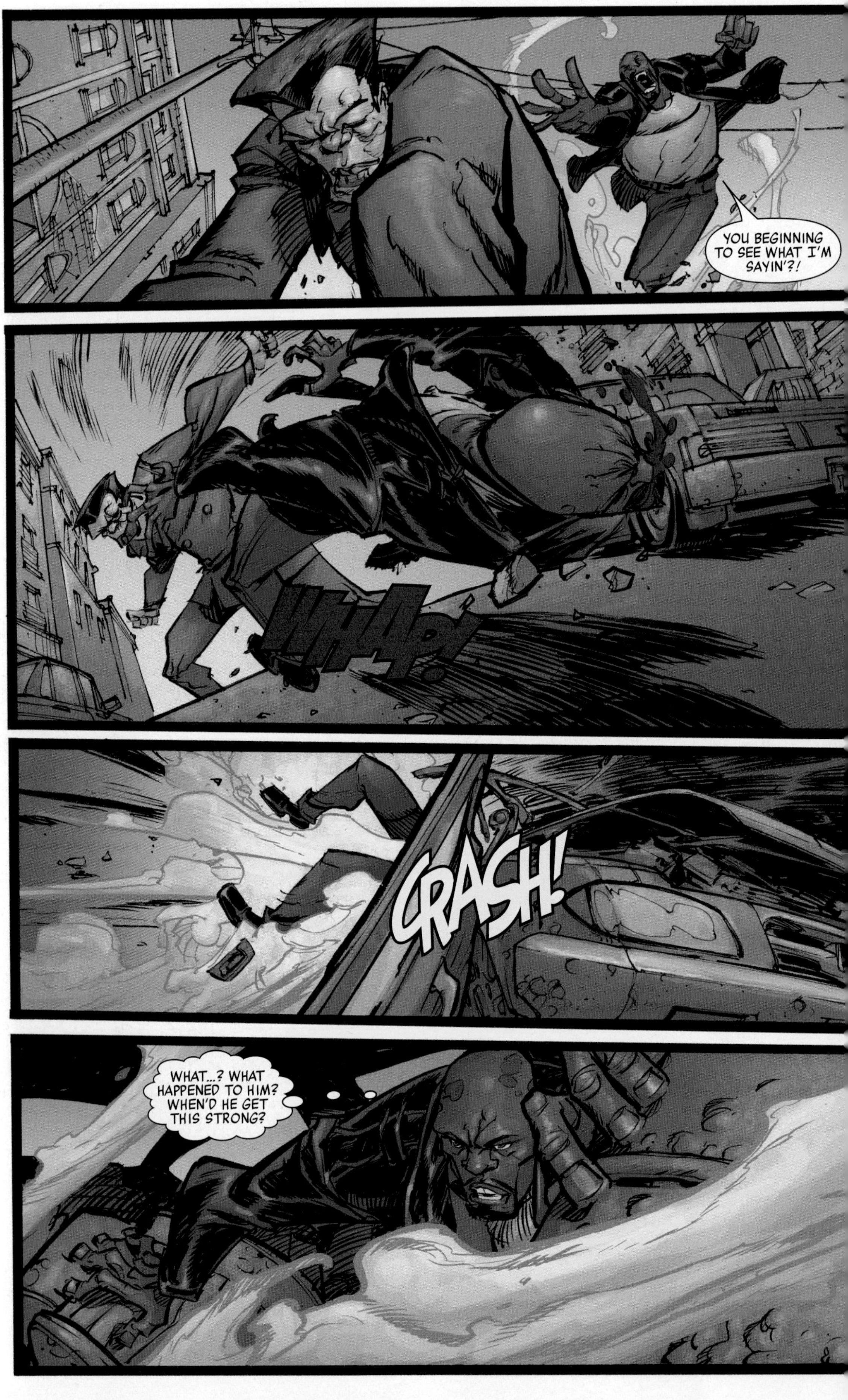

YOU BEGINNING TO SEE WHAT I'M SAYIN'?!
WHAP!
CRASH!
WHAT...? WHAT HAPPENED TO HIM? WHEN'D HE GET THIS STRONG?

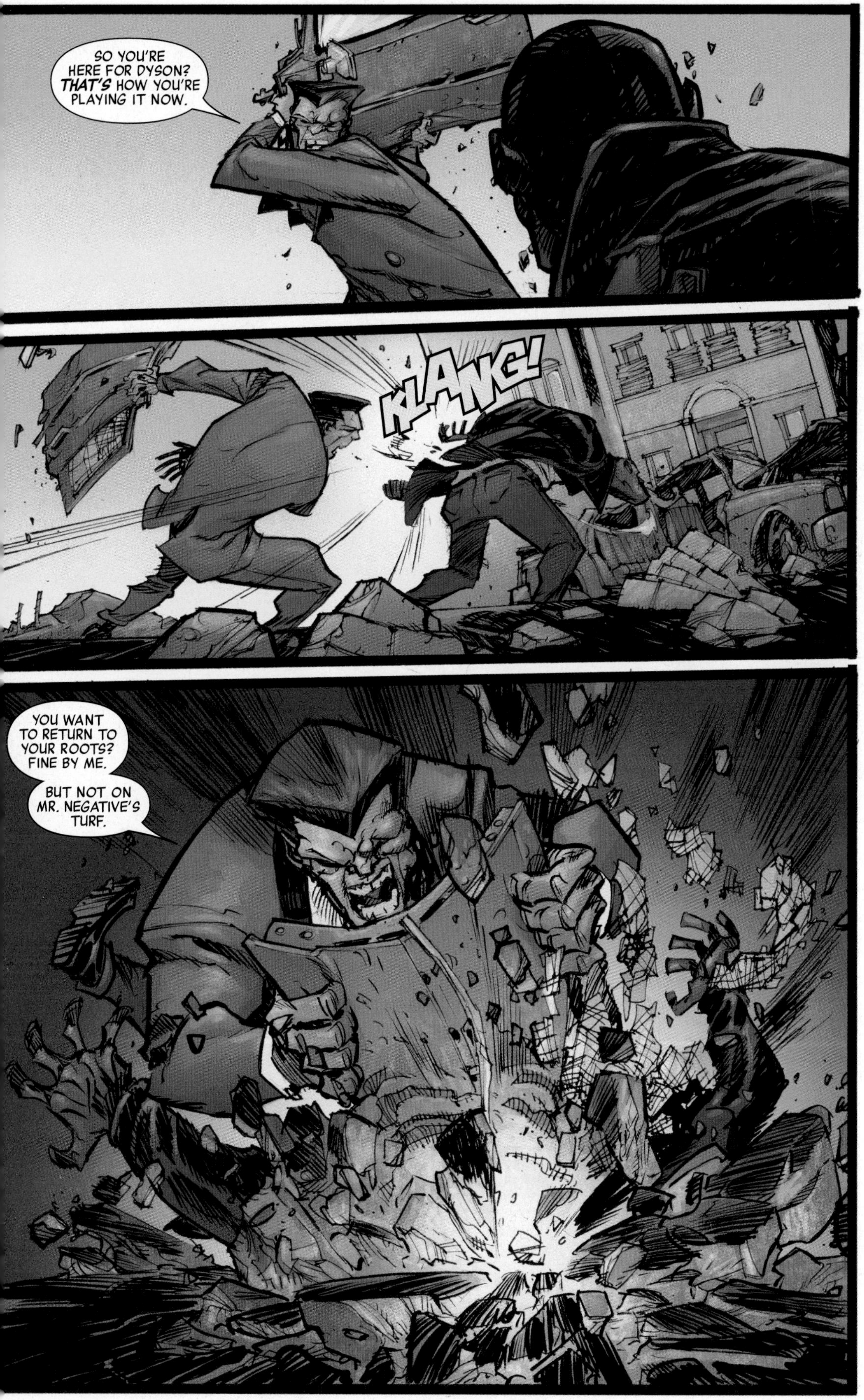
SO YOU'RE HERE FOR DYSON? THAT'S HOW YOU'RE PLAYING IT NOW.
KLANG!
YOU WANT TO RETURN TO YOUR ROOTS? FINE BY ME.
BUT NOT ON MR. NEGATIVE'S TURF.

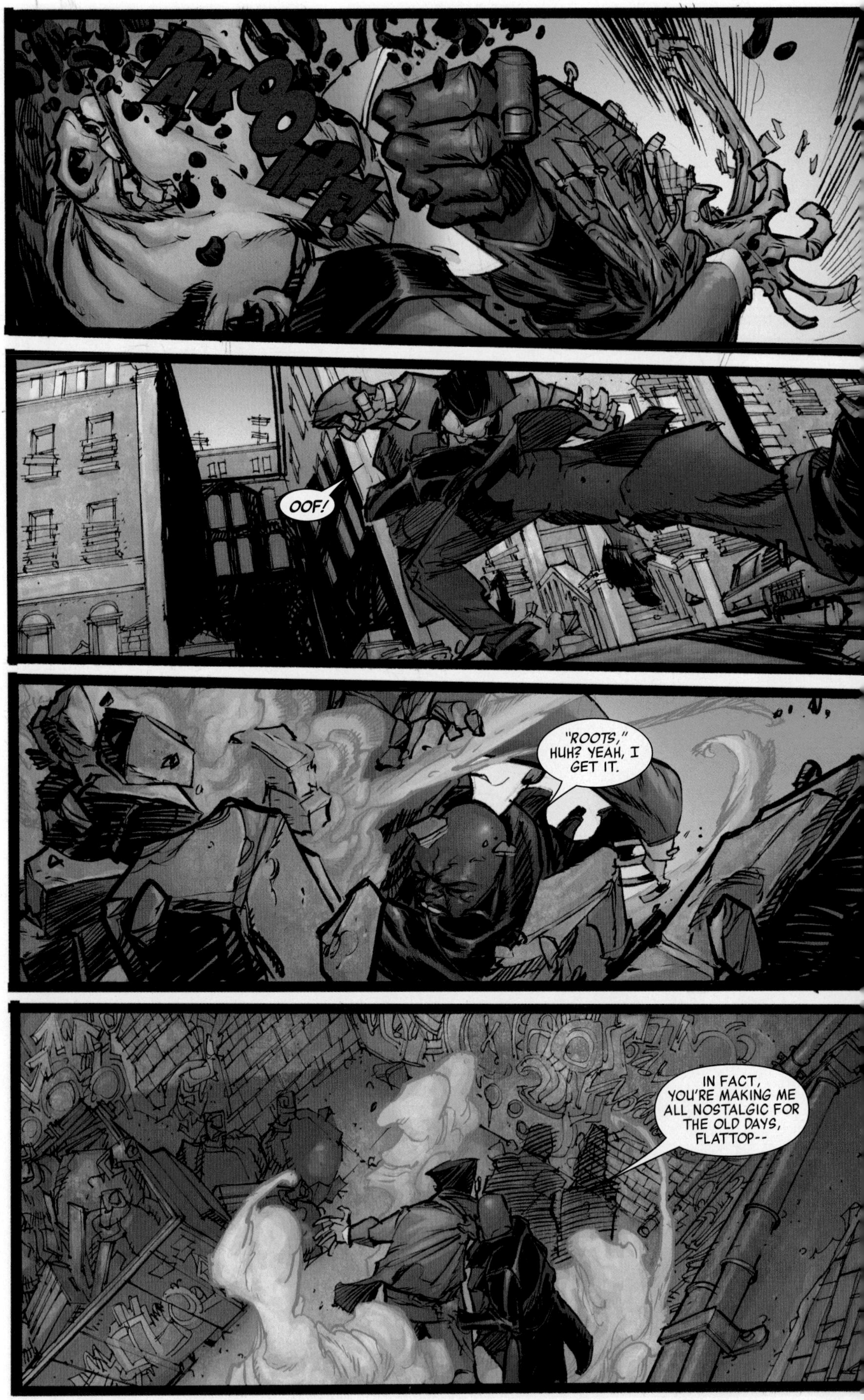
PAKOOMPH!
OOF!
"ROOTS," HUH? YEAH, I GET IT.
IN FACT, YOU'RE MAKING ME ALL NOSTALGIC FOR THE OLD DAYS, FLATTOP--

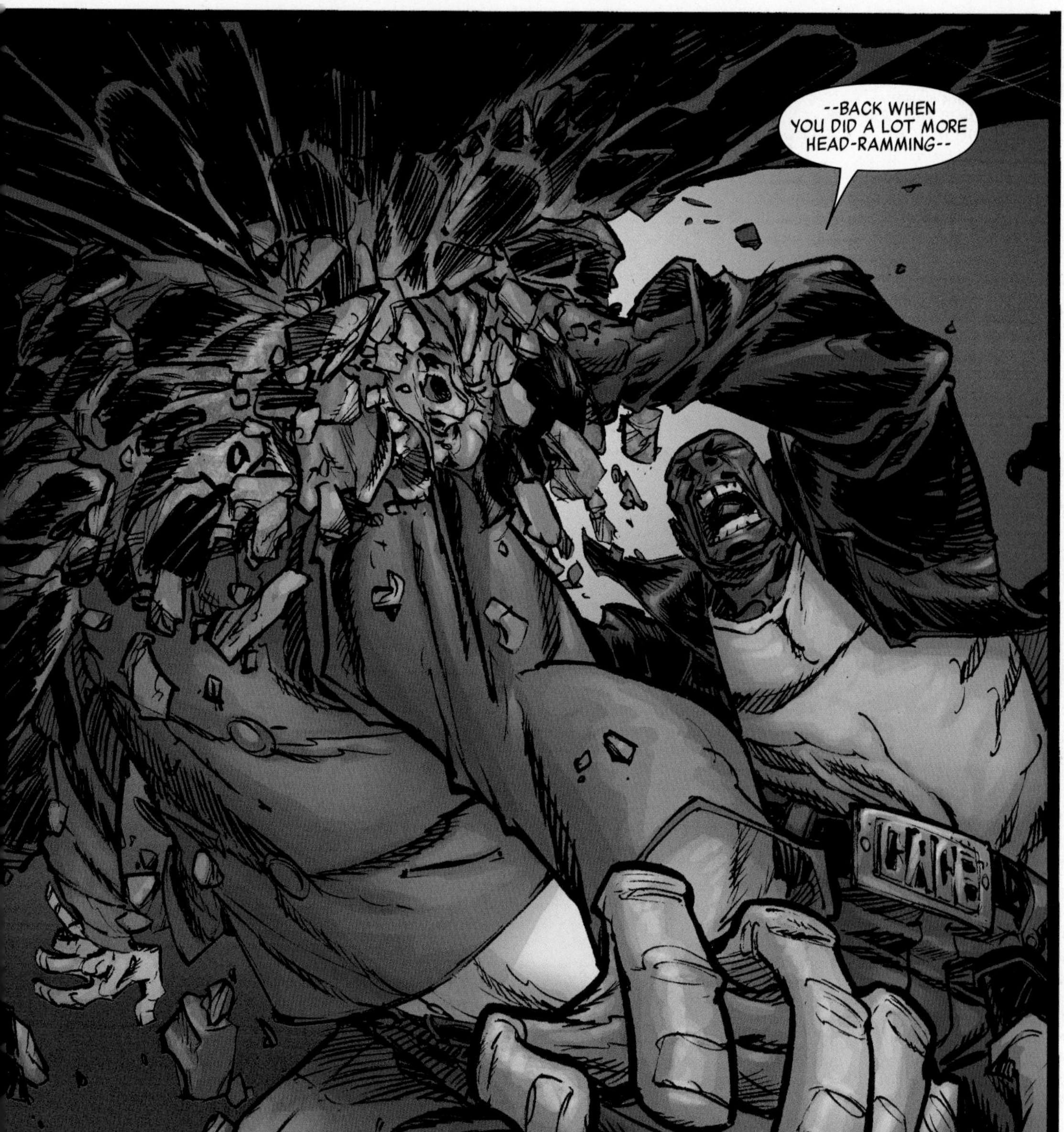
--BACK WHEN YOU DID A LOT MORE HEAD-RAMMING--
CAGE

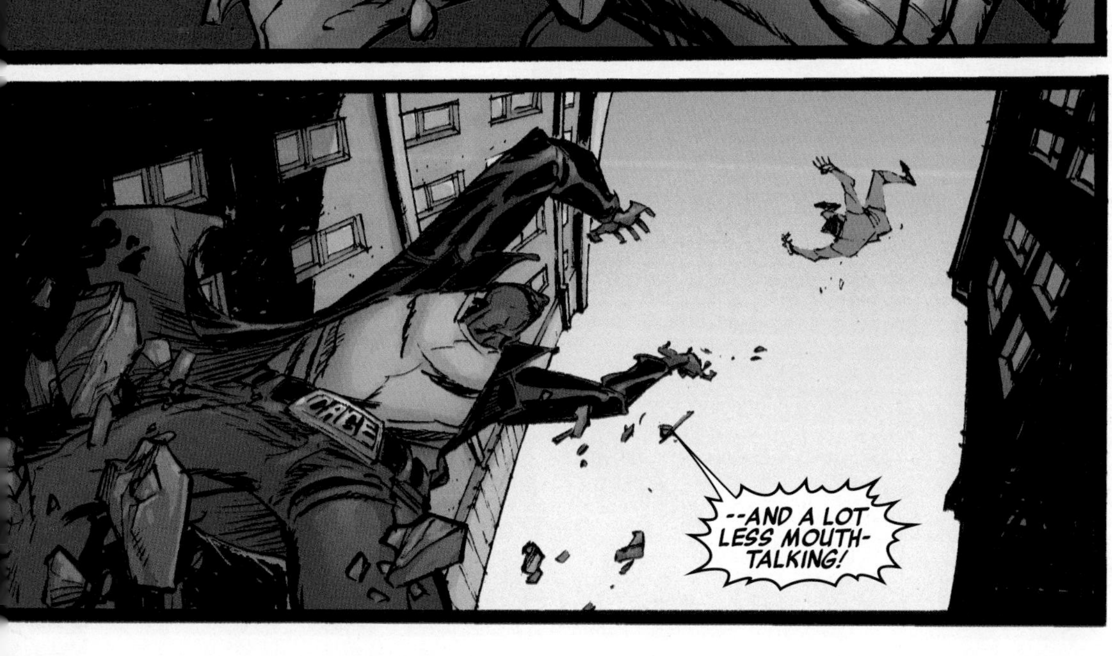
CAGE
--AND A LOT LESS MOUTH-TALKING!

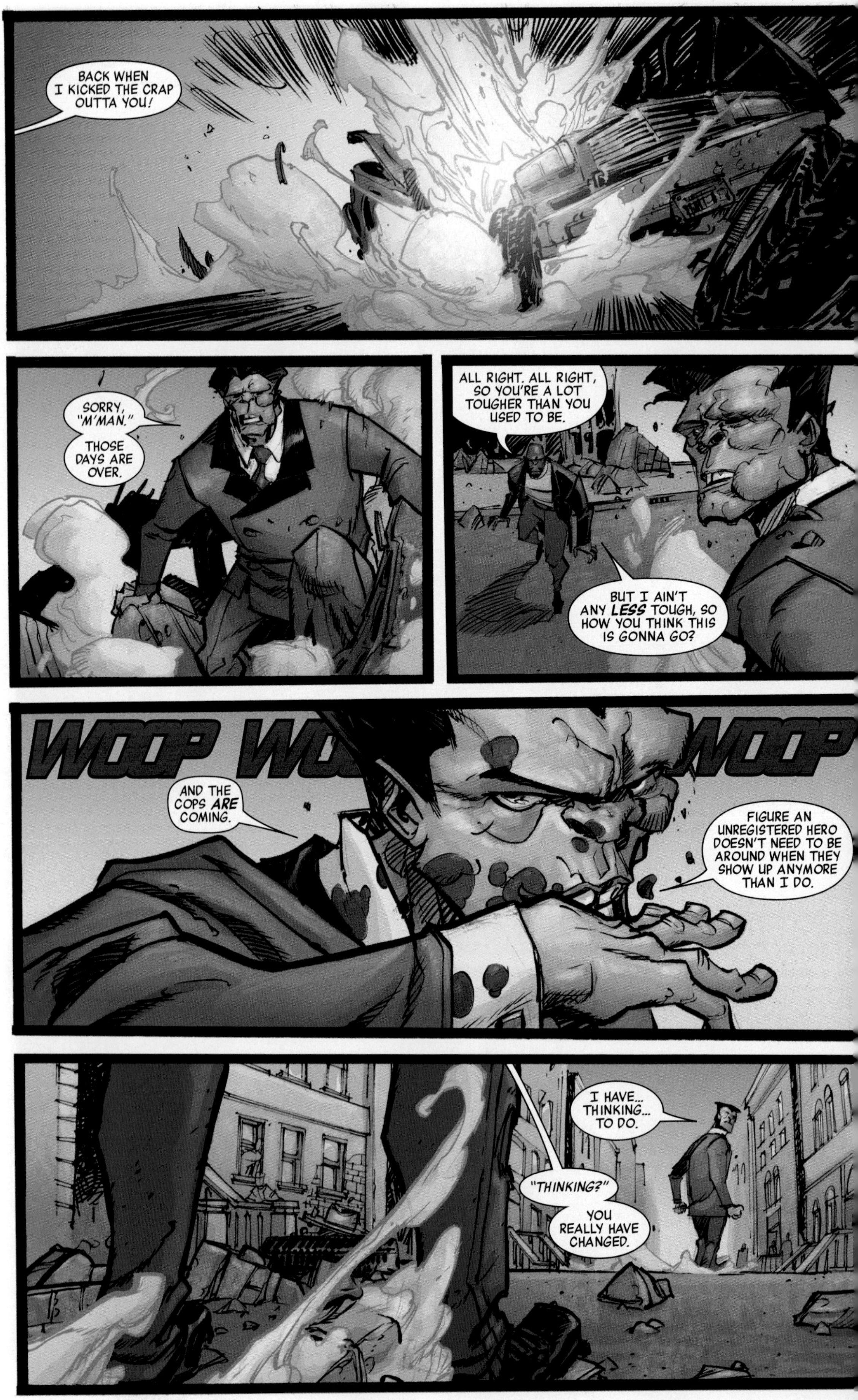
BACK WHEN I KICKED THE CRAP OUTTA YOU!
SORRY, "M'MAN."
THOSE DAYS ARE OVER.
ALL RIGHT. ALL RIGHT, SO YOU'RE A LOT TOUGHER THAN YOU USED TO BE.
BUT I AIN'T ANY LESS TOUGH, SO HOW YOU THINK THIS IS GONNA GO?
WOOP WOO WOOP
AND THE COPS ARE COMING.
FIGURE AN UNREGISTERED HERO DOESN'T NEED TO BE AROUND WHEN THEY SHOW UP ANYMORE THAN I DO.
I HAVE... THINKING... TO DO.
"THINKING?"
YOU REALLY HAVE CHANGED.

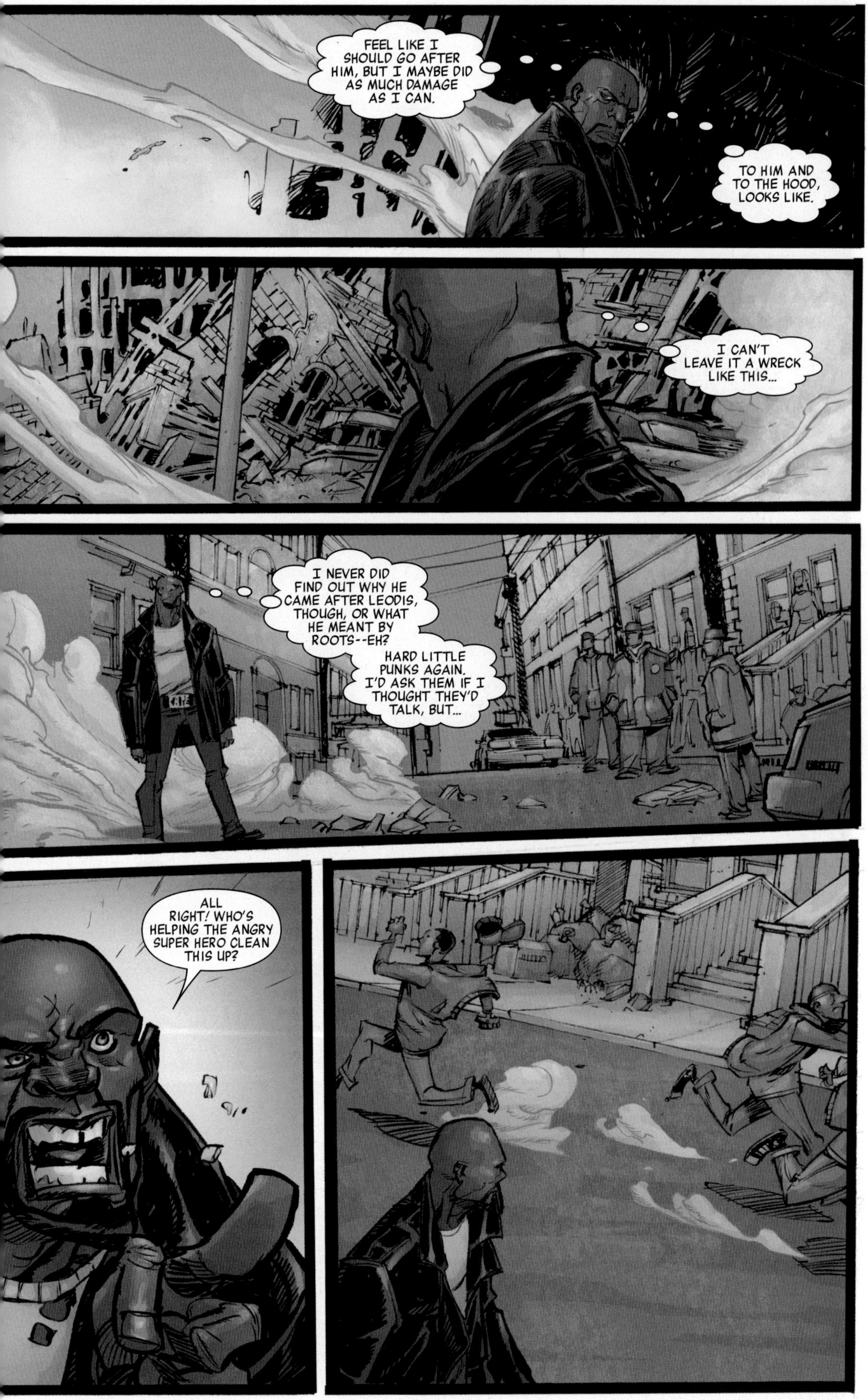
FEEL LIKE I SHOULD GO AFTER HIM, BUT I MAYBE DID AS MUCH DAMAGE AS I CAN.
TO HIM AND TO THE HOOD, LOOKS LIKE.
I CAN'T LEAVE IT A WRECK LIKE THIS...
I NEVER DID FIND OUT WHY HE CAME AFTER LEODIS, THOUGH, OR WHAT HE MEANT BY ROOTS--EH?
HARD LITTLE PUNKS AGAIN. I'D ASK THEM IF I THOUGHT THEY'D TALK, BUT...
ALL RIGHT! WHO'S HELPING THE ANGRY SUPER HERO CLEAN THIS UP?

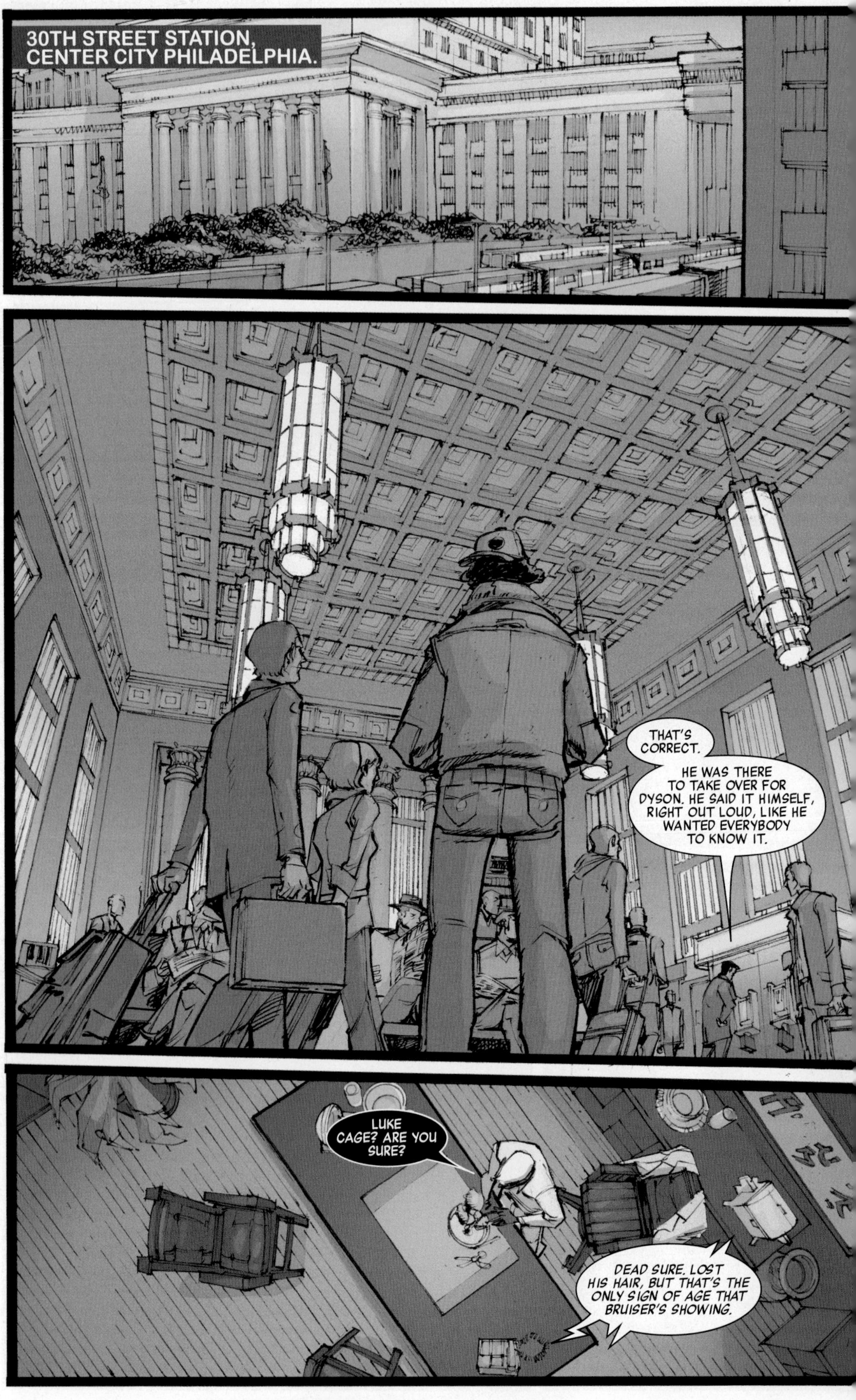
30TH STREET STATION, CENTER CITY PHILADELPHIA.
THAT'S CORRECT.
HE WAS THERE TO TAKE OVER FOR DYSON. HE SAID IT HIMSELF, RIGHT OUT LOUD, LIKE HE WANTED EVERYBODY TO KNOW IT.
LUKE CAGE? ARE YOU SURE?
DEAD SURE. LOST HIS HAIR, BUT THAT'S THE ONLY SIGN OF AGE THAT BRUISER'S SHOWING.

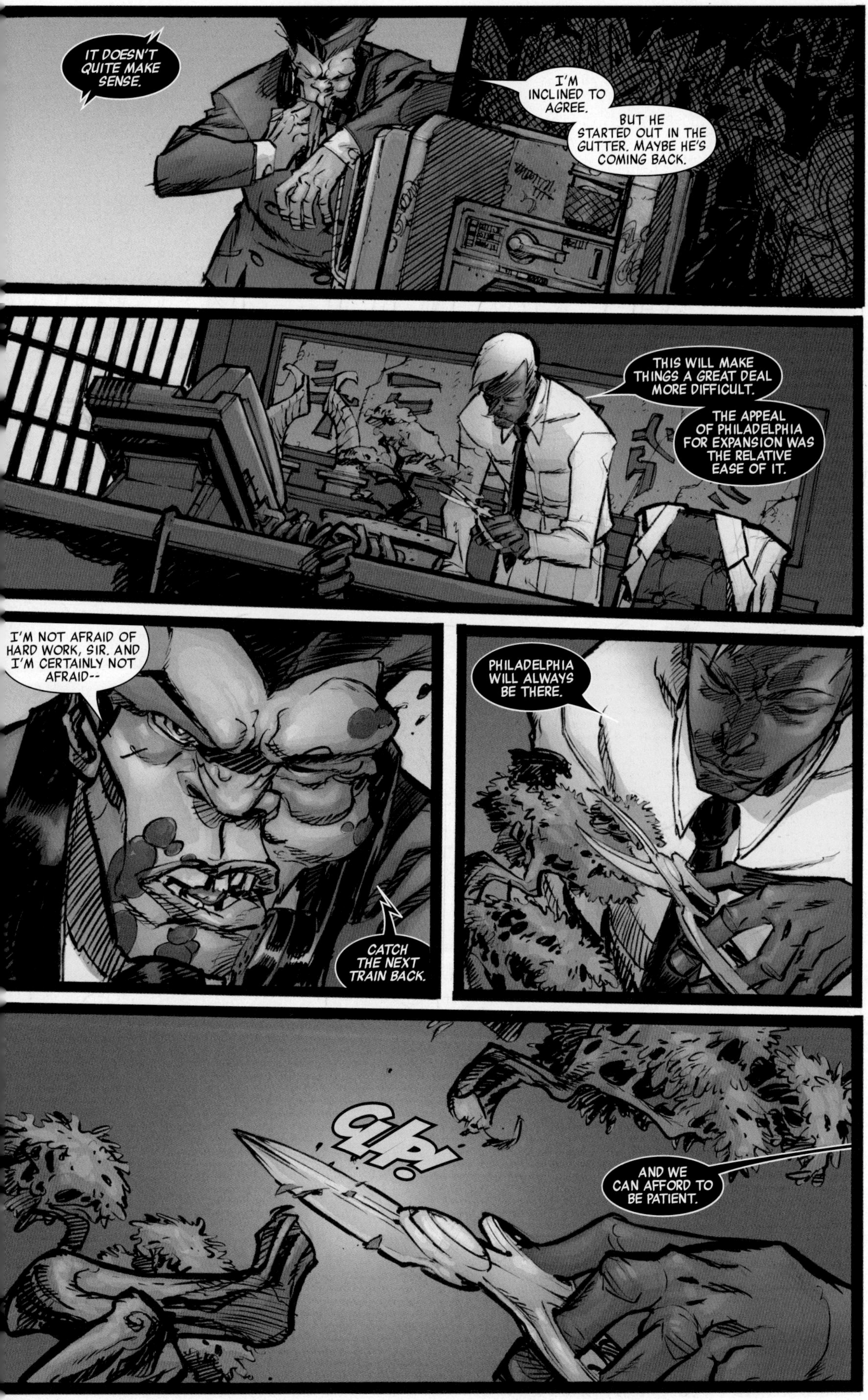
IT DOESN'T QUITE MAKE SENSE.
I'M INCLINED TO AGREE.
BUT HE STARTED OUT IN THE GUTTER. MAYBE HE'S COMING BACK.
THIS WILL MAKE THINGS A GREAT DEAL MORE DIFFICULT.
THE APPEAL OF PHILADELPHIA FOR EXPANSION WAS THE RELATIVE EASE OF IT.
I'M NOT AFRAID OF HARD WORK, SIR. AND I'M CERTAINLY NOT AFRAID--
CATCH THE NEXT TRAIN BACK.
PHILADELPHIA WILL ALWAYS BE THERE.
CLIP!
AND WE CAN AFFORD TO BE PATIENT.

MR. CAGE, LOOK AT YOU!

WHAT HAVE YOU BEEN UP TO? I SAID I WANTED TO YOU TO COME DOWN AND SEE LEODIS. NOTHING ELSE.

I'M SORRY, MRS. DYSON. I WENT TO CHECK OUT LEODIS'S OFFICE, AND... BELIEVE ME, I DIDN'T PLAN IT THIS WAY.

HOW IS HE?

THEY TOOK THAT TUBE OUT OF HIS MOUTH, SO HE'S BREATHING ON HIS OWN AGAIN.

THEY TELL ME THAT'S A GOOD SIGN--

"--BUT I'LL KEEP PRAYING JUST THE SAME."

HEY, SON. BEEN AWHILE, HUH?

MR. CAGE!... WHAT ARE YOU--

TAKE IT EASY, NOW. DOCTORS DON'T WANT YOU GETTING WORKED UP.

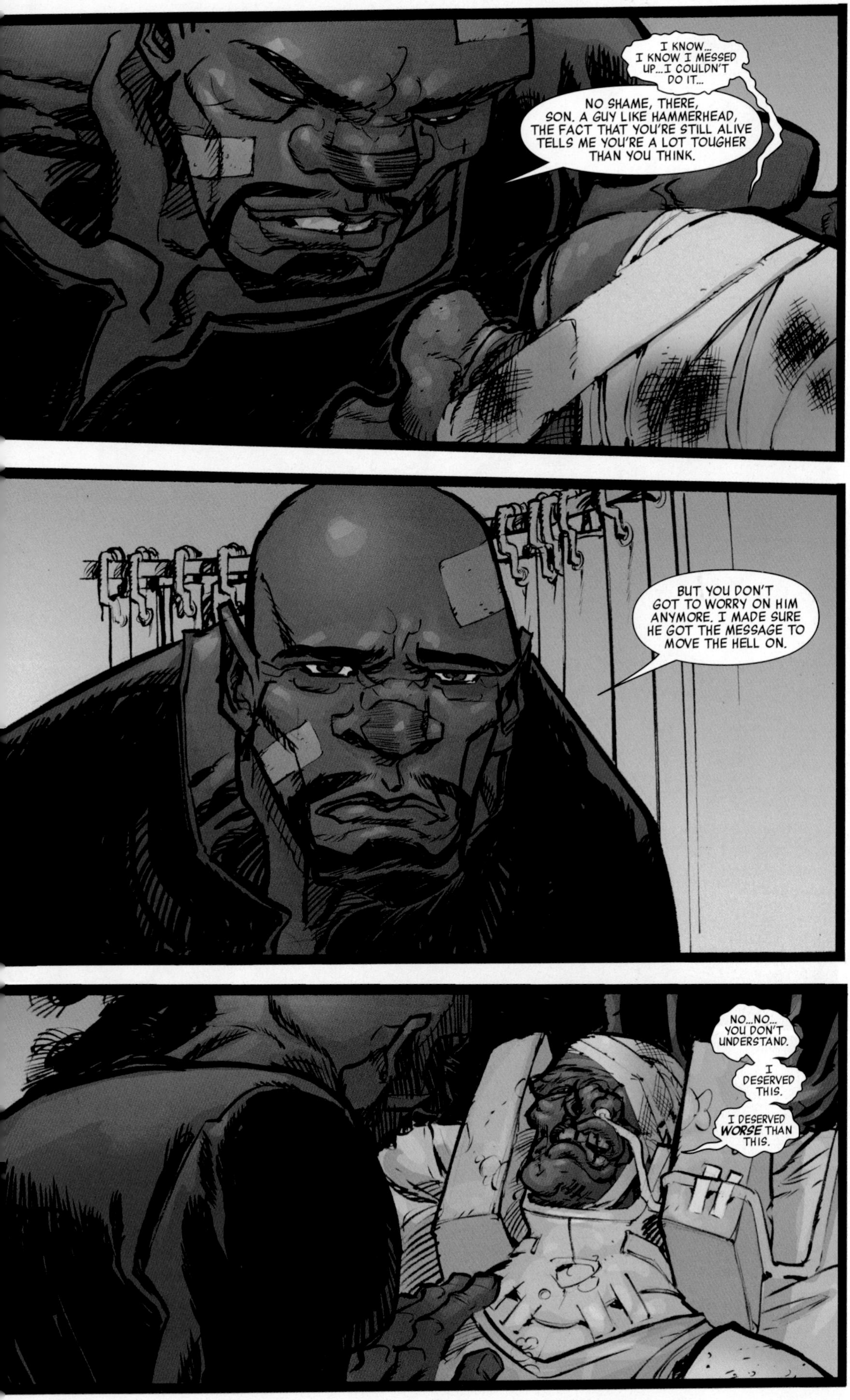
I KNOW... I KNOW I MESSED UP...I COULDN'T DO IT...
NO SHAME, THERE, SON. A GUY LIKE HAMMERHEAD, THE FACT THAT YOU'RE STILL ALIVE TELLS ME YOU'RE A LOT TOUGHER THAN YOU THINK.
BUT YOU DON'T GOT TO WORRY ON HIM ANYMORE. I MADE SURE HE GOT THE MESSAGE TO MOVE THE HELL ON.
NO...NO... YOU DON'T UNDERSTAND.
I DESERVED THIS.
I DESERVED *WORSE* THAN THIS.

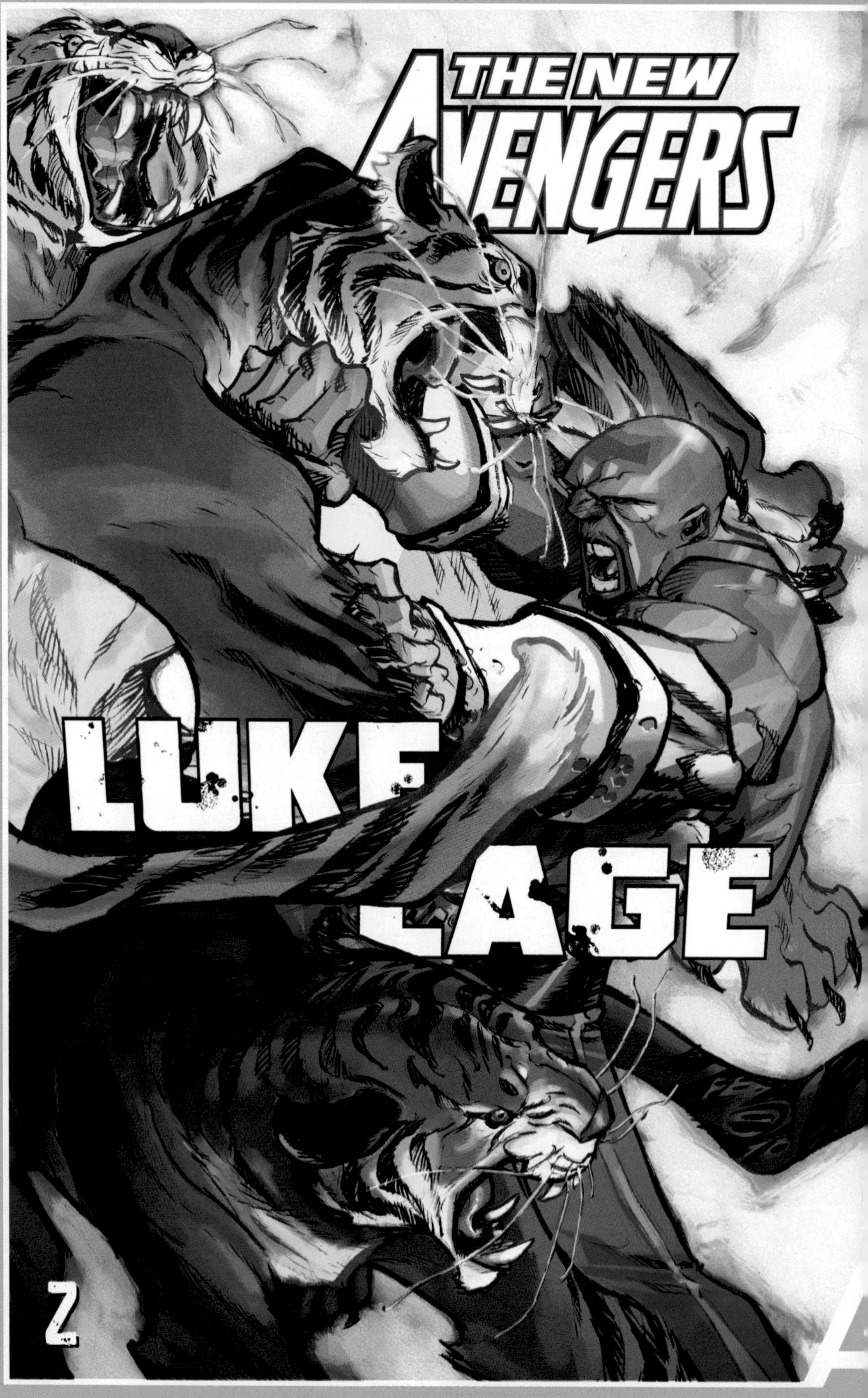
THE NEW AVENGERS
LUKE CAGE
2

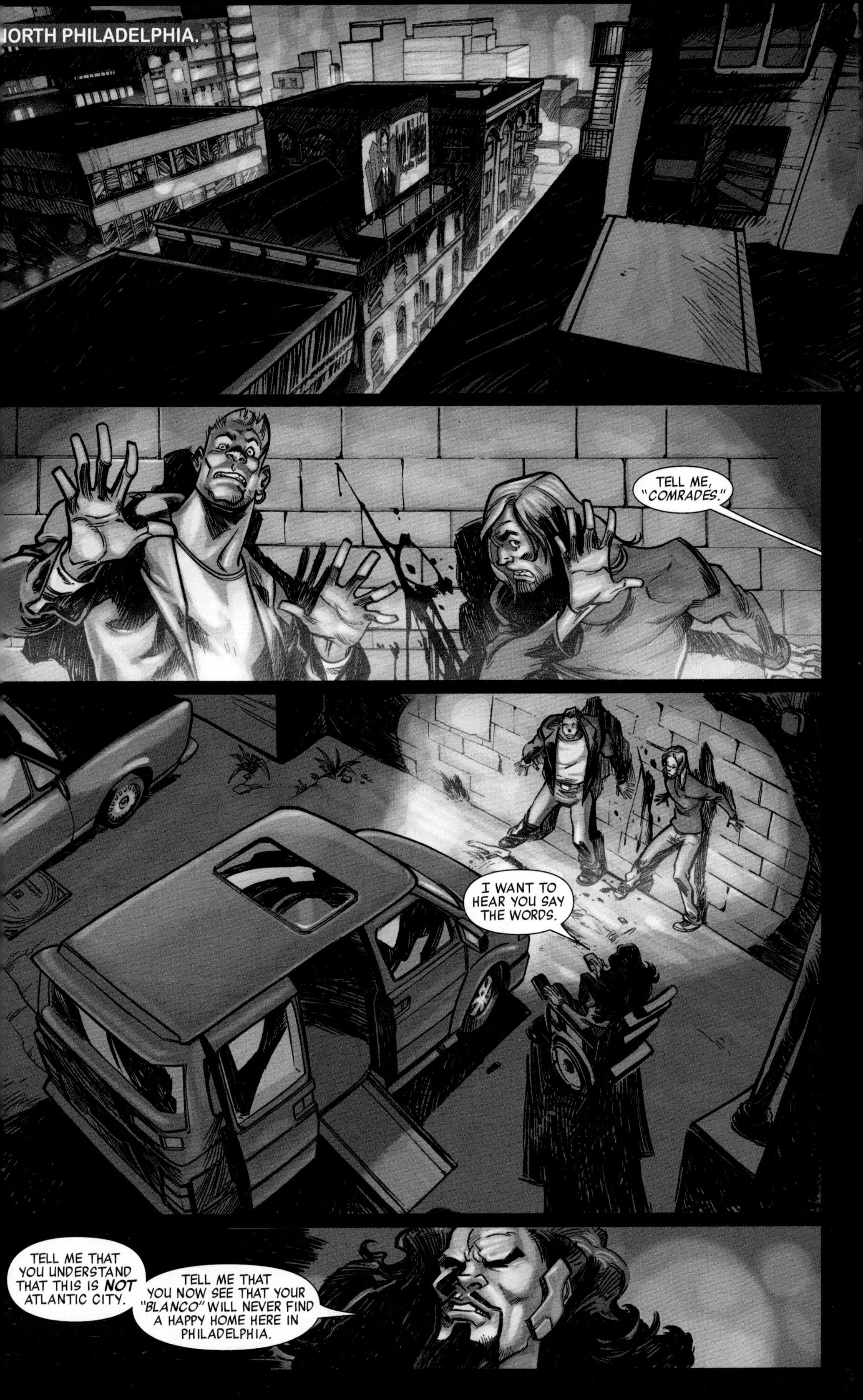
NORTH PHILADELPHIA.
TELL ME, "COMRADES."
I WANT TO HEAR YOU SAY THE WORDS.
TELL ME THAT YOU UNDERSTAND THAT THIS IS *NOT* ATLANTIC CITY.
TELL ME THAT YOU NOW SEE THAT YOUR "*BLANCO*" WILL NEVER FIND A HAPPY HOME HERE IN PHILADELPHIA.

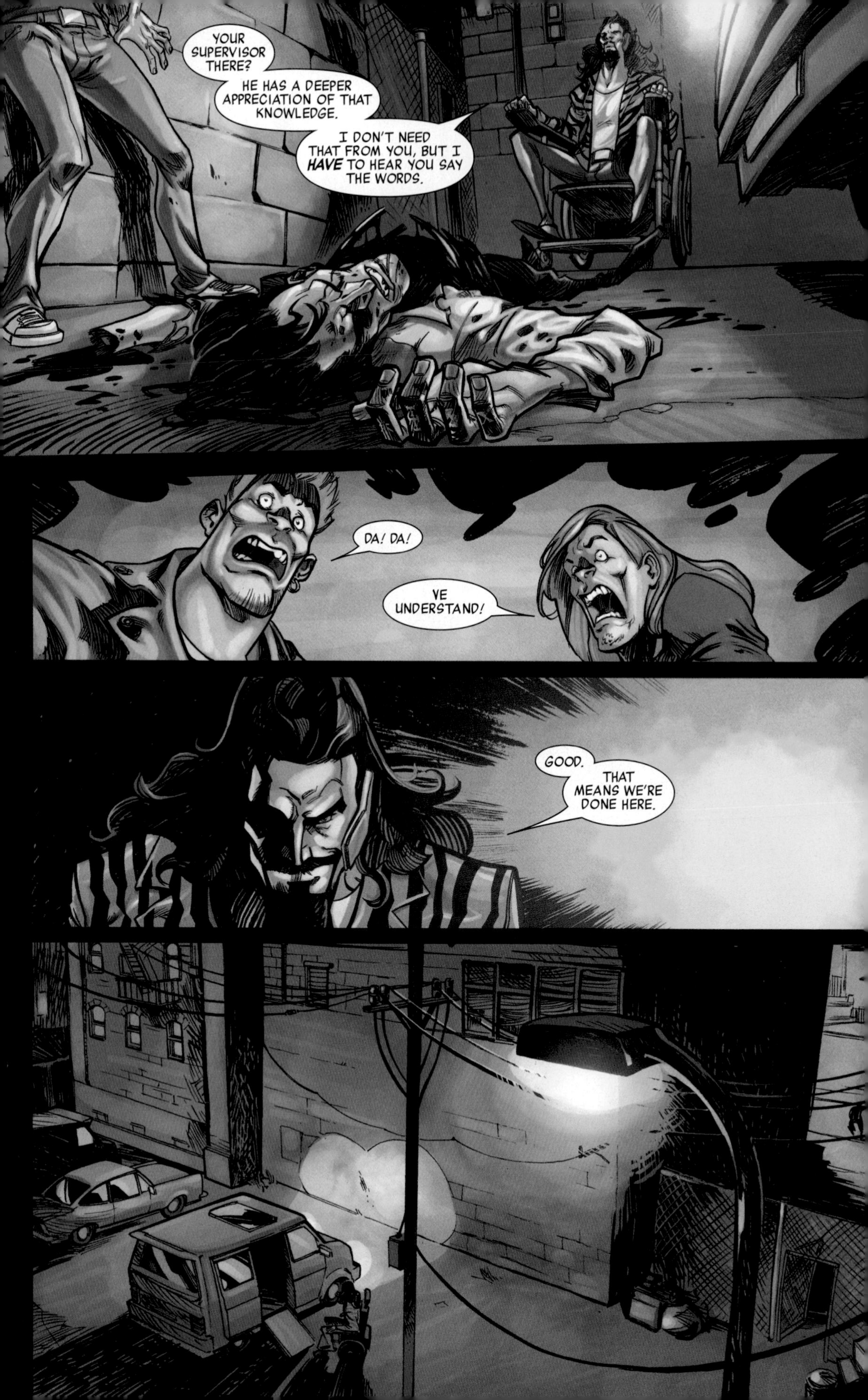
YOUR SUPERVISOR THERE?
HE HAS A DEEPER APPRECIATION OF THAT KNOWLEDGE.
I DON'T NEED THAT FROM YOU, BUT I HAVE TO HEAR YOU SAY THE WORDS.
DA! DA!
VE UNDERSTAND!
GOOD.
THAT MEANS WE'RE DONE HERE.

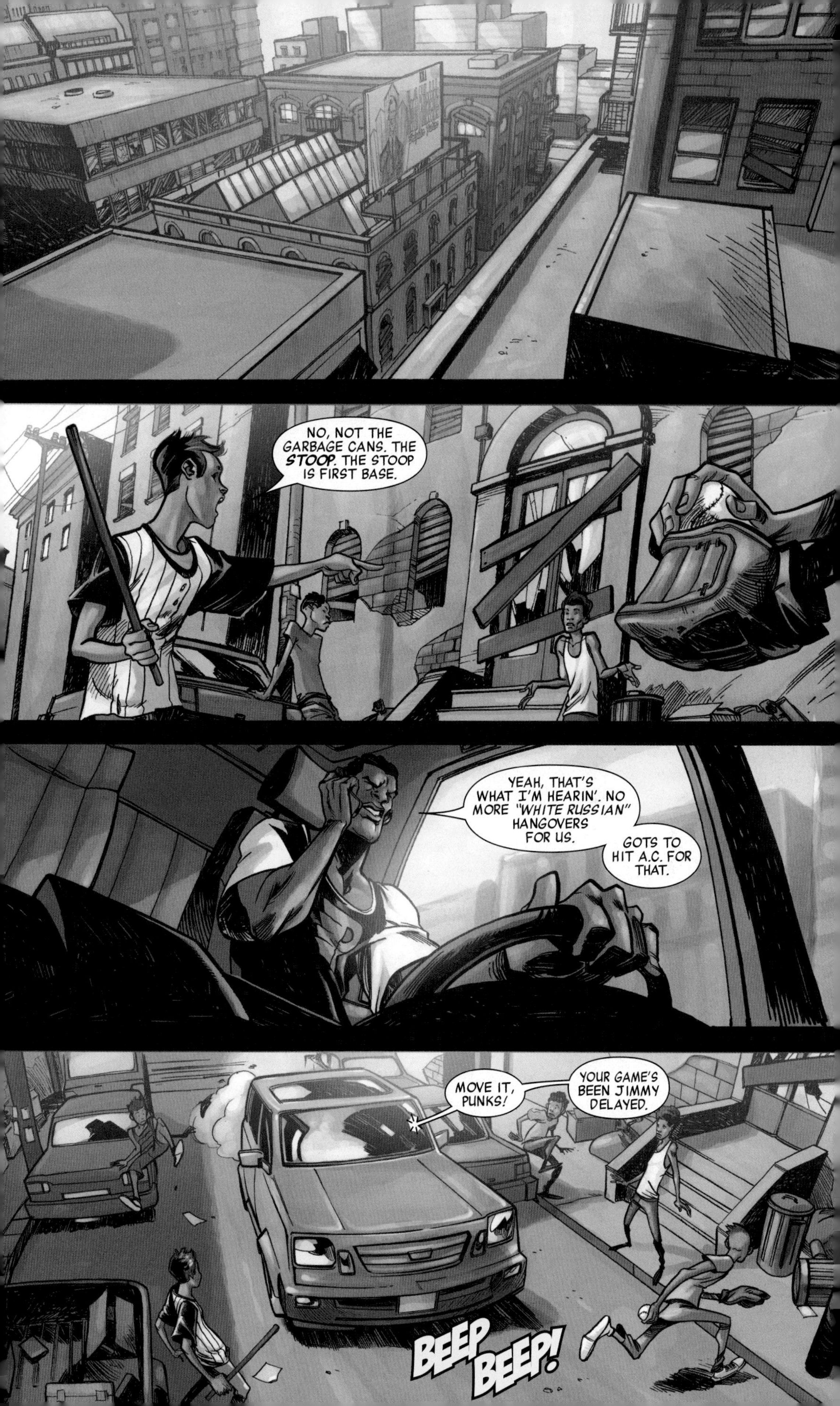
NO, NOT THE GARBAGE CANS. THE *STOOP*. THE STOOP IS FIRST BASE.
YEAH, THAT'S WHAT I'M HEARIN'. NO MORE *"WHITE RUSSIAN"* HANGOVERS FOR US.
GOTS TO HIT A.C. FOR THAT.
MOVE IT, PUNKS!
YOUR GAME'S BEEN JIMMY DELAYED.
BEEP BEEP!

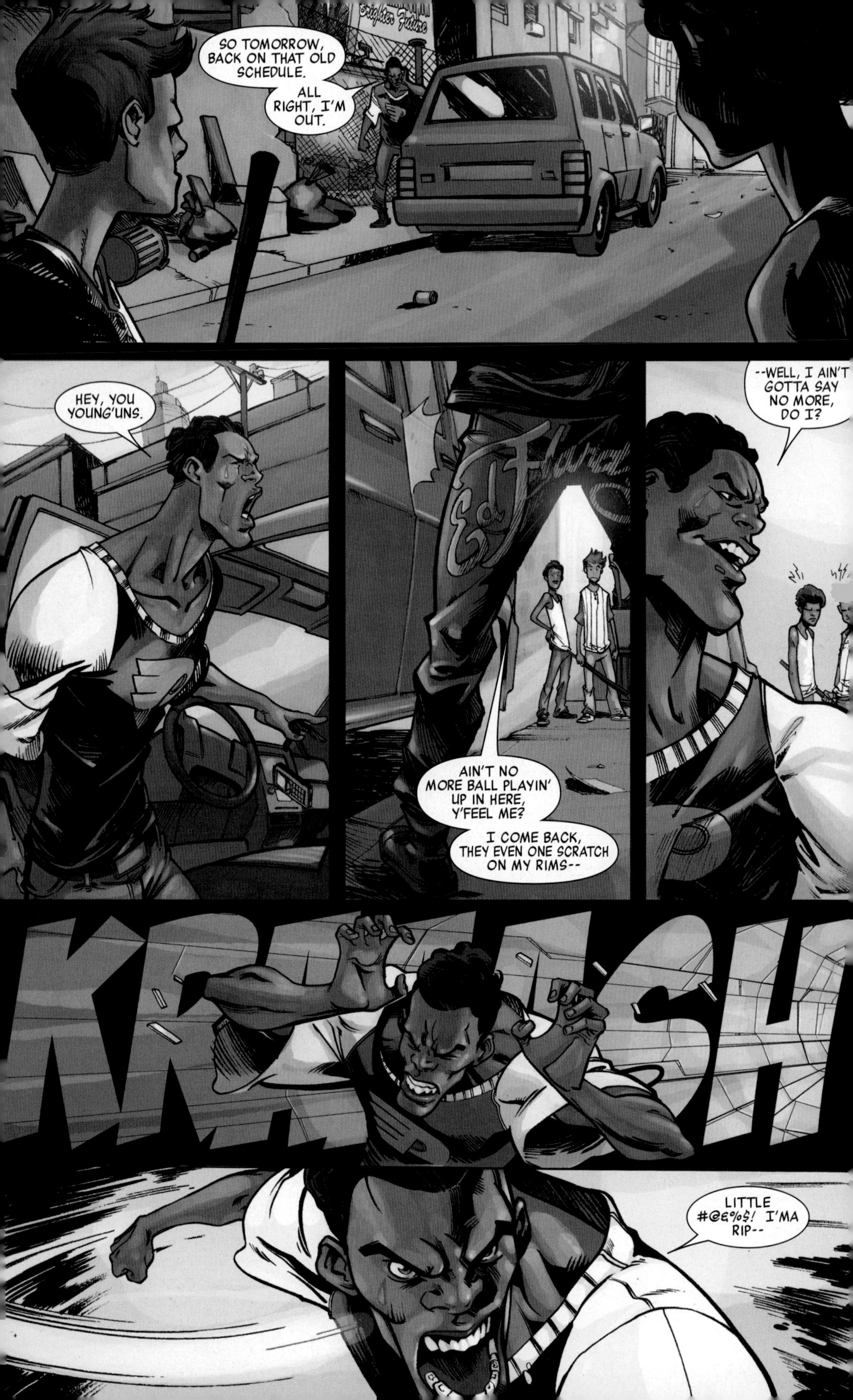
Brighter Future
SO TOMORROW, BACK ON THAT OLD SCHEDULE.
ALL RIGHT, I'M OUT.
HEY, YOU YOUNG'UNS.
AIN'T NO MORE BALL PLAYIN' UP IN HERE, Y'FEEL ME?
I COME BACK, THEY EVEN ONE SCRATCH ON MY RIMS--
--WELL, I AIN'T GOTTA SAY NO MORE, DO I?
LITTLE #@€%$! I'MA RIP--

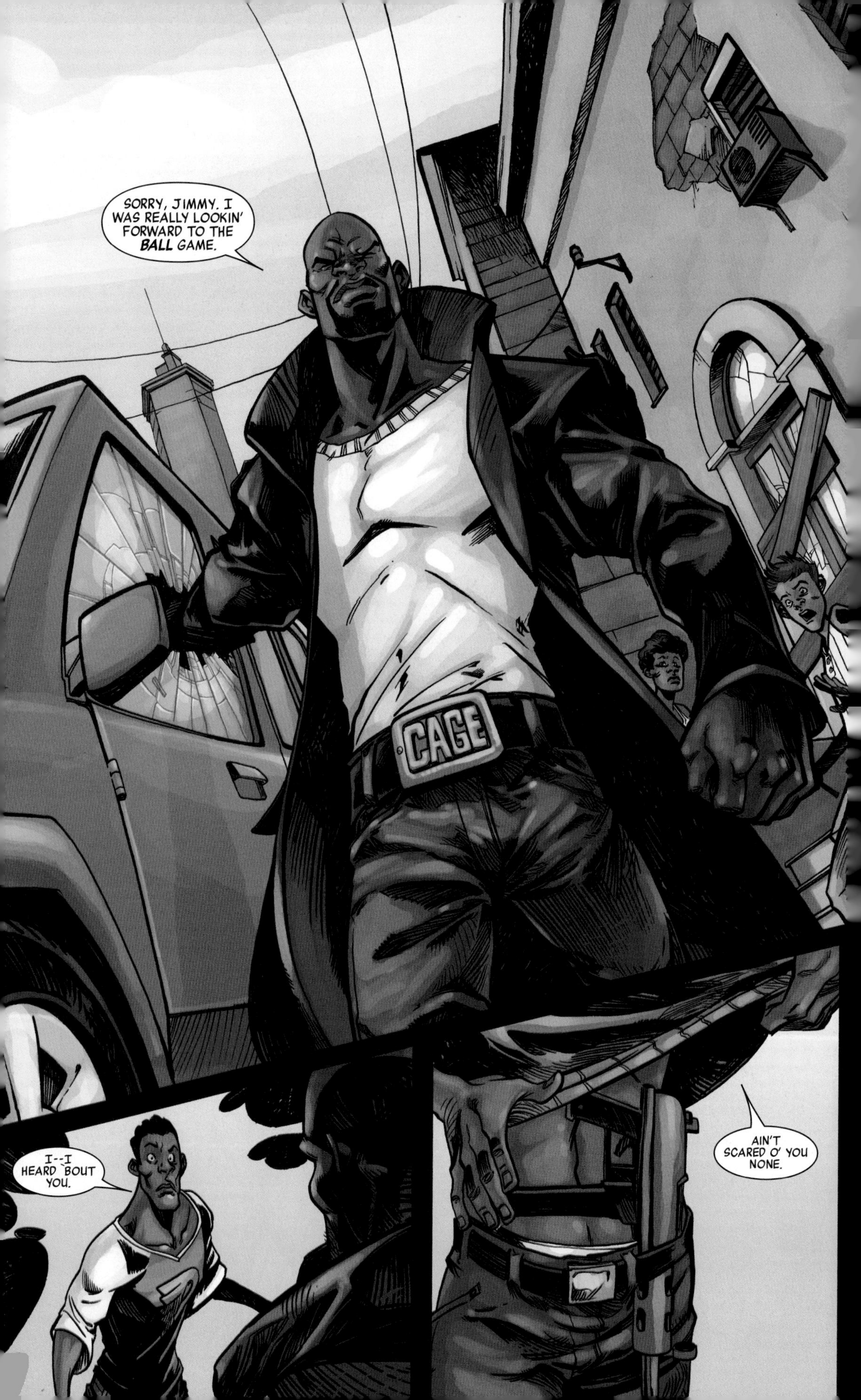
SORRY, JIMMY. I WAS REALLY LOOKIN' FORWARD TO THE BALL GAME.
CAGE
I--I HEARD 'BOUT YOU.
AIN'T SCARED O' YOU NONE.

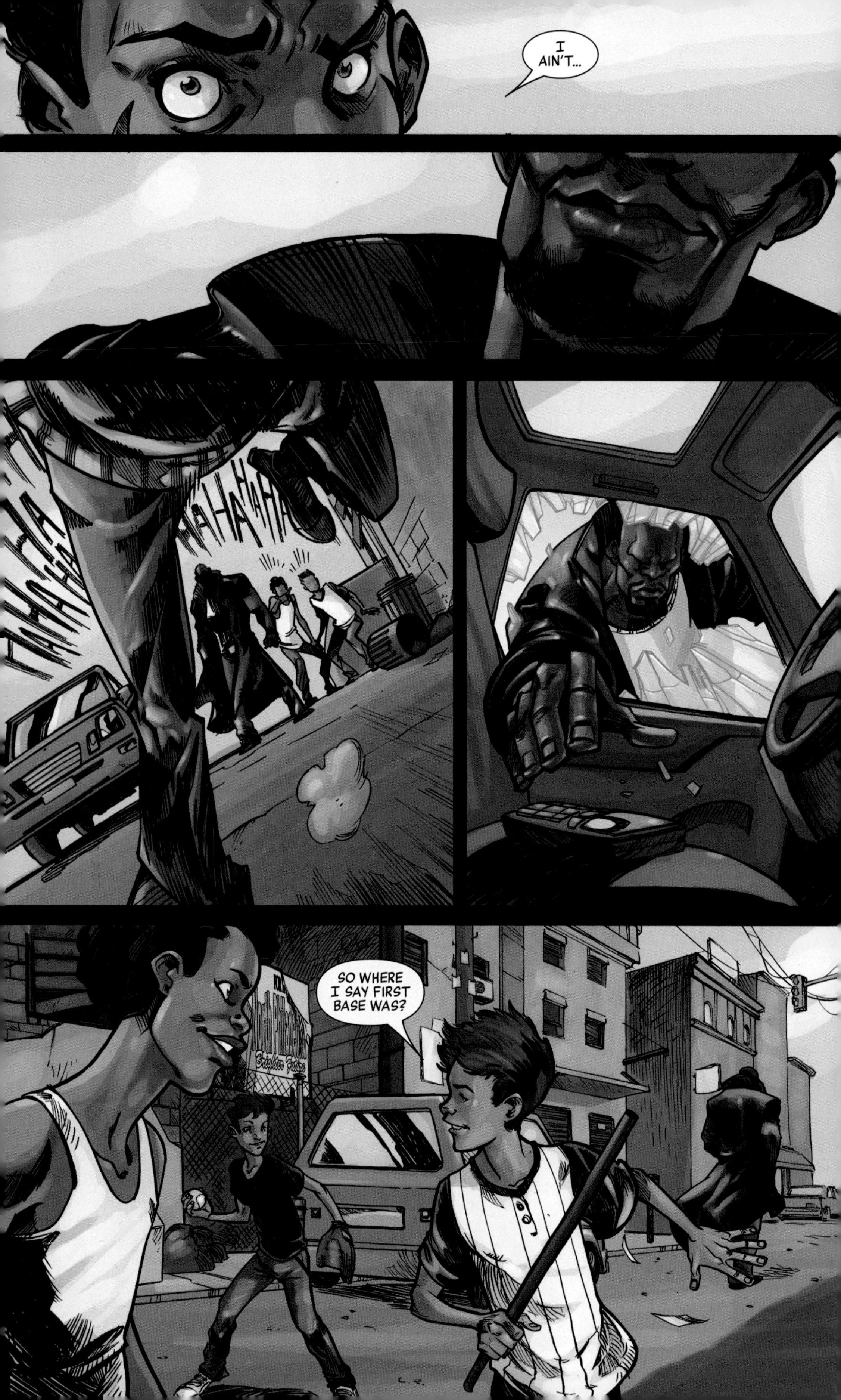

I AIN'T...
HAHAHAHA
HAHAHAHA
SO WHERE I SAY FIRST BASE WAS?

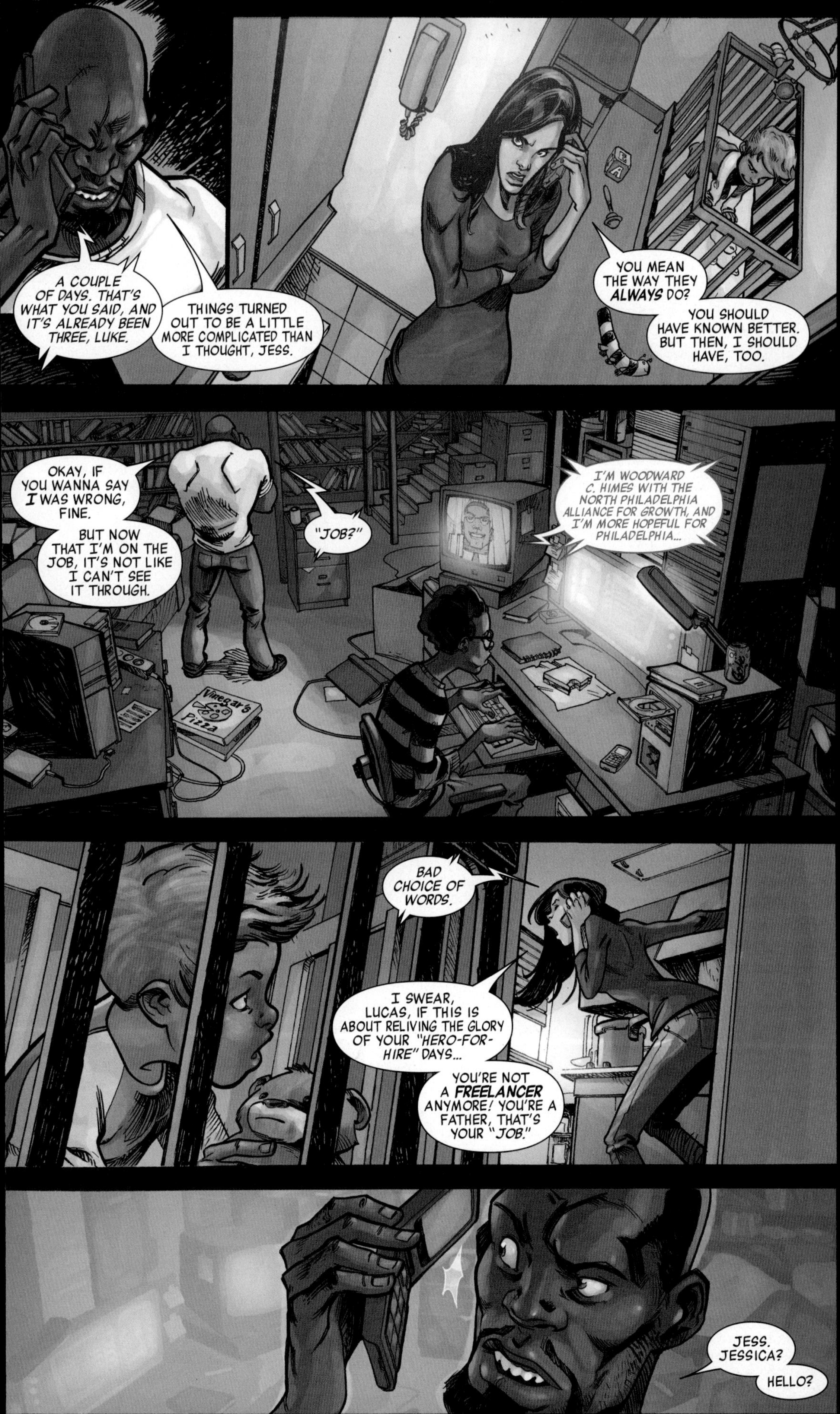

A COUPLE OF DAYS. THAT'S WHAT YOU SAID, AND IT'S ALREADY BEEN THREE, LUKE.
THINGS TURNED OUT TO BE A LITTLE MORE COMPLICATED THAN I THOUGHT, JESS.
YOU MEAN THE WAY THEY ALWAYS DO?
YOU SHOULD HAVE KNOWN BETTER. BUT THEN, I SHOULD HAVE, TOO.
OKAY, IF YOU WANNA SAY I WAS WRONG, FINE.
BUT NOW THAT I'M ON THE JOB, IT'S NOT LIKE I CAN'T SEE IT THROUGH.
"JOB?"
I'M WOODWARD C. HIMES WITH THE NORTH PHILADELPHIA ALLIANCE FOR GROWTH, AND I'M MORE HOPEFUL FOR PHILADELPHIA...
Vinegar's Pizza
BAD CHOICE OF WORDS.
I SWEAR, LUCAS, IF THIS IS ABOUT RELIVING THE GLORY OF YOUR "HERO-FOR-HIRE" DAYS...
YOU'RE NOT A FREELANCER ANYMORE! YOU'RE A FATHER, THAT'S YOUR "JOB."
JESS. JESSICA?
HELLO?

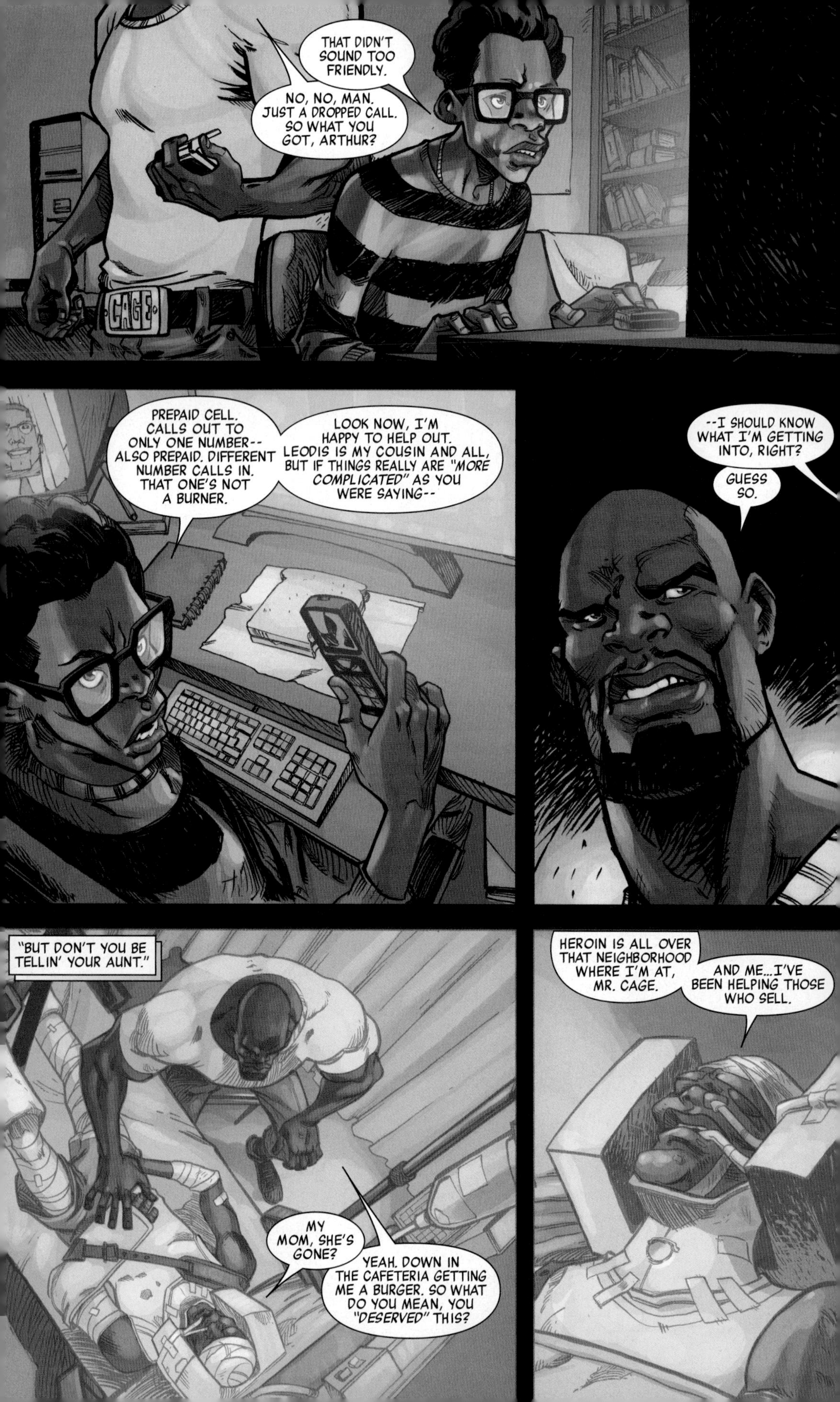
THAT DIDN'T SOUND TOO FRIENDLY.
NO, NO, MAN. JUST A DROPPED CALL. SO WHAT YOU GOT, ARTHUR?
CAGE
PREPAID CELL. CALLS OUT TO ONLY ONE NUMBER-- ALSO PREPAID. DIFFERENT NUMBER CALLS IN. THAT ONE'S NOT A BURNER.
LOOK NOW, I'M HAPPY TO HELP OUT. LEODIS IS MY COUSIN AND ALL, BUT IF THINGS REALLY ARE "MORE COMPLICATED" AS YOU WERE SAYING--
--I SHOULD KNOW WHAT I'M GETTING INTO, RIGHT?
GUESS SO.
"BUT DON'T YOU BE TELLIN' YOUR AUNT."
MY MOM, SHE'S GONE?
YEAH. DOWN IN THE CAFETERIA GETTING ME A BURGER. SO WHAT DO YOU MEAN, YOU "DESERVED" THIS?
HEROIN IS ALL OVER THAT NEIGHBORHOOD WHERE I'M AT, MR. CAGE.
AND ME...I'VE BEEN HELPING THOSE WHO SELL.

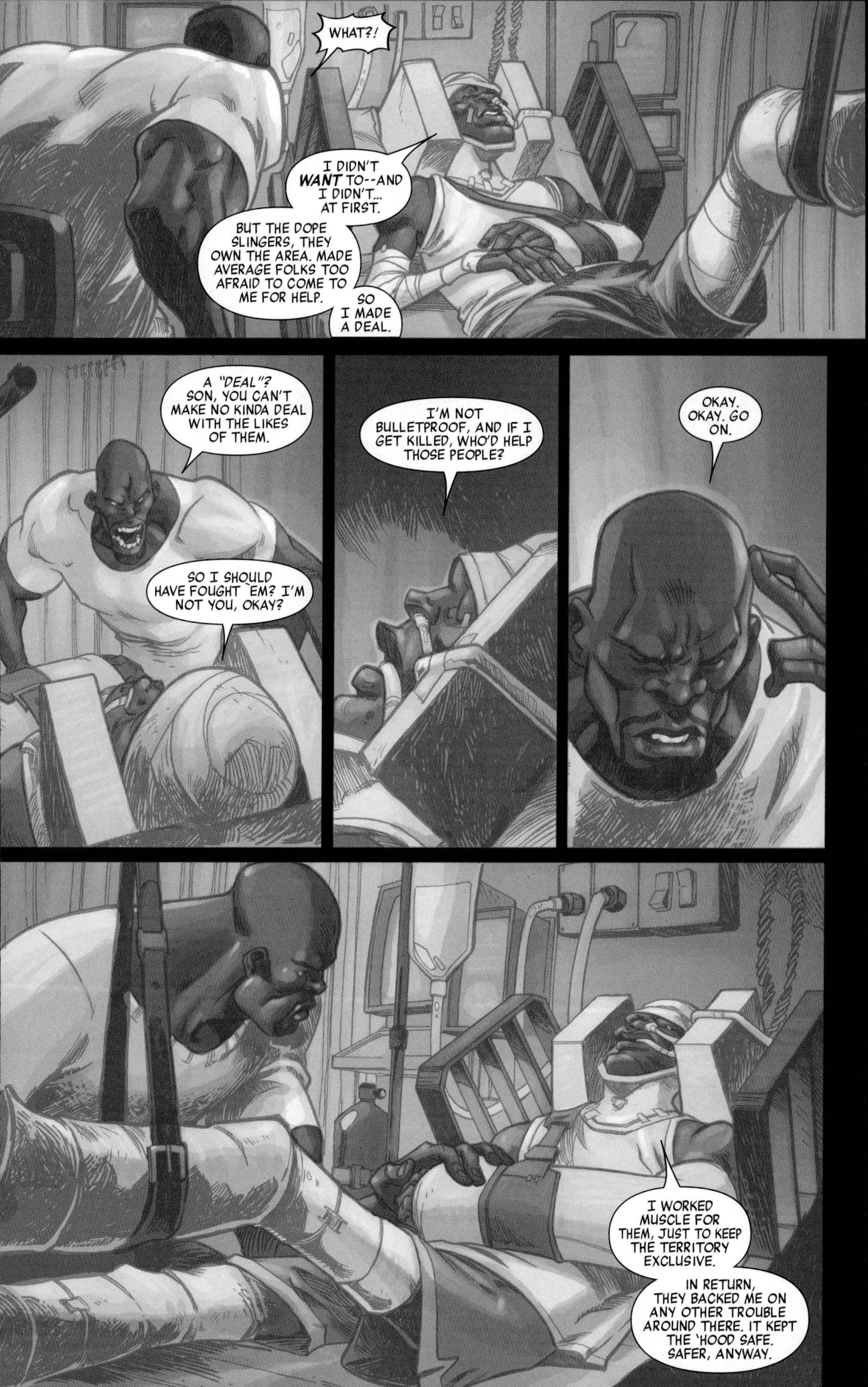
WHAT?!
I DIDN'T WANT TO--AND I DIDN'T... AT FIRST.
BUT THE DOPE SLINGERS, THEY OWN THE AREA. MADE AVERAGE FOLKS TOO AFRAID TO COME TO ME FOR HELP.
SO I MADE A DEAL.
A "DEAL"? SON, YOU CAN'T MAKE NO KINDA DEAL WITH THE LIKES OF THEM.
SO I SHOULD HAVE FOUGHT 'EM? I'M NOT YOU, OKAY?
I'M NOT BULLETPROOF, AND IF I GET KILLED, WHO'D HELP THOSE PEOPLE?
OKAY. OKAY. GO ON.
I WORKED MUSCLE FOR THEM, JUST TO KEEP THE TERRITORY EXCLUSIVE.
IN RETURN, THEY BACKED ME ON ANY OTHER TROUBLE AROUND THERE. IT KEPT THE 'HOOD SAFE. SAFER, ANYWAY.

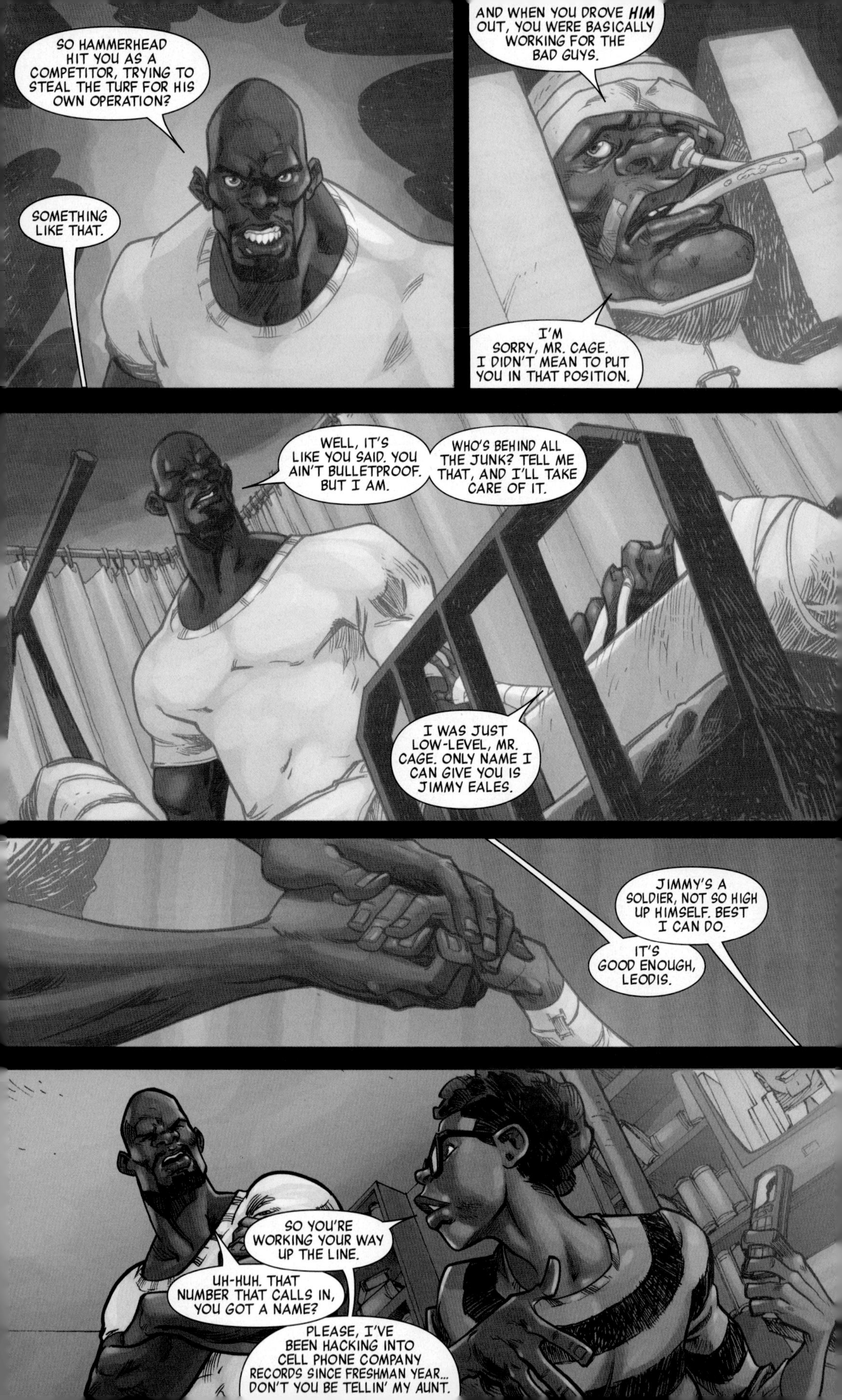
SO HAMMERHEAD HIT YOU AS A COMPETITOR, TRYING TO STEAL THE TURF FOR HIS OWN OPERATION?
SOMETHING LIKE THAT.
AND WHEN YOU DROVE HIM OUT, YOU WERE BASICALLY WORKING FOR THE BAD GUYS.
I'M SORRY, MR. CAGE. I DIDN'T MEAN TO PUT YOU IN THAT POSITION.
WELL, IT'S LIKE YOU SAID. YOU AIN'T BULLETPROOF. BUT I AM.
WHO'S BEHIND ALL THE JUNK? TELL ME THAT, AND I'LL TAKE CARE OF IT.
I WAS JUST LOW-LEVEL, MR. CAGE. ONLY NAME I CAN GIVE YOU IS JIMMY EALES.
JIMMY'S A SOLDIER, NOT SO HIGH UP HIMSELF. BEST I CAN DO.
IT'S GOOD ENOUGH, LEODIS.
SO YOU'RE WORKING YOUR WAY UP THE LINE.
UH-HUH. THAT NUMBER THAT CALLS IN, YOU GOT A NAME?
PLEASE, I'VE BEEN HACKING INTO CELL PHONE COMPANY RECORDS SINCE FRESHMAN YEAR... DON'T YOU BE TELLIN' MY AUNT.

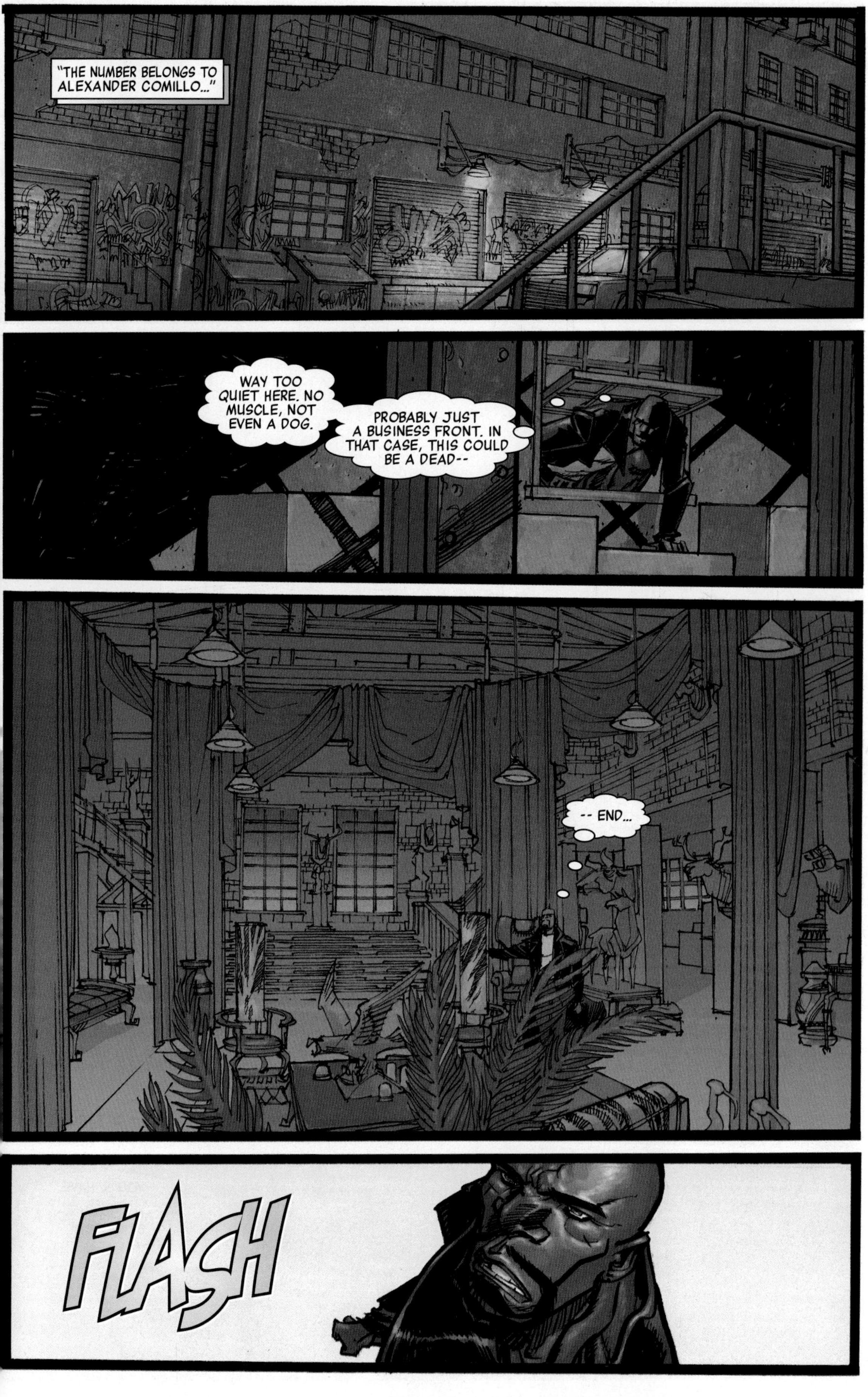
"THE NUMBER BELONGS TO ALEXANDER COMILLO..."
WAY TOO QUIET HERE. NO MUSCLE, NOT EVEN A DOG.
PROBABLY JUST A BUSINESS FRONT. IN THAT CASE, THIS COULD BE A DEAD--
-- END...
FLASH

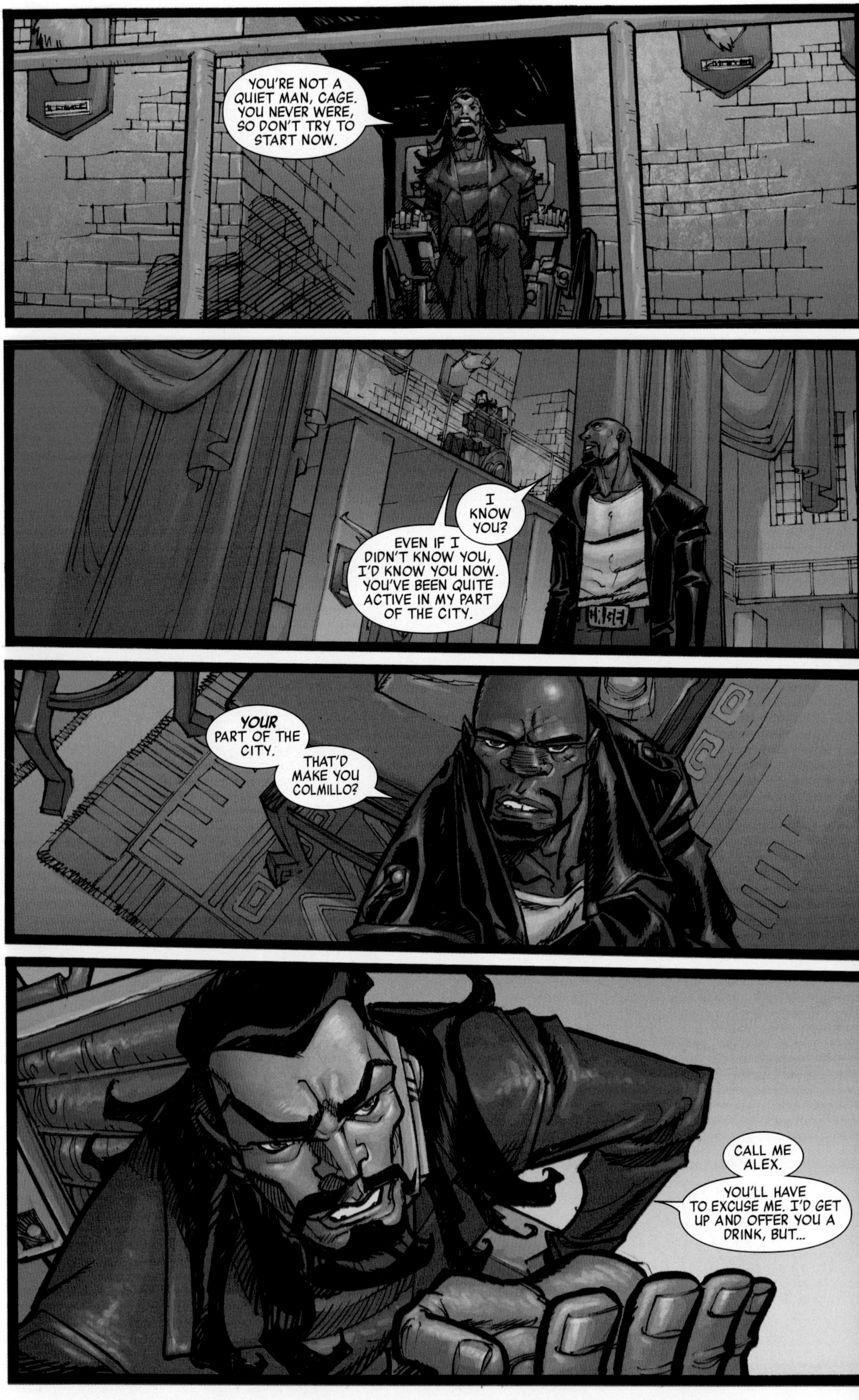
YOU'RE NOT A QUIET MAN, CAGE. YOU NEVER WERE, SO DON'T TRY TO START NOW.
I KNOW YOU?
EVEN IF I DIDN'T KNOW YOU, I'D KNOW YOU NOW. YOU'VE BEEN QUITE ACTIVE IN MY PART OF THE CITY.
YOUR PART OF THE CITY.
THAT'D MAKE YOU COLMILLO?
CALL ME ALEX.
YOU'LL HAVE TO EXCUSE ME. I'D GET UP AND OFFER YOU A DRINK, BUT...

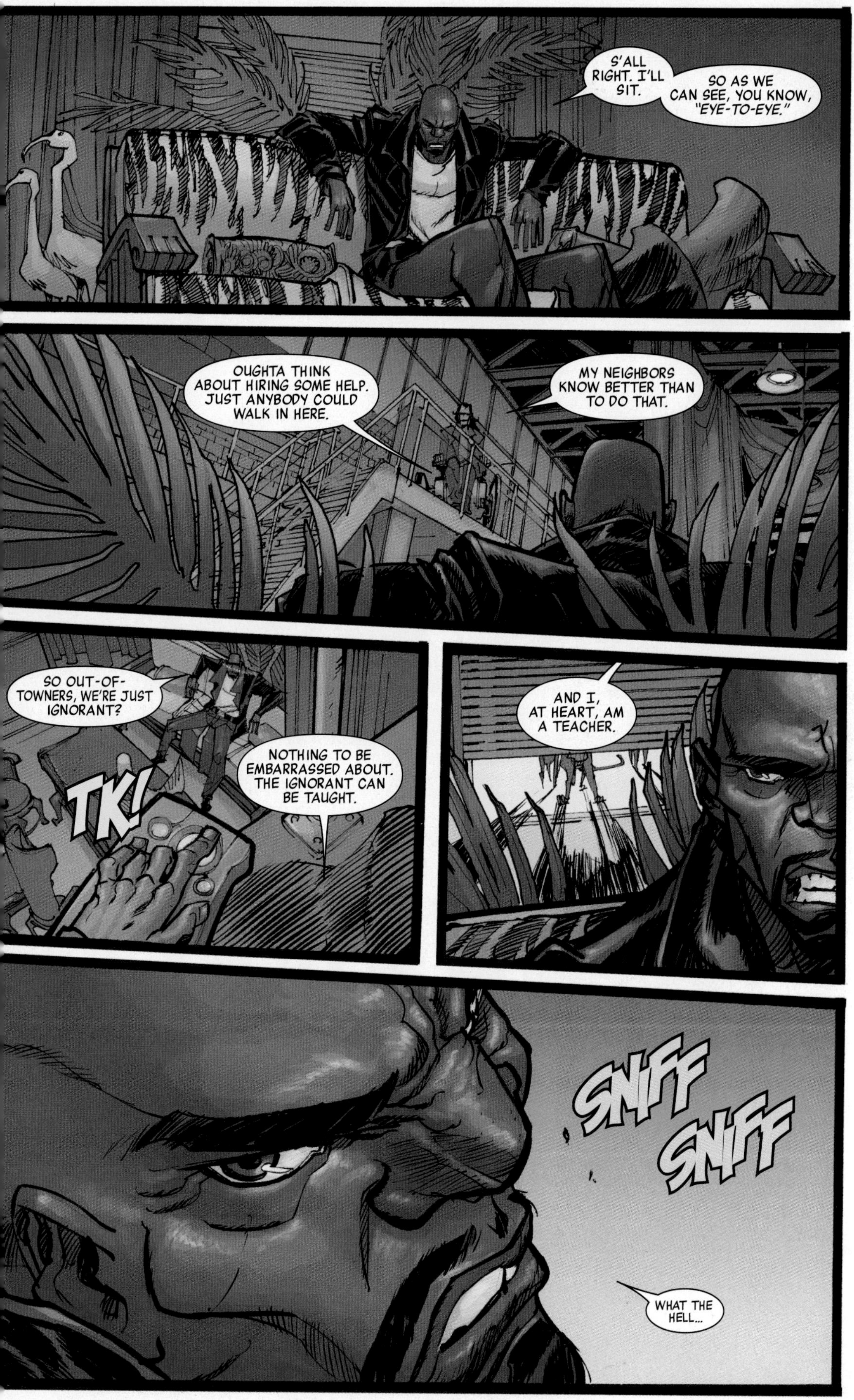
S'ALL RIGHT. I'LL SIT.
SO AS WE CAN SEE, YOU KNOW, "EYE-TO-EYE."
OUGHTA THINK ABOUT HIRING SOME HELP. JUST ANYBODY COULD WALK IN HERE.
MY NEIGHBORS KNOW BETTER THAN TO DO THAT.
SO OUT-OF-TOWNERS, WE'RE JUST IGNORANT?
TK!
NOTHING TO BE EMBARRASSED ABOUT. THE IGNORANT CAN BE TAUGHT.
AND I, AT HEART, AM A TEACHER.
SNIFF
SNIFF
WHAT THE HELL...

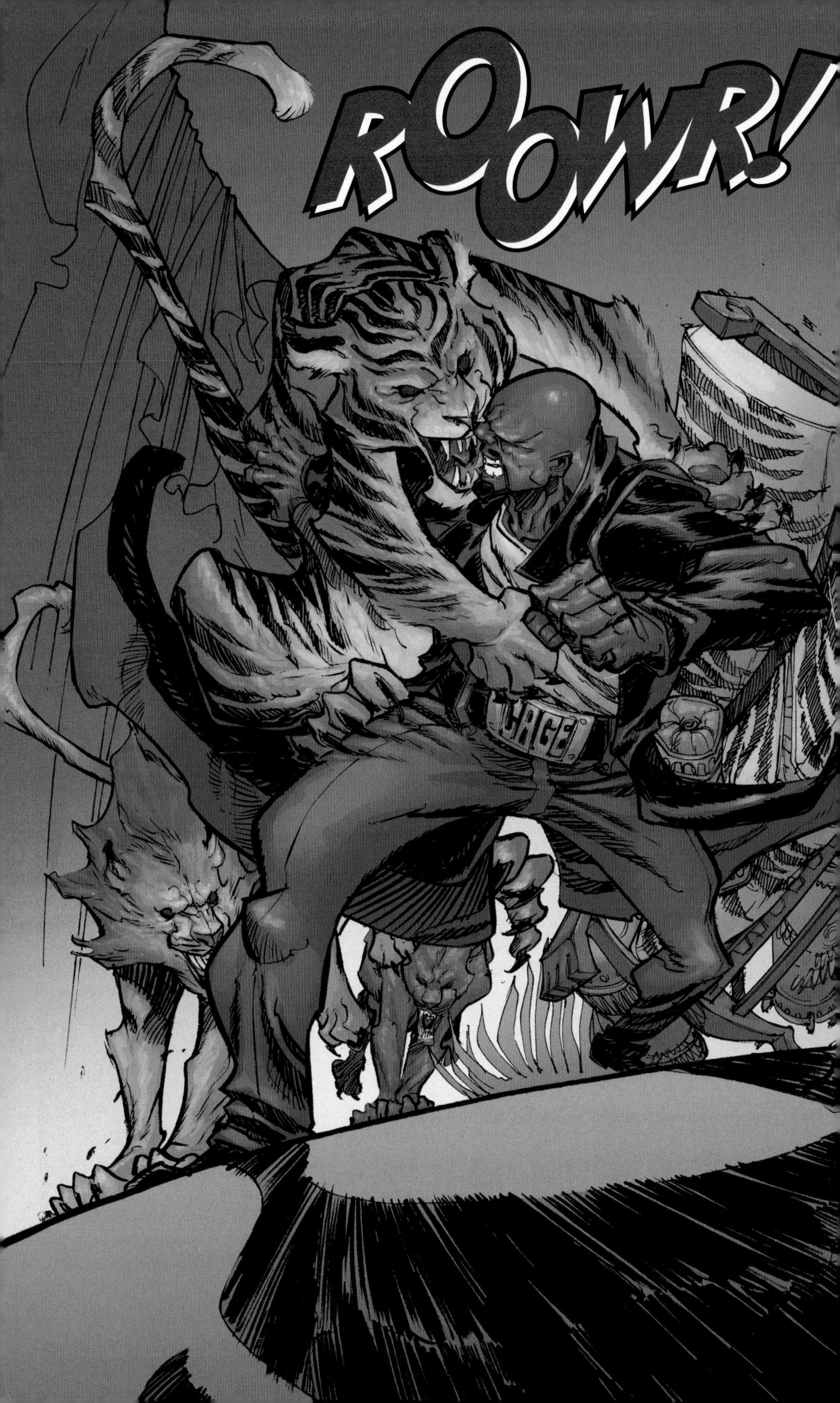
ROOWR!
CAGE

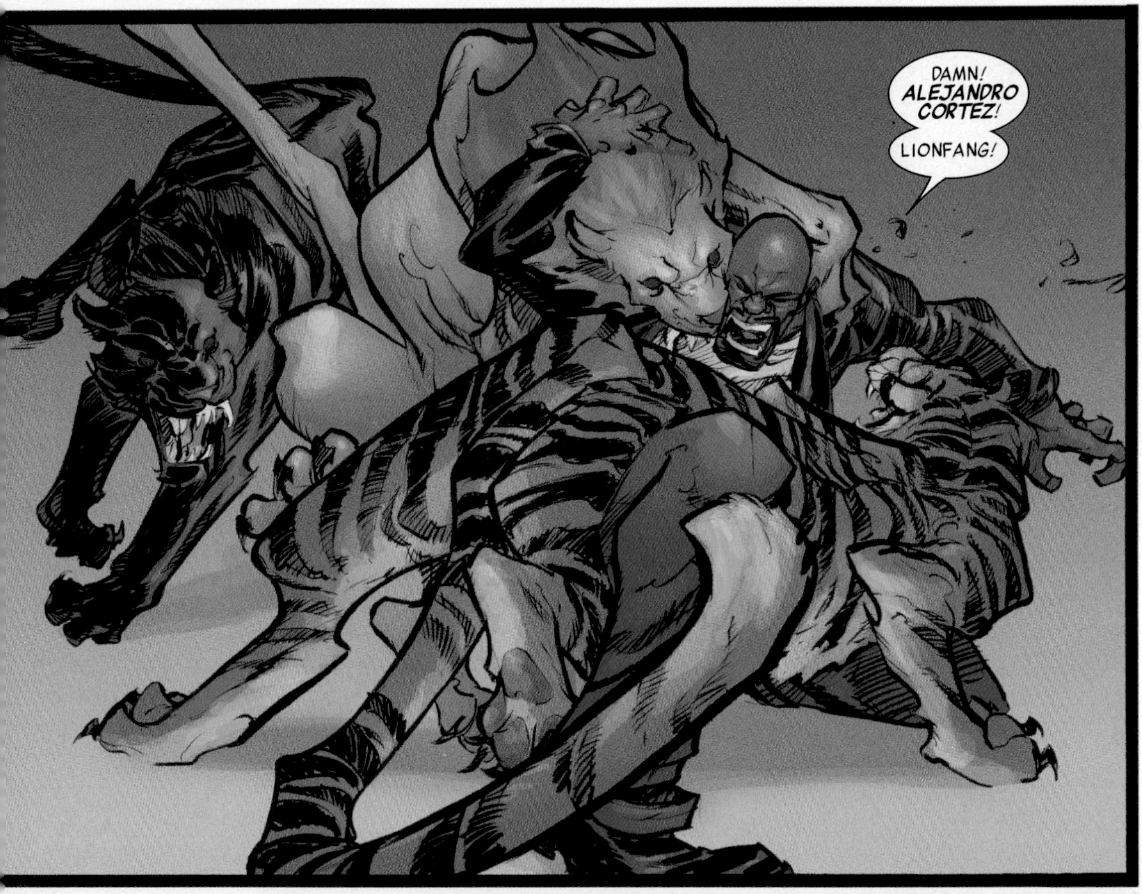
DAMN! ALEJANDRO CORTEZ!
LIONFANG!

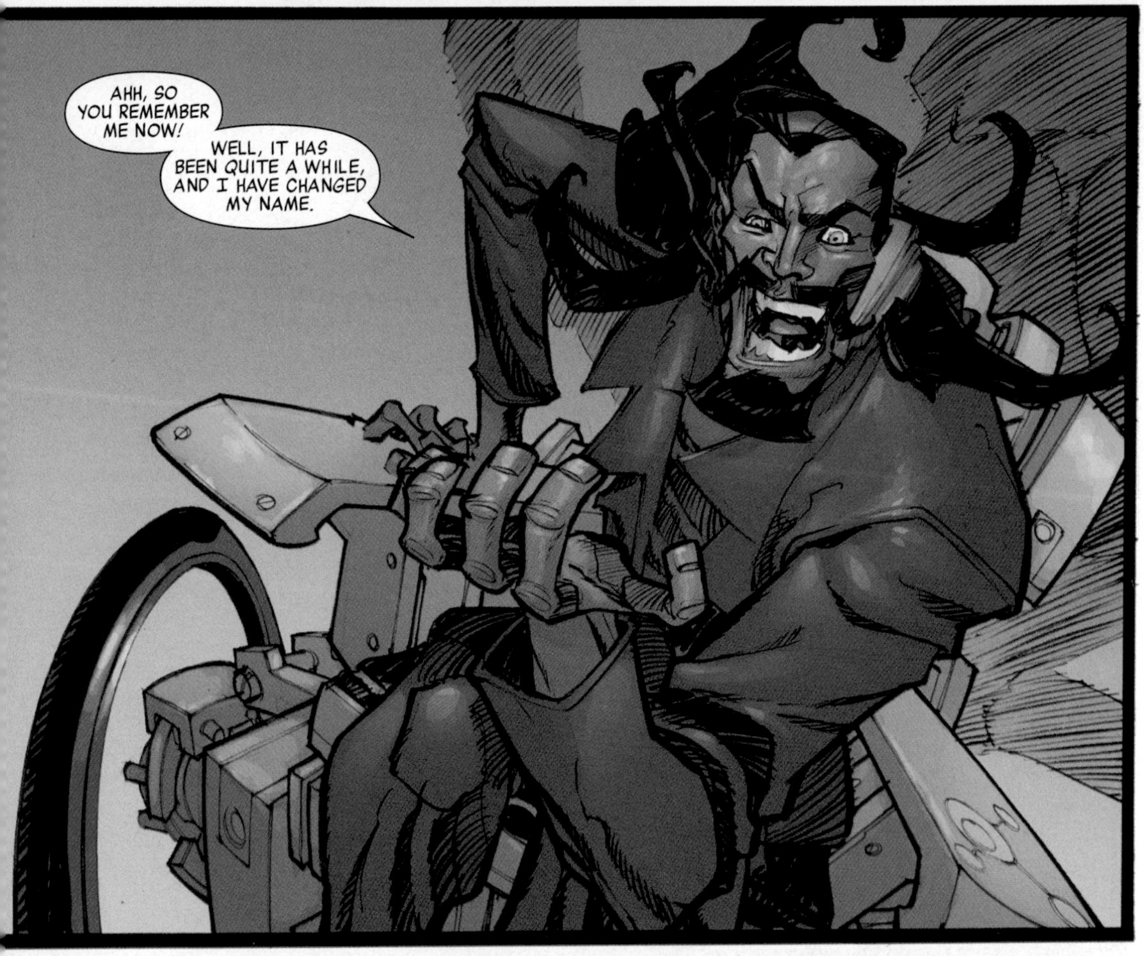
AHH, SO YOU REMEMBER ME NOW!
WELL, IT HAS BEEN QUITE A WHILE, AND I HAVE CHANGED MY NAME.

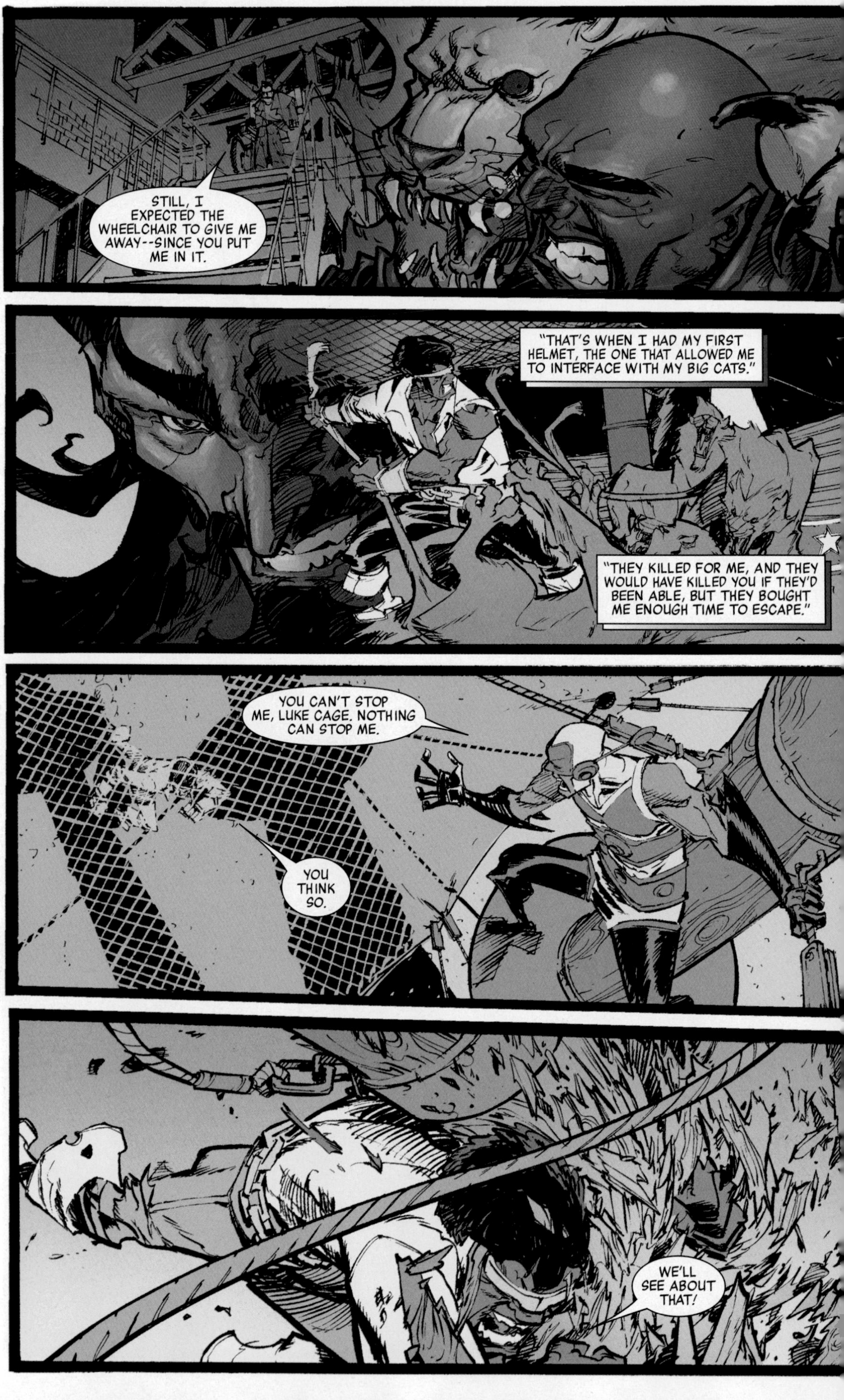

STILL, I EXPECTED THE WHEELCHAIR TO GIVE ME AWAY--SINCE YOU PUT ME IN IT.
"THAT'S WHEN I HAD MY FIRST HELMET, THE ONE THAT ALLOWED ME TO INTERFACE WITH MY BIG CATS."
"THEY KILLED FOR ME, AND THEY WOULD HAVE KILLED YOU IF THEY'D BEEN ABLE, BUT THEY BOUGHT ME ENOUGH TIME TO ESCAPE."
YOU CAN'T STOP ME, LUKE CAGE. NOTHING CAN STOP ME.
YOU THINK SO.
WE'LL SEE ABOUT THAT!

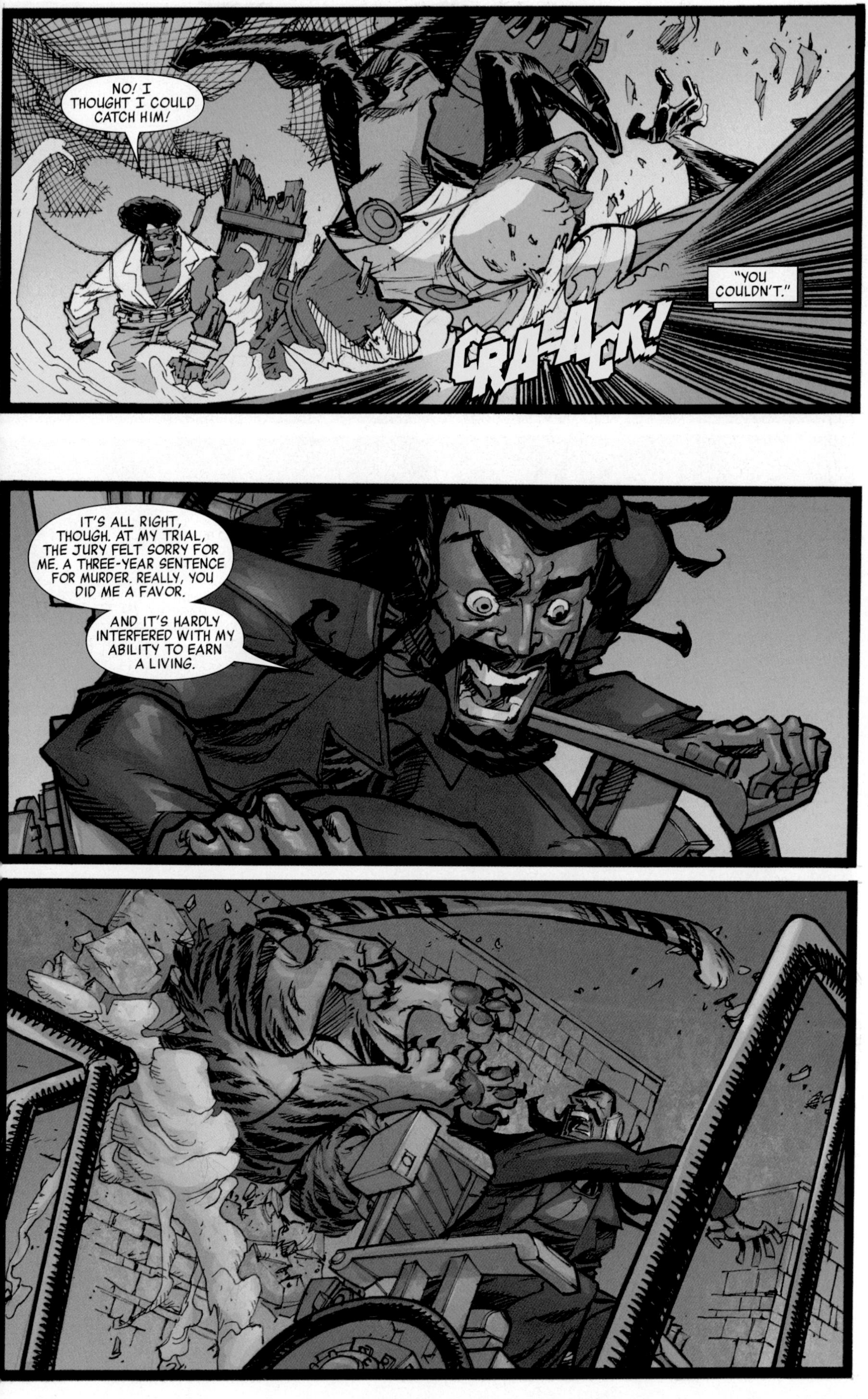
NO! I THOUGHT I COULD CATCH HIM!
"YOU COULDN'T."
CRA-ACK!
IT'S ALL RIGHT, THOUGH. AT MY TRIAL, THE JURY FELT SORRY FOR ME. A THREE-YEAR SENTENCE FOR MURDER. REALLY, YOU DID ME A FAVOR.
AND IT'S HARDLY INTERFERED WITH MY ABILITY TO EARN A LIVING.

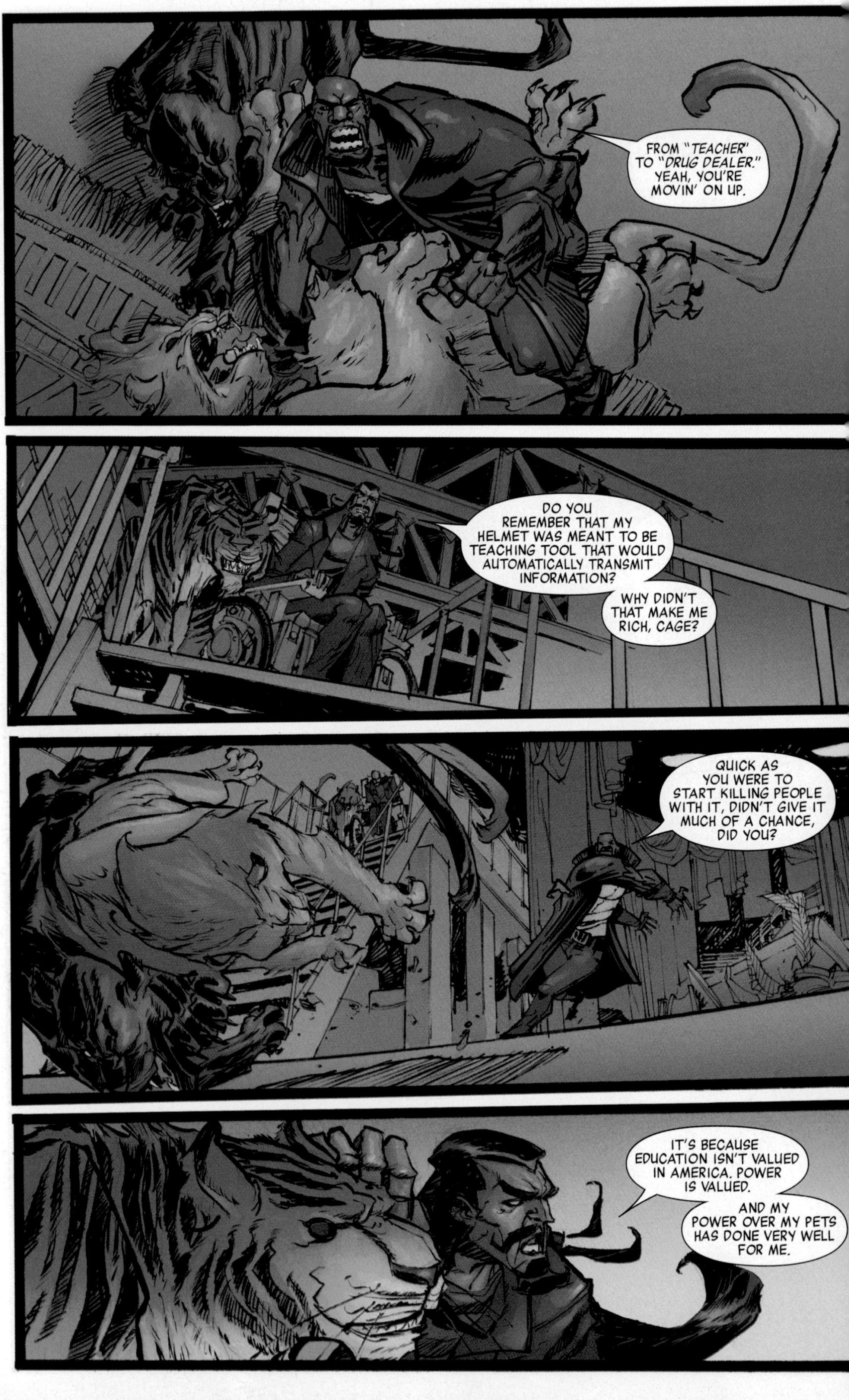
FROM "TEACHER" TO "DRUG DEALER." YEAH, YOU'RE MOVIN' ON UP.
DO YOU REMEMBER THAT MY HELMET WAS MEANT TO BE TEACHING TOOL THAT WOULD AUTOMATICALLY TRANSMIT INFORMATION?
WHY DIDN'T THAT MAKE ME RICH, CAGE?
QUICK AS YOU WERE TO START KILLING PEOPLE WITH IT, DIDN'T GIVE IT MUCH OF A CHANCE, DID YOU?
IT'S BECAUSE EDUCATION ISN'T VALUED IN AMERICA. POWER IS VALUED.
AND MY POWER OVER MY PETS HAS DONE VERY WELL FOR ME.

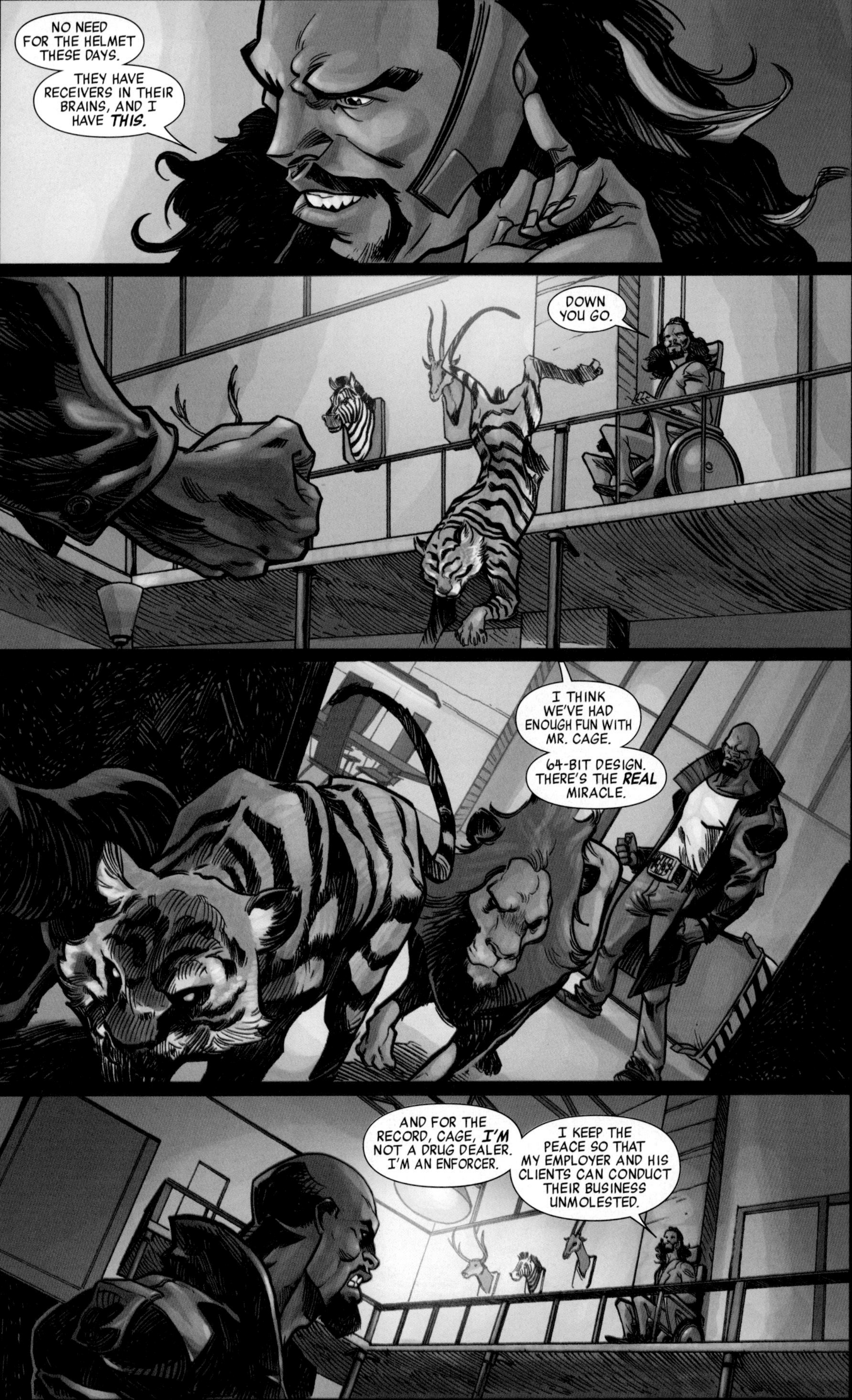
NO NEED FOR THE HELMET THESE DAYS.
THEY HAVE RECEIVERS IN THEIR BRAINS, AND I HAVE THIS.
DOWN YOU GO.
I THINK WE'VE HAD ENOUGH FUN WITH MR. CAGE.
64-BIT DESIGN. THERE'S THE REAL MIRACLE.
AND FOR THE RECORD, CAGE, I'M NOT A DRUG DEALER. I'M AN ENFORCER.
I KEEP THE PEACE SO THAT MY EMPLOYER AND HIS CLIENTS CAN CONDUCT THEIR BUSINESS UNMOLESTED.

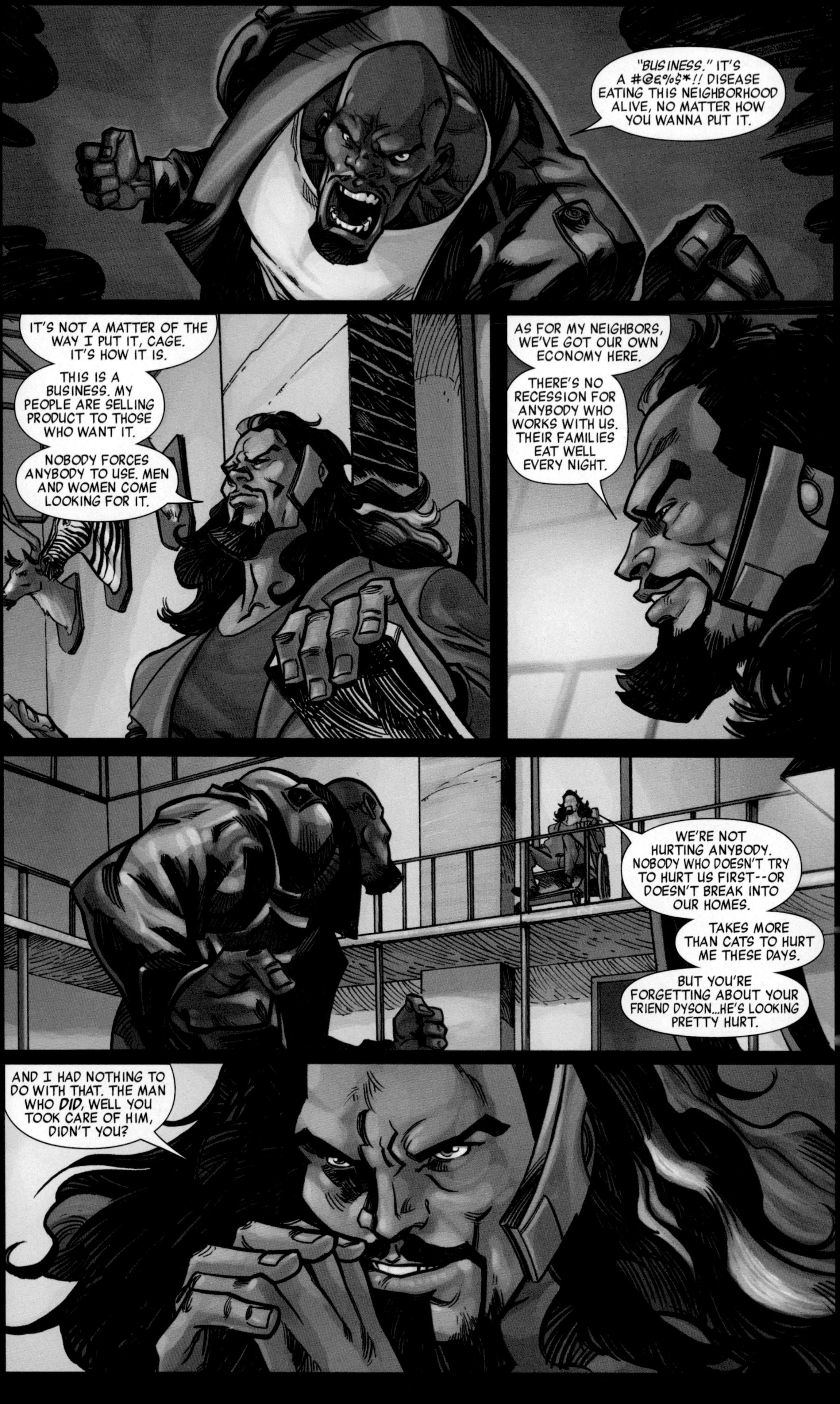
"BUSINESS." IT'S A #@&%$*!! DISEASE EATING THIS NEIGHBORHOOD ALIVE, NO MATTER HOW YOU WANNA PUT IT.
IT'S NOT A MATTER OF THE WAY I PUT IT, CAGE. IT'S HOW IT IS.
THIS IS A BUSINESS. MY PEOPLE ARE SELLING PRODUCT TO THOSE WHO WANT IT.
NOBODY FORCES ANYBODY TO USE. MEN AND WOMEN COME LOOKING FOR IT.
AS FOR MY NEIGHBORS, WE'VE GOT OUR OWN ECONOMY HERE.
THERE'S NO RECESSION FOR ANYBODY WHO WORKS WITH US. THEIR FAMILIES EAT WELL EVERY NIGHT.
WE'RE NOT HURTING ANYBODY. NOBODY WHO DOESN'T TRY TO HURT US FIRST--OR DOESN'T BREAK INTO OUR HOMES.
TAKES MORE THAN CATS TO HURT ME THESE DAYS.
BUT YOU'RE FORGETTING ABOUT YOUR FRIEND DYSON...HE'S LOOKING PRETTY HURT.
AND I HAD NOTHING TO DO WITH THAT. THE MAN WHO DID, WELL YOU TOOK CARE OF HIM, DIDN'T YOU?

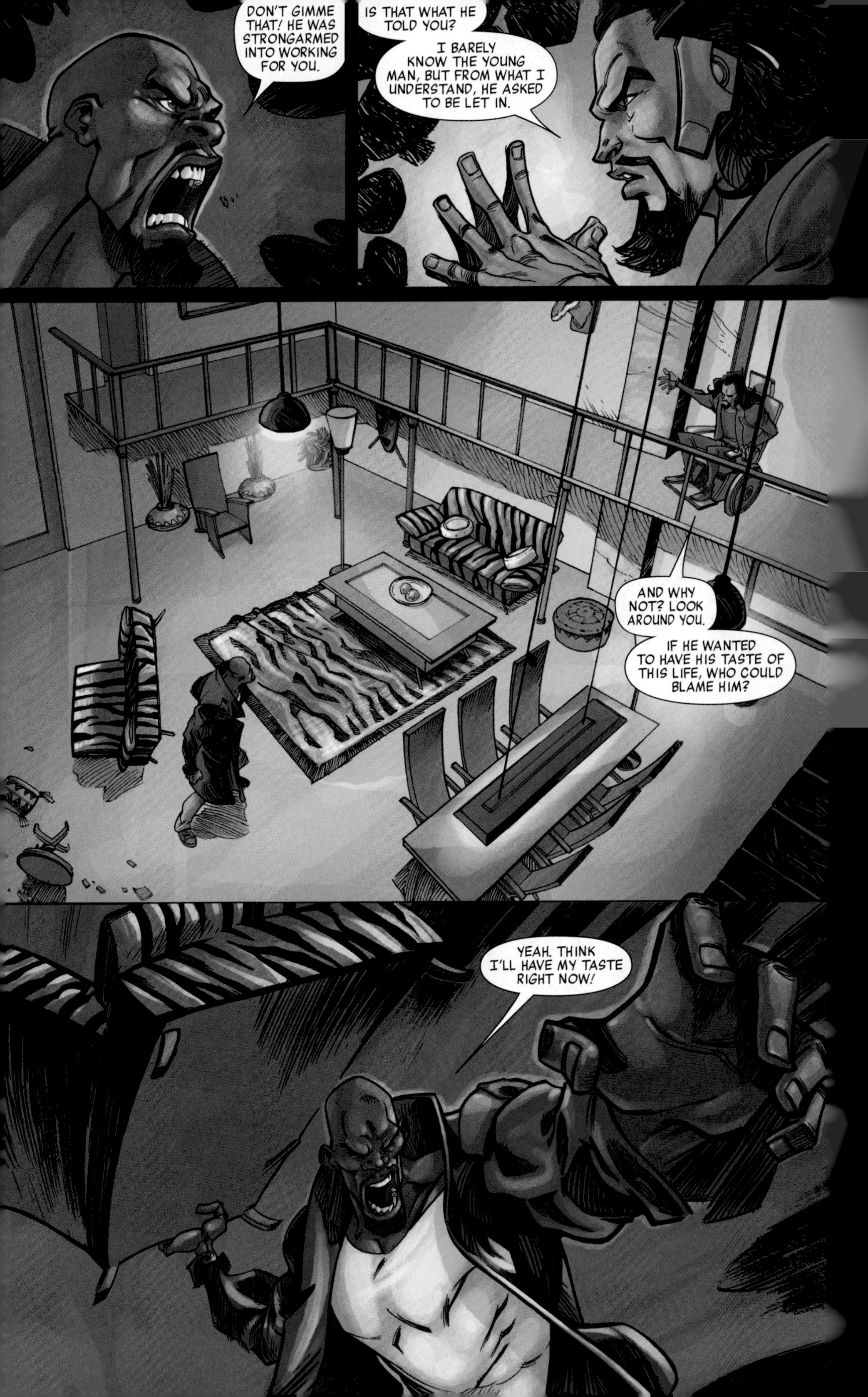
DON'T GIMME THAT! HE WAS STRONGARMED INTO WORKING FOR YOU.
IS THAT WHAT HE TOLD YOU?
I BARELY KNOW THE YOUNG MAN, BUT FROM WHAT I UNDERSTAND, HE ASKED TO BE LET IN.
AND WHY NOT? LOOK AROUND YOU.
IF HE WANTED TO HAVE HIS TASTE OF THIS LIFE, WHO COULD BLAME HIM?
YEAH. THINK I'LL HAVE MY TASTE RIGHT NOW!

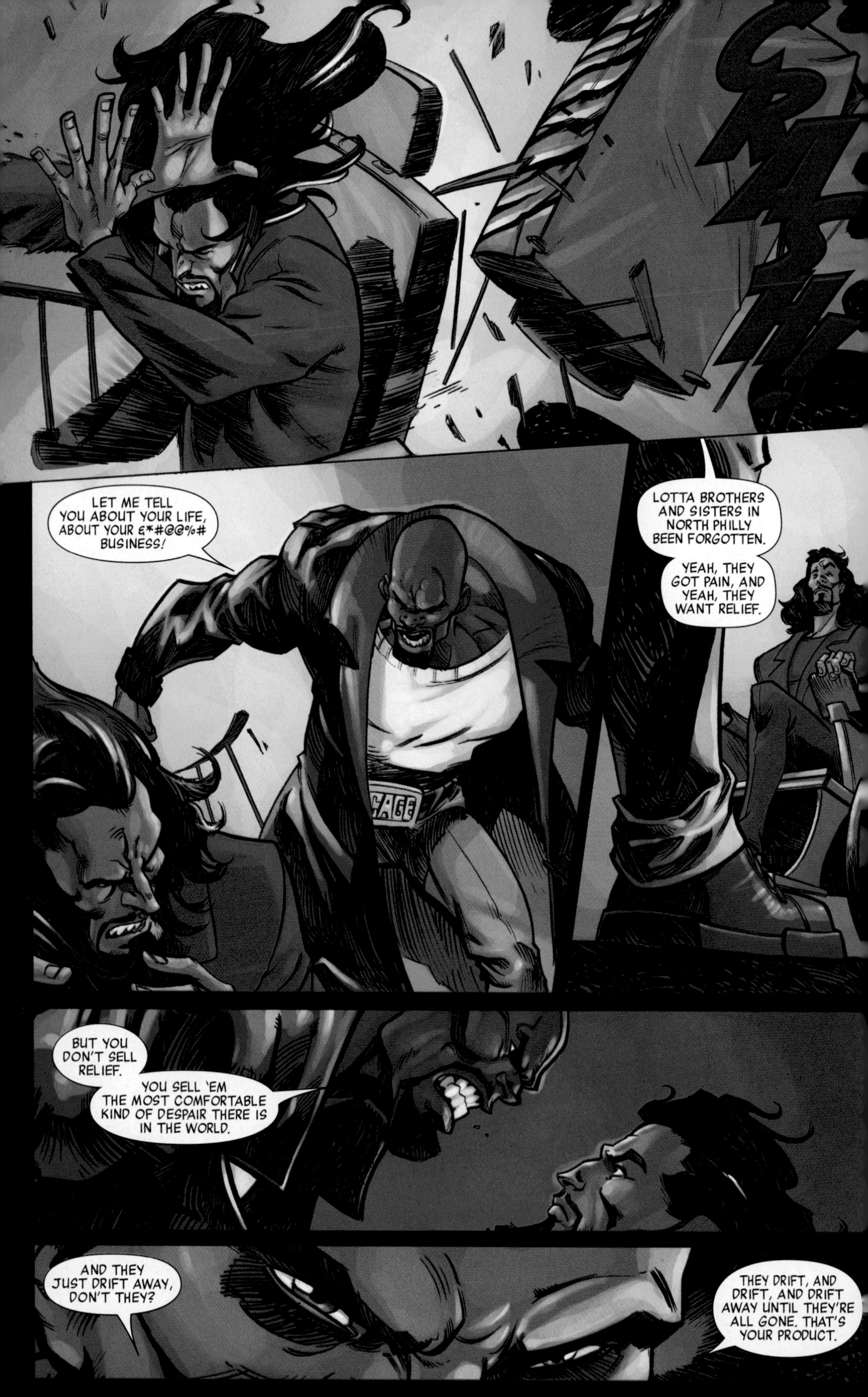
LET ME TELL YOU ABOUT YOUR LIFE, ABOUT YOUR &*#@@%# BUSINESS!
LOTTA BROTHERS AND SISTERS IN NORTH PHILLY BEEN FORGOTTEN.
YEAH, THEY GOT PAIN, AND YEAH, THEY WANT RELIEF.
CAGE
BUT YOU DON'T SELL RELIEF.
YOU SELL 'EM THE MOST COMFORTABLE KIND OF DESPAIR THERE IS IN THE WORLD.
AND THEY JUST DRIFT AWAY, DON'T THEY?
THEY DRIFT, AND DRIFT, AND DRIFT AWAY UNTIL THEY'RE ALL GONE. THAT'S YOUR PRODUCT.

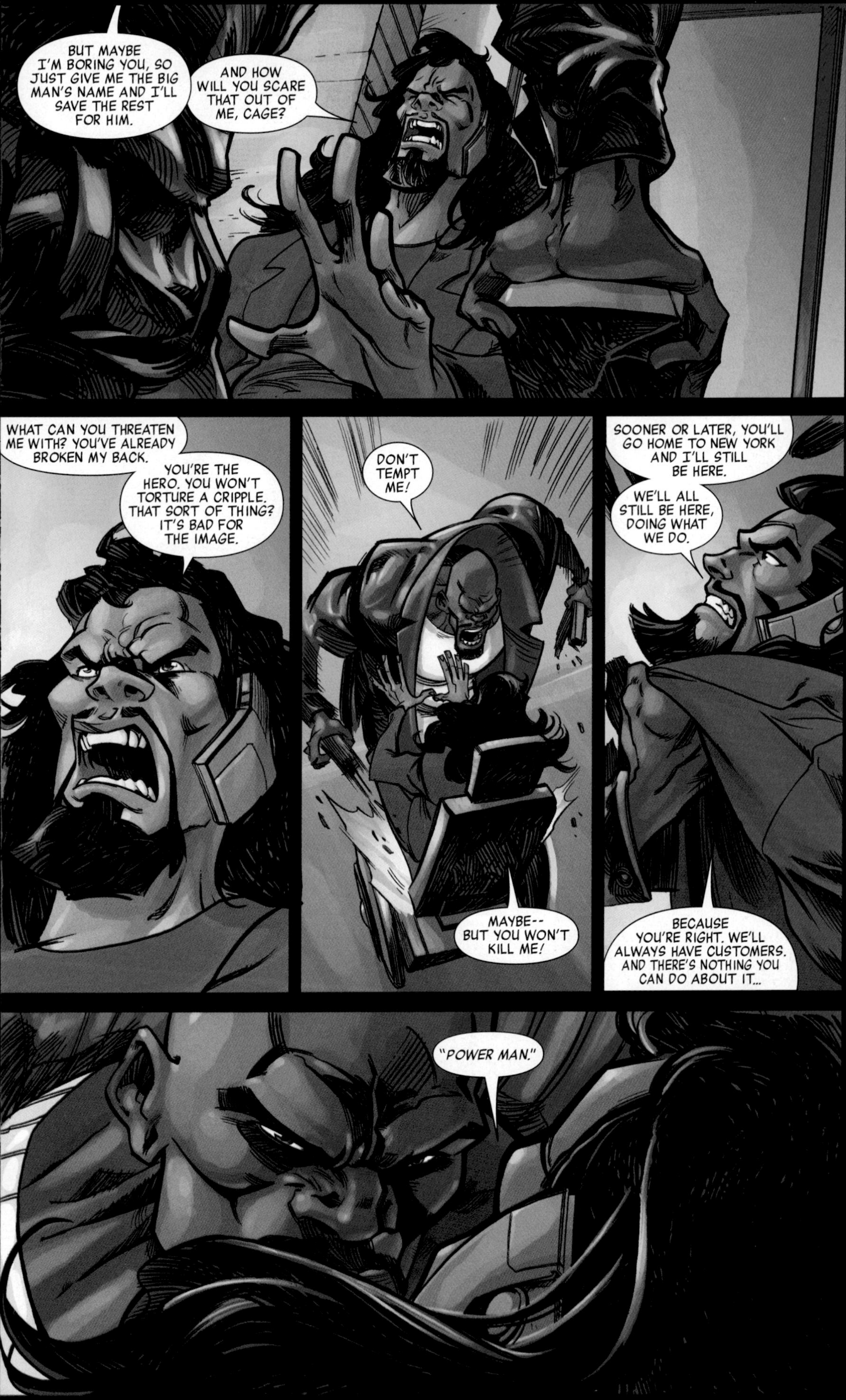
BUT MAYBE I'M BORING YOU, SO JUST GIVE ME THE BIG MAN'S NAME AND I'LL SAVE THE REST FOR HIM.
AND HOW WILL YOU SCARE THAT OUT OF ME, CAGE?
WHAT CAN YOU THREATEN ME WITH? YOU'VE ALREADY BROKEN MY BACK.
YOU'RE THE HERO. YOU WON'T TORTURE A CRIPPLE. THAT SORT OF THING? IT'S BAD FOR THE IMAGE.
DON'T TEMPT ME!
MAYBE-- BUT YOU WON'T KILL ME!
SOONER OR LATER, YOU'LL GO HOME TO NEW YORK AND I'LL STILL BE HERE.
WE'LL ALL STILL BE HERE, DOING WHAT WE DO.
BECAUSE YOU'RE RIGHT. WE'LL ALWAYS HAVE CUSTOMERS. AND THERE'S NOTHING YOU CAN DO ABOUT IT...
"POWER MAN."

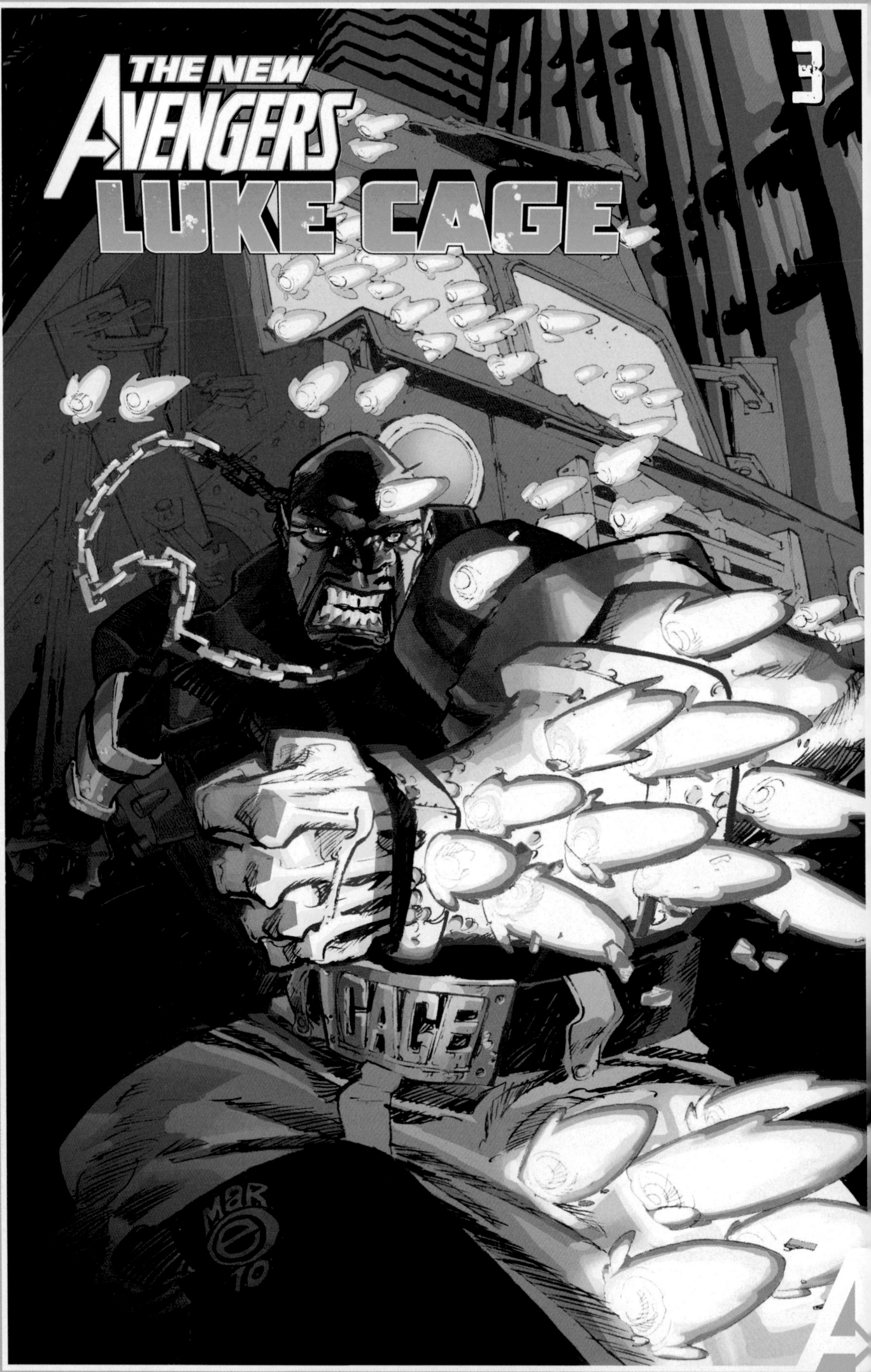
THE NEW AVENGERS
LUKE CAGE
3
CAGE

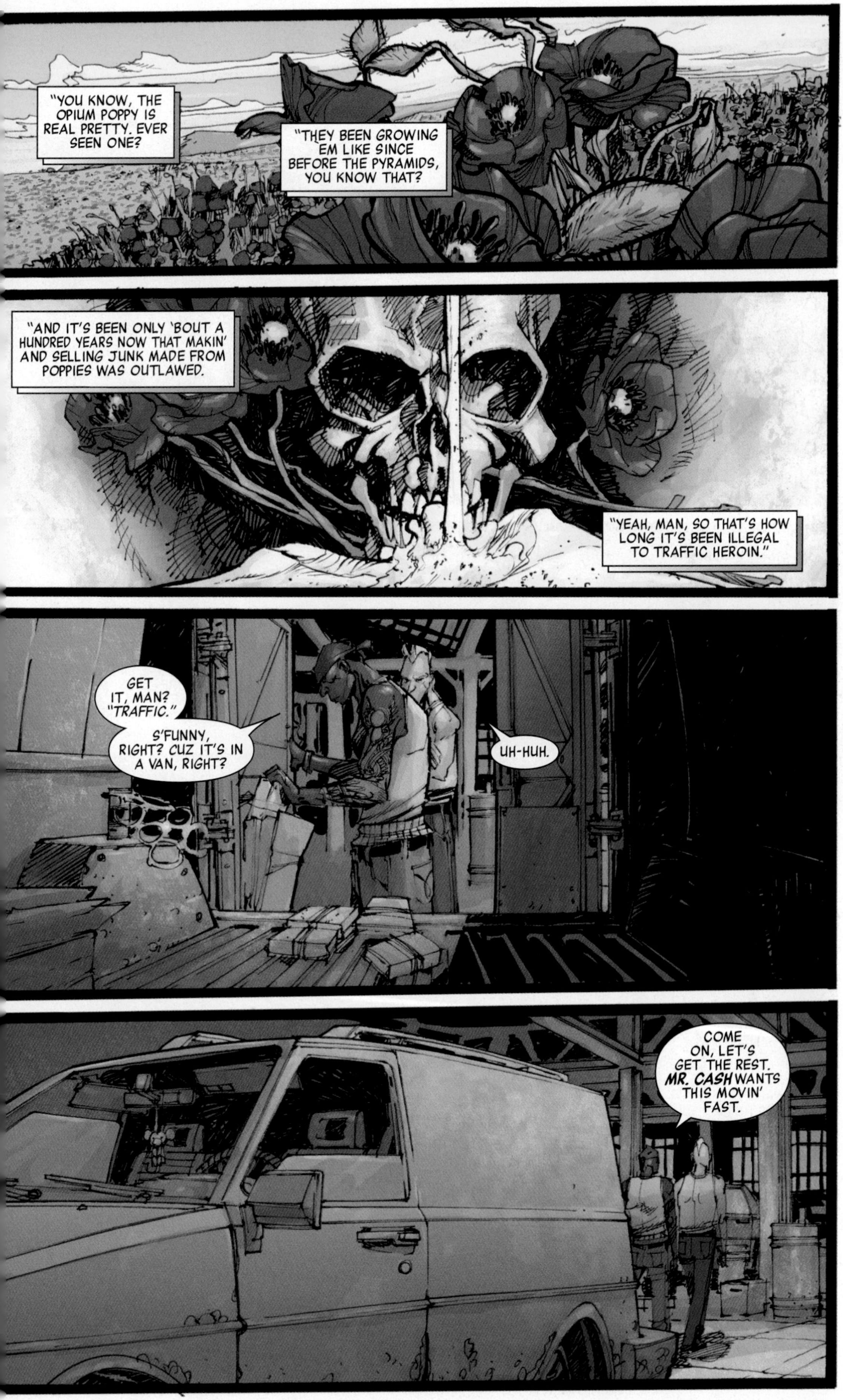
"YOU KNOW, THE OPIUM POPPY IS REAL PRETTY. EVER SEEN ONE?
"THEY BEEN GROWING EM LIKE SINCE BEFORE THE PYRAMIDS, YOU KNOW THAT?
"AND IT'S BEEN ONLY 'BOUT A HUNDRED YEARS NOW THAT MAKIN' AND SELLING JUNK MADE FROM POPPIES WAS OUTLAWED.
"YEAH, MAN, SO THAT'S HOW LONG IT'S BEEN ILLEGAL TO TRAFFIC HEROIN."
GET IT, MAN? "TRAFFIC."
S'FUNNY, RIGHT? CUZ IT'S IN A VAN, RIGHT?
UH-HUH.
COME ON, LET'S GET THE REST. MR. CASH WANTS THIS MOVIN' FAST.

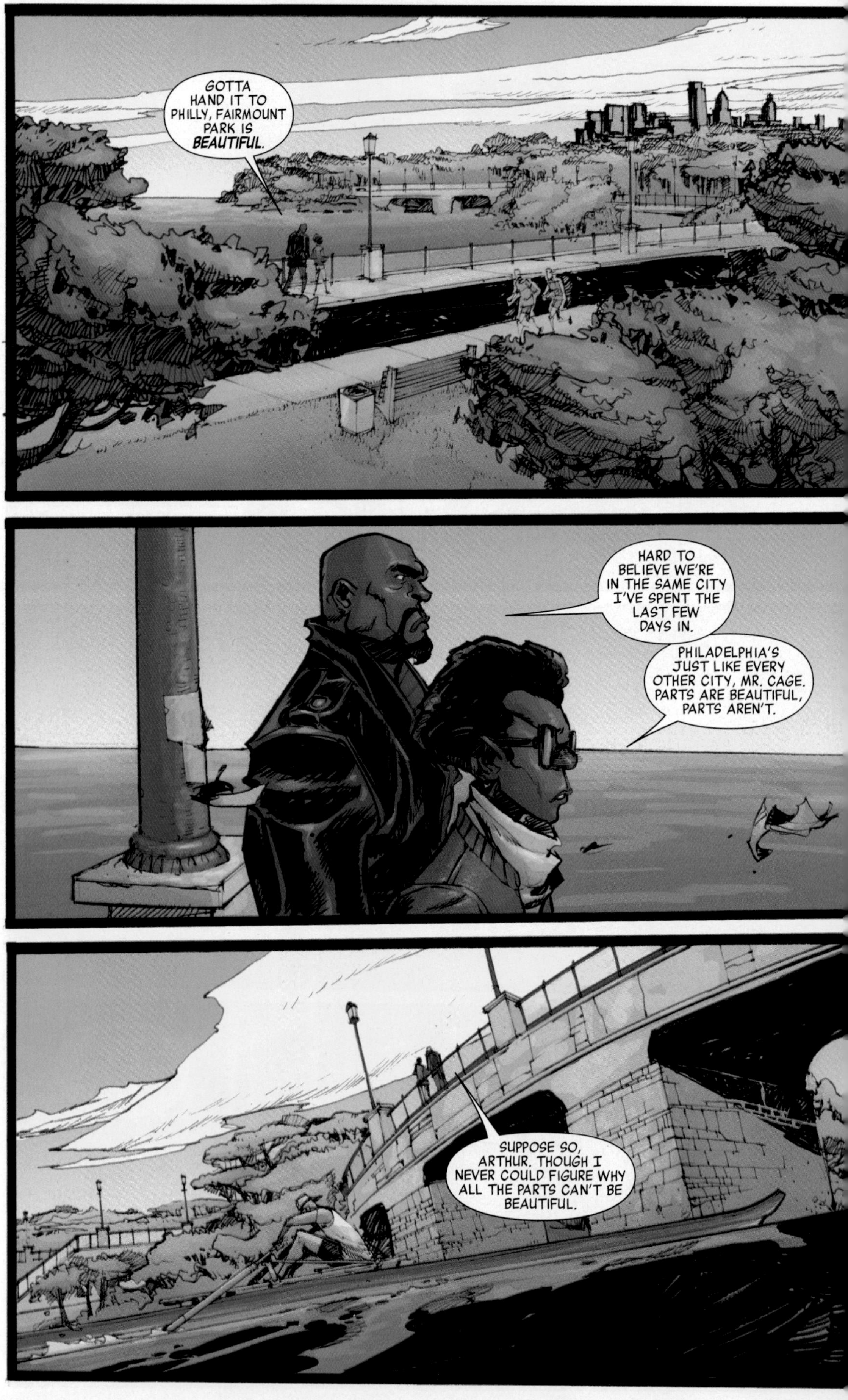
GOTTA HAND IT TO PHILLY, FAIRMOUNT PARK IS *BEAUTIFUL*.
HARD TO BELIEVE WE'RE IN THE SAME CITY I'VE SPENT THE LAST FEW DAYS IN.
PHILADELPHIA'S JUST LIKE EVERY OTHER CITY, MR. CAGE. PARTS ARE BEAUTIFUL, PARTS AREN'T.
SUPPOSE SO, ARTHUR. THOUGH I NEVER COULD FIGURE WHY ALL THE PARTS CAN'T BE BEAUTIFUL.

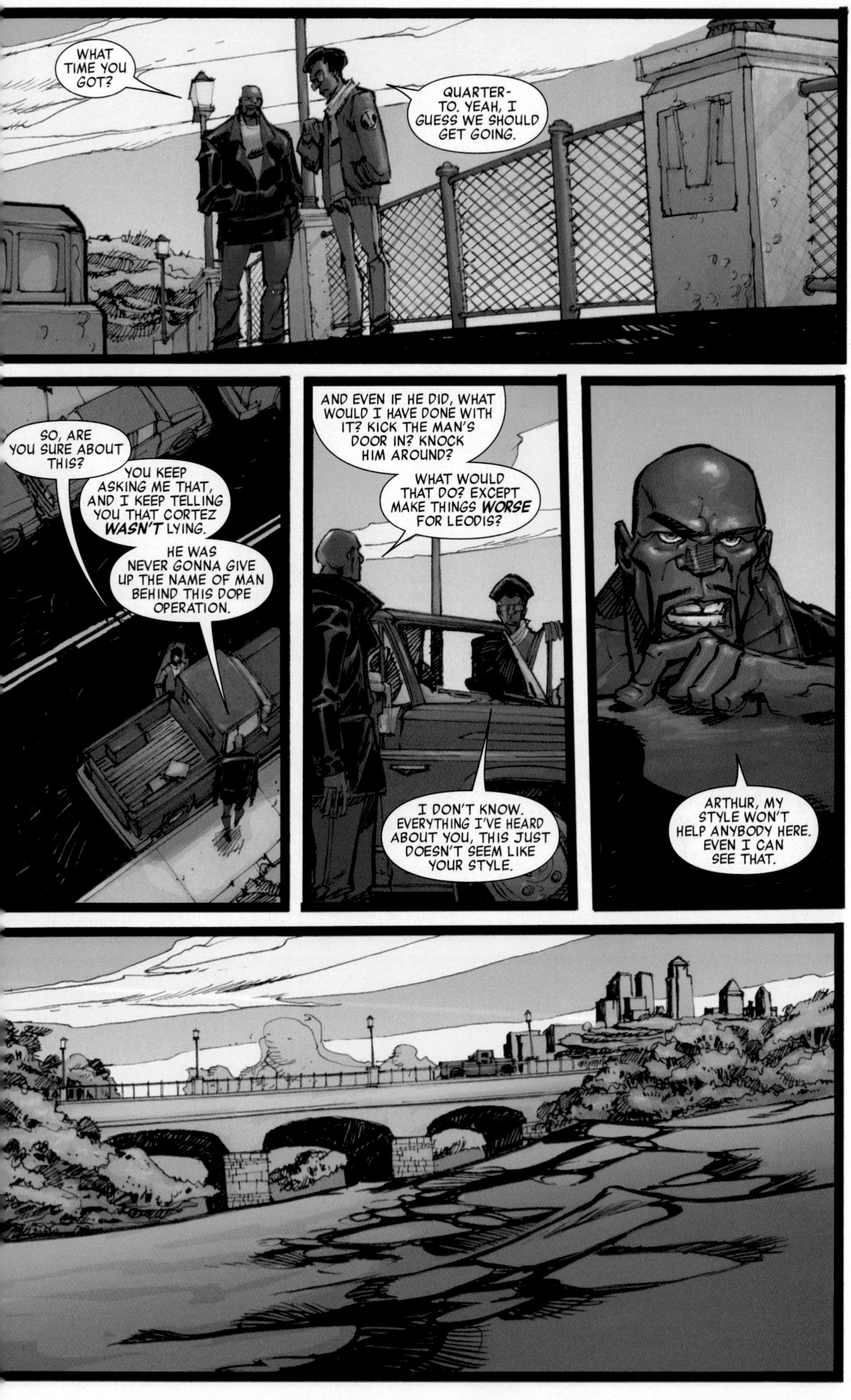
WHAT TIME YOU GOT?
QUARTER-TO. YEAH, I GUESS WE SHOULD GET GOING.
SO, ARE YOU SURE ABOUT THIS?
YOU KEEP ASKING ME THAT, AND I KEEP TELLING YOU THAT CORTEZ **WASN'T** LYING.
HE WAS NEVER GONNA GIVE UP THE NAME OF MAN BEHIND THIS DOPE OPERATION.
AND EVEN IF HE DID, WHAT WOULD I HAVE DONE WITH IT? KICK THE MAN'S DOOR IN? KNOCK HIM AROUND?
WHAT WOULD THAT DO? EXCEPT MAKE THINGS **WORSE** FOR LEODIS?
I DON'T KNOW. EVERYTHING I'VE HEARD ABOUT YOU, THIS JUST DOESN'T SEEM LIKE YOUR STYLE.
ARTHUR, MY STYLE WON'T HELP ANYBODY HERE. EVEN I CAN SEE THAT.

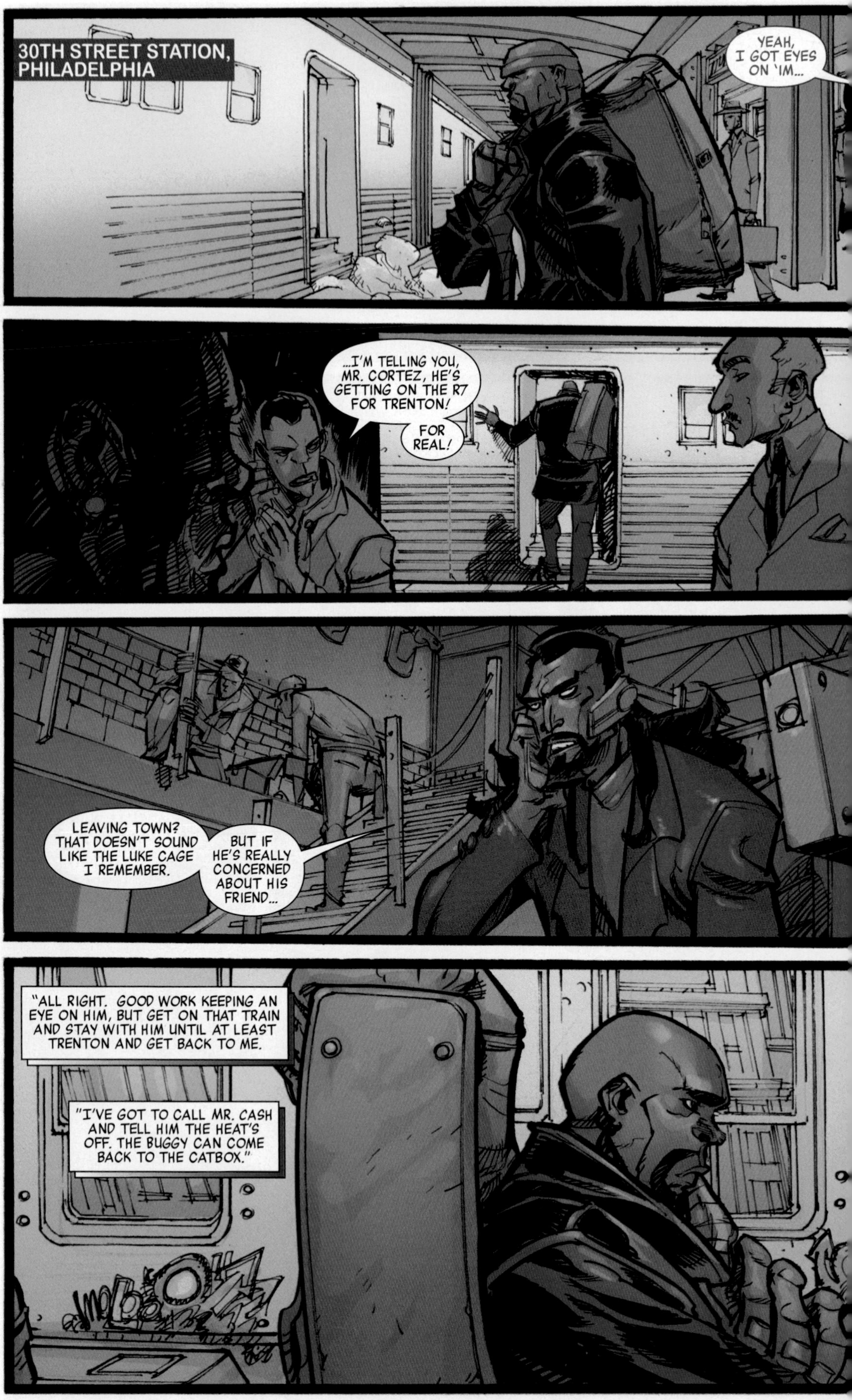

30TH STREET STATION, PHILADELPHIA
YEAH, I GOT EYES ON 'IM...
...I'M TELLING YOU, MR. CORTEZ, HE'S GETTING ON THE R7 FOR TRENTON!
FOR REAL!
LEAVING TOWN? THAT DOESN'T SOUND LIKE THE LUKE CAGE I REMEMBER.
BUT IF HE'S REALLY CONCERNED ABOUT HIS FRIEND...
"ALL RIGHT. GOOD WORK KEEPING AN EYE ON HIM, BUT GET ON THAT TRAIN AND STAY WITH HIM UNTIL AT LEAST TRENTON AND GET BACK TO ME.
"I'VE GOT TO CALL MR. CASH AND TELL HIM THE HEAT'S OFF. THE BUGGY CAN COME BACK TO THE CATBOX."

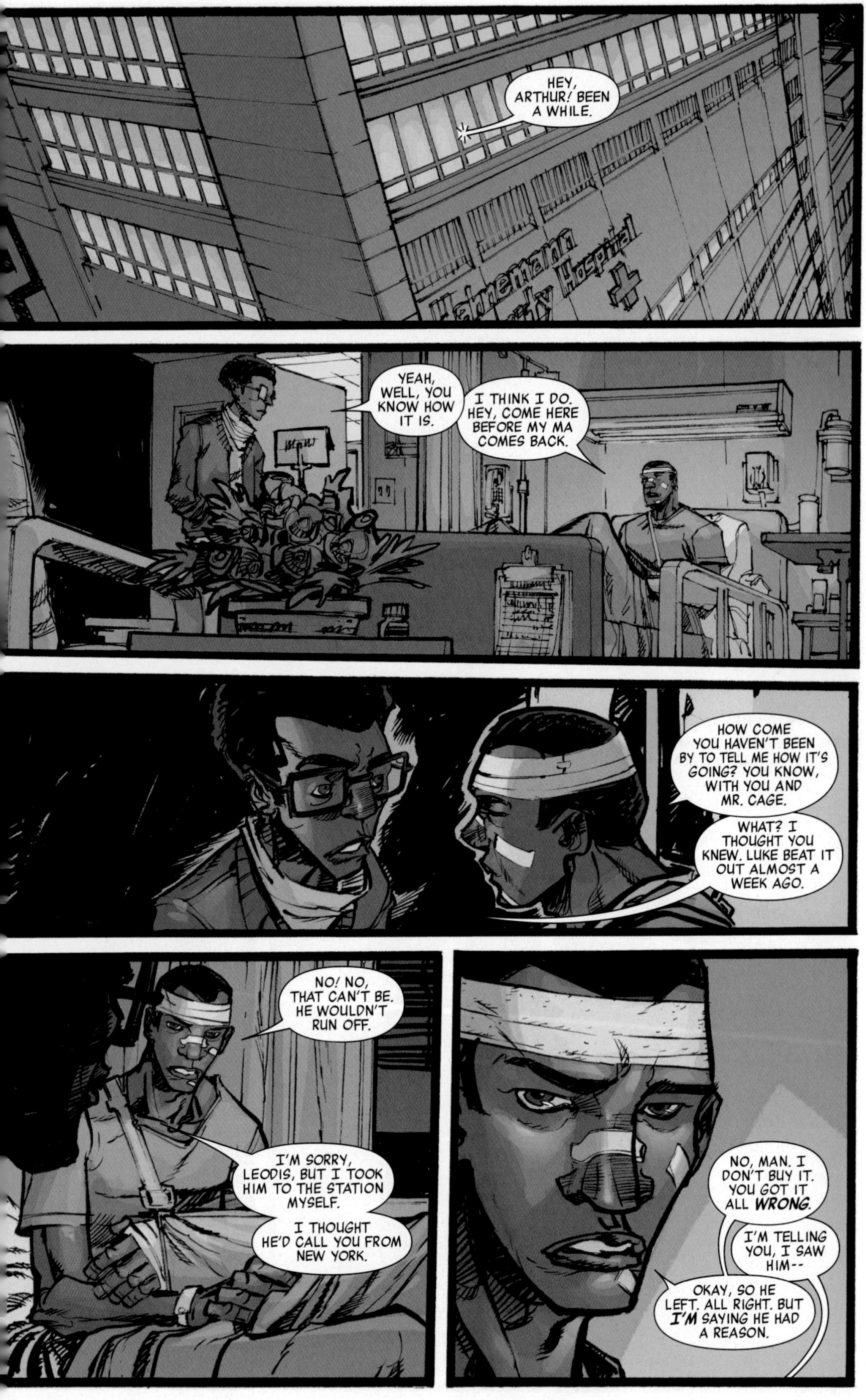
HEY, ARTHUR! BEEN A WHILE.
Hahnemann University Hospital
YEAH, WELL, YOU KNOW HOW IT IS.
I THINK I DO. HEY, COME HERE BEFORE MY MA COMES BACK.
HOW COME YOU HAVEN'T BEEN BY TO TELL ME HOW IT'S GOING? YOU KNOW, WITH YOU AND MR. CAGE.
WHAT? I THOUGHT YOU KNEW. LUKE BEAT IT OUT ALMOST A WEEK AGO.
NO! NO, THAT CAN'T BE. HE WOULDN'T RUN OFF.
I'M SORRY, LEODIS, BUT I TOOK HIM TO THE STATION MYSELF.
I THOUGHT HE'D CALL YOU FROM NEW YORK.
NO, MAN. I DON'T BUY IT. YOU GOT IT ALL WRONG.
I'M TELLING YOU, I SAW HIM--
OKAY, SO HE LEFT. ALL RIGHT. BUT I'M SAYING HE HAD A REASON.

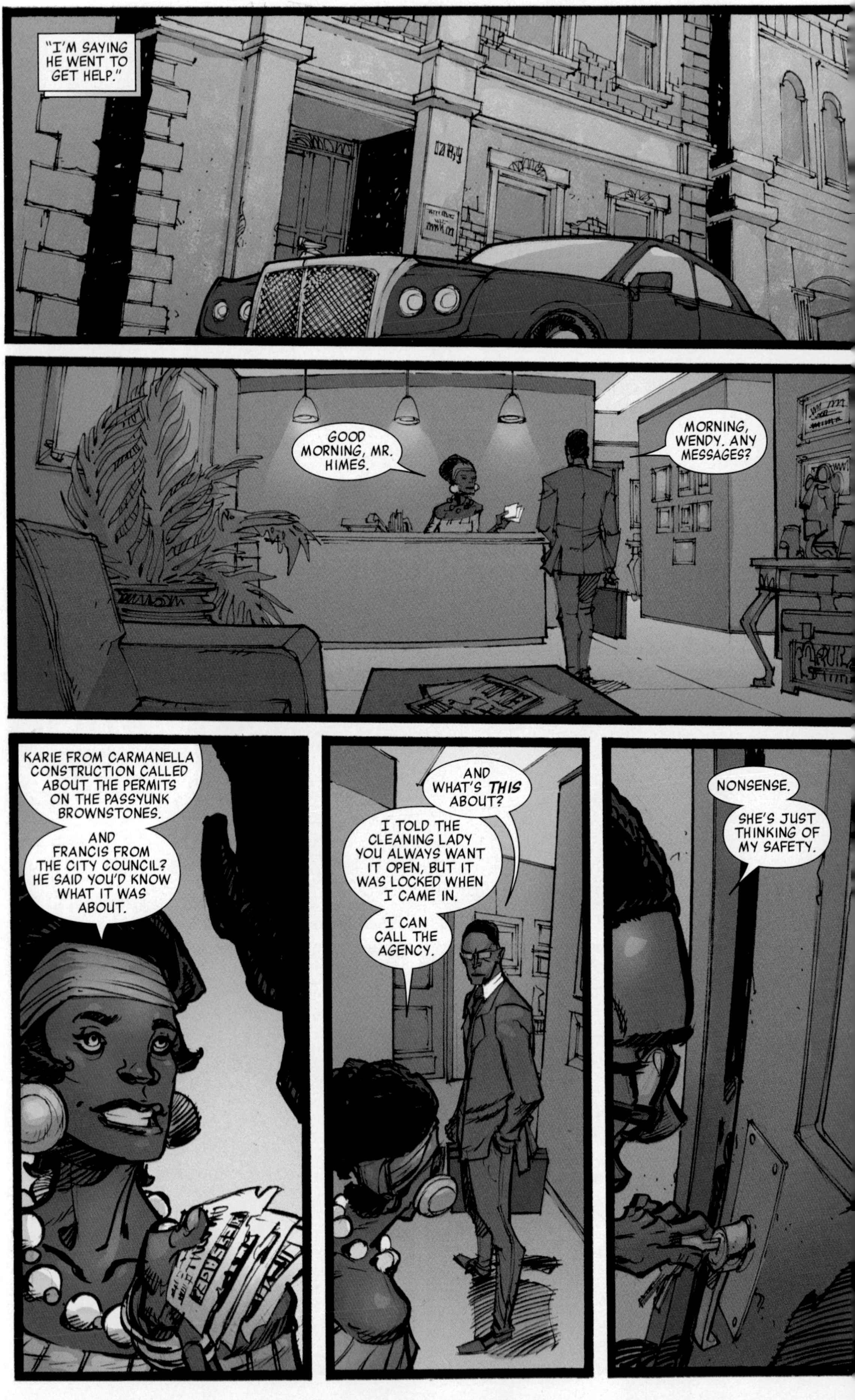
"I'M SAYING HE WENT TO GET HELP."
GOOD MORNING, MR. HIMES.
MORNING, WENDY. ANY MESSAGES?
KARIE FROM CARMANELLA CONSTRUCTION CALLED ABOUT THE PERMITS ON THE PASSYUNK BROWNSTONES.
AND FRANCIS FROM THE CITY COUNCIL? HE SAID YOU'D KNOW WHAT IT WAS ABOUT.
AND WHAT'S *THIS* ABOUT?
I TOLD THE CLEANING LADY YOU ALWAYS WANT IT OPEN, BUT IT WAS LOCKED WHEN I CAME IN.
I CAN CALL THE AGENCY.
NONSENSE.
SHE'S JUST THINKING OF MY SAFETY.

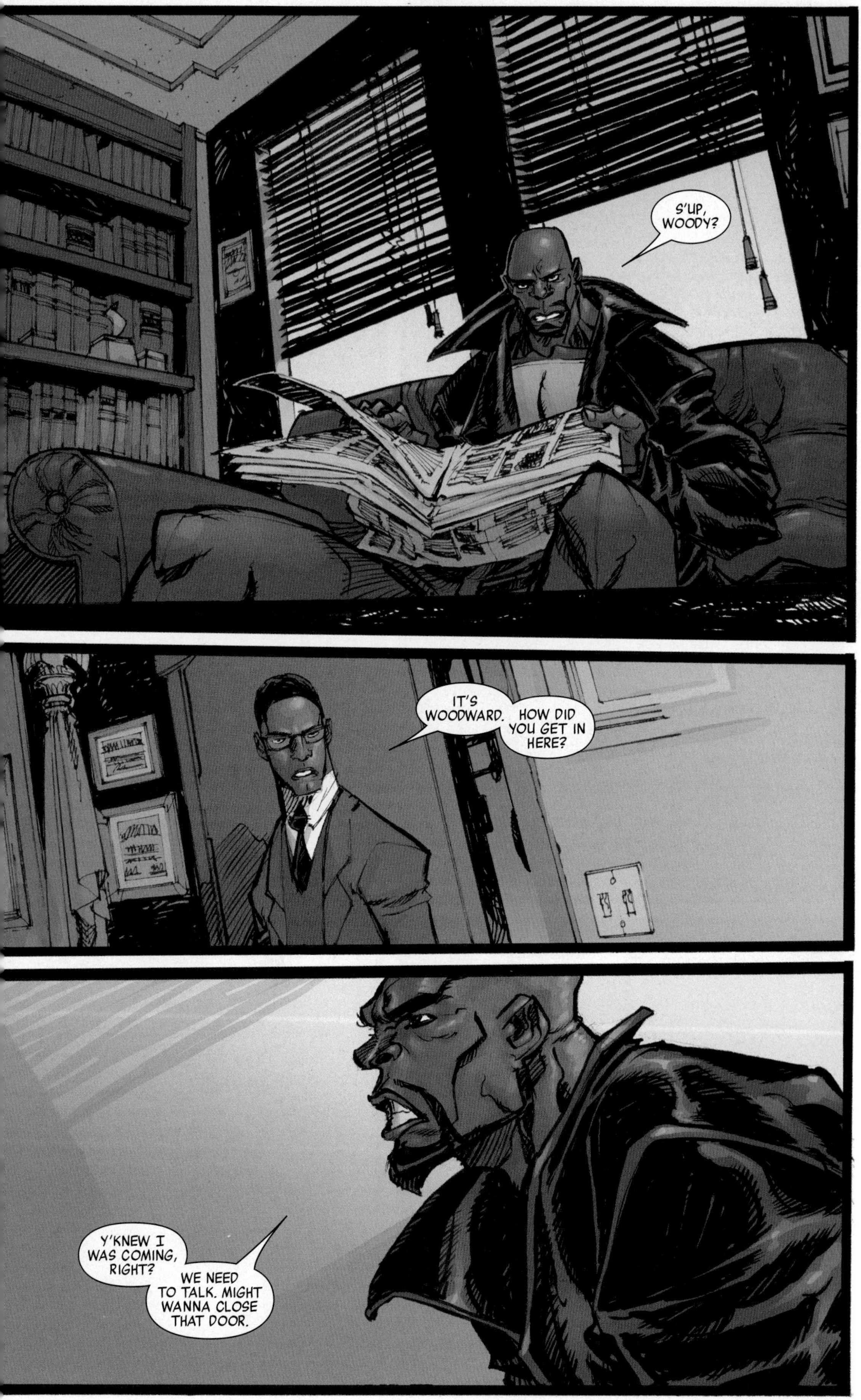
S'UP, WOODY?
IT'S WOODWARD.
HOW DID YOU GET IN HERE?
Y'KNEW I WAS COMING, RIGHT?
WE NEED TO TALK. MIGHT WANNA CLOSE THAT DOOR.

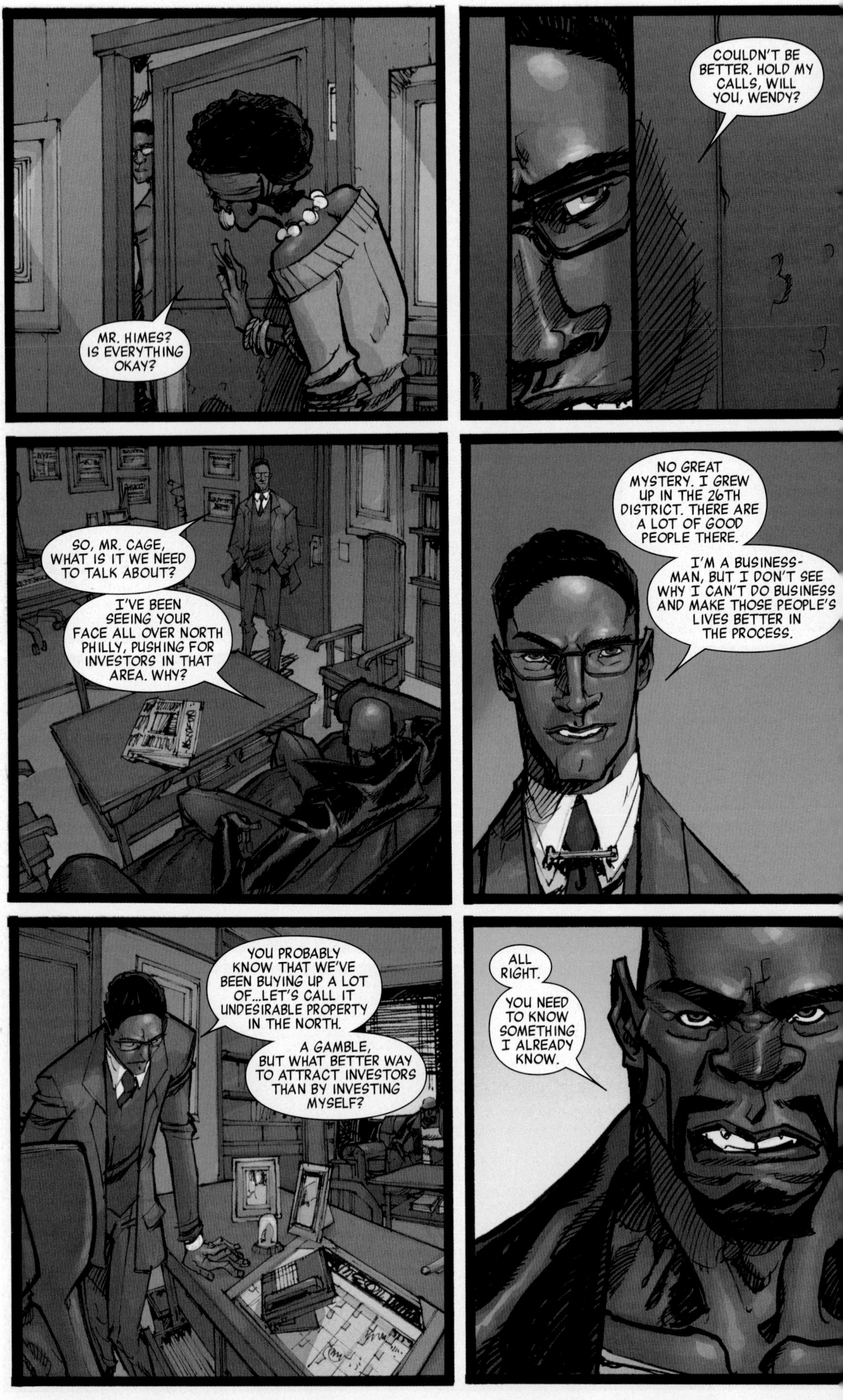
MR. HIMES? IS EVERYTHING OKAY?
COULDN'T BE BETTER. HOLD MY CALLS, WILL YOU, WENDY?
SO, MR. CAGE, WHAT IS IT WE NEED TO TALK ABOUT?
I'VE BEEN SEEING YOUR FACE ALL OVER NORTH PHILLY, PUSHING FOR INVESTORS IN THAT AREA. WHY?
NO GREAT MYSTERY. I GREW UP IN THE 26TH DISTRICT. THERE ARE A LOT OF GOOD PEOPLE THERE.
I'M A BUSINESS-MAN, BUT I DON'T SEE WHY I CAN'T DO BUSINESS AND MAKE THOSE PEOPLE'S LIVES BETTER IN THE PROCESS.
YOU PROBABLY KNOW THAT WE'VE BEEN BUYING UP A LOT OF...LET'S CALL IT UNDESIRABLE PROPERTY IN THE NORTH.
A GAMBLE, BUT WHAT BETTER WAY TO ATTRACT INVESTORS THAN BY INVESTING MYSELF?
ALL RIGHT.
YOU NEED TO KNOW SOMETHING I ALREADY KNOW.

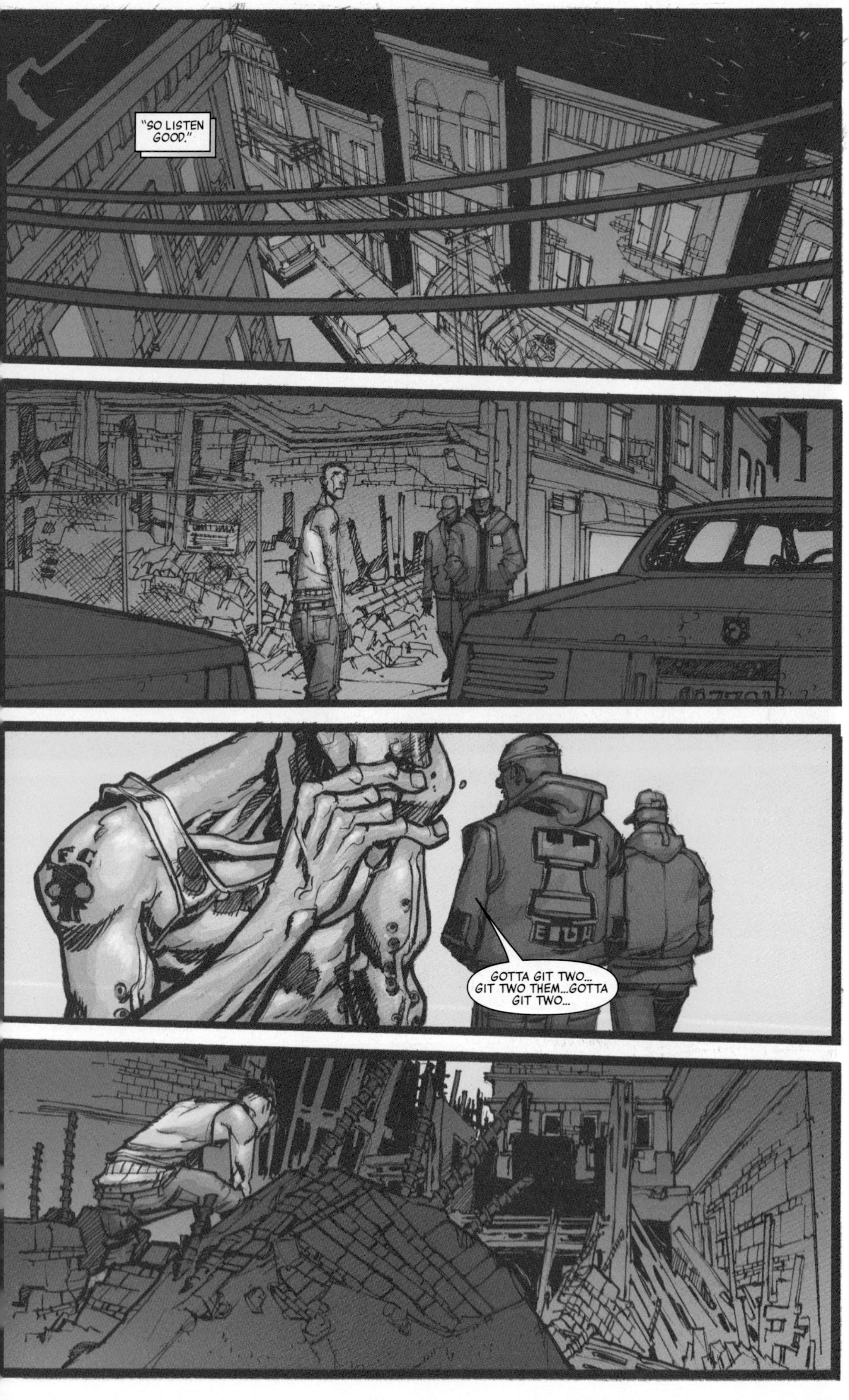

"SO LISTEN GOOD."
GOTTA GIT TWO... GIT TWO THEM...GOTTA GIT TWO...

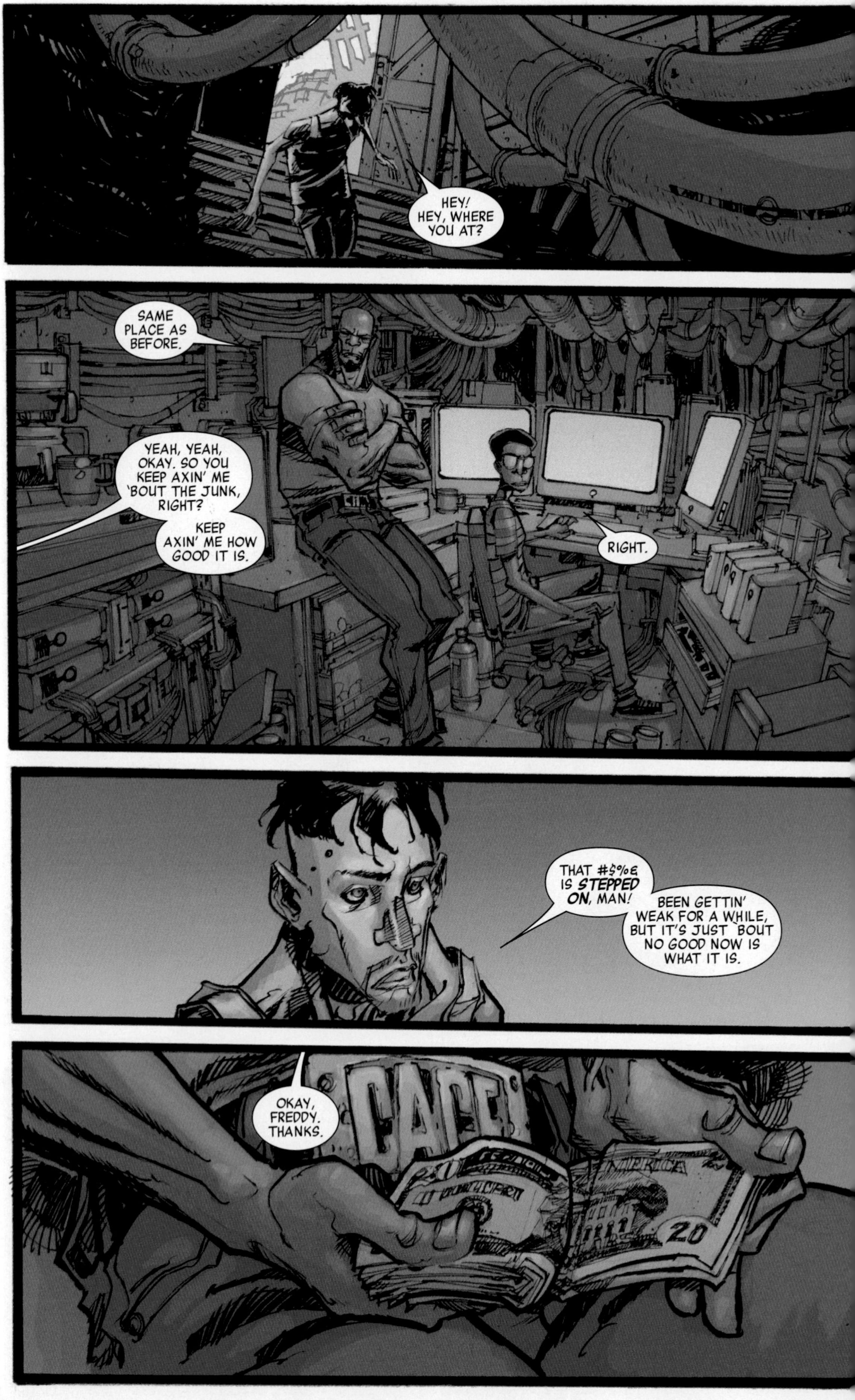
HEY! HEY, WHERE YOU AT?
SAME PLACE AS BEFORE.
YEAH, YEAH, OKAY. SO YOU KEEP AXIN' ME 'BOUT THE JUNK, RIGHT?
KEEP AXIN' ME HOW GOOD IT IS.
RIGHT.
THAT #$%€ IS **STEPPED ON**, MAN!
BEEN GETTIN' WEAK FOR A WHILE, BUT IT'S JUST 'BOUT NO GOOD NOW IS WHAT IT IS.
OKAY, FREDDY. THANKS.
20

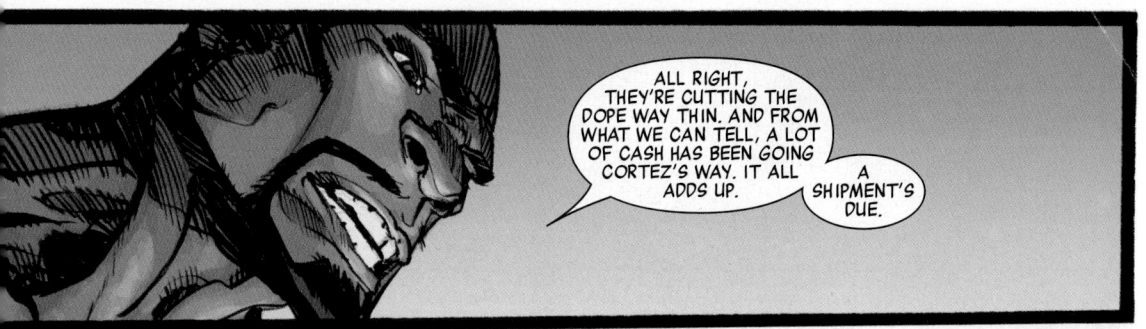

ALL RIGHT, THEY'RE CUTTING THE DOPE WAY THIN. AND FROM WHAT WE CAN TELL, A LOT OF CASH HAS BEEN GOING CORTEZ'S WAY. IT ALL ADDS UP.

A SHIPMENT'S DUE.

YOU KNOW, I DON'T FEEL SO GREAT ABOUT PUTTING CASH INTO A JUNKIE'S HANDS--

OR LYING TO MY COUSIN ABOUT YOU LEAVING TOWN.

FOCUS, ARTHUR. WE PULL THIS OFF, THE ONLY THING FREDDY CAN BUY WITH THAT PAPER WILL BE FRUIT PIES.

WELL, KNOWING THE DOPE'S COMING, I SHOULD BE ABLE TO SPOT SOME PATTERNS IN THEIR PHONE CHATTER, FIGURE OUT THEIR CODE.

I CAN PROBABLY COME UP WITH A TIME FOR DELIVERY.

ALREADY WE'VE SEEN "CATBOX" TOSSED AROUND A LOT. I'M BETTING THE DELIVERY SITE IS CORTEZ'S TIGER-GUARDED WAREHOUSE.

THAT'LL MAKE IT PRETTY EASY TO INTERCEPT THE STUFF.

GREAT. JUST ONE MORE THING.

CORTEZ HAS BEEN CALLING ONE NUMBER A LOT SINCE I "LEFT TOWN." THAT'S OUR "CEO," NO DOUBT.

SO GET ME A NAME.

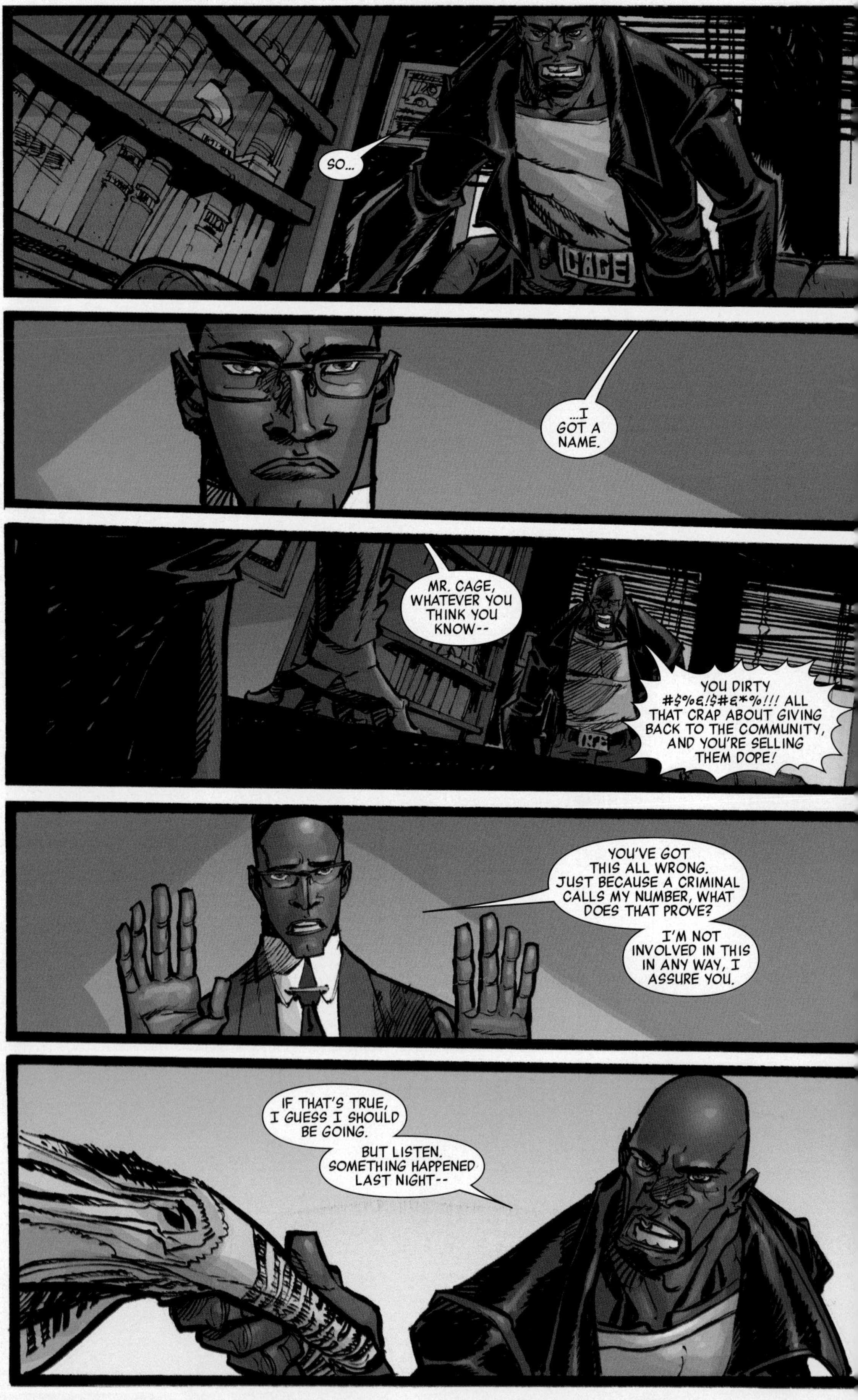
SO...
...I GOT A NAME.
MR. CAGE, WHATEVER YOU THINK YOU KNOW--
YOU DIRTY #$%&!$#&*%!!! ALL THAT CRAP ABOUT GIVING BACK TO THE COMMUNITY, AND YOU'RE SELLING THEM DOPE!
YOU'VE GOT THIS ALL WRONG. JUST BECAUSE A CRIMINAL CALLS MY NUMBER, WHAT DOES THAT PROVE?
I'M NOT INVOLVED IN THIS IN ANY WAY, I ASSURE YOU.
IF THAT'S TRUE, I GUESS I SHOULD BE GOING.
BUT LISTEN. SOMETHING HAPPENED LAST NIGHT--

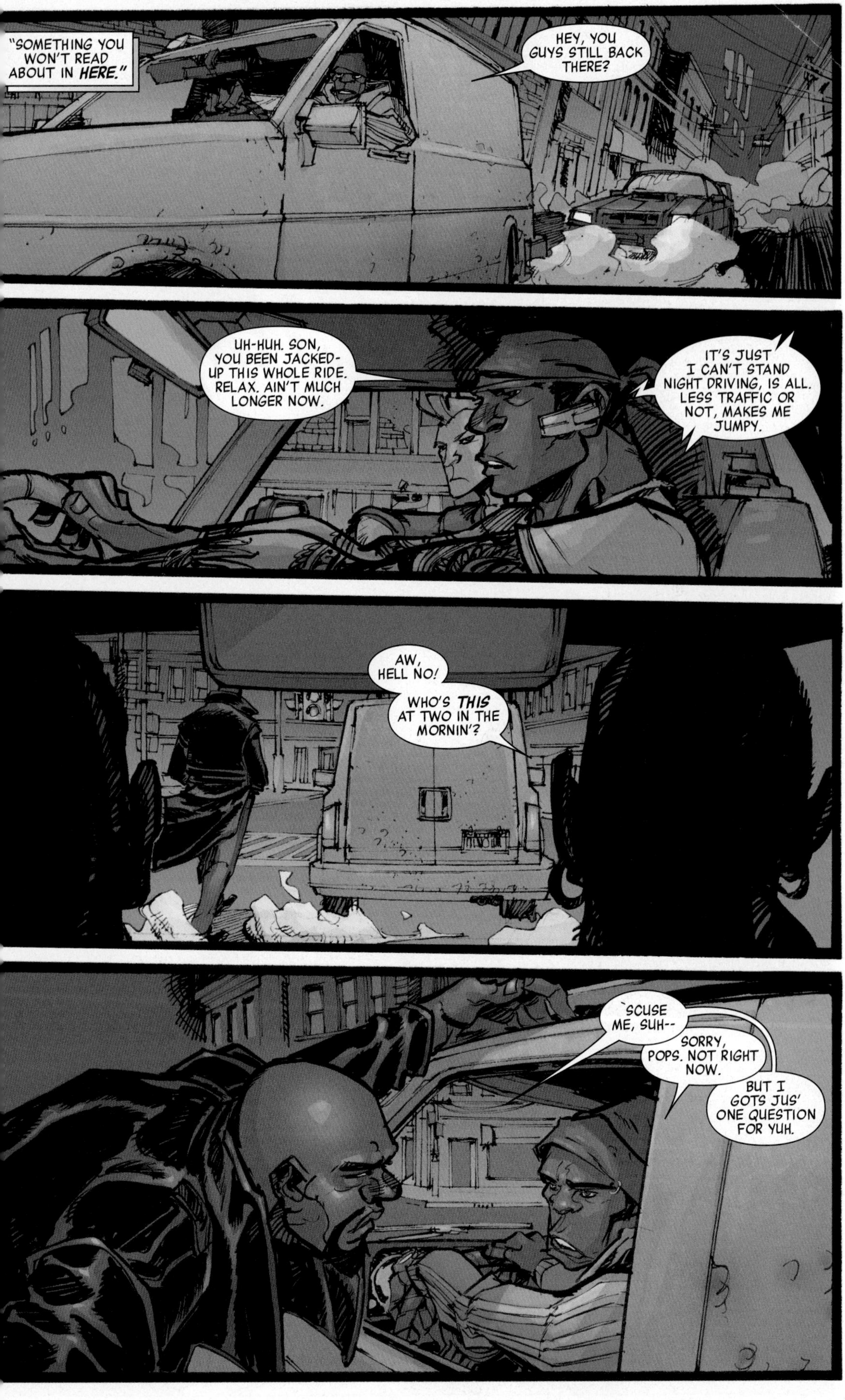
"SOMETHING YOU WON'T READ ABOUT IN *HERE.*"
HEY, YOU GUYS STILL BACK THERE?
UH-HUH. SON, YOU BEEN JACKED-UP THIS WHOLE RIDE. RELAX. AIN'T MUCH LONGER NOW.
IT'S JUST I CAN'T STAND NIGHT DRIVING, IS ALL. LESS TRAFFIC OR NOT, MAKES ME JUMPY.
AW, HELL NO!
WHO'S *THIS* AT TWO IN THE MORNIN'?
`SCUSE ME, SUH--
SORRY, POPS. NOT RIGHT NOW.
BUT I GOTS JUS' ONE QUESTION FOR YUH.

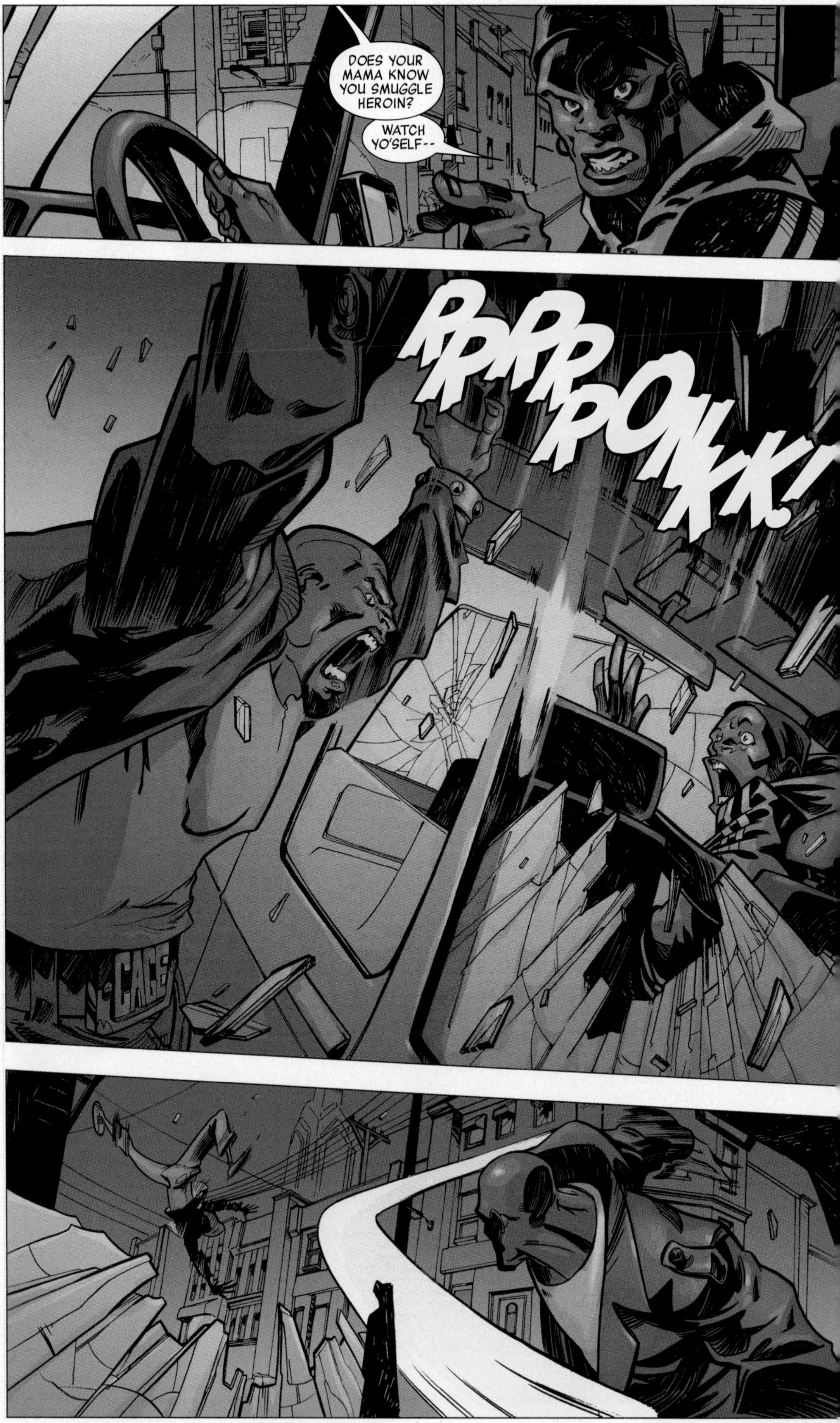
DOES YOUR MAMA KNOW YOU SMUGGLE HEROIN?
WATCH YO'SELF--
RRRRRONKK!
CAGE

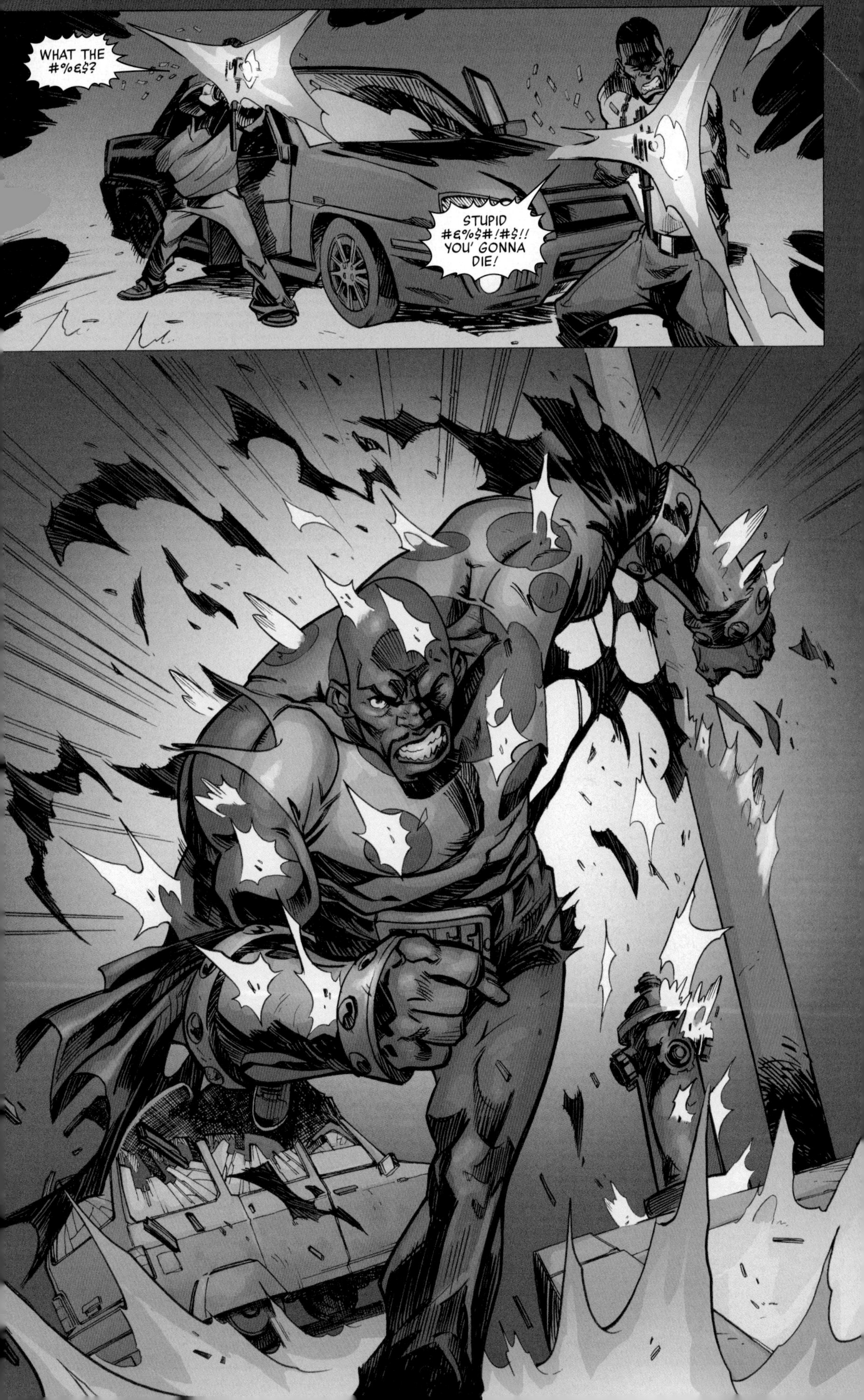
WHAT THE #%&$?
STUPID #&%$#!#$!! YOU' GONNA DIE!

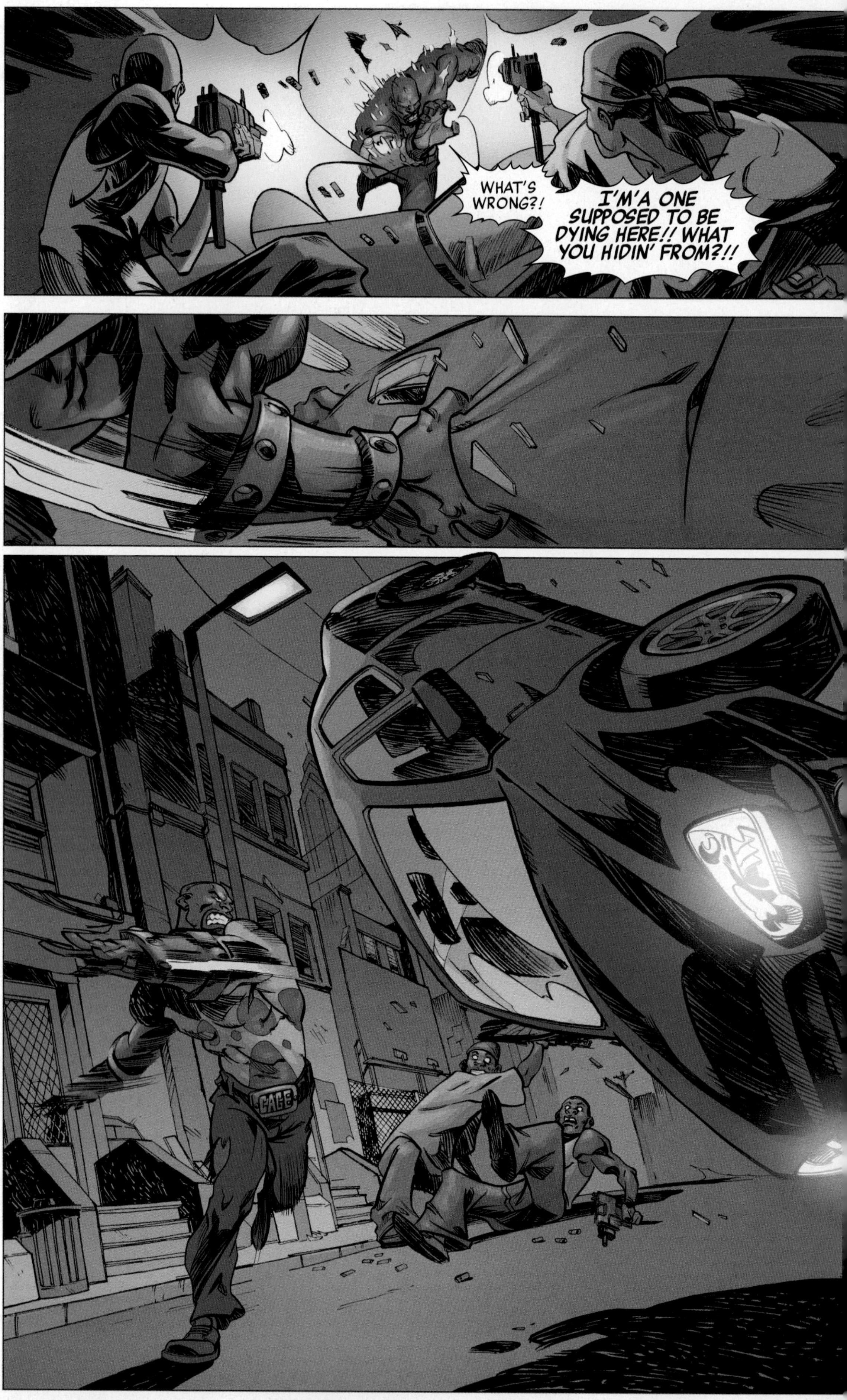
WHAT'S WRONG?!
I'M'A ONE SUPPOSED TO BE DYING HERE!! WHAT YOU HIDIN' FROM?!!
CAGE

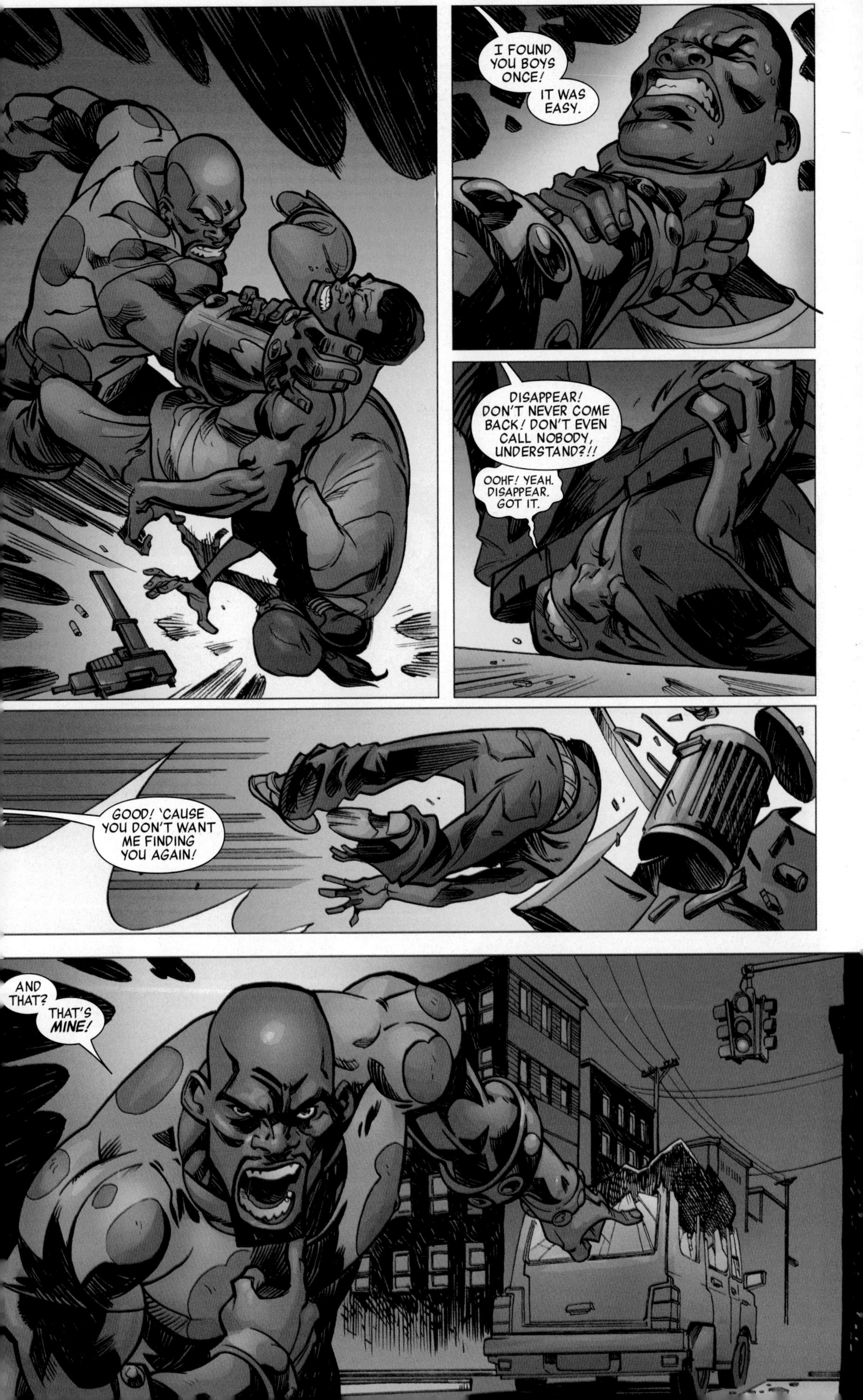
I FOUND YOU BOYS ONCE!
IT WAS EASY.
DISAPPEAR! DON'T NEVER COME BACK! DON'T EVEN CALL NOBODY, UNDERSTAND?!!
OOHF! YEAH. DISAPPEAR. GOT IT.
GOOD! 'CAUSE YOU DON'T WANT ME FINDING YOU AGAIN!
AND THAT?
THAT'S *MINE!*

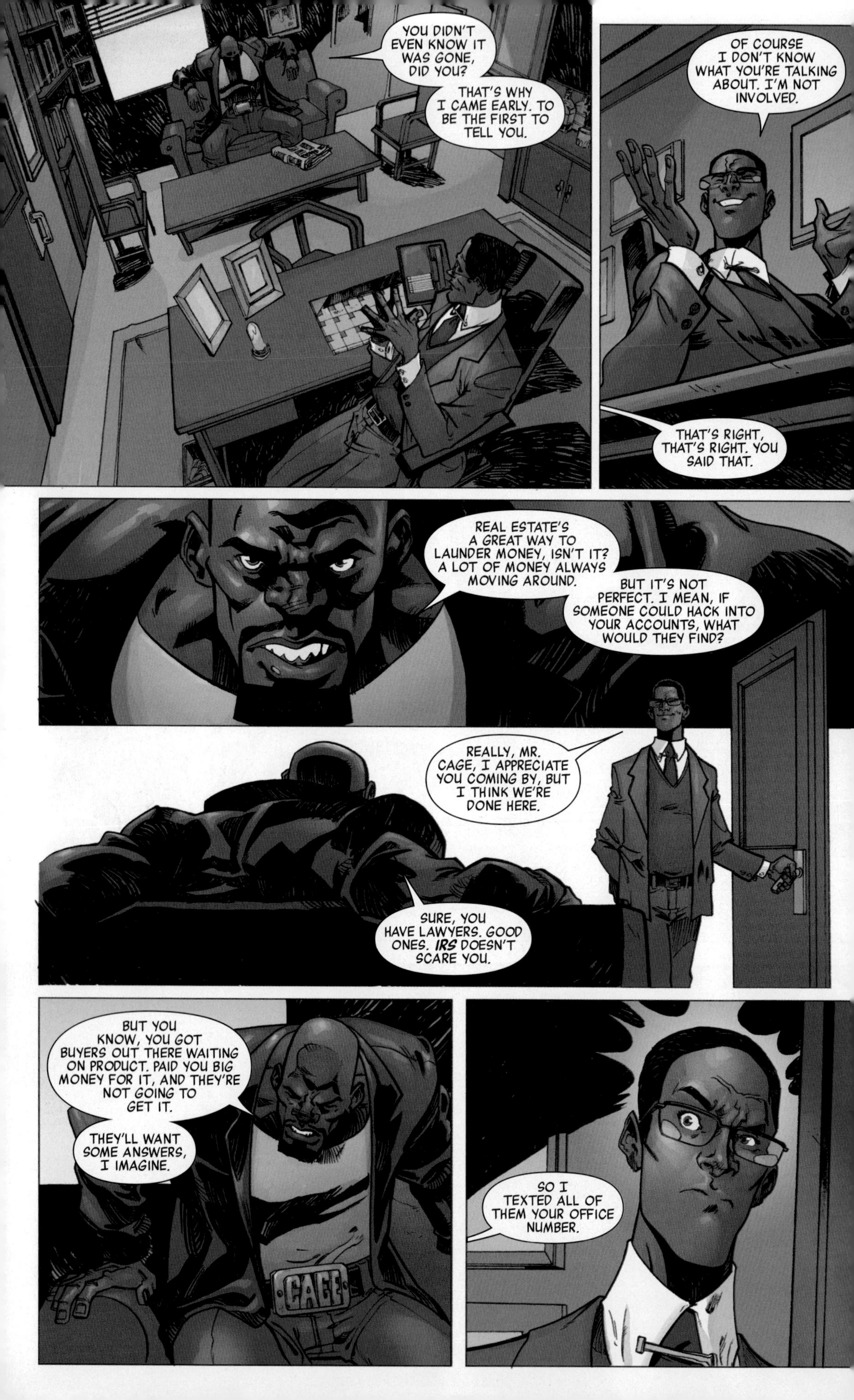
YOU DIDN'T EVEN KNOW IT WAS GONE, DID YOU?
THAT'S WHY I CAME EARLY. TO BE THE FIRST TO TELL YOU.
OF COURSE I DON'T KNOW WHAT YOU'RE TALKING ABOUT. I'M NOT INVOLVED.
THAT'S RIGHT, THAT'S RIGHT. YOU SAID THAT.
REAL ESTATE'S A GREAT WAY TO LAUNDER MONEY, ISN'T IT? A LOT OF MONEY ALWAYS MOVING AROUND.
BUT IT'S NOT PERFECT. I MEAN, IF SOMEONE COULD HACK INTO YOUR ACCOUNTS, WHAT WOULD THEY FIND?
REALLY, MR. CAGE, I APPRECIATE YOU COMING BY, BUT I THINK WE'RE DONE HERE.
SURE, YOU HAVE LAWYERS. GOOD ONES. IRS DOESN'T SCARE YOU.
BUT YOU KNOW, YOU GOT BUYERS OUT THERE WAITING ON PRODUCT. PAID YOU BIG MONEY FOR IT, AND THEY'RE NOT GOING TO GET IT.
THEY'LL WANT SOME ANSWERS, I IMAGINE.
CAGE
SO I TEXTED ALL OF THEM YOUR OFFICE NUMBER.

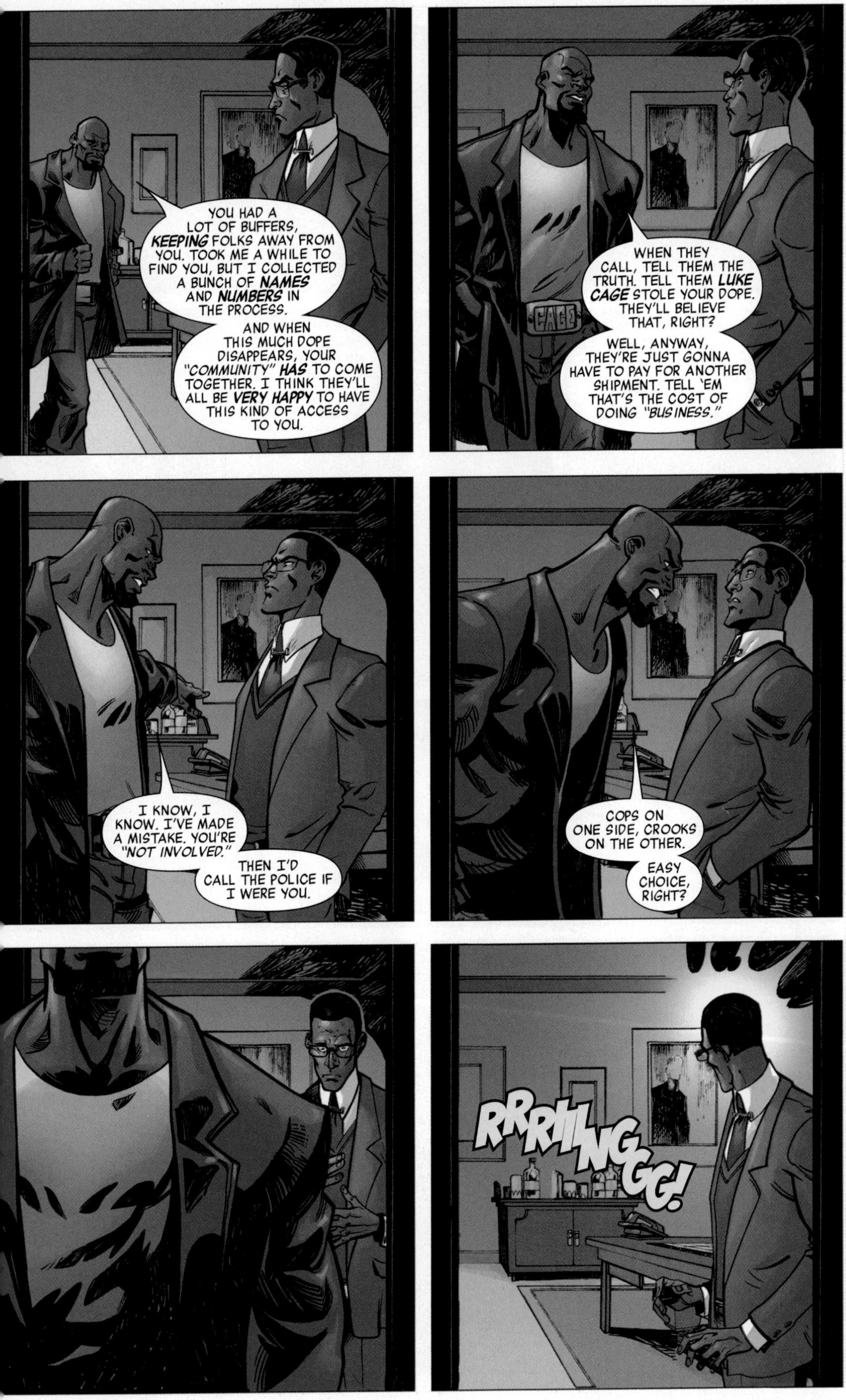
YOU HAD A LOT OF BUFFERS, KEEPING FOLKS AWAY FROM YOU. TOOK ME A WHILE TO FIND YOU, BUT I COLLECTED A BUNCH OF NAMES AND NUMBERS IN THE PROCESS.
AND WHEN THIS MUCH DOPE DISAPPEARS, YOUR "COMMUNITY" HAS TO COME TOGETHER. I THINK THEY'LL ALL BE VERY HAPPY TO HAVE THIS KIND OF ACCESS TO YOU.
CAGE
WHEN THEY CALL, TELL THEM THE TRUTH. TELL THEM LUKE CAGE STOLE YOUR DOPE. THEY'LL BELIEVE THAT, RIGHT?
WELL, ANYWAY, THEY'RE JUST GONNA HAVE TO PAY FOR ANOTHER SHIPMENT. TELL 'EM THAT'S THE COST OF DOING "BUSINESS."
I KNOW, I KNOW. I'VE MADE A MISTAKE. YOU'RE "NOT INVOLVED."
THEN I'D CALL THE POLICE IF I WERE YOU.
COPS ON ONE SIDE, CROOKS ON THE OTHER.
EASY CHOICE, RIGHT?
RRRIIINGGG!

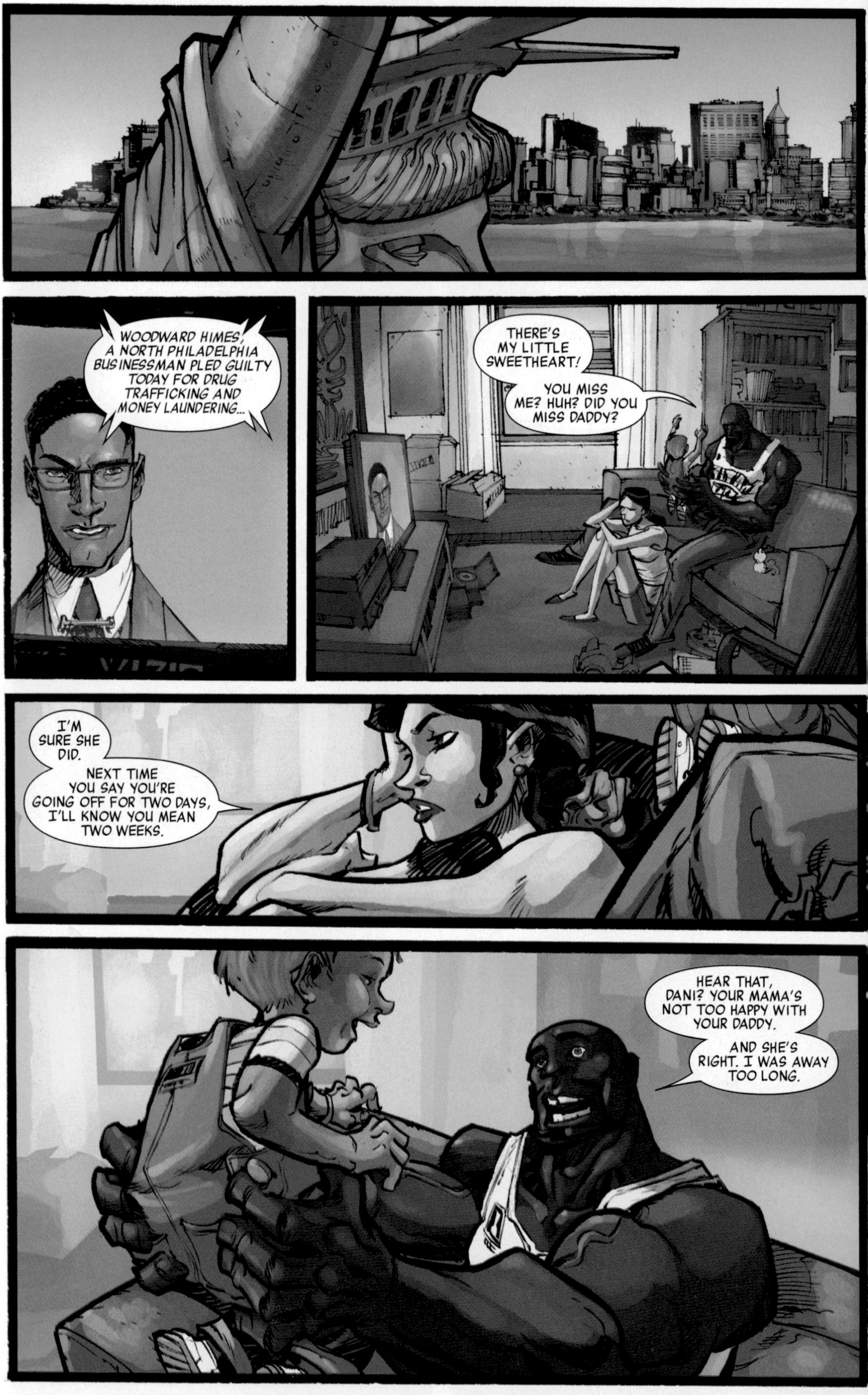
WOODWARD HIMES, A NORTH PHILADELPHIA BUSINESSMAN PLED GUILTY TODAY FOR DRUG TRAFFICKING AND MONEY LAUNDERING...
THERE'S MY LITTLE SWEETHEART!
YOU MISS ME? HUH? DID YOU MISS DADDY?
I'M SURE SHE DID.
NEXT TIME YOU SAY YOU'RE GOING OFF FOR TWO DAYS, I'LL KNOW YOU MEAN TWO WEEKS.
HEAR THAT, DANI? YOUR MAMA'S NOT TOO HAPPY WITH YOUR DADDY.
AND SHE'S RIGHT. I WAS AWAY TOO LONG.

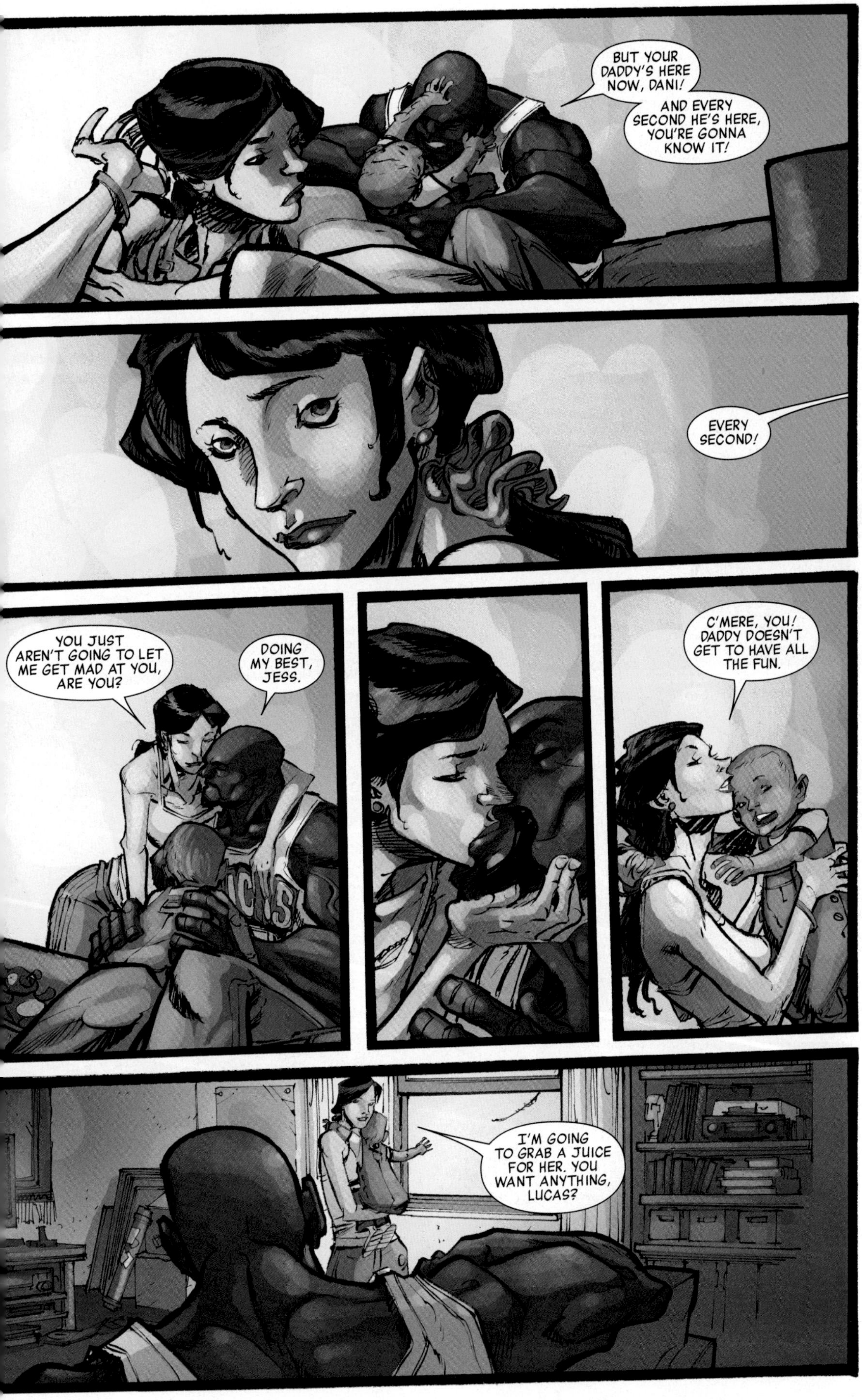
BUT YOUR DADDY'S HERE NOW, DANI!
AND EVERY SECOND HE'S HERE, YOU'RE GONNA KNOW IT!
EVERY SECOND!
YOU JUST AREN'T GOING TO LET ME GET MAD AT YOU, ARE YOU?
DOING MY BEST, JESS.
C'MERE, YOU! DADDY DOESN'T GET TO HAVE ALL THE FUN.
I'M GOING TO GRAB A JUICE FOR HER. YOU WANT ANYTHING, LUCAS?

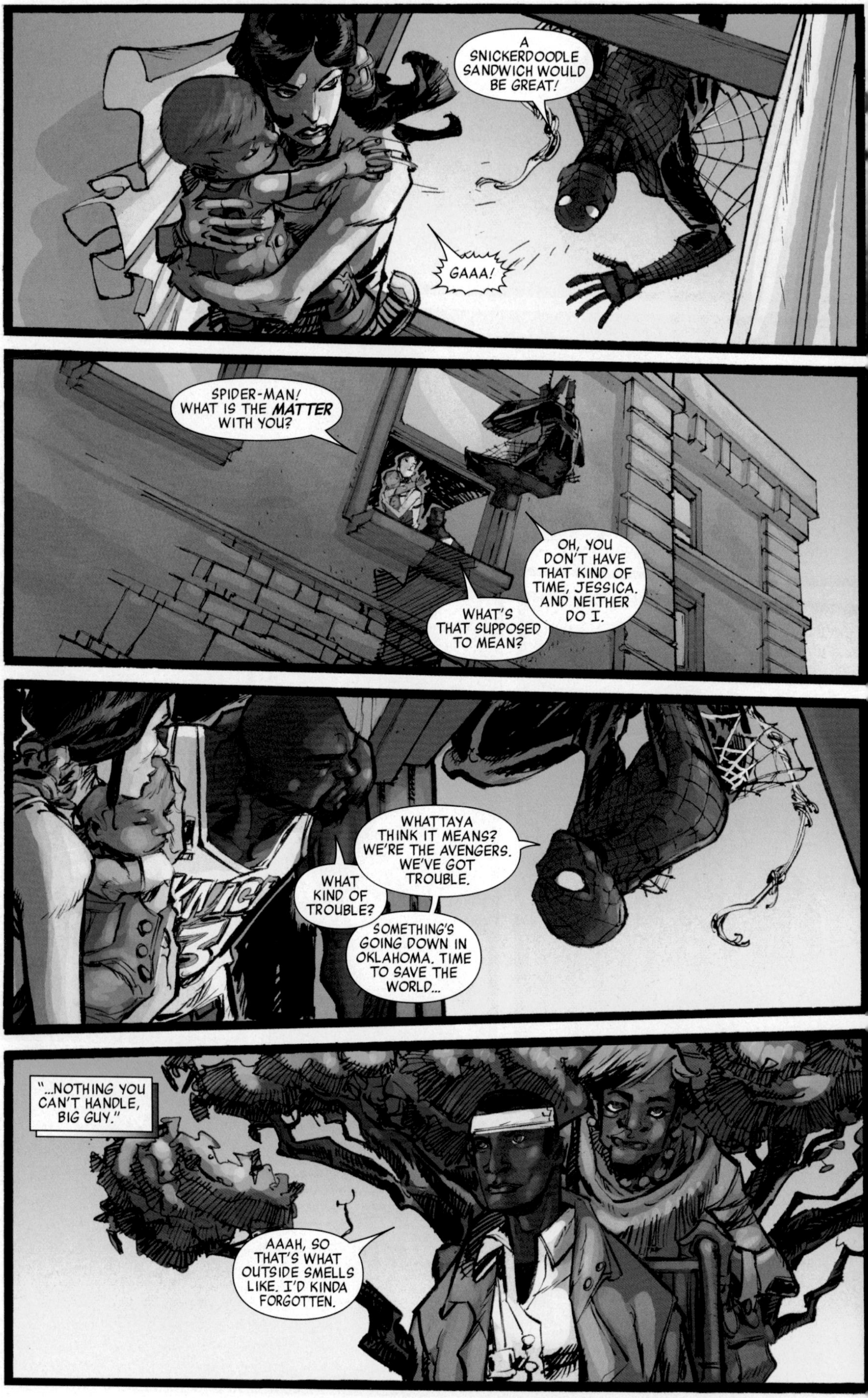
A SNICKERDOODLE SANDWICH WOULD BE GREAT!
GAAA!
SPIDER-MAN! WHAT IS THE MATTER WITH YOU?
OH, YOU DON'T HAVE THAT KIND OF TIME, JESSICA. AND NEITHER DO I.
WHAT'S THAT SUPPOSED TO MEAN?
WHATTAYA THINK IT MEANS? WE'RE THE AVENGERS. WE'VE GOT TROUBLE.
WHAT KIND OF TROUBLE?
SOMETHING'S GOING DOWN IN OKLAHOMA. TIME TO SAVE THE WORLD...
"...NOTHING YOU CAN'T HANDLE, BIG GUY."
AAAH, SO THAT'S WHAT OUTSIDE SMELLS LIKE. I'D KINDA FORGOTTEN.

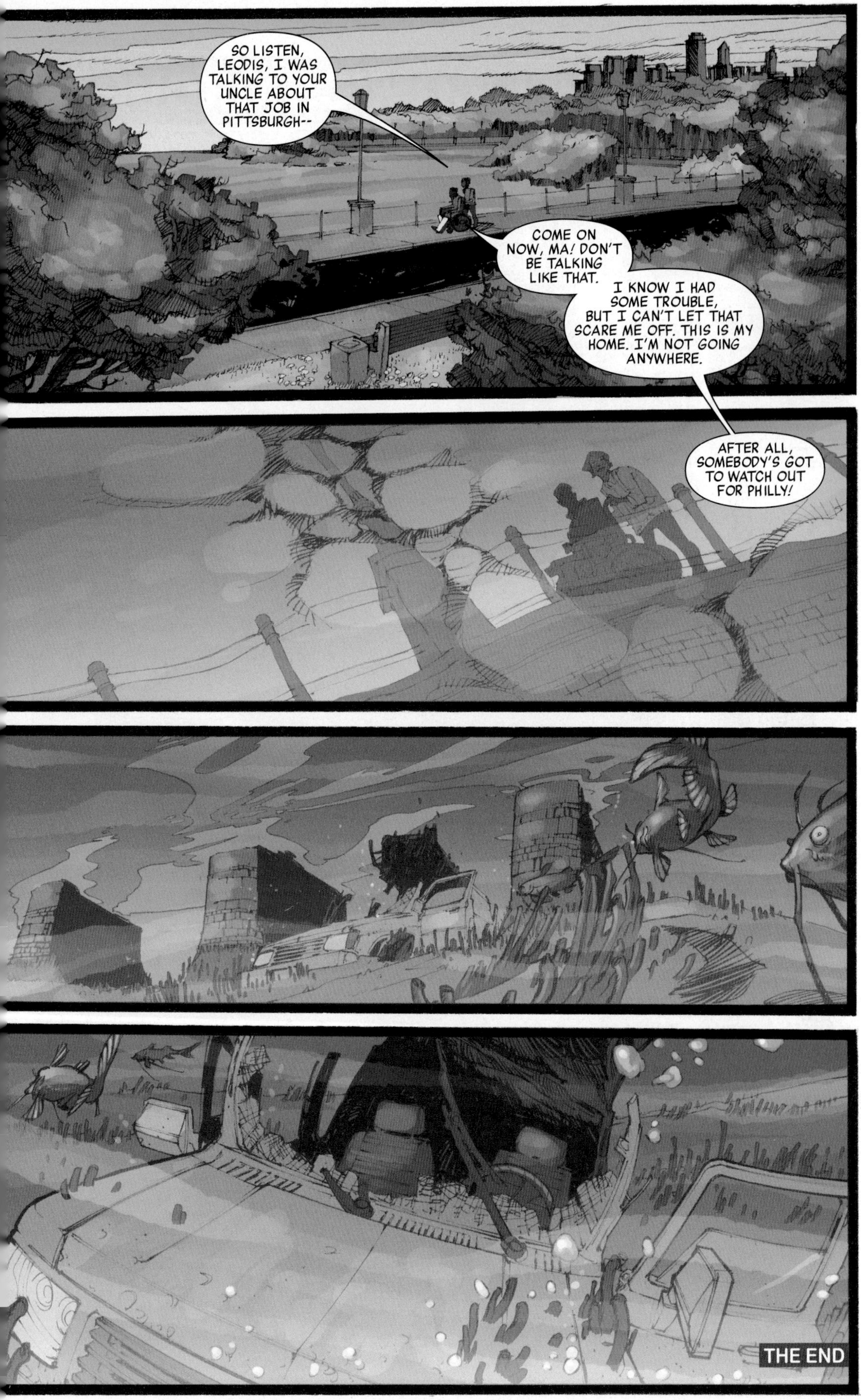
SO LISTEN, LEODIS, I WAS TALKING TO YOUR UNCLE ABOUT THAT JOB IN PITTSBURGH--
COME ON NOW, MA! DON'T BE TALKING LIKE THAT.
I KNOW I HAD SOME TROUBLE, BUT I CAN'T LET THAT SCARE ME OFF. THIS IS MY HOME. I'M NOT GOING ANYWHERE.
AFTER ALL, SOMEBODY'S GOT TO WATCH OUT FOR PHILLY!
THE END

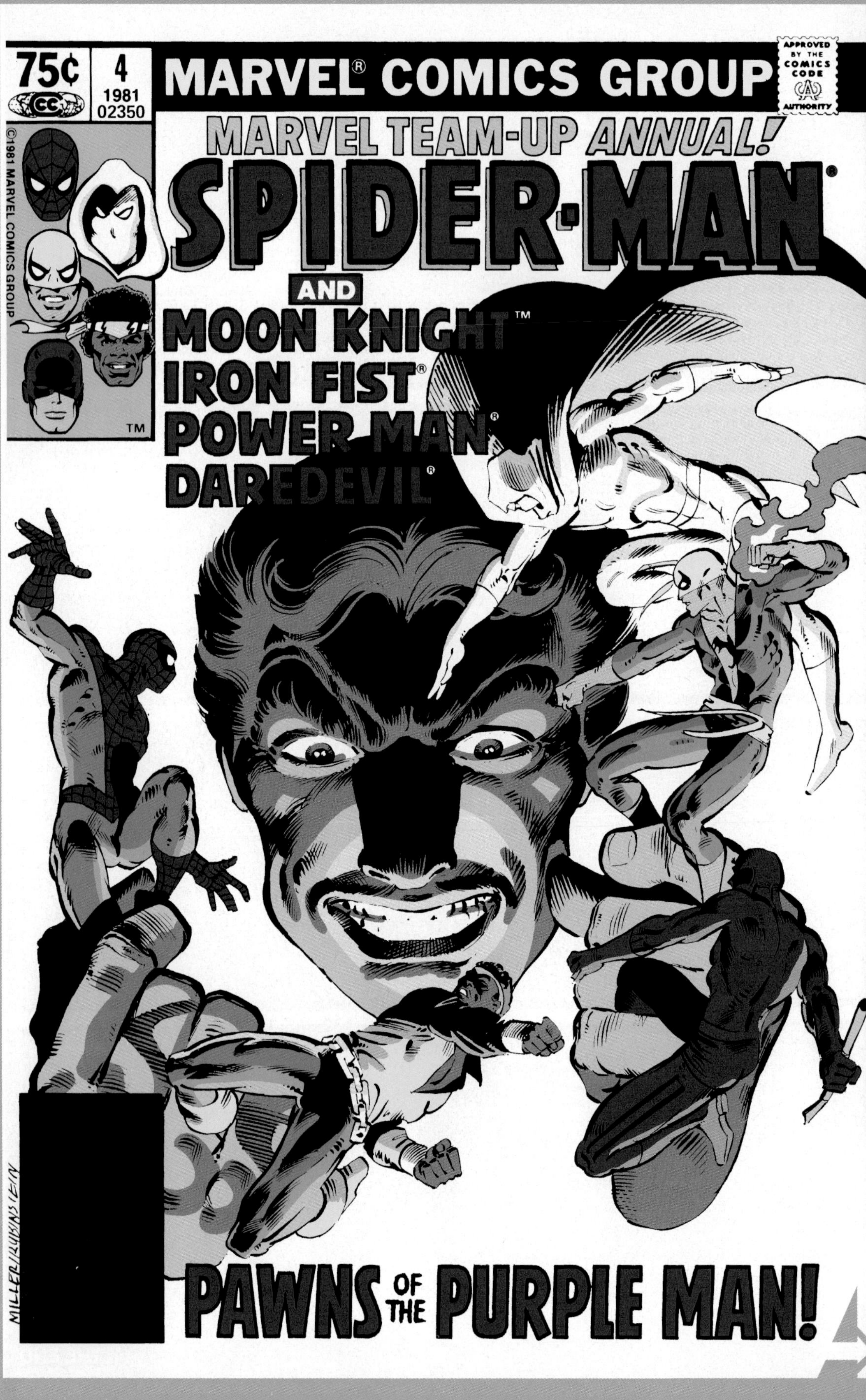
75¢
4
1981
02350
MARVEL® COMICS GROUP
APPROVED BY THE COMICS CODE AUTHORITY
©1981 MARVEL COMICS GROUP
TM
MARVEL TEAM-UP ANNUAL!
SPIDER-MAN®
AND
MOON KNIGHT™
IRON FIST®
POWER MAN®
DAREDEVIL®
PAWNS OF THE PURPLE MAN!

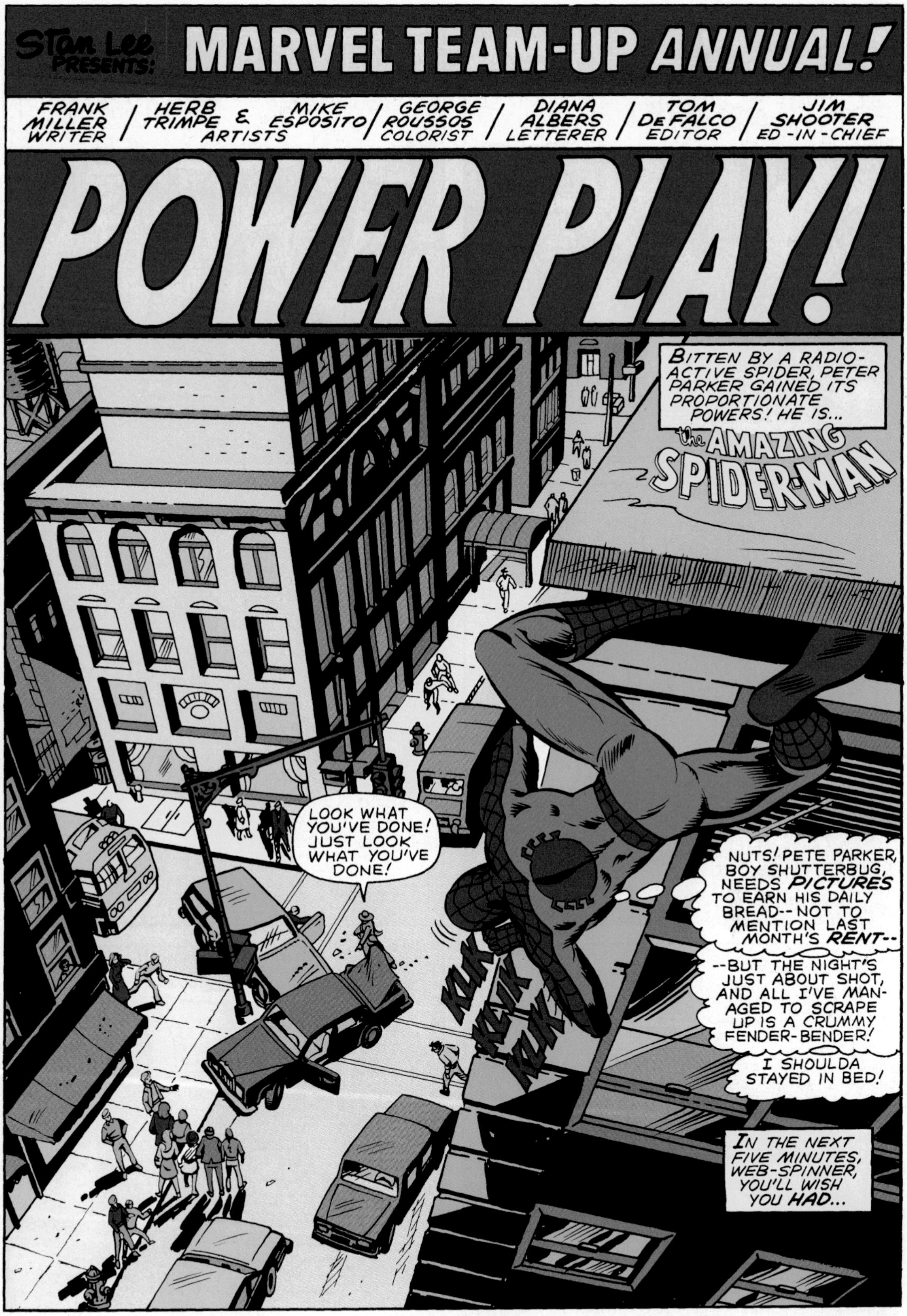
Stan Lee PRESENTS:
MARVEL TEAM-UP ANNUAL!
FRANK MILLER WRITER
HERB TRIMPE & MIKE ESPOSITO ARTISTS
GEORGE ROUSSOS COLORIST
DIANA ALBERS LETTERER
TOM DEFALCO EDITOR
JIM SHOOTER ED-IN-CHIEF
POWER PLAY!
BITTEN BY A RADIO-ACTIVE SPIDER, PETER PARKER GAINED ITS PROPORTIONATE POWERS! HE IS...
the AMAZING SPIDER-MAN
LOOK WHAT YOU'VE DONE! JUST LOOK WHAT YOU'VE DONE!
NUTS! PETE PARKER, BOY SHUTTERBUG, NEEDS PICTURES TO EARN HIS DAILY BREAD-- NOT TO MENTION LAST MONTH'S RENT--
--BUT THE NIGHT'S JUST ABOUT SHOT, AND ALL I'VE MAN-AGED TO SCRAPE UP IS A CRUMMY FENDER-BENDER!
I SHOULDA STAYED IN BED!
KLIK KLIK KLIK
IN THE NEXT FIVE MINUTES, WEB-SPINNER, YOU'LL WISH YOU HAD...

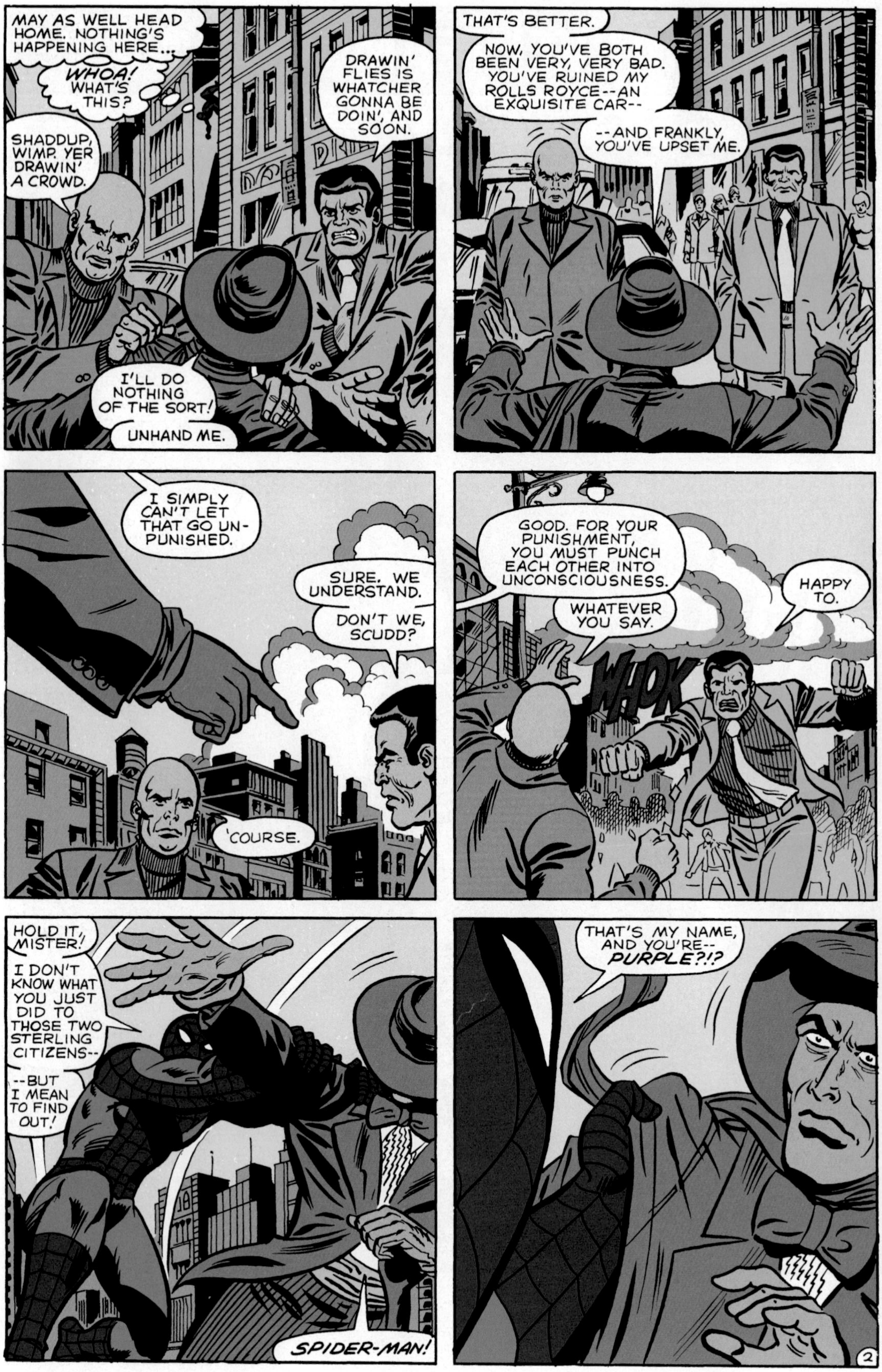
MAY AS WELL HEAD HOME. NOTHING'S HAPPENING HERE...
WHOA! WHAT'S THIS?
SHADDUP, WIMP. YER DRAWIN' A CROWD.
DRAWIN' FLIES IS WHATCHER GONNA BE DOIN', AND SOON.
I'LL DO NOTHING OF THE SORT!
UNHAND ME.
THAT'S BETTER.
NOW, YOU'VE BOTH BEEN VERY, VERY BAD. YOU'VE RUINED MY ROLLS ROYCE--AN EXQUISITE CAR--
--AND FRANKLY, YOU'VE UPSET ME.
I SIMPLY CAN'T LET THAT GO UN-PUNISHED.
SURE. WE UNDERSTAND.
DON'T WE, SCUDD?
'COURSE.
GOOD. FOR YOUR PUNISHMENT, YOU MUST PUNCH EACH OTHER INTO UNCONSCIOUSNESS.
WHATEVER YOU SAY.
HAPPY TO.
WHOK
HOLD IT, MISTER!
I DON'T KNOW WHAT YOU JUST DID TO THOSE TWO STERLING CITIZENS--
--BUT I MEAN TO FIND OUT!
SPIDER-MAN!
THAT'S MY NAME, AND YOU'RE-- PURPLE?!?
2

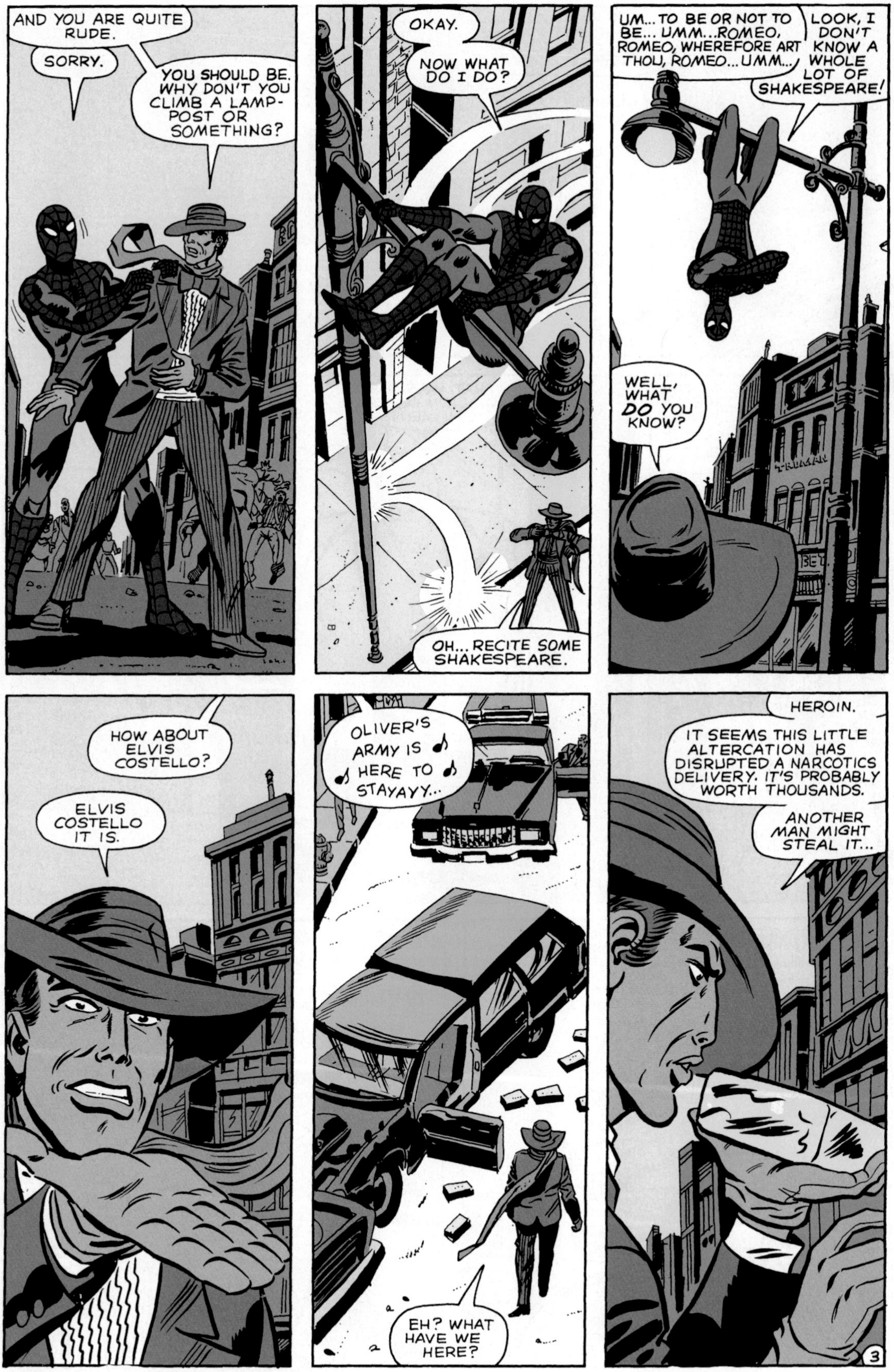
AND YOU ARE QUITE RUDE.
SORRY.
YOU SHOULD BE. WHY DON'T YOU CLIMB A LAMP-POST OR SOMETHING?
OKAY.
NOW WHAT DO I DO?
OH... RECITE SOME SHAKESPEARE.
UM... TO BE OR NOT TO BE... UMM...ROMEO, ROMEO, WHEREFORE ART THOU, ROMEO... UMM...
LOOK, I DON'T KNOW A WHOLE LOT OF SHAKESPEARE!
WELL, WHAT DO YOU KNOW?
TRUMAN
HOW ABOUT ELVIS COSTELLO?
ELVIS COSTELLO IT IS.
OLIVER'S ARMY IS HERE TO STAYAYY...
EH? WHAT HAVE WE HERE?
HEROIN.
IT SEEMS THIS LITTLE ALTERCATION HAS DISRUPTED A NARCOTICS DELIVERY. IT'S PROBABLY WORTH THOUSANDS.
ANOTHER MAN MIGHT STEAL IT...
3

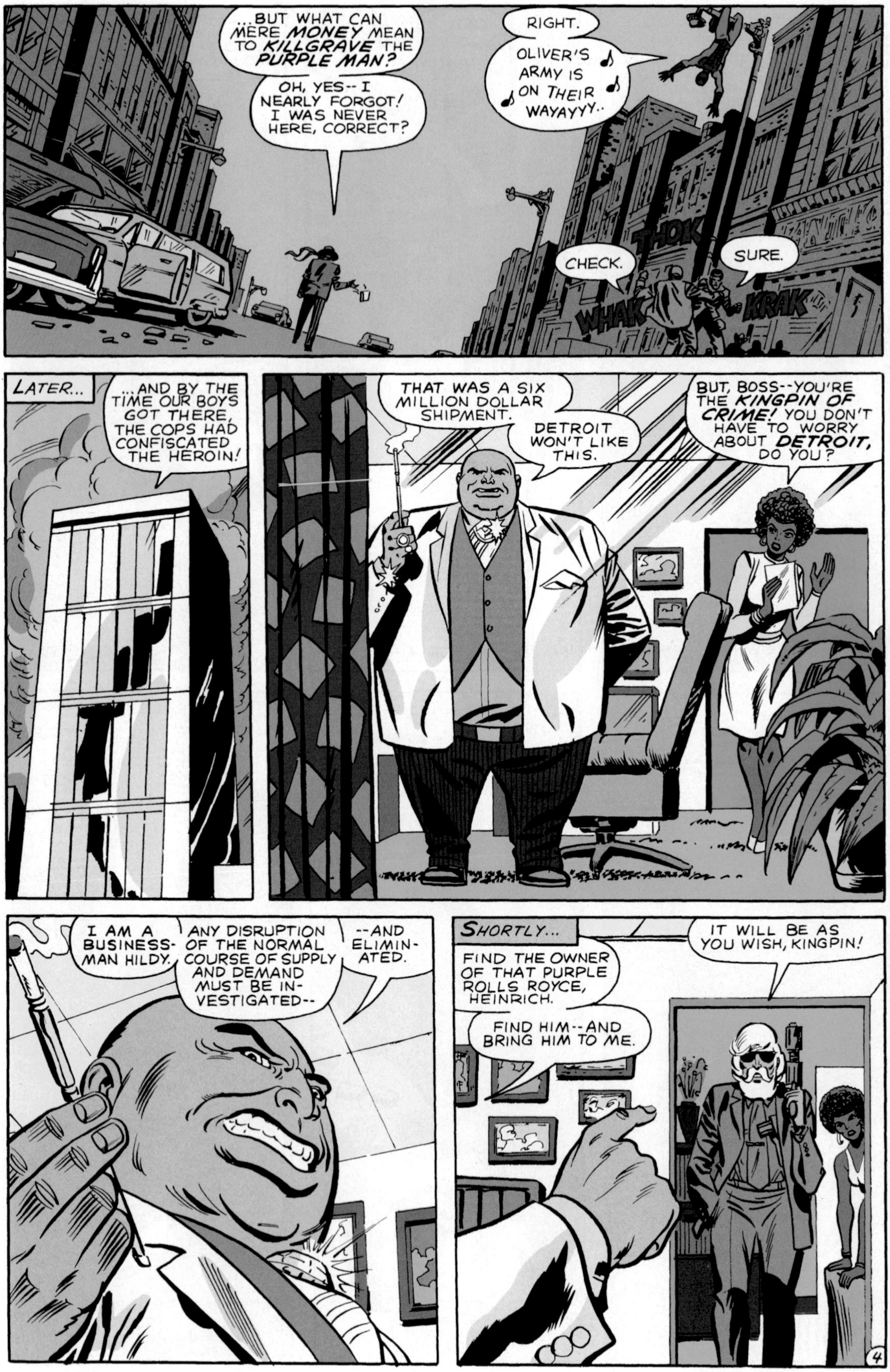

...BUT WHAT CAN MERE MONEY MEAN TO KILLGRAVE THE PURPLE MAN?
OH, YES-- I NEARLY FORGOT! I WAS NEVER HERE, CORRECT?
RIGHT.
OLIVER'S ARMY IS ON THEIR WAYAYYY..
THOK
CHECK.
SURE.
WHAK
KRAK
LATER...
...AND BY THE TIME OUR BOYS GOT THERE, THE COPS HAD CONFISCATED THE HEROIN!
THAT WAS A SIX MILLION DOLLAR SHIPMENT.
DETROIT WON'T LIKE THIS.
BUT, BOSS--YOU'RE THE KINGPIN OF CRIME! YOU DON'T HAVE TO WORRY ABOUT DETROIT, DO YOU?
I AM A BUSINESS-MAN HILDY.
ANY DISRUPTION OF THE NORMAL COURSE OF SUPPLY AND DEMAND MUST BE IN-VESTIGATED--
--AND ELIMIN-ATED.
SHORTLY...
FIND THE OWNER OF THAT PURPLE ROLLS ROYCE, HEINRICH.
FIND HIM--AND BRING HIM TO ME.
IT WILL BE AS YOU WISH, KINGPIN!
4

MEAN-WHILE...

YOU DON'T REMEMBER? YOU DON'T REMEMBER?

POLICE

YOU SPEND TWO HOURS DUKIN' IT OUT ON FIFTH AVENUE, AND YA SIT THERE AND TELL ME YA DON'T REMEMBER *WHY?*

C'MON, LOOTENANT! YA KNOW WE'D TELL YA IF'N WE KNEW!

YEAH! WE'RE LAW-ABIDIN' CITIZENS!

LAW ABIDING MY--

DON'T BE TOO HARD ON THEM, NICK.

DAREDEVIL!? WHATTA YOU WANT?

I KNOW THE *PURPLE MAN.* I FOUGHT HIM MANY TIMES.

THOSE MEN ARE TELLING THE TRUTH.

WHATTA *YOU* KNOW?

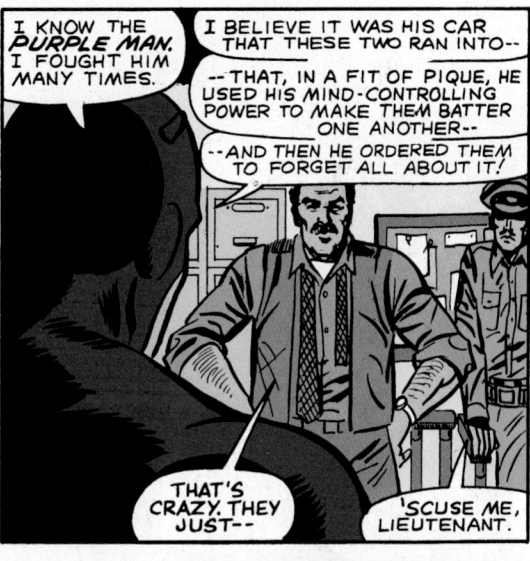

I BELIEVE IT WAS HIS CAR THAT THESE TWO RAN INTO--

--THAT, IN A FIT OF PIQUE, HE USED HIS MIND-CONTROLLING POWER TO MAKE THEM BATTER ONE ANOTHER--

--AND THEN HE ORDERED THEM TO FORGET ALL ABOUT IT!

THAT'S CRAZY. THEY JUST--

'SCUSE ME, LIEUTENANT.

WE'VE TRACED THE REGISTRATION ON THE PURPLE ROLLS. IT'S OWNED BY A *ZEBEDIAH KILLGRAVE.* HIS ADDRESS CHECKS OUT TO BE THREE BLOCKS IN THE EAST RIVER--

--SO WE CHECKED THE LOCAL HOTEL REGISTERS, AND FOUND HIM BOOKED AT THE MOST EXPENSIVE SUITE AT THE PLAZA!

NICE WORK DELANY.

HEY, HORNHEAD-- HOW'D YOU KNOW ABOUT ALL THIS?

HORNHEAD?

BLAST HIM! HE ALWAYS DOES THAT TO ME!

5

159

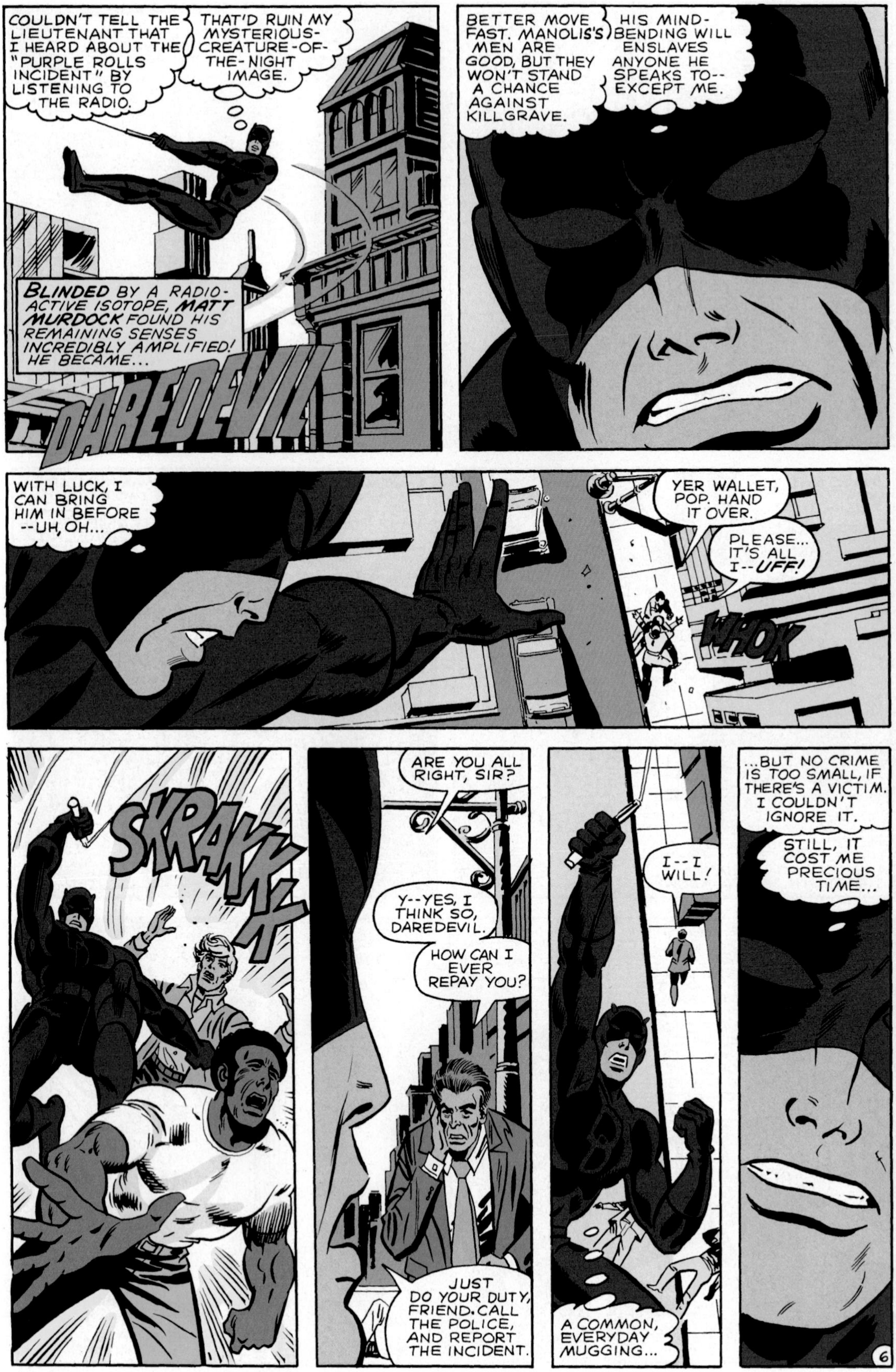
COULDN'T TELL THE LIEUTENANT THAT I HEARD ABOUT THE "PURPLE ROLLS INCIDENT" BY LISTENING TO THE RADIO.
THAT'D RUIN MY MYSTERIOUS-CREATURE-OF-THE-NIGHT IMAGE.
BLINDED BY A RADIO-ACTIVE ISOTOPE, MATT MURDOCK FOUND HIS REMAINING SENSES INCREDIBLY AMPLIFIED! HE BECAME...
DAREDEVIL
BETTER MOVE FAST. MANOLIS'S MEN ARE GOOD, BUT THEY WON'T STAND A CHANCE AGAINST KILLGRAVE.
HIS MIND-BENDING WILL ENSLAVES ANYONE HE SPEAKS TO--EXCEPT ME.
WITH LUCK, I CAN BRING HIM IN BEFORE --UH, OH...
YER WALLET, POP. HAND IT OVER.
PLEASE... IT'S ALL I--UFF!
WHOK
SKRAKKK
ARE YOU ALL RIGHT, SIR?
Y--YES, I THINK SO, DAREDEVIL.
HOW CAN I EVER REPAY YOU?
JUST DO YOUR DUTY, FRIEND. CALL THE POLICE, AND REPORT THE INCIDENT.
I--I WILL!
A COMMON, EVERYDAY MUGGING...
...BUT NO CRIME IS TOO SMALL, IF THERE'S A VICTIM. I COULDN'T IGNORE IT.
STILL, IT COST ME PRECIOUS TIME...
6

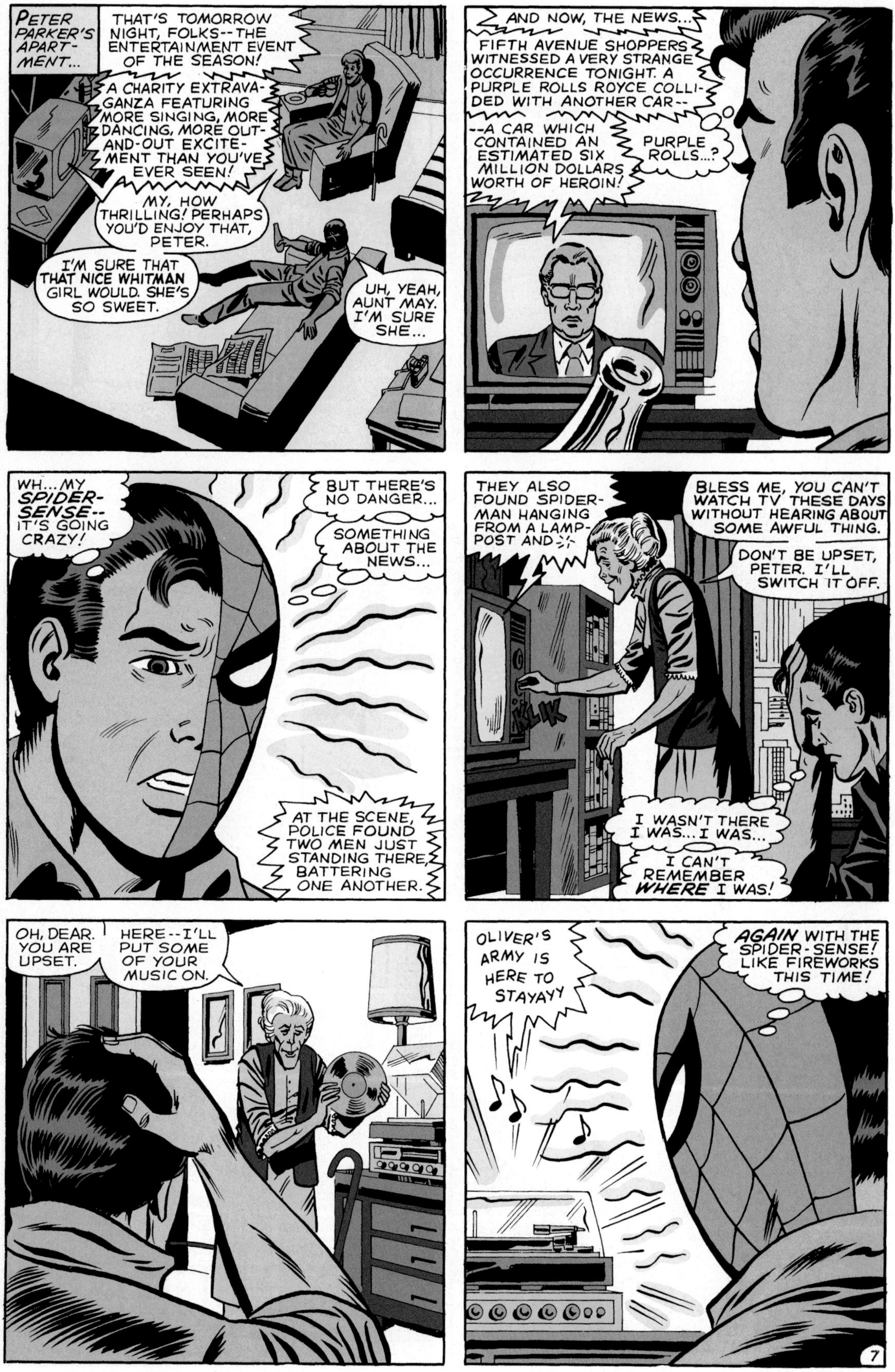
PETER PARKER'S APARTMENT...
THAT'S TOMORROW NIGHT, FOLKS--THE ENTERTAINMENT EVENT OF THE SEASON!
A CHARITY EXTRAVAGANZA FEATURING MORE SINGING, MORE DANCING, MORE OUT-AND-OUT EXCITEMENT THAN YOU'VE EVER SEEN!
MY, HOW THRILLING! PERHAPS YOU'D ENJOY THAT, PETER.
I'M SURE THAT THAT NICE WHITMAN GIRL WOULD. SHE'S SO SWEET.
UH, YEAH, AUNT MAY. I'M SURE SHE...
AND NOW, THE NEWS...
FIFTH AVENUE SHOPPERS WITNESSED A VERY STRANGE OCCURRENCE TONIGHT. A PURPLE ROLLS ROYCE COLLIDED WITH ANOTHER CAR--
--A CAR WHICH CONTAINED AN ESTIMATED SIX MILLION DOLLARS WORTH OF HEROIN!
PURPLE ROLLS...?
WH... MY SPIDER-SENSE-- IT'S GOING CRAZY!
BUT THERE'S NO DANGER...
SOMETHING ABOUT THE NEWS...
AT THE SCENE, POLICE FOUND TWO MEN JUST STANDING THERE, BATTERING ONE ANOTHER.
THEY ALSO FOUND SPIDER-MAN HANGING FROM A LAMP-POST AND
BLESS ME, YOU CAN'T WATCH TV THESE DAYS WITHOUT HEARING ABOUT SOME AWFUL THING.
DON'T BE UPSET, PETER. I'LL SWITCH IT OFF.
KLIK
I WASN'T THERE I WAS... I WAS...
I CAN'T REMEMBER WHERE I WAS!
OH, DEAR. YOU ARE UPSET.
HERE--I'LL PUT SOME OF YOUR MUSIC ON.
OLIVER'S ARMY IS HERE TO STAYAYY
AGAIN WITH THE SPIDER-SENSE! LIKE FIREWORKS THIS TIME!
7

NO WAY AROUND IT. SOMETHING HAPPENED TO ME TONIGHT-- SOMETHING I CAN'T REMEMBER.

MAYBE--JUST MAYBE--I TOOK PICTURES OF IT!

PETER! WHAT'S WRONG?

UH...NOTHING, AUNT MAY! I JUST REMEMBERED--I'VE GOT TO RUSH SOME PICTURES OVER TO THE DAILY BUGLE, OR JONAH JAMESON-- MY FRIENDLY NEIGHBORHOOD NEWSPAPER PUBLISHER--WILL HAVE MY HEAD!

POOR BOY. HE'S SO HIGH STRUNG, AND SENSITIVE!

THERE'S AN EXTRA SHOT ON THIS ROLL.

THE PLOT THICKENS.

YES... IT'S ALL COMING BACK NOW...

THE FENDER-BENDER...THE PURPLE ROLLS...

...AND THE PURPLE MAN...

MY SPIDER-SENSE SEEMS TO BE SET OFF BY THIS PURPLE GUY. I MAY BE ABLE TO FIND HIM WITH IT, IF I COVER ENOUGH OF THE CITY.

IF I WERE DAREDEVIL, I'D PROBABLY KNOW WHICH HOODS TO PUNCH OUT TO FIND WHAT I NEED.

BUT I'M NOT. SO I'LL JUST BLUNDER ALONG...

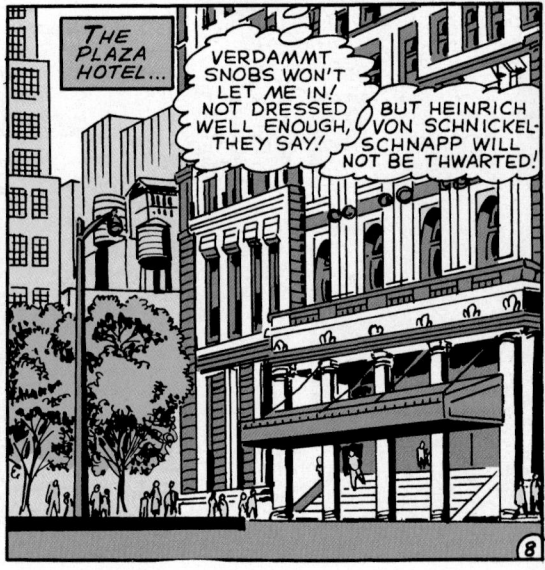

THE PLAZA HOTEL...

VERDAMMT SNOBS WON'T LET ME IN! NOT DRESSED WELL ENOUGH, THEY SAY!

BUT HEINRICH VON SCHNICKEL-SCHNAPP WILL NOT BE THWARTED!

8

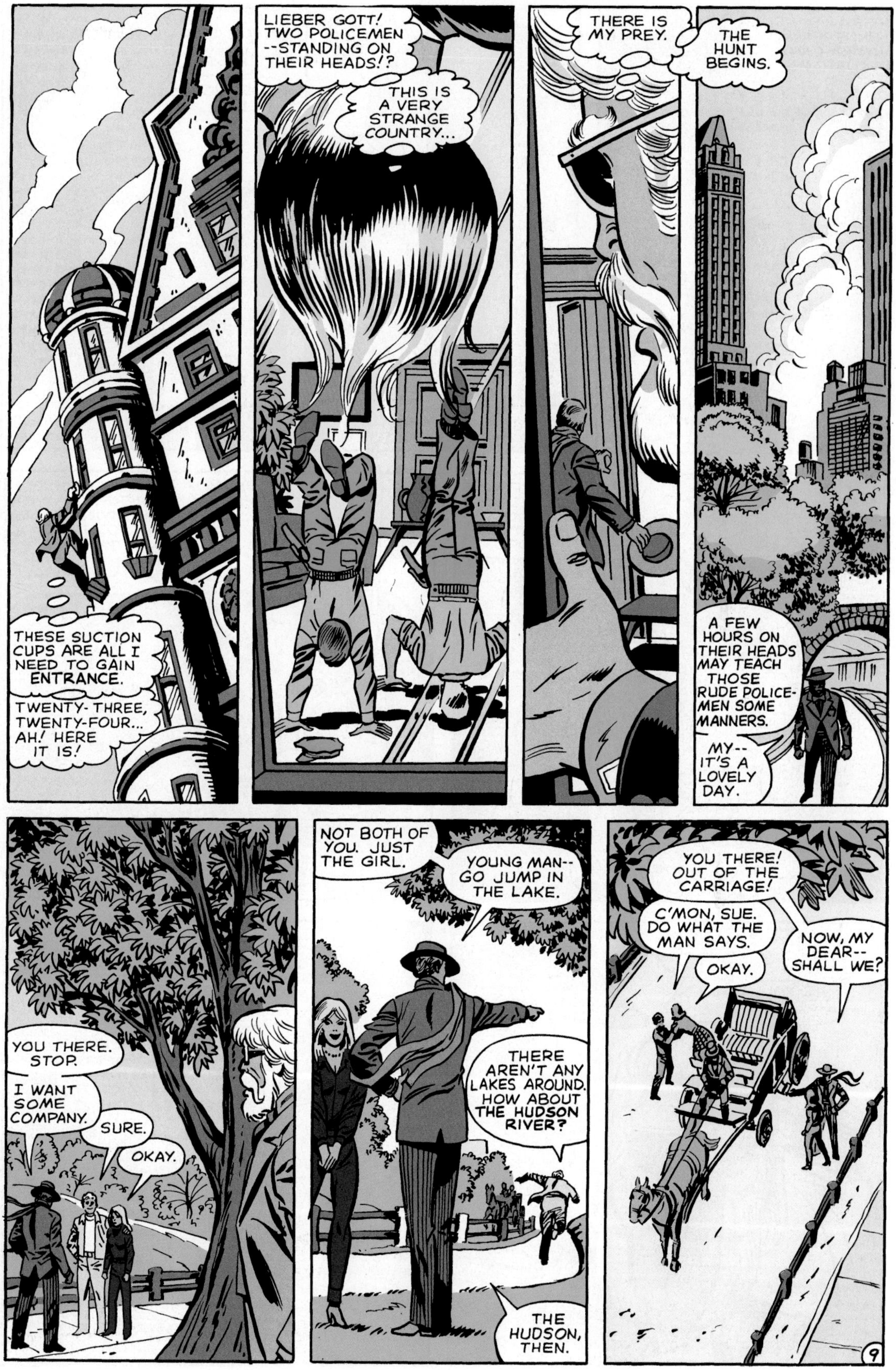
THESE SUCTION CUPS ARE ALL I NEED TO GAIN ENTRANCE.
TWENTY-THREE, TWENTY-FOUR... AH! HERE IT IS!
LIEBER GOTT! TWO POLICEMEN --STANDING ON THEIR HEADS!?
THIS IS A VERY STRANGE COUNTRY...
THERE IS MY PREY.
THE HUNT BEGINS.
A FEW HOURS ON THEIR HEADS MAY TEACH THOSE RUDE POLICEMEN SOME MANNERS.
MY-- IT'S A LOVELY DAY.
YOU THERE. STOP.
I WANT SOME COMPANY.
SURE.
OKAY.
NOT BOTH OF YOU. JUST THE GIRL.
YOUNG MAN-- GO JUMP IN THE LAKE.
THERE AREN'T ANY LAKES AROUND. HOW ABOUT THE HUDSON RIVER?
THE HUDSON, THEN.
YOU THERE! OUT OF THE CARRIAGE!
C'MON, SUE. DO WHAT THE MAN SAYS.
OKAY.
NOW, MY DEAR-- SHALL WE?
9

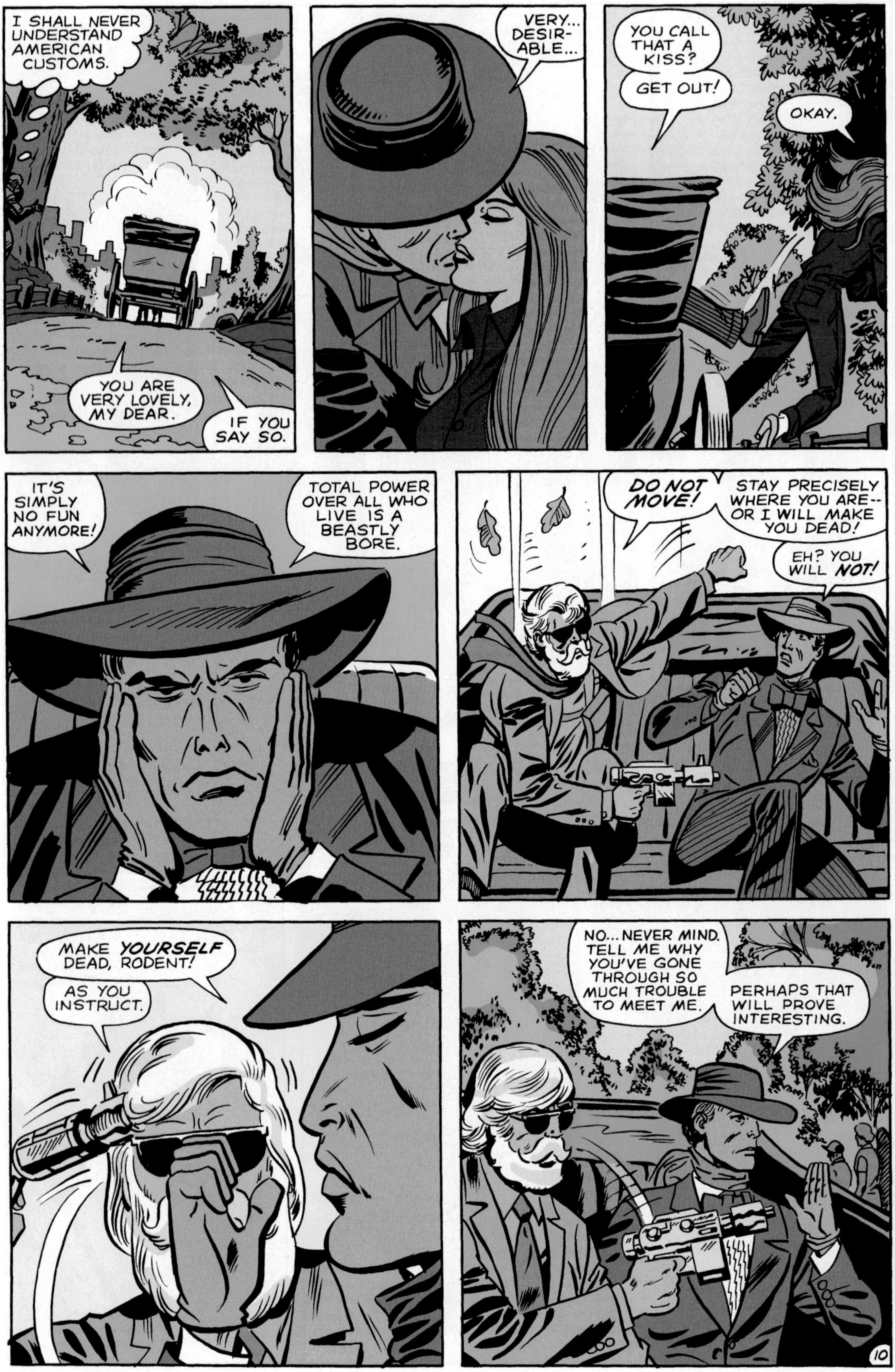
I SHALL NEVER UNDERSTAND AMERICAN CUSTOMS.
YOU ARE VERY LOVELY, MY DEAR.
IF YOU SAY SO.
VERY... DESIR-ABLE...
YOU CALL THAT A KISS?
GET OUT!
OKAY.
IT'S SIMPLY NO FUN ANYMORE!
TOTAL POWER OVER ALL WHO LIVE IS A BEASTLY BORE.
DO NOT MOVE!
STAY PRECISELY WHERE YOU ARE-- OR I WILL MAKE YOU DEAD!
EH? YOU WILL NOT!
MAKE YOURSELF DEAD, RODENT!
AS YOU INSTRUCT.
NO... NEVER MIND. TELL ME WHY YOU'VE GONE THROUGH SO MUCH TROUBLE TO MEET ME.
PERHAPS THAT WILL PROVE INTERESTING.
10

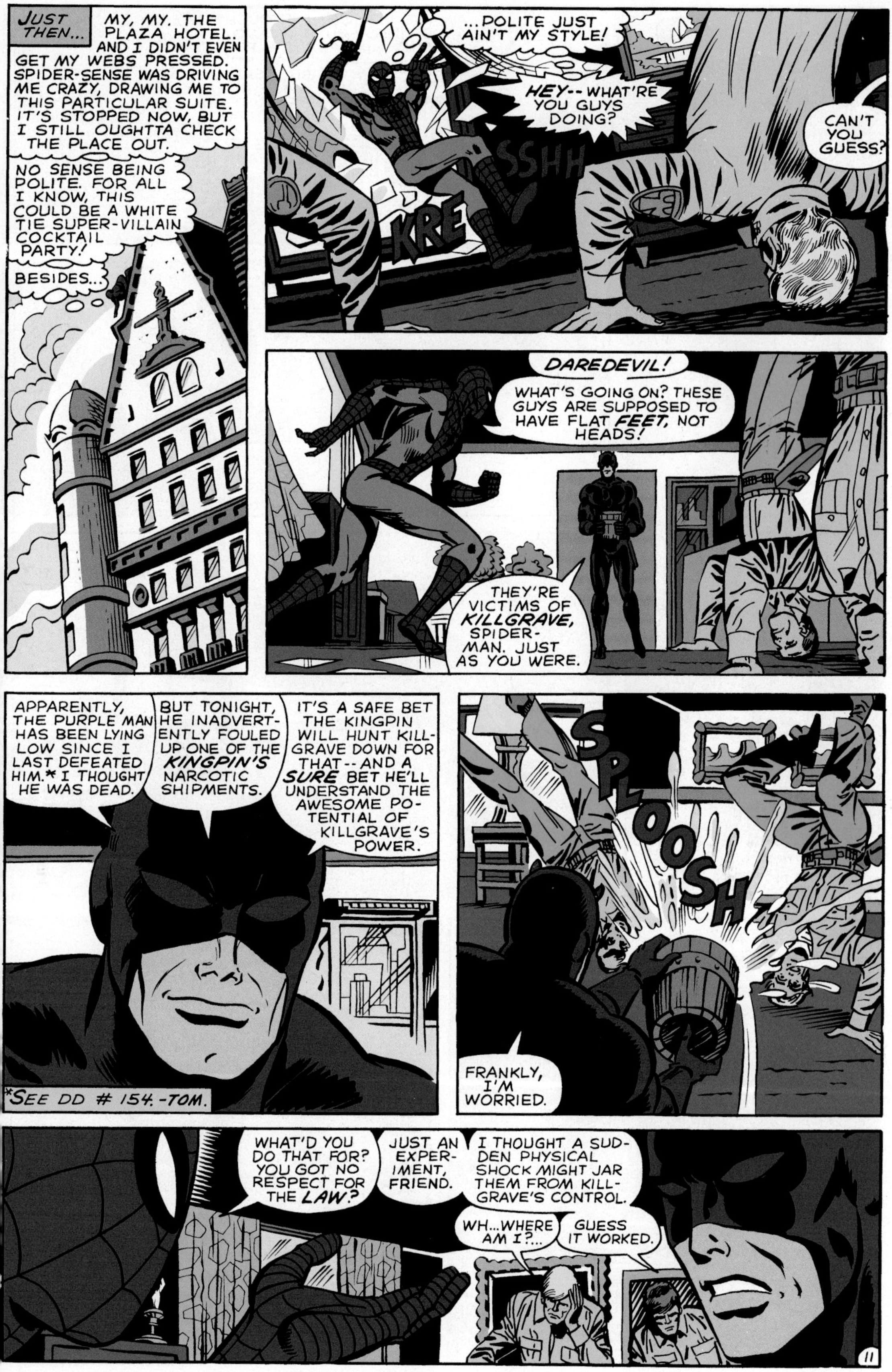
JUST THEN...
MY, MY. THE PLAZA HOTEL. AND I DIDN'T EVEN GET MY WEBS PRESSED. SPIDER-SENSE WAS DRIVING ME CRAZY, DRAWING ME TO THIS PARTICULAR SUITE. IT'S STOPPED NOW, BUT I STILL OUGHTTA CHECK THE PLACE OUT.
NO SENSE BEING POLITE. FOR ALL I KNOW, THIS COULD BE A WHITE TIE SUPER-VILLAIN COCKTAIL PARTY!
BESIDES...
...POLITE JUST AIN'T MY STYLE!
KRESSHH
HEY-- WHAT'RE YOU GUYS DOING?
CAN'T YOU GUESS?
DAREDEVIL!
WHAT'S GOING ON? THESE GUYS ARE SUPPOSED TO HAVE FLAT FEET, NOT HEADS!
THEY'RE VICTIMS OF KILLGRAVE, SPIDER-MAN. JUST AS YOU WERE.
APPARENTLY, THE PURPLE MAN HAS BEEN LYING LOW SINCE I LAST DEFEATED HIM.* I THOUGHT HE WAS DEAD.
BUT TONIGHT, HE INADVERTENTLY FOULED UP ONE OF THE KINGPIN'S NARCOTIC SHIPMENTS.
IT'S A SAFE BET THE KINGPIN WILL HUNT KILLGRAVE DOWN FOR THAT-- AND A SURE BET HE'LL UNDERSTAND THE AWESOME POTENTIAL OF KILLGRAVE'S POWER.
*SEE DD # 154. -TOM.
SPLOOSH
FRANKLY, I'M WORRIED.
WHAT'D YOU DO THAT FOR? YOU GOT NO RESPECT FOR THE LAW?
JUST AN EXPERIMENT, FRIEND.
I THOUGHT A SUDDEN PHYSICAL SHOCK MIGHT JAR THEM FROM KILLGRAVE'S CONTROL.
WH...WHERE AM I?...
GUESS IT WORKED.
11

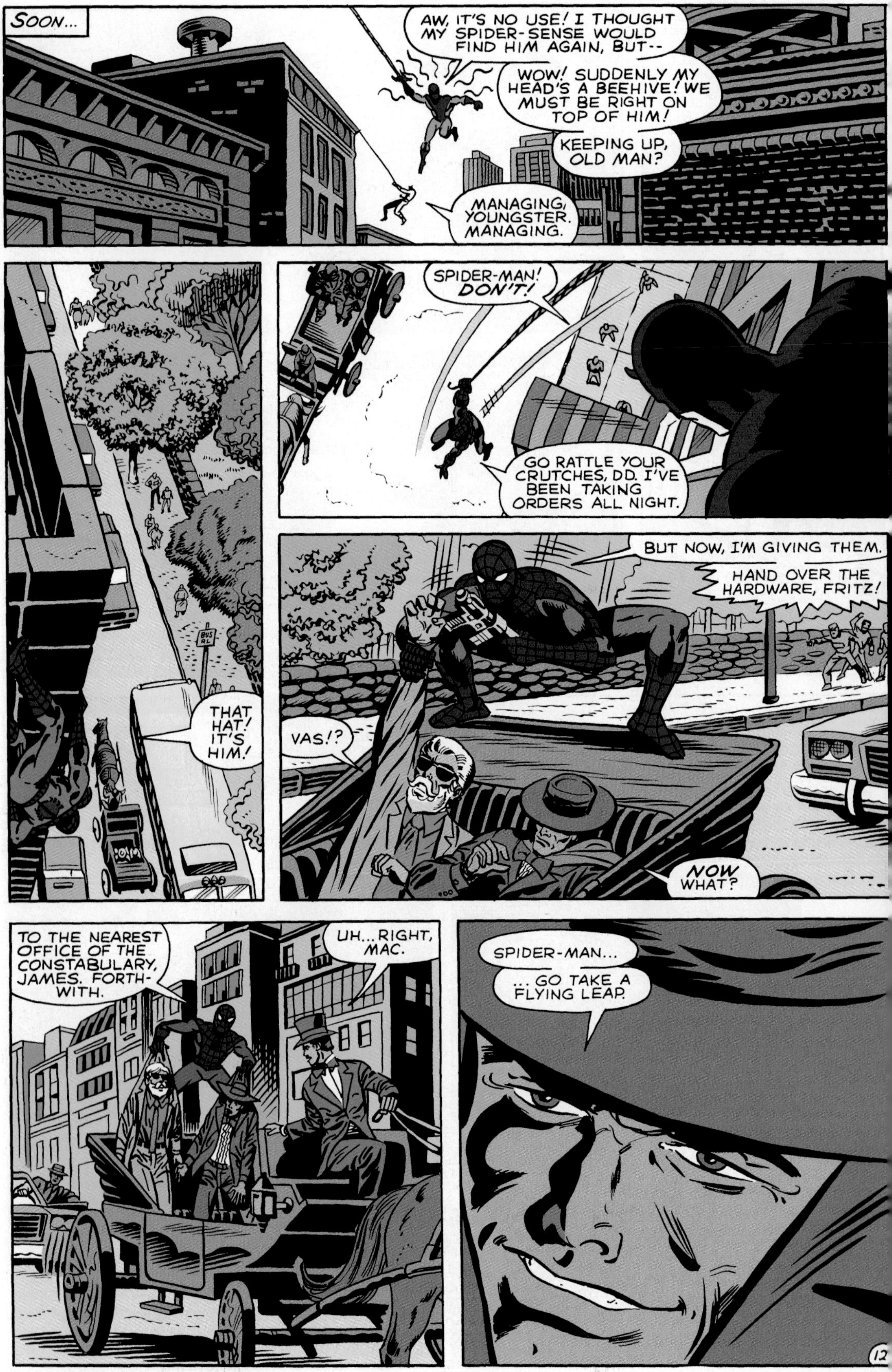
SOON...
AW, IT'S NO USE! I THOUGHT MY SPIDER-SENSE WOULD FIND HIM AGAIN, BUT--
WOW! SUDDENLY MY HEAD'S A BEEHIVE! WE MUST BE RIGHT ON TOP OF HIM!
KEEPING UP, OLD MAN?
MANAGING, YOUNGSTER. MANAGING.
THAT HAT! IT'S HIM!
SPIDER-MAN! DON'T!
GO RATTLE YOUR CRUTCHES, DD. I'VE BEEN TAKING ORDERS ALL NIGHT.
BUT NOW, I'M GIVING THEM.
HAND OVER THE HARDWARE, FRITZ!
VAS!?
NOW WHAT?
TO THE NEAREST OFFICE OF THE CONSTABULARY, JAMES. FORTH-WITH.
UH... RIGHT, MAC.
SPIDER-MAN...
... GO TAKE A FLYING LEAP.
12

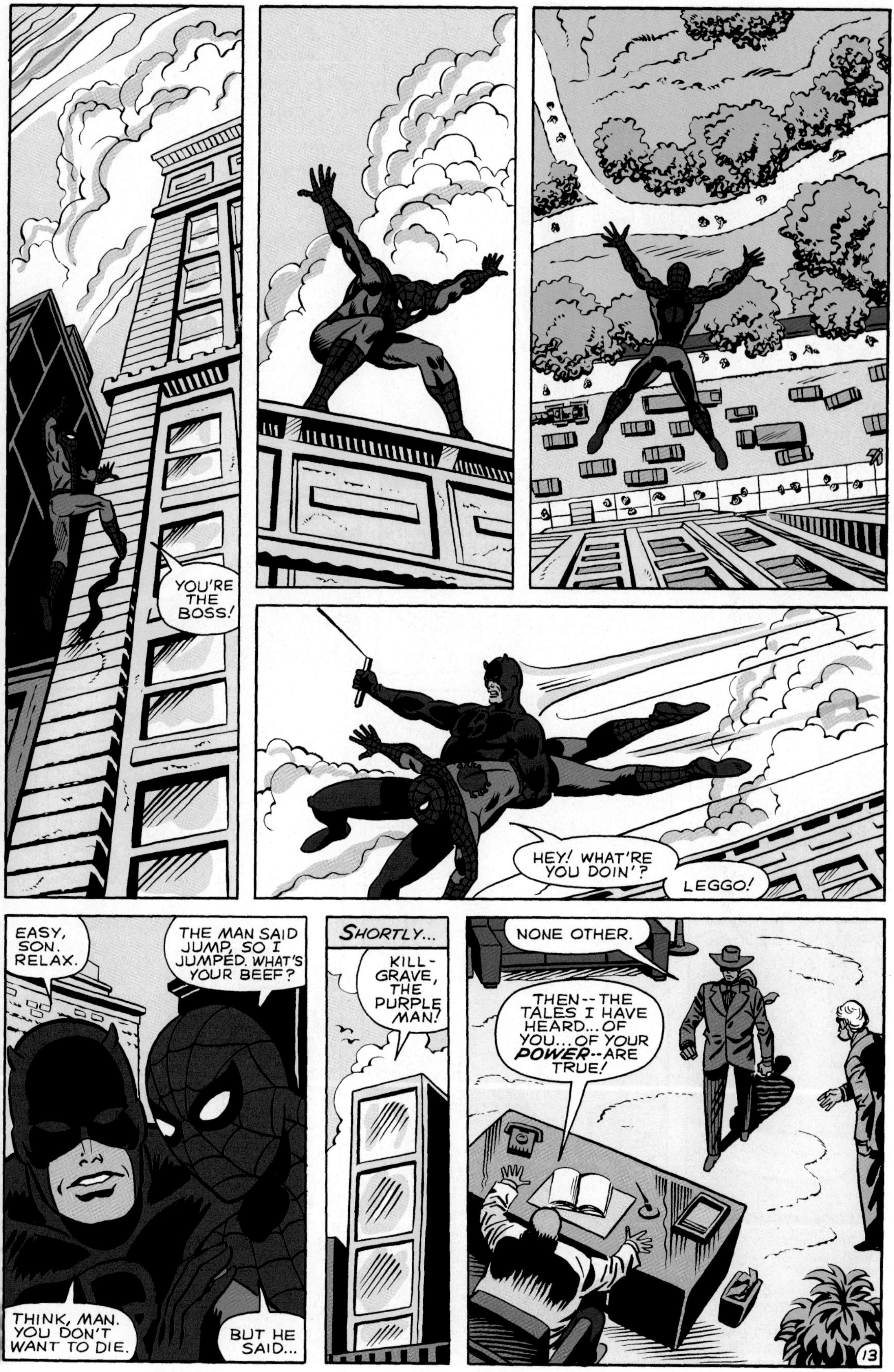
YOU'RE THE BOSS!
HEY! WHAT'RE YOU DOIN'?
LEGGO!
EASY, SON. RELAX.
THE MAN SAID JUMP, SO I JUMPED. WHAT'S YOUR BEEF?
THINK, MAN. YOU DON'T WANT TO DIE.
BUT HE SAID...
SHORTLY...
KILL-GRAVE, THE PURPLE MAN?
NONE OTHER.
THEN--THE TALES I HAVE HEARD... OF YOU... OF YOUR POWER--ARE TRUE!
13

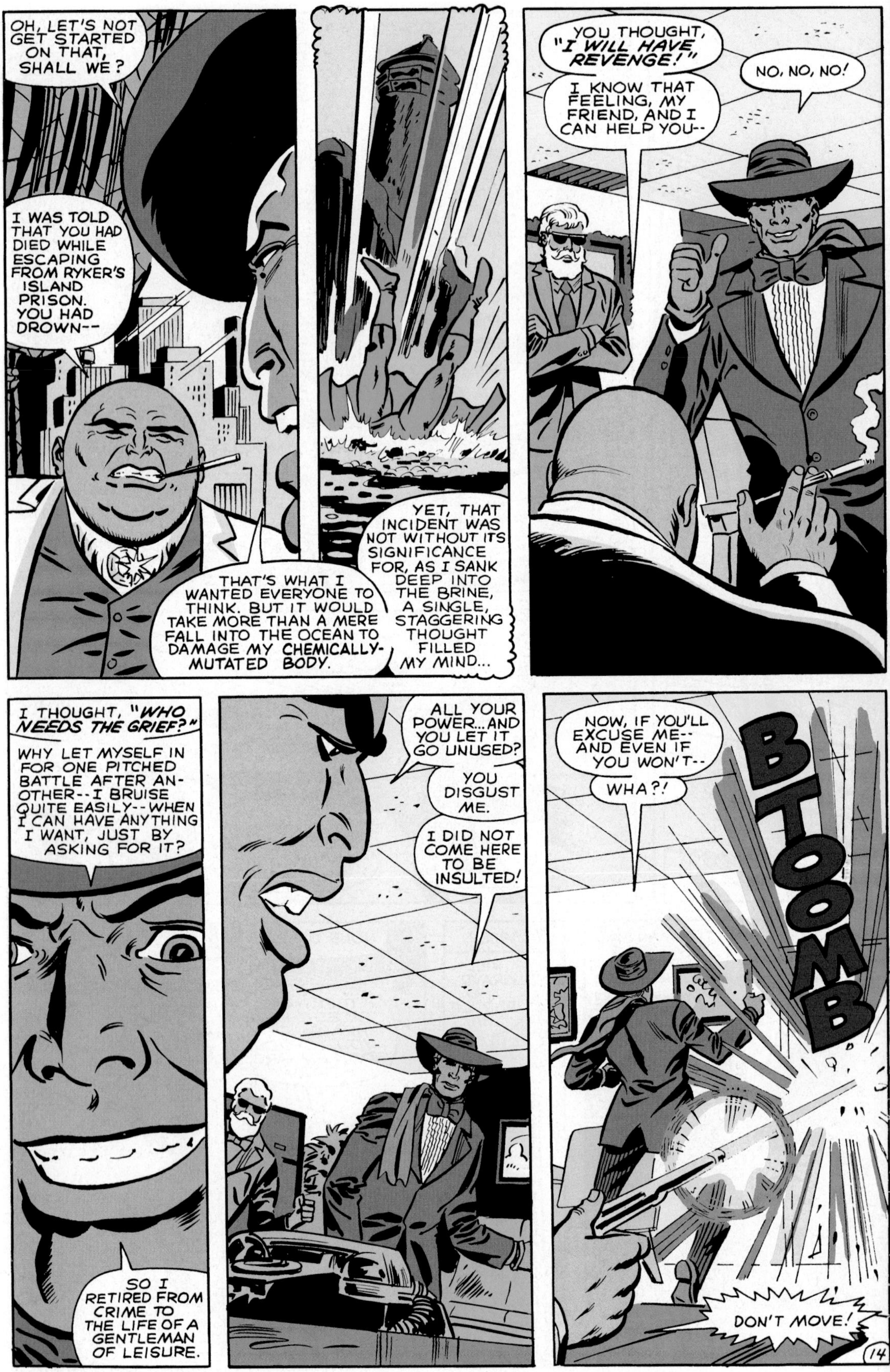

OH, LET'S NOT GET STARTED ON THAT, SHALL WE?
I WAS TOLD THAT YOU HAD DIED WHILE ESCAPING FROM RYKER'S ISLAND PRISON. YOU HAD DROWN--
THAT'S WHAT I WANTED EVERYONE TO THINK. BUT IT WOULD TAKE MORE THAN A MERE FALL INTO THE OCEAN TO DAMAGE MY CHEMICALLY-MUTATED BODY.
YET, THAT INCIDENT WAS NOT WITHOUT ITS SIGNIFICANCE FOR, AS I SANK DEEP INTO THE BRINE, A SINGLE, STAGGERING THOUGHT FILLED MY MIND...
YOU THOUGHT, "I WILL HAVE REVENGE!"
I KNOW THAT FEELING, MY FRIEND, AND I CAN HELP YOU--
NO, NO, NO!
I THOUGHT, "WHO NEEDS THE GRIEF?"
WHY LET MYSELF IN FOR ONE PITCHED BATTLE AFTER ANOTHER--I BRUISE QUITE EASILY--WHEN I CAN HAVE ANYTHING I WANT, JUST BY ASKING FOR IT?
SO I RETIRED FROM CRIME TO THE LIFE OF A GENTLEMAN OF LEISURE.
ALL YOUR POWER...AND YOU LET IT GO UNUSED?
YOU DISGUST ME.
I DID NOT COME HERE TO BE INSULTED!
NOW, IF YOU'LL EXCUSE ME--AND EVEN IF YOU WON'T--
WHA?!
BTOOMB
DON'T MOVE!
14

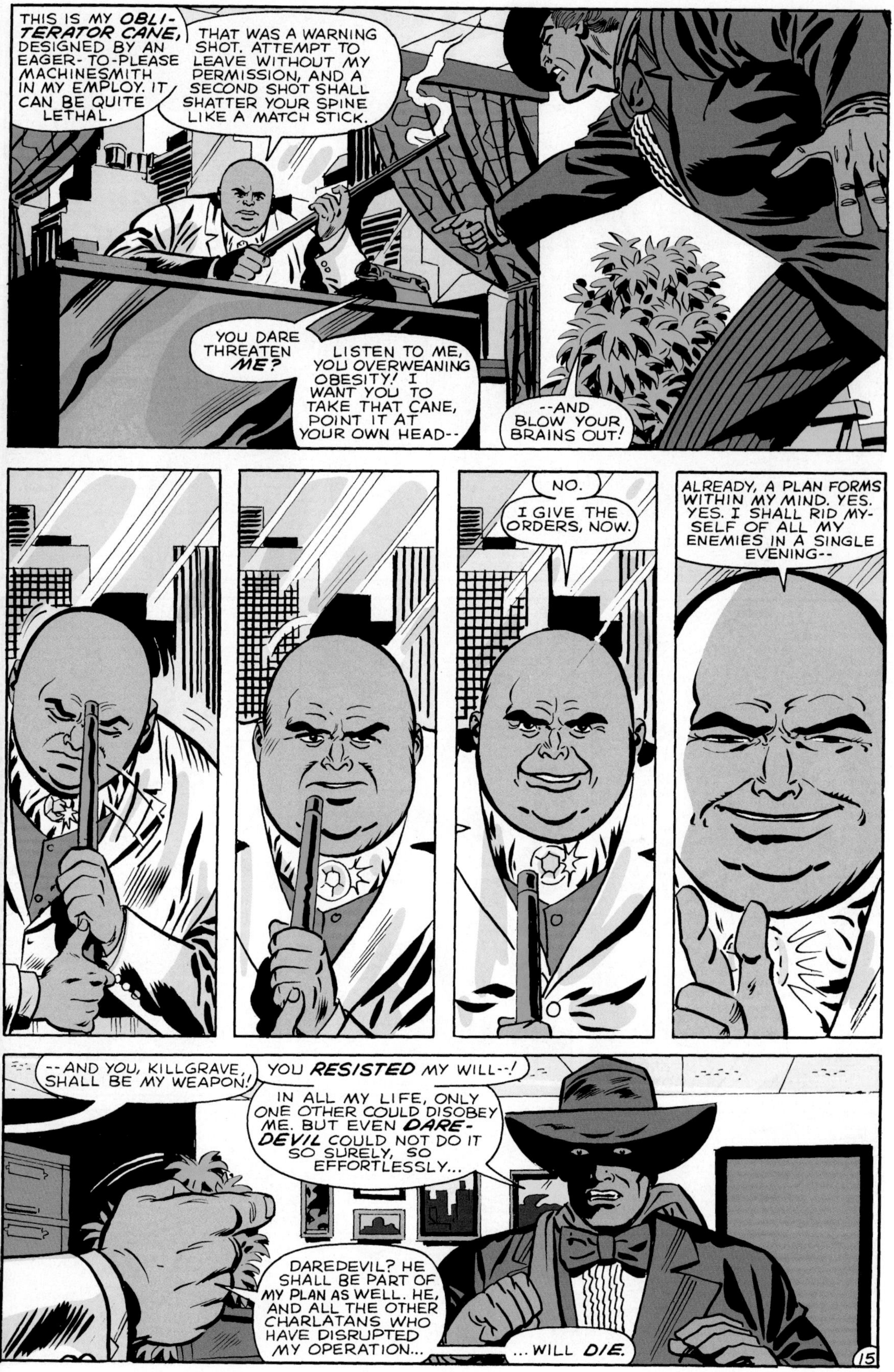
THIS IS MY OBLITERATOR CANE, DESIGNED BY AN EAGER-TO-PLEASE MACHINESMITH IN MY EMPLOY. IT CAN BE QUITE LETHAL.
THAT WAS A WARNING SHOT. ATTEMPT TO LEAVE WITHOUT MY PERMISSION, AND A SECOND SHOT SHALL SHATTER YOUR SPINE LIKE A MATCH STICK.
YOU DARE THREATEN ME?
LISTEN TO ME, YOU OVERWEANING OBESITY! I WANT YOU TO TAKE THAT CANE, POINT IT AT YOUR OWN HEAD--
--AND BLOW YOUR BRAINS OUT!
NO.
I GIVE THE ORDERS, NOW.
ALREADY, A PLAN FORMS WITHIN MY MIND. YES. YES. I SHALL RID MYSELF OF ALL MY ENEMIES IN A SINGLE EVENING--
--AND YOU, KILLGRAVE, SHALL BE MY WEAPON!
YOU RESISTED MY WILL--!
IN ALL MY LIFE, ONLY ONE OTHER COULD DISOBEY ME. BUT EVEN DAREDEVIL COULD NOT DO IT SO SURELY, SO EFFORTLESSLY...
DAREDEVIL? HE SHALL BE PART OF MY PLAN AS WELL. HE, AND ALL THE OTHER CHARLATANS WHO HAVE DISRUPTED MY OPERATION...
...WILL DIE.
15

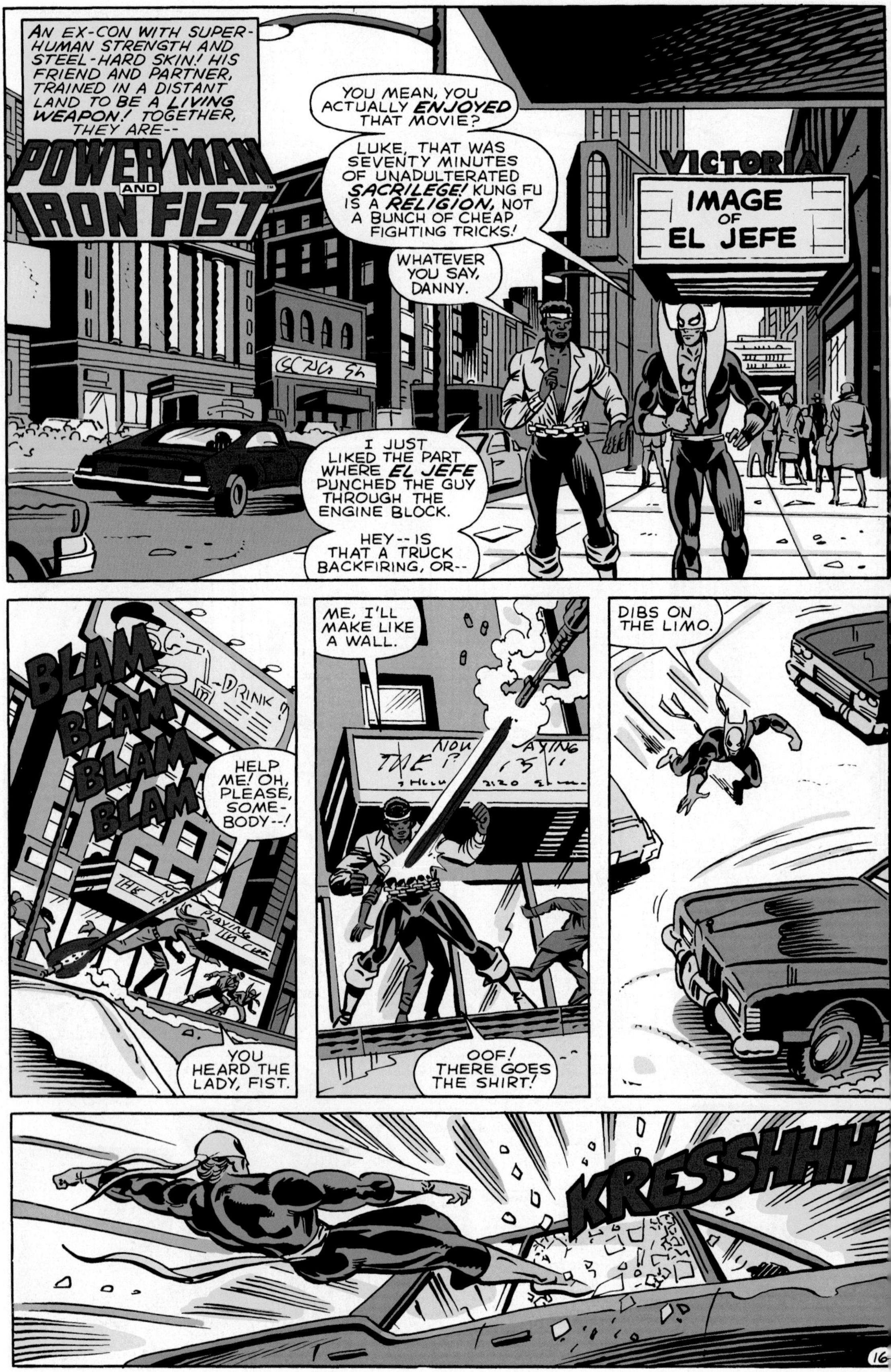
AN EX-CON WITH SUPER-HUMAN STRENGTH AND STEEL-HARD SKIN! HIS FRIEND AND PARTNER, TRAINED IN A DISTANT LAND TO BE A LIVING WEAPON! TOGETHER, THEY ARE--
POWER MAN AND IRON FIST
YOU MEAN, YOU ACTUALLY ENJOYED THAT MOVIE?
LUKE, THAT WAS SEVENTY MINUTES OF UNADULTERATED SACRILEGE! KUNG FU IS A RELIGION, NOT A BUNCH OF CHEAP FIGHTING TRICKS!
WHATEVER YOU SAY, DANNY.
VICTORIA
IMAGE OF EL JEFE
I JUST LIKED THE PART WHERE EL JEFE PUNCHED THE GUY THROUGH THE ENGINE BLOCK.
HEY--IS THAT A TRUCK BACKFIRING, OR--
BLAM BLAM BLAM BLAM
DRINK
HELP ME! OH, PLEASE, SOME-BODY--!
YOU HEARD THE LADY, FIST.
ME, I'LL MAKE LIKE A WALL.
OOF! THERE GOES THE SHIRT!
DIBS ON THE LIMO.
KRESSHHH
16

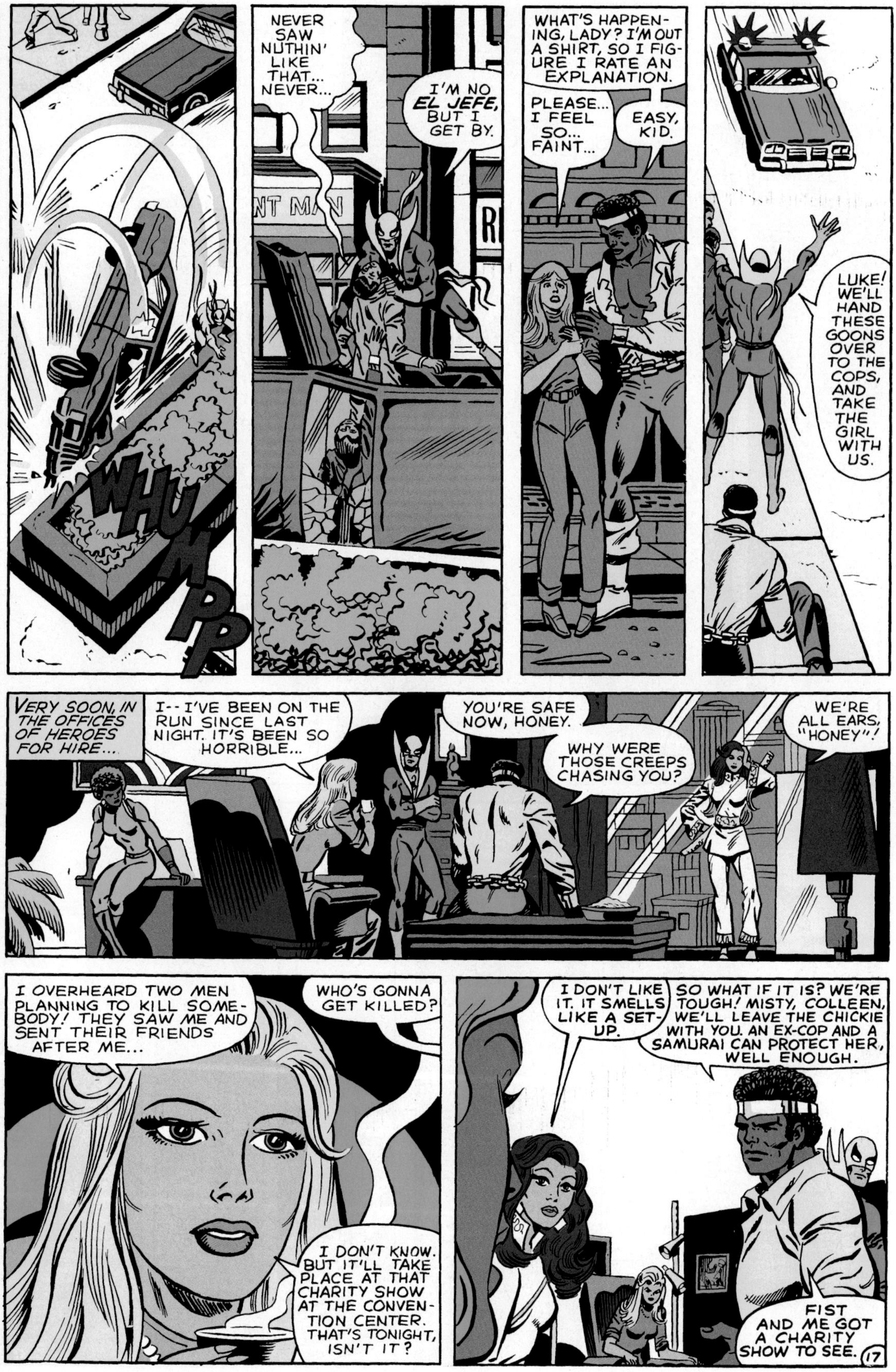
WHUMPP
NEVER SAW NUTHIN' LIKE THAT... NEVER...
I'M NO EL JEFE, BUT I GET BY.
WHAT'S HAPPENING, LADY? I'M OUT A SHIRT, SO I FIGURE I RATE AN EXPLANATION.
PLEASE... I FEEL SO... FAINT...
EASY, KID.
LUKE! WE'LL HAND THESE GOONS OVER TO THE COPS, AND TAKE THE GIRL WITH US.
VERY SOON, IN THE OFFICES OF HEROES FOR HIRE...
I-- I'VE BEEN ON THE RUN SINCE LAST NIGHT. IT'S BEEN SO HORRIBLE...
YOU'RE SAFE NOW, HONEY.
WHY WERE THOSE CREEPS CHASING YOU?
WE'RE ALL EARS, "HONEY"!
I OVERHEARD TWO MEN PLANNING TO KILL SOMEBODY! THEY SAW ME AND SENT THEIR FRIENDS AFTER ME...
WHO'S GONNA GET KILLED?
I DON'T KNOW. BUT IT'LL TAKE PLACE AT THAT CHARITY SHOW AT THE CONVENTION CENTER. THAT'S TONIGHT, ISN'T IT?
I DON'T LIKE IT. IT SMELLS LIKE A SET-UP.
SO WHAT IF IT IS? WE'RE TOUGH! MISTY, COLLEEN, WE'LL LEAVE THE CHICKIE WITH YOU. AN EX-COP AND A SAMURAI CAN PROTECT HER, WELL ENOUGH.
FIST AND ME GOT A CHARITY SHOW TO SEE.
17

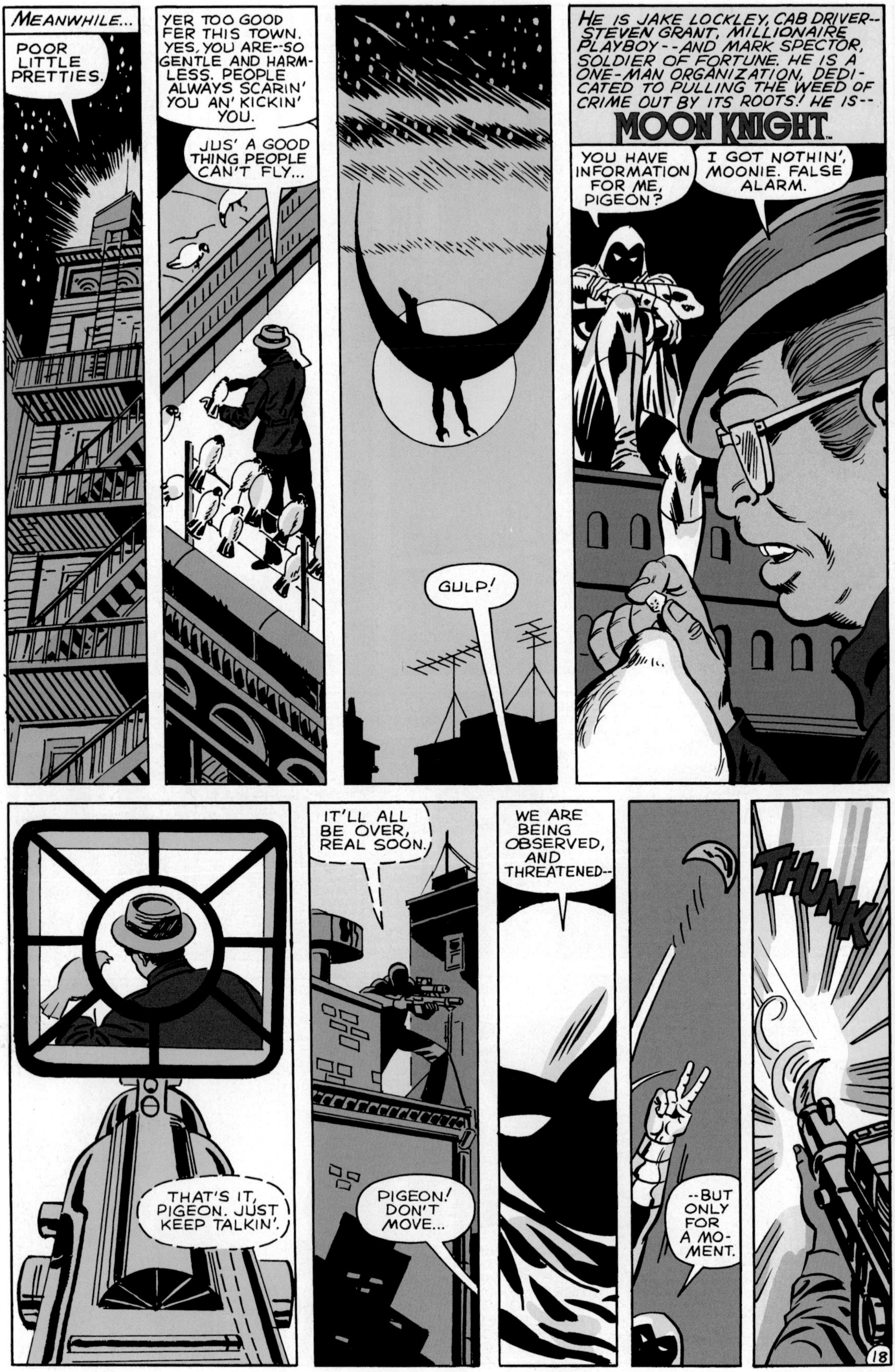
MEANWHILE...
POOR LITTLE PRETTIES.
YER TOO GOOD FER THIS TOWN. YES, YOU ARE--SO GENTLE AND HARMLESS. PEOPLE ALWAYS SCARIN' YOU AN' KICKIN' YOU.
JUS' A GOOD THING PEOPLE CAN'T FLY...
GULP!
HE IS JAKE LOCKLEY, CAB DRIVER--STEVEN GRANT, MILLIONAIRE PLAYBOY--AND MARK SPECTOR, SOLDIER OF FORTUNE. HE IS A ONE-MAN ORGANIZATION, DEDICATED TO PULLING THE WEED OF CRIME OUT BY ITS ROOTS! HE IS--
MOON KNIGHT
YOU HAVE INFORMATION FOR ME, PIGEON?
I GOT NOTHIN', MOONIE. FALSE ALARM.
THAT'S IT, PIGEON. JUST KEEP TALKIN'.
IT'LL ALL BE OVER, REAL SOON.
PIGEON! DON'T MOVE...
WE ARE BEING OBSERVED, AND THREATENED--
--BUT ONLY FOR A MOMENT.
THUNK
18

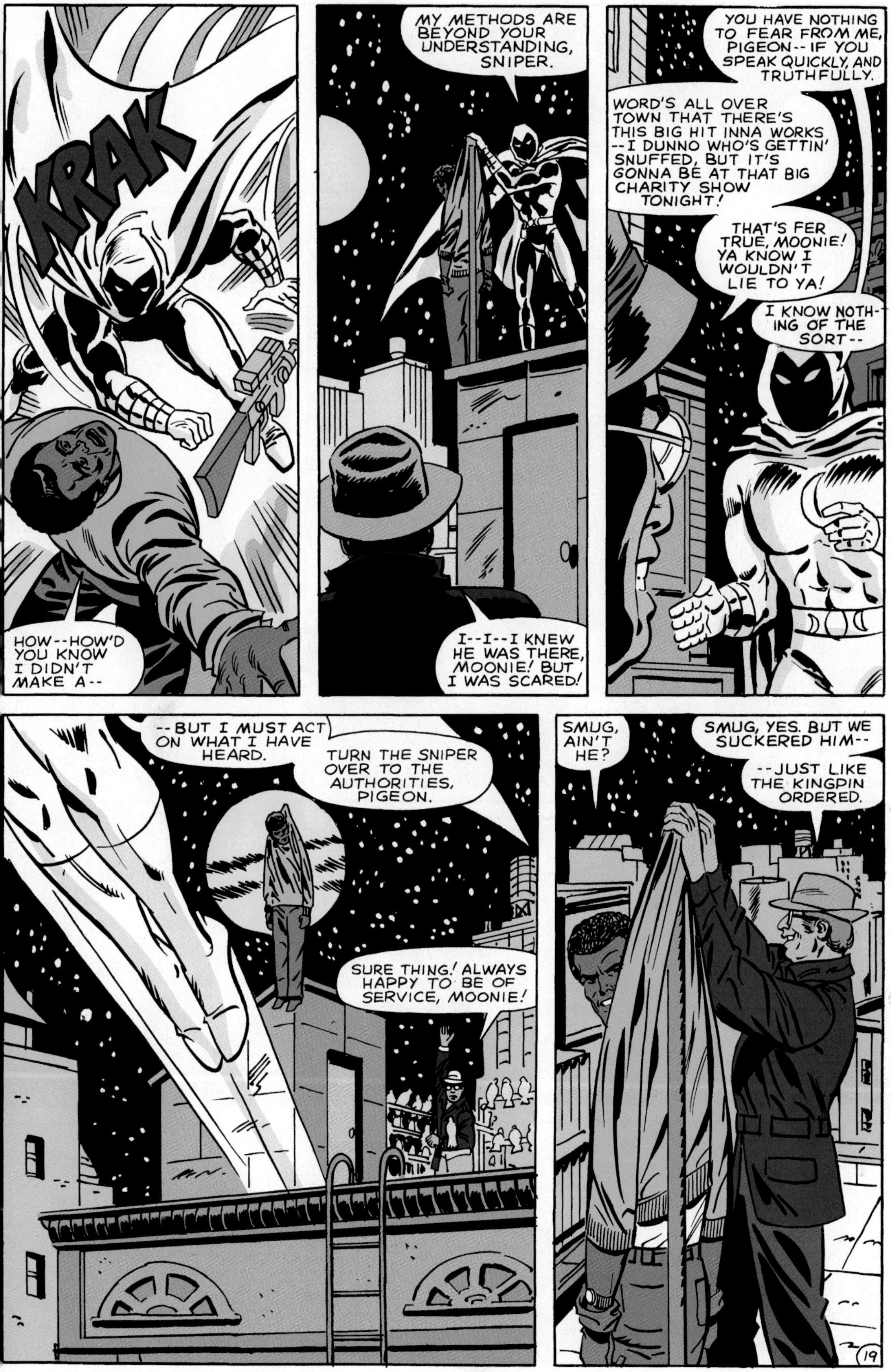
KRAK
HOW--HOW'D YOU KNOW I DIDN'T MAKE A--
MY METHODS ARE BEYOND YOUR UNDERSTANDING, SNIPER.
I--I--I KNEW HE WAS THERE, MOONIE! BUT I WAS SCARED!
YOU HAVE NOTHING TO FEAR FROM ME, PIGEON--IF YOU SPEAK QUICKLY, AND TRUTHFULLY.
WORD'S ALL OVER TOWN THAT THERE'S THIS BIG HIT INNA WORKS--I DUNNO WHO'S GETTIN' SNUFFED, BUT IT'S GONNA BE AT THAT BIG CHARITY SHOW TONIGHT!
THAT'S FER TRUE, MOONIE! YA KNOW I WOULDN'T LIE TO YA!
I KNOW NOTHING OF THE SORT--
--BUT I MUST ACT ON WHAT I HAVE HEARD.
TURN THE SNIPER OVER TO THE AUTHORITIES, PIGEON.
SURE THING! ALWAYS HAPPY TO BE OF SERVICE, MOONIE!
SMUG, AIN'T HE?
SMUG, YES. BUT WE SUCKERED HIM--
--JUST LIKE THE KINGPIN ORDERED.
19

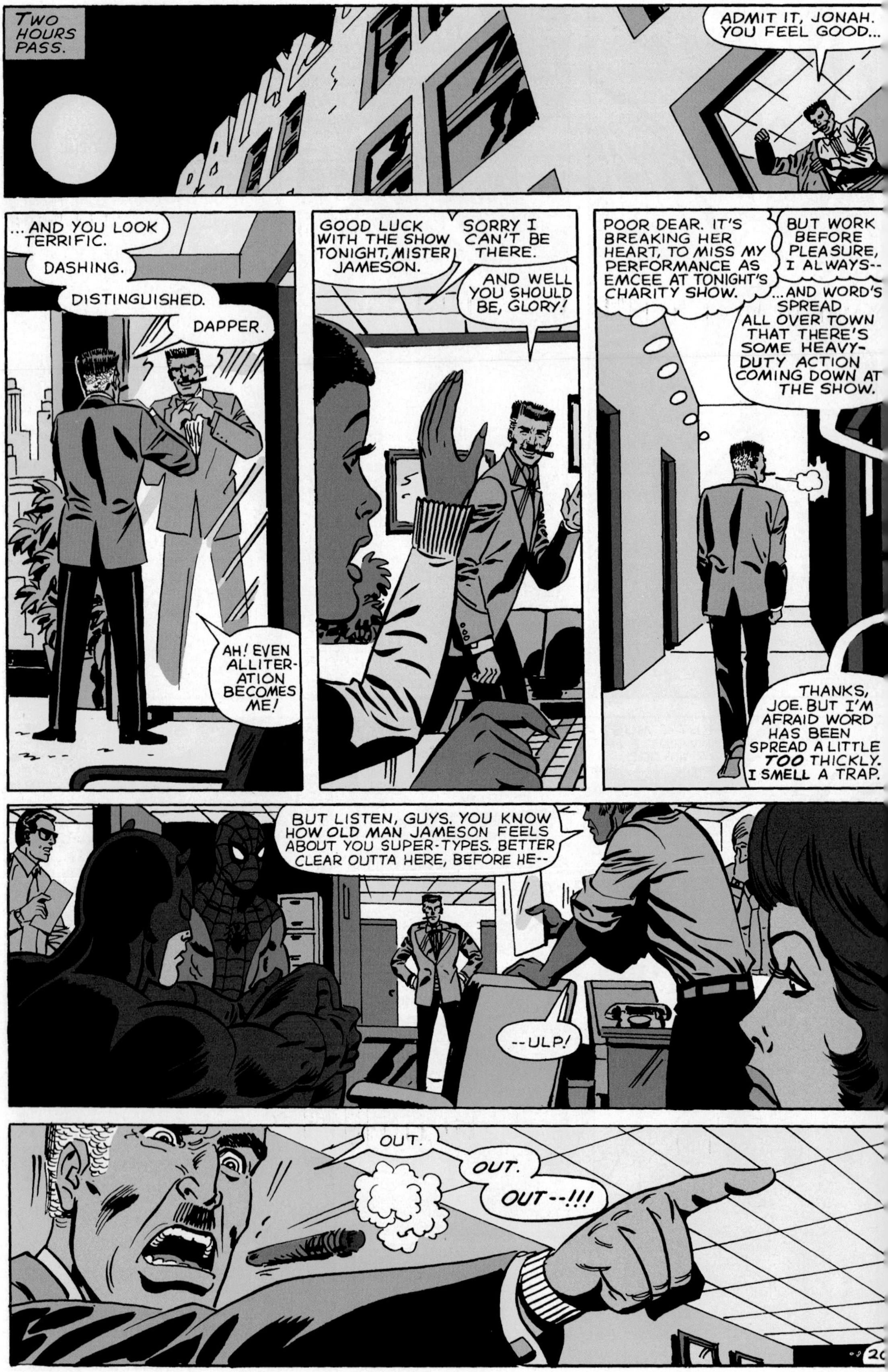
TWO HOURS PASS.
ADMIT IT, JONAH. YOU FEEL GOOD...
...AND YOU LOOK TERRIFIC.
DASHING.
DISTINGUISHED.
DAPPER.
AH! EVEN ALLITERATION BECOMES ME!
GOOD LUCK WITH THE SHOW TONIGHT, MISTER JAMESON.
SORRY I CAN'T BE THERE.
AND WELL YOU SHOULD BE, GLORY!
POOR DEAR. IT'S BREAKING HER HEART, TO MISS MY PERFORMANCE AS EMCEE AT TONIGHT'S CHARITY SHOW.
BUT WORK BEFORE PLEASURE, I ALWAYS--
...AND WORD'S SPREAD ALL OVER TOWN THAT THERE'S SOME HEAVY-DUTY ACTION COMING DOWN AT THE SHOW.
THANKS, JOE. BUT I'M AFRAID WORD HAS BEEN SPREAD A LITTLE TOO THICKLY. I SMELL A TRAP.
BUT LISTEN, GUYS. YOU KNOW HOW OLD MAN JAMESON FEELS ABOUT YOU SUPER-TYPES. BETTER CLEAR OUTTA HERE, BEFORE HE--
--ULP!
OUT.
OUT.
OUT--!!!

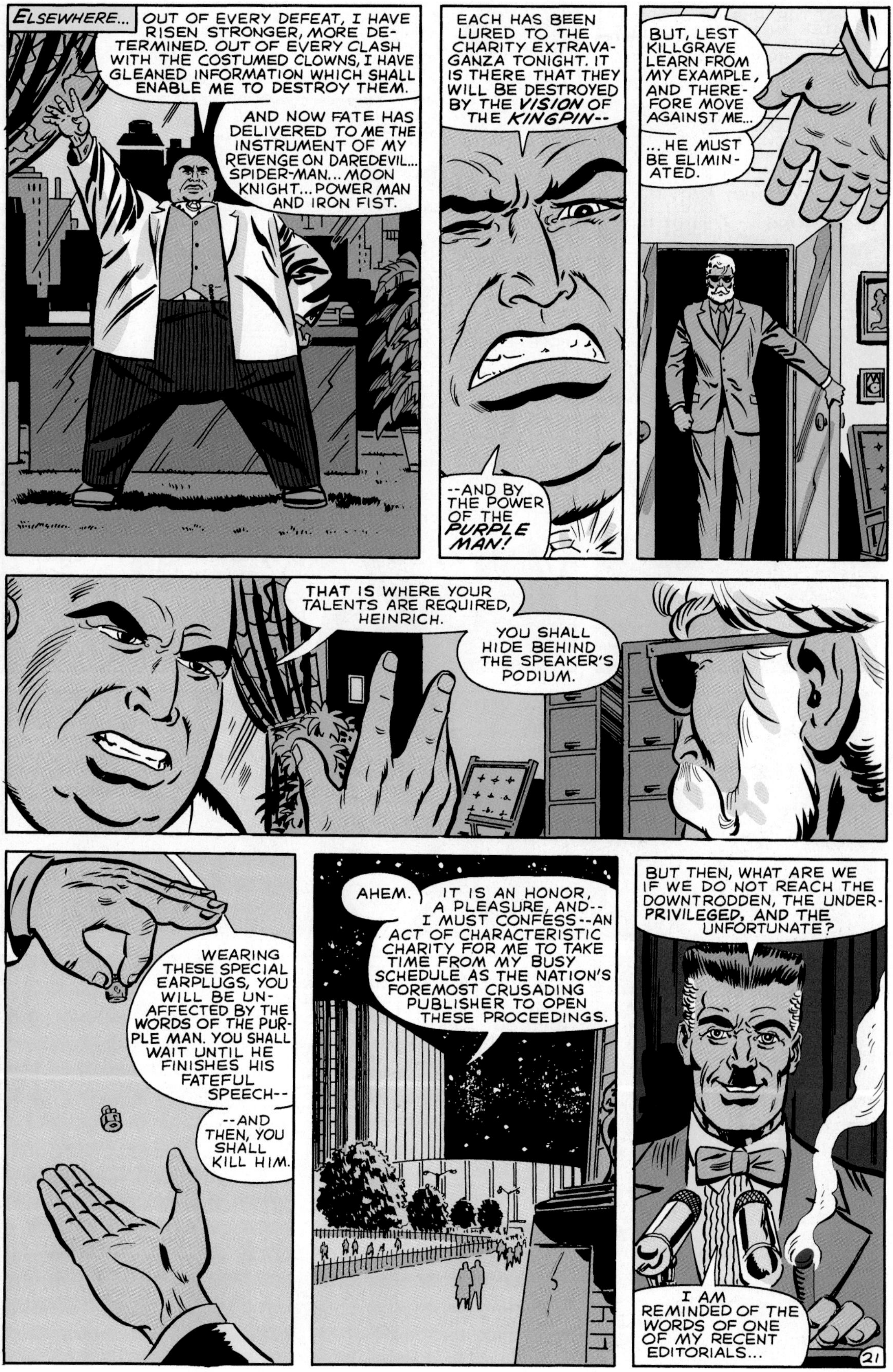
ELSEWHERE...
OUT OF EVERY DEFEAT, I HAVE RISEN STRONGER, MORE DETERMINED. OUT OF EVERY CLASH WITH THE COSTUMED CLOWNS, I HAVE GLEANED INFORMATION WHICH SHALL ENABLE ME TO DESTROY THEM.
AND NOW FATE HAS DELIVERED TO ME THE INSTRUMENT OF MY REVENGE ON DAREDEVIL... SPIDER-MAN... MOON KNIGHT... POWER MAN AND IRON FIST.
EACH HAS BEEN LURED TO THE CHARITY EXTRAVAGANZA TONIGHT. IT IS THERE THAT THEY WILL BE DESTROYED BY THE VISION OF THE KINGPIN--
--AND BY THE POWER OF THE PURPLE MAN!
BUT, LEST KILLGRAVE LEARN FROM MY EXAMPLE, AND THEREFORE MOVE AGAINST ME...
... HE MUST BE ELIMINATED.
THAT IS WHERE YOUR TALENTS ARE REQUIRED, HEINRICH.
YOU SHALL HIDE BEHIND THE SPEAKER'S PODIUM.
WEARING THESE SPECIAL EARPLUGS, YOU WILL BE UNAFFECTED BY THE WORDS OF THE PURPLE MAN. YOU SHALL WAIT UNTIL HE FINISHES HIS FATEFUL SPEECH--
--AND THEN, YOU SHALL KILL HIM.
AHEM.
IT IS AN HONOR, A PLEASURE, AND-- I MUST CONFESS--AN ACT OF CHARACTERISTIC CHARITY FOR ME TO TAKE TIME FROM MY BUSY SCHEDULE AS THE NATION'S FOREMOST CRUSADING PUBLISHER TO OPEN THESE PROCEEDINGS.
BUT THEN, WHAT ARE WE IF WE DO NOT REACH THE DOWNTRODDEN, THE UNDERPRIVILEGED, AND THE UNFORTUNATE?
I AM REMINDED OF THE WORDS OF ONE OF MY RECENT EDITORIALS...
21

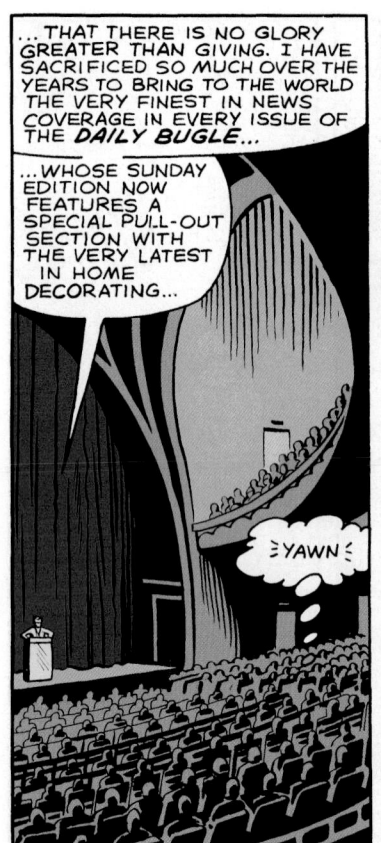

...THAT THERE IS NO GLORY GREATER THAN GIVING. I HAVE SACRIFICED SO MUCH OVER THE YEARS TO BRING TO THE WORLD THE VERY FINEST IN NEWS COVERAGE IN EVERY ISSUE OF THE *DAILY BUGLE*...

...WHOSE SUNDAY EDITION NOW FEATURES A SPECIAL PULL-OUT SECTION WITH THE VERY LATEST IN HOME DECORATING...

≷YAWN≷

I HESITATE TO MENTION THE GENEROUS CASH CONTRIBUTION I MADE TO MAKE THIS ALL POSSIBLE. TRUE, IT IS TAX-DEDUCTABLE, BUT WHY QUIBBLE?

YOU MAY NOT GET A CHANCE TO BECOME *MOON KNIGHT*, STEVEN. JAMESON MIGHT *BORE* THE BAD GUYS TO DEATH.

KEEP YOUR EYES OPEN, FIST.

ALWAYS, LUKE.

SHEESH. OLD FLAT-TOP IS IN RARE FORM TONIGHT. JUST HOPE HE DOESN'T GET STARTED ON *SPIDER-MAN*...

EXCUSE ME, SIR. THAT CIGAR SMELLS AWFUL.

ESPECIALLY TO THE HYPER-SENSES OF A CERTAIN *MAN WITHOUT FEAR!*

AND NOW, WITHOUT FURTHER ADO, LET ME INTRODUCE OUR FIRST GUEST...

...KILLGRAVE, THE PURPLE MAN!

WHO?

CA-MON! WE WERE EXPECTING STEVE MARTIN!

BOO!

QUIET.

THAT'S BETTER. NOW, BEFORE I BEGIN MY... ACT ...I'D LIKE TO POINT OUT A CE-LEBRITY IN THE AUDIENCE.

THERE HE IS IN THE THIRD ROW-- MATT MURDOCK. YOU MAY KNOW HIM AS A FAMOUS LAWYER--

--BUT THAT'S ONLY HALF THE STORY, ISN'T IT, MATT?

HE'S TOYING WITH ME. HE KNOWS I'M DAREDEVIL, AND HE'S GOING TO TELL THEM.

HEY....!

HAVE TO MOVE FAST--!

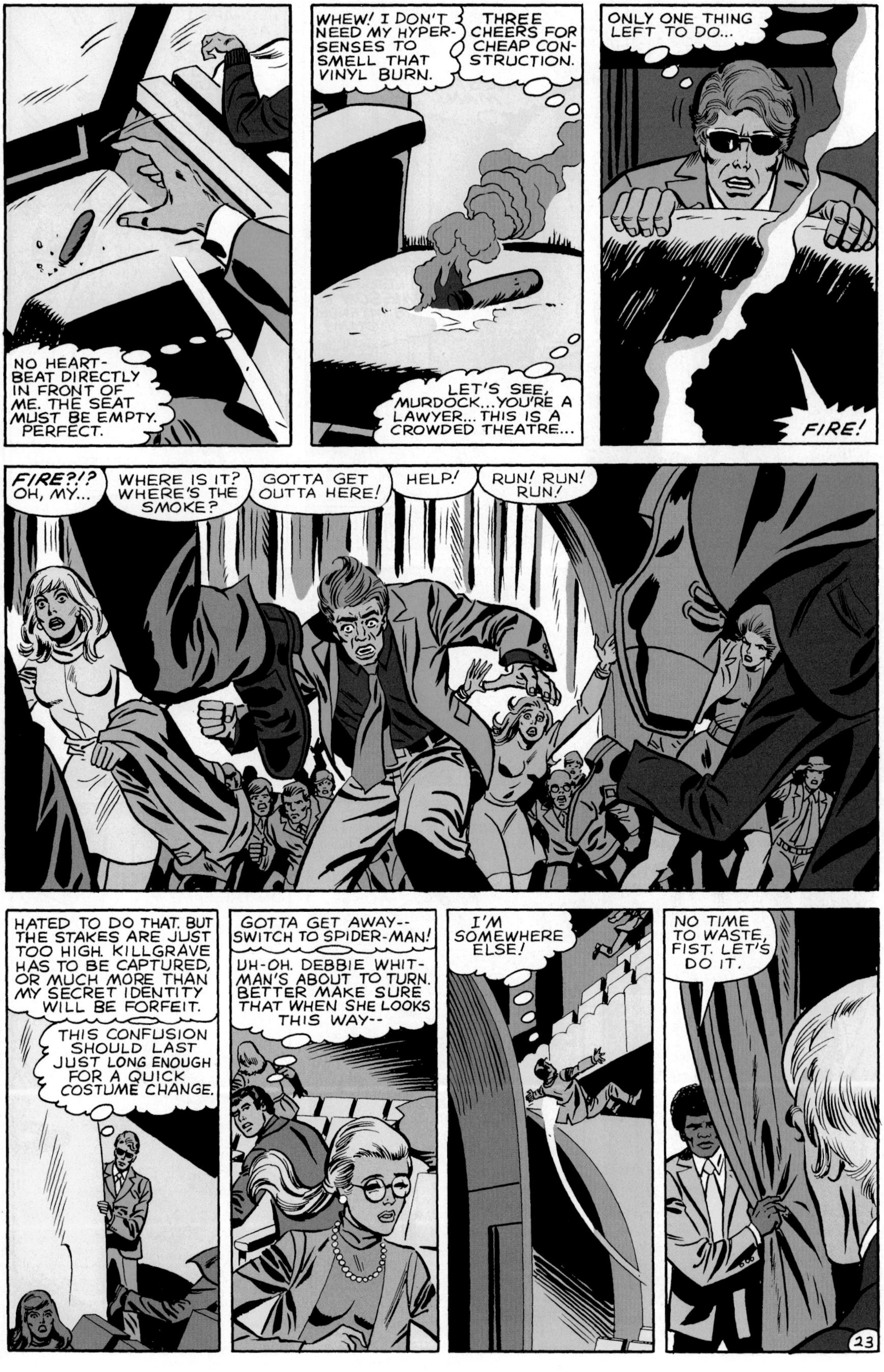
NO HEART-BEAT DIRECTLY IN FRONT OF ME. THE SEAT MUST BE EMPTY. PERFECT.
WHEW! I DON'T NEED MY HYPER-SENSES TO SMELL THAT VINYL BURN.
THREE CHEERS FOR CHEAP CON-STRUCTION.
LET'S SEE, MURDOCK... YOU'RE A LAWYER... THIS IS A CROWDED THEATRE...
ONLY ONE THING LEFT TO DO...
FIRE!
FIRE?!? OH, MY...
WHERE IS IT? WHERE'S THE SMOKE?
GOTTA GET OUTTA HERE!
HELP!
RUN! RUN! RUN!
HATED TO DO THAT. BUT THE STAKES ARE JUST TOO HIGH. KILLGRAVE HAS TO BE CAPTURED, OR MUCH MORE THAN MY SECRET IDENTITY WILL BE FORFEIT.
THIS CONFUSION SHOULD LAST JUST LONG ENOUGH FOR A QUICK COSTUME CHANGE.
GOTTA GET AWAY-- SWITCH TO SPIDER-MAN!
UH-OH. DEBBIE WHIT-MAN'S ABOUT TO TURN. BETTER MAKE SURE THAT WHEN SHE LOOKS THIS WAY--
I'M SOMEWHERE ELSE!
NO TIME TO WASTE, FIST. LET'S DO IT.
23

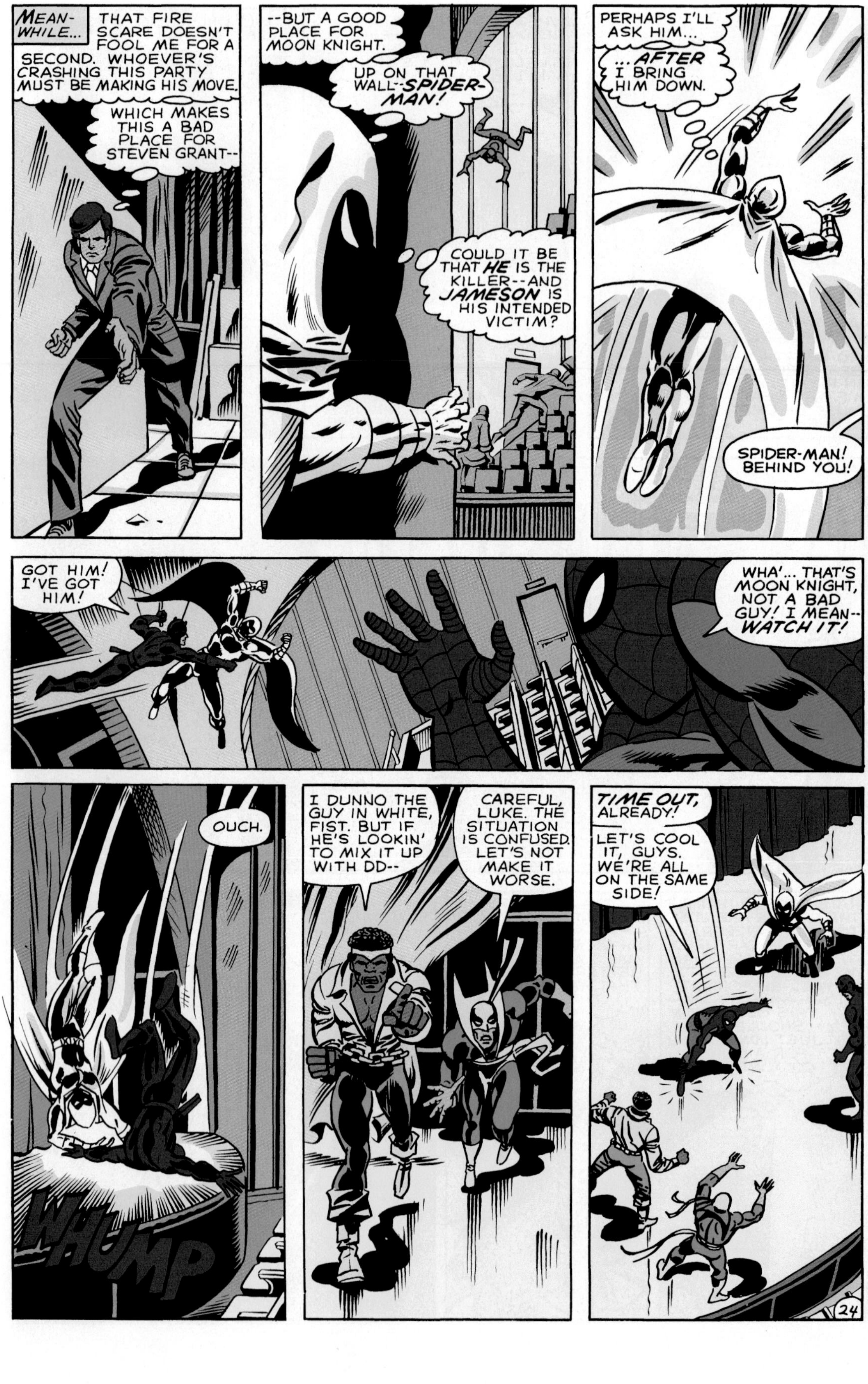
MEAN-WHILE...
THAT FIRE SCARE DOESN'T FOOL ME FOR A SECOND. WHOEVER'S CRASHING THIS PARTY MUST BE MAKING HIS MOVE.
WHICH MAKES THIS A BAD PLACE FOR STEVEN GRANT--
--BUT A GOOD PLACE FOR MOON KNIGHT.
UP ON THAT WALL--SPIDER-MAN!
COULD IT BE THAT HE IS THE KILLER--AND JAMESON IS HIS INTENDED VICTIM?
PERHAPS I'LL ASK HIM...
...AFTER I BRING HIM DOWN.
SPIDER-MAN! BEHIND YOU!
GOT HIM! I'VE GOT HIM!
WHA'... THAT'S MOON KNIGHT, NOT A BAD GUY! I MEAN--WATCH IT!
OUCH.
WHUMP
I DUNNO THE GUY IN WHITE, FIST. BUT IF HE'S LOOKIN' TO MIX IT UP WITH DD--
CAREFUL, LUKE. THE SITUATION IS CONFUSED. LET'S NOT MAKE IT WORSE.
TIME OUT, ALREADY!
LET'S COOL IT, GUYS. WE'RE ALL ON THE SAME SIDE!
24

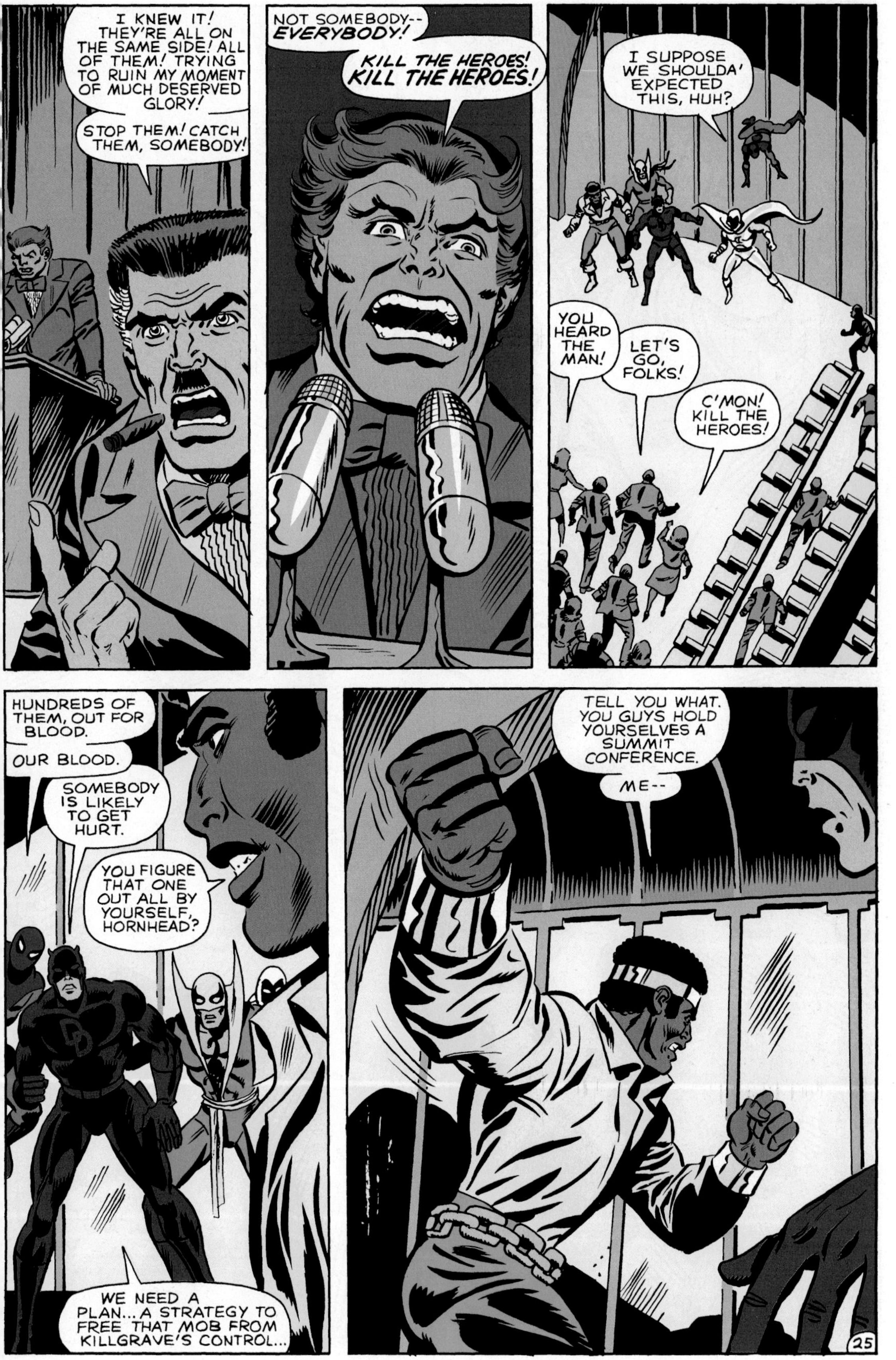
I KNEW IT! THEY'RE ALL ON THE SAME SIDE! ALL OF THEM! TRYING TO RUIN MY MOMENT OF MUCH DESERVED GLORY!
STOP THEM! CATCH THEM, SOMEBODY!
NOT SOMEBODY-- EVERYBODY!
KILL THE HEROES! KILL THE HEROES!
I SUPPOSE WE SHOULDA' EXPECTED THIS, HUH?
YOU HEARD THE MAN!
LET'S GO, FOLKS!
C'MON! KILL THE HEROES!
HUNDREDS OF THEM, OUT FOR BLOOD.
OUR BLOOD.
SOMEBODY IS LIKELY TO GET HURT.
YOU FIGURE THAT ONE OUT ALL BY YOURSELF, HORNHEAD?
WE NEED A PLAN... A STRATEGY TO FREE THAT MOB FROM KILLGRAVE'S CONTROL...
TELL YOU WHAT. YOU GUYS HOLD YOURSELVES A SUMMIT CONFERENCE.
ME--
25

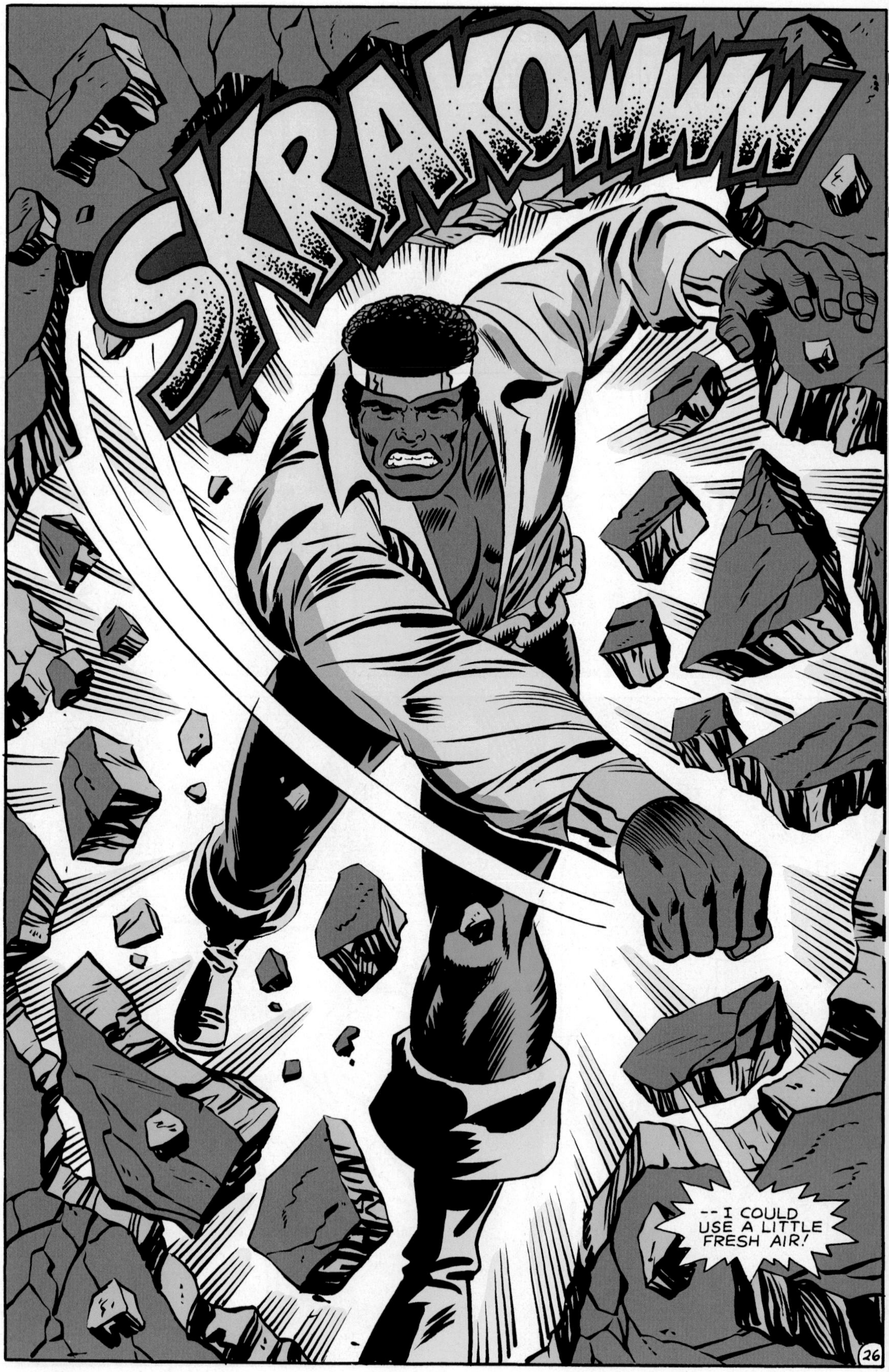
SKRAKOWWW
-- I COULD USE A LITTLE FRESH AIR!
26

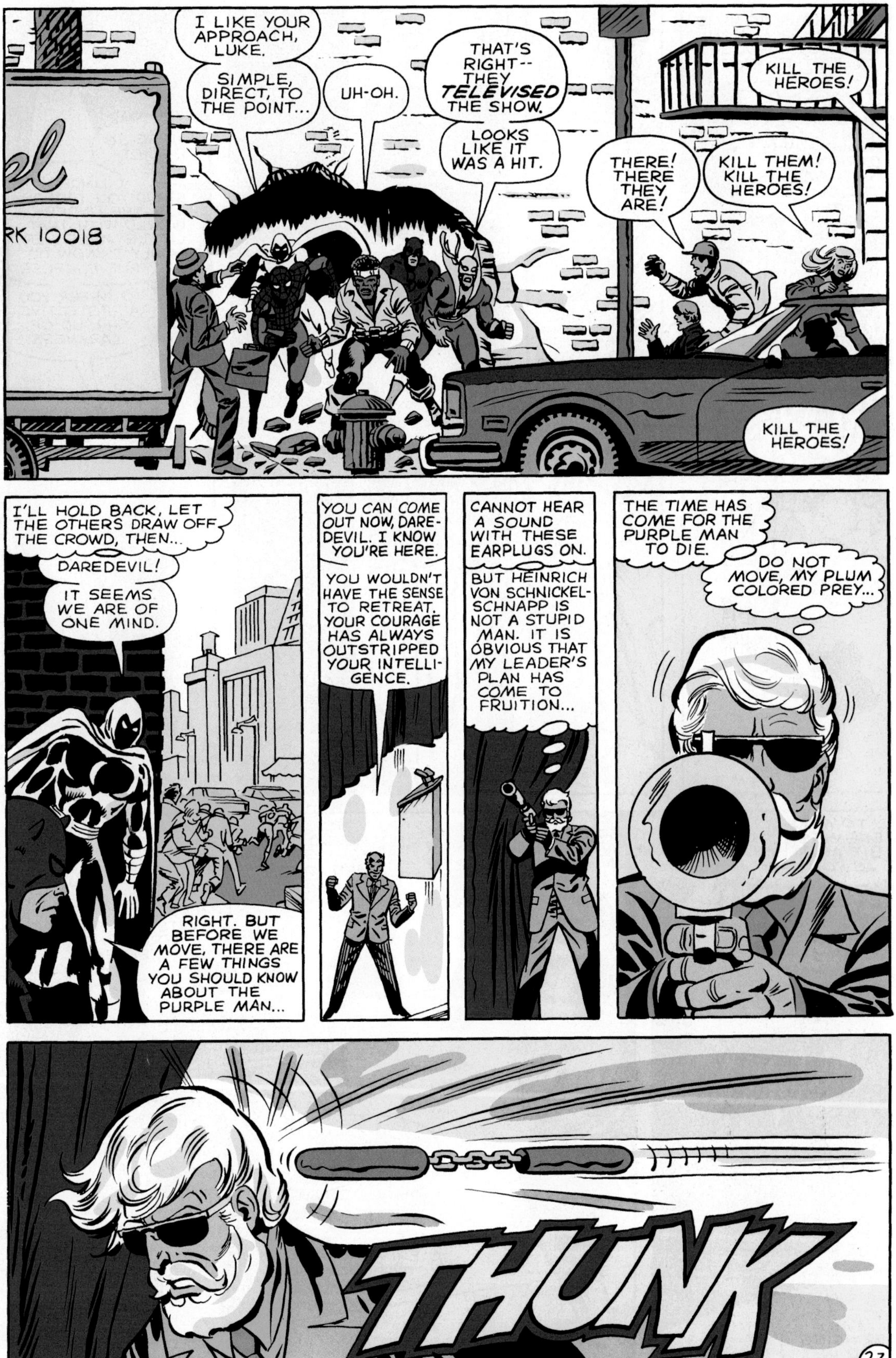
I LIKE YOUR APPROACH, LUKE.
SIMPLE, DIRECT, TO THE POINT...
UH-OH.
THAT'S RIGHT-- THEY *TELEVISED* THE SHOW.
LOOKS LIKE IT WAS A HIT.
RK 10018
KILL THE HEROES!
THERE! THERE THEY ARE!
KILL THEM! KILL THE HEROES!
KILL THE HEROES!
I'LL HOLD BACK, LET THE OTHERS DRAW OFF THE CROWD, THEN...
DAREDEVIL!
IT SEEMS WE ARE OF ONE MIND.
RIGHT. BUT BEFORE WE MOVE, THERE ARE A FEW THINGS YOU SHOULD KNOW ABOUT THE PURPLE MAN...
YOU CAN COME OUT NOW, DAREDEVIL. I KNOW YOU'RE HERE.
YOU WOULDN'T HAVE THE SENSE TO RETREAT. YOUR COURAGE HAS ALWAYS OUTSTRIPPED YOUR INTELLIGENCE.
CANNOT HEAR A SOUND WITH THESE EARPLUGS ON.
BUT HEINRICH VON SCHNICKELSCHNAPP IS NOT A STUPID MAN. IT IS OBVIOUS THAT MY LEADER'S PLAN HAS COME TO FRUITION...
THE TIME HAS COME FOR THE PURPLE MAN TO DIE.
DO NOT MOVE, MY PLUM COLORED PREY...
THUNK
27

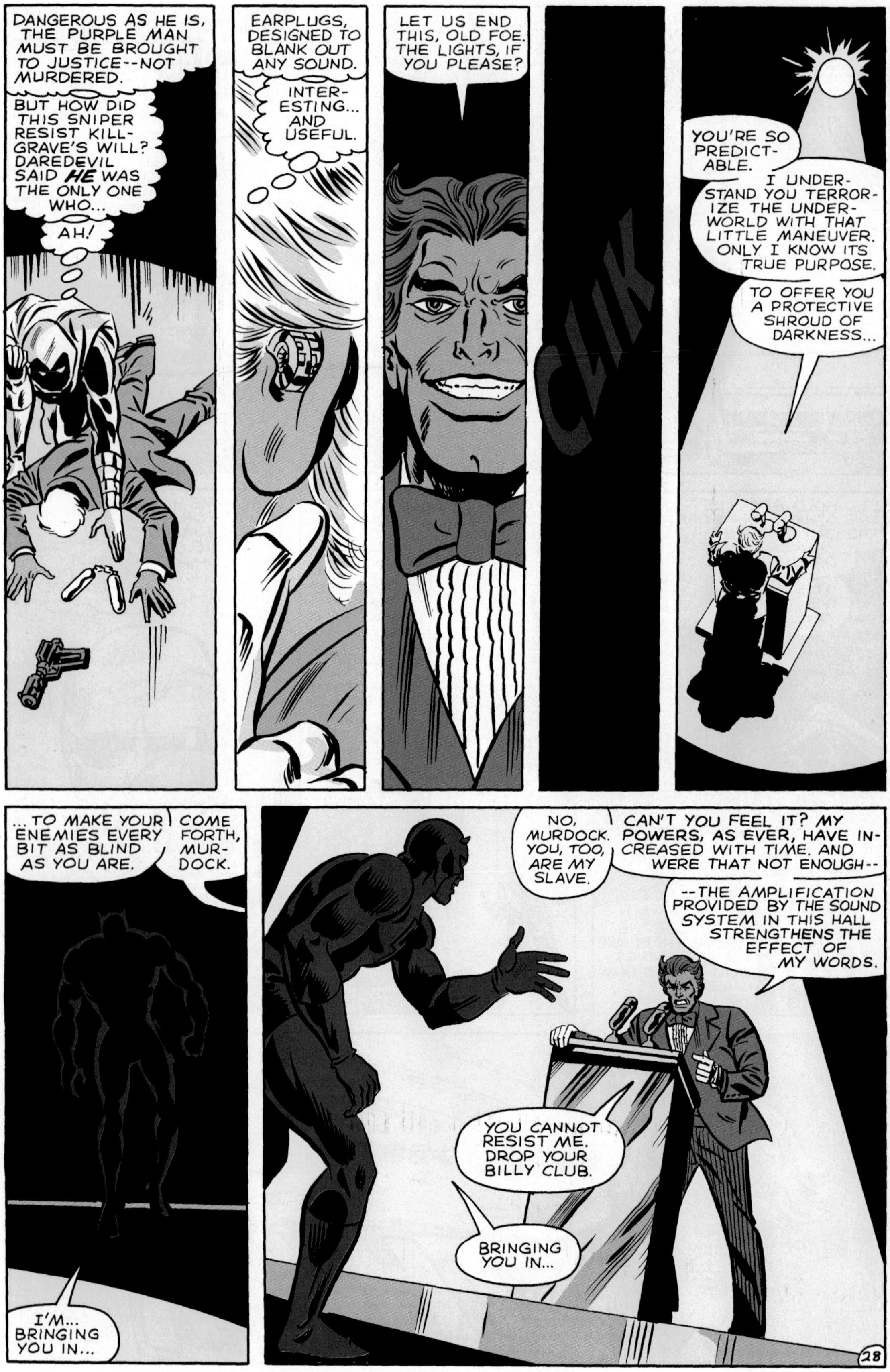
DANGEROUS AS HE IS, THE PURPLE MAN MUST BE BROUGHT TO JUSTICE--NOT MURDERED.
BUT HOW DID THIS SNIPER RESIST KILL-GRAVE'S WILL? DAREDEVIL SAID HE WAS THE ONLY ONE WHO...
AH!
EARPLUGS, DESIGNED TO BLANK OUT ANY SOUND.
INTERESTING... AND USEFUL.
LET US END THIS, OLD FOE. THE LIGHTS, IF YOU PLEASE?
CLIK
YOU'RE SO PREDICTABLE.
I UNDERSTAND YOU TERRORIZE THE UNDERWORLD WITH THAT LITTLE MANEUVER. ONLY I KNOW ITS TRUE PURPOSE.
TO OFFER YOU A PROTECTIVE SHROUD OF DARKNESS...
...TO MAKE YOUR ENEMIES EVERY BIT AS BLIND AS YOU ARE.
COME FORTH, MUR-DOCK.
I'M... BRINGING YOU IN...
NO, MURDOCK. YOU, TOO, ARE MY SLAVE.
CAN'T YOU FEEL IT? MY POWERS, AS EVER, HAVE IN-CREASED WITH TIME. AND WERE THAT NOT ENOUGH--
--THE AMPLIFICATION PROVIDED BY THE SOUND SYSTEM IN THIS HALL STRENGTHENS THE EFFECT OF MY WORDS.
YOU CANNOT RESIST ME. DROP YOUR BILLY CLUB.
BRINGING YOU IN...
28

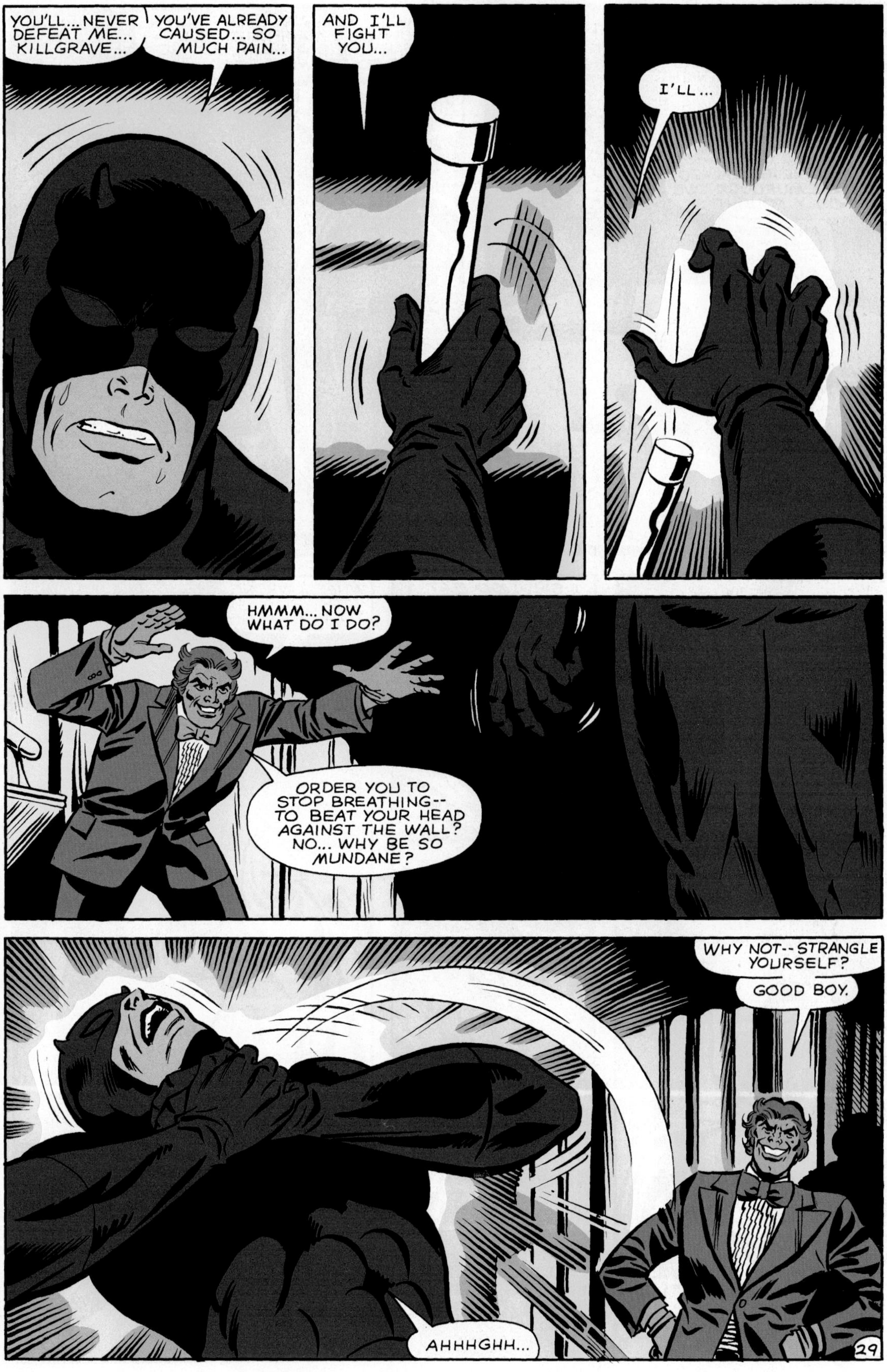
YOU'LL... NEVER DEFEAT ME... KILLGRAVE...
YOU'VE ALREADY CAUSED... SO MUCH PAIN...
AND I'LL FIGHT YOU...
I'LL...
HMMM... NOW WHAT DO I DO?
ORDER YOU TO STOP BREATHING-- TO BEAT YOUR HEAD AGAINST THE WALL? NO... WHY BE SO MUNDANE?
WHY NOT--STRANGLE YOURSELF?
GOOD BOY.
AHHHGHH...
29

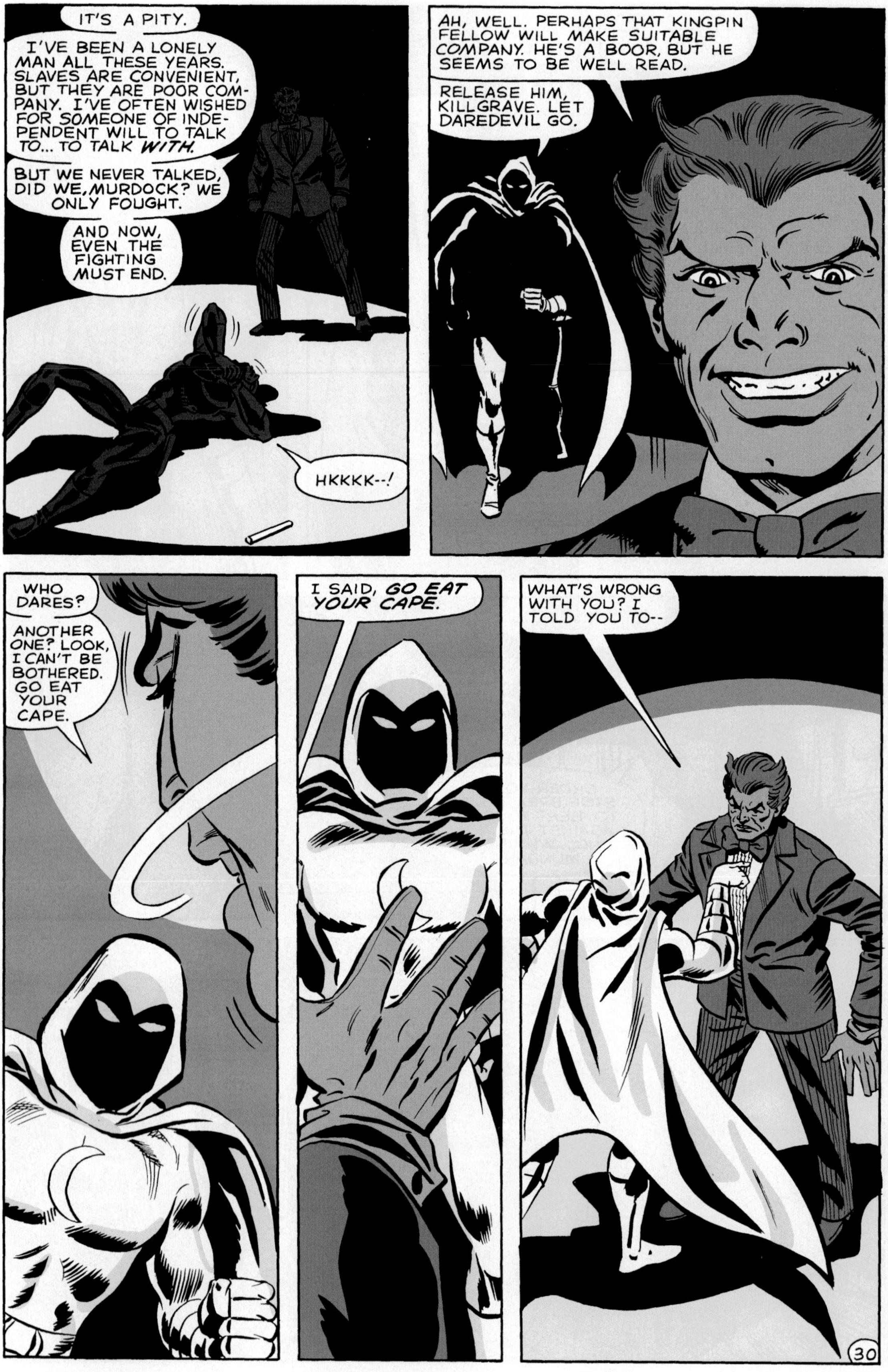
IT'S A PITY.
I'VE BEEN A LONELY MAN ALL THESE YEARS. SLAVES ARE CONVENIENT, BUT THEY ARE POOR COMPANY. I'VE OFTEN WISHED FOR SOMEONE OF INDEPENDENT WILL TO TALK TO... TO TALK WITH.
BUT WE NEVER TALKED, DID WE, MURDOCK? WE ONLY FOUGHT.
AND NOW, EVEN THE FIGHTING MUST END.
HKKKK--!
AH, WELL. PERHAPS THAT KINGPIN FELLOW WILL MAKE SUITABLE COMPANY. HE'S A BOOR, BUT HE SEEMS TO BE WELL READ.
RELEASE HIM, KILLGRAVE. LET DAREDEVIL GO.
WHO DARES?
ANOTHER ONE? LOOK, I CAN'T BE BOTHERED. GO EAT YOUR CAPE.
I SAID, GO EAT YOUR CAPE.
WHAT'S WRONG WITH YOU? I TOLD YOU TO--
30

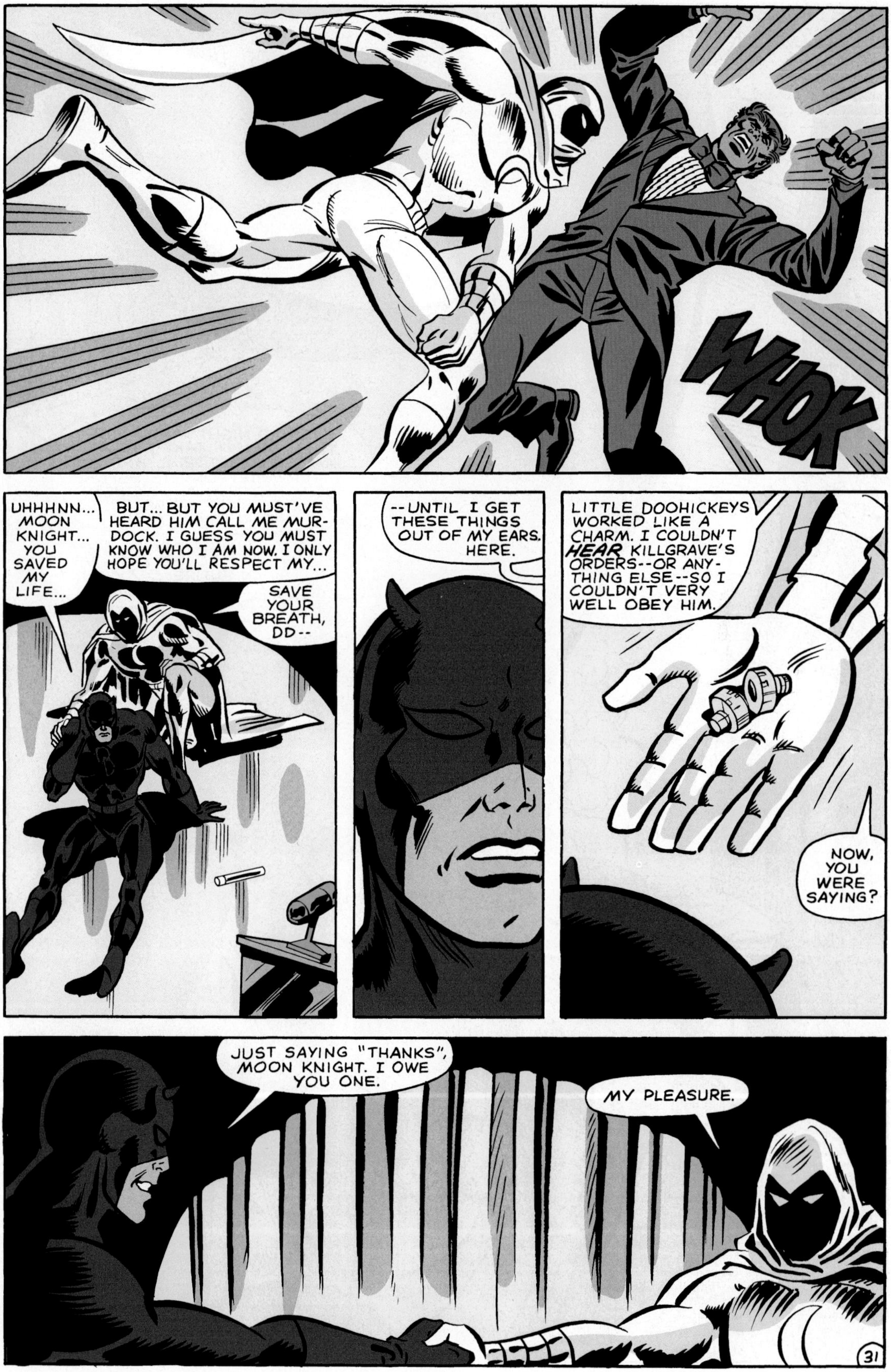
WHOK
UHHHNN... MOON KNIGHT... YOU SAVED MY LIFE...
BUT... BUT YOU MUST'VE HEARD HIM CALL ME MURDOCK. I GUESS YOU MUST KNOW WHO I AM NOW. I ONLY HOPE YOU'LL RESPECT MY...
SAVE YOUR BREATH, DD--
--UNTIL I GET THESE THINGS OUT OF MY EARS. HERE.
LITTLE DOOHICKEYS WORKED LIKE A CHARM. I COULDN'T HEAR KILLGRAVE'S ORDERS--OR ANYTHING ELSE--SO I COULDN'T VERY WELL OBEY HIM.
NOW, YOU WERE SAYING?
JUST SAYING "THANKS", MOON KNIGHT. I OWE YOU ONE.
MY PLEASURE.
31

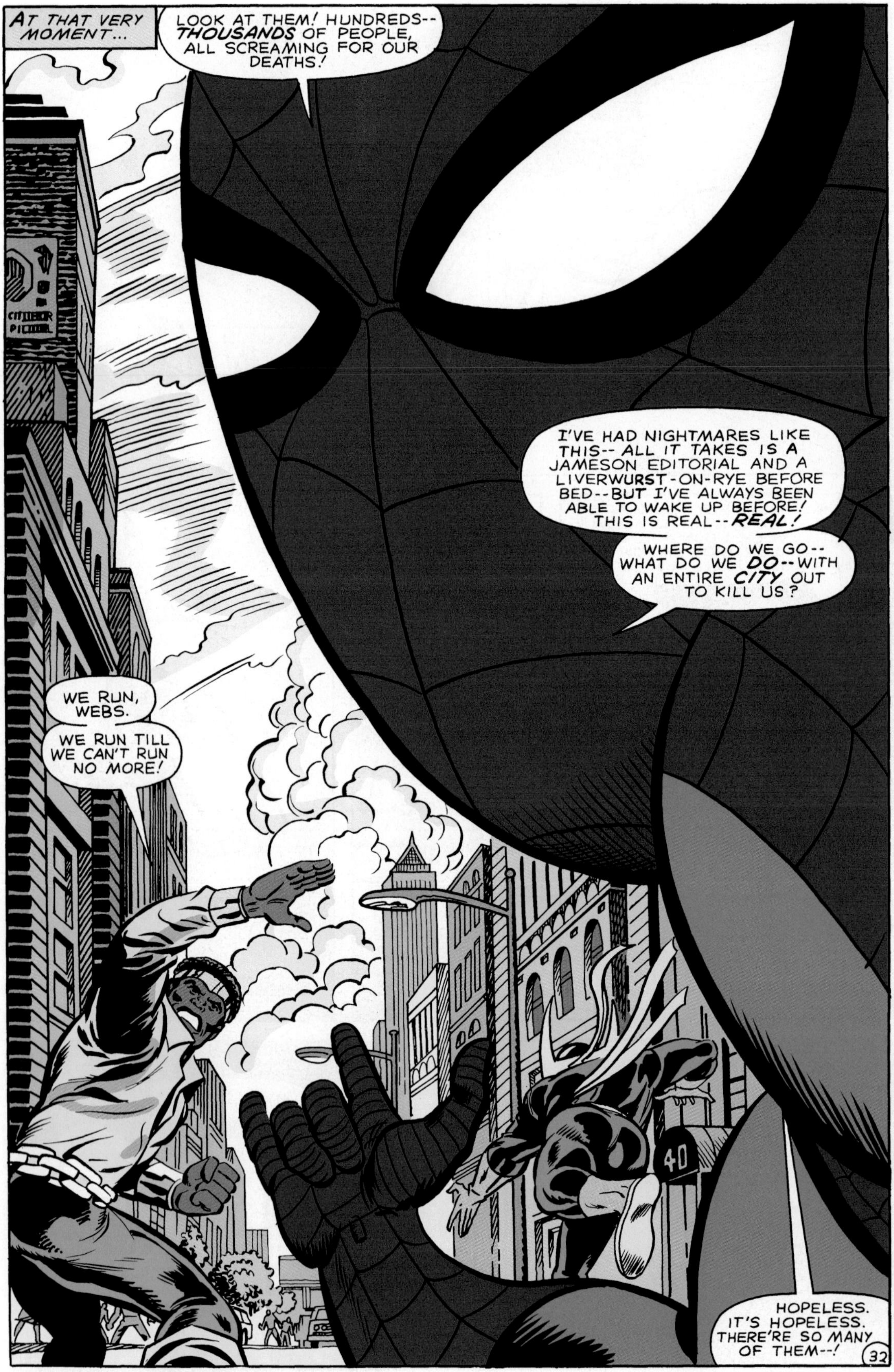
AT THAT VERY MOMENT...
LOOK AT THEM! HUNDREDS-- THOUSANDS OF PEOPLE, ALL SCREAMING FOR OUR DEATHS!
I'VE HAD NIGHTMARES LIKE THIS-- ALL IT TAKES IS A JAMESON EDITORIAL AND A LIVERWURST-ON-RYE BEFORE BED--BUT I'VE ALWAYS BEEN ABLE TO WAKE UP BEFORE! THIS IS REAL--REAL!
WHERE DO WE GO-- WHAT DO WE DO--WITH AN ENTIRE CITY OUT TO KILL US?
WE RUN, WEBS.
WE RUN TILL WE CAN'T RUN NO MORE!
40
HOPELESS. IT'S HOPELESS. THERE'RE SO MANY OF THEM--!
32

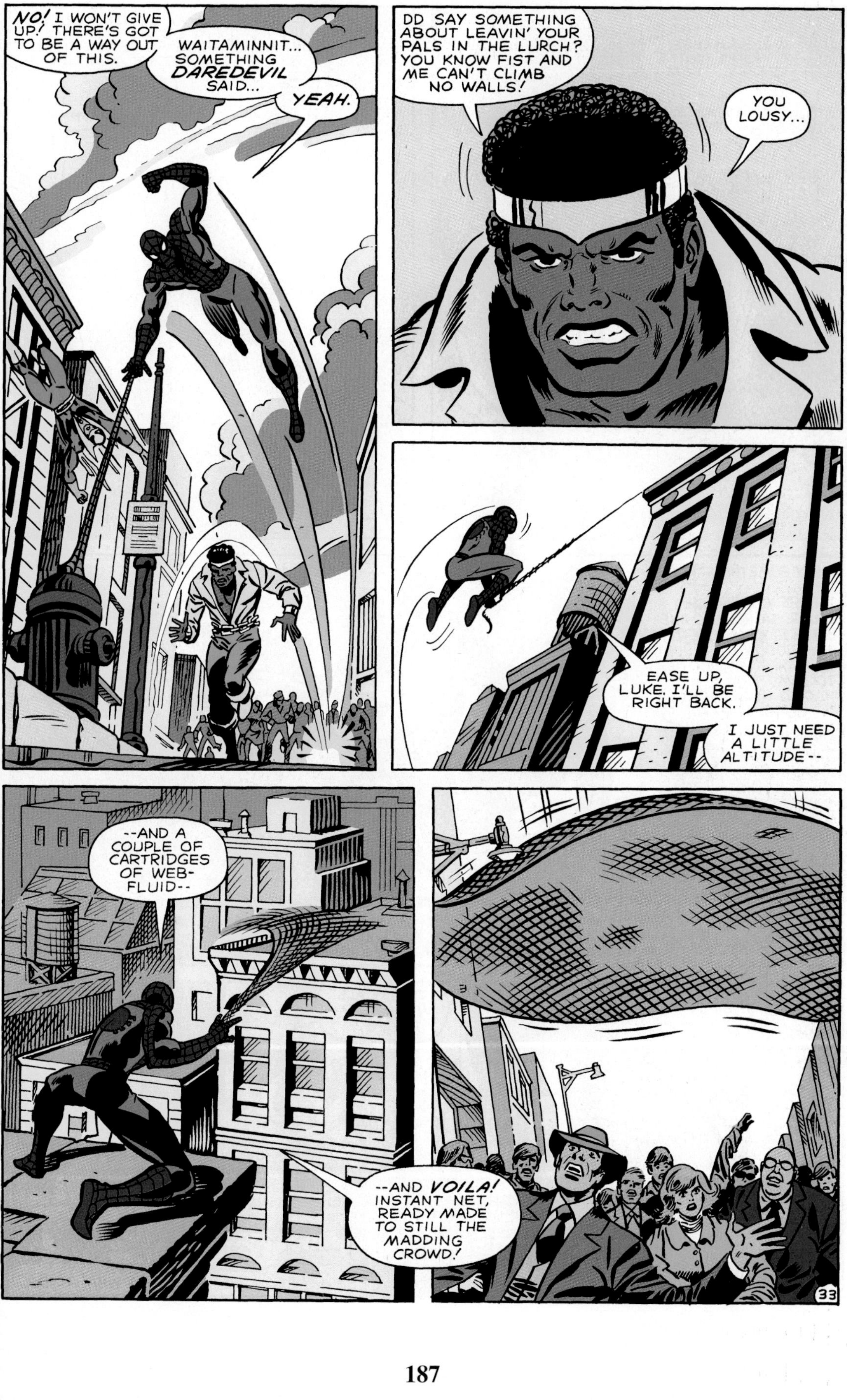
NO! I WON'T GIVE UP! THERE'S GOT TO BE A WAY OUT OF THIS.
WAITAMINNIT... SOMETHING DAREDEVIL SAID...
YEAH.
DD SAY SOMETHING ABOUT LEAVIN' YOUR PALS IN THE LURCH? YOU KNOW FIST AND ME CAN'T CLIMB NO WALLS!
YOU LOUSY...
EASE UP, LUKE. I'LL BE RIGHT BACK.
I JUST NEED A LITTLE ALTITUDE--
--AND A COUPLE OF CARTRIDGES OF WEB-FLUID--
--AND VOILA! INSTANT NET, READY MADE TO STILL THE MADDING CROWD!
33

WELL, MAYBE IT WON'T QUITE *STILL* THEM--

--BUT IT'LL SURE AS HECK SLOW THEM DOWN!

OKAY, GENTS. THIS IS IT. DO AS I SAY, OR WE'RE AS DEAD AS LAST WEEK'S MEATLOAF!

SO *SAY* SOMETHING, MAN!

"SAY SOMETHING"? I HOPE YOU REALIZE YOU'RE TALKING TO THE BIGGEST **CHATTERBOX** IN HERODOM! WHY JUST THE OTHER DAY, DOC OCK TOLD ME THAT IF HE HAD TO HEAR ANOTHER WORD, HE'D--

SO SHUT UP!

THAT'S MORE LIKE IT!

WATCH THE SHIRT, WEBS!

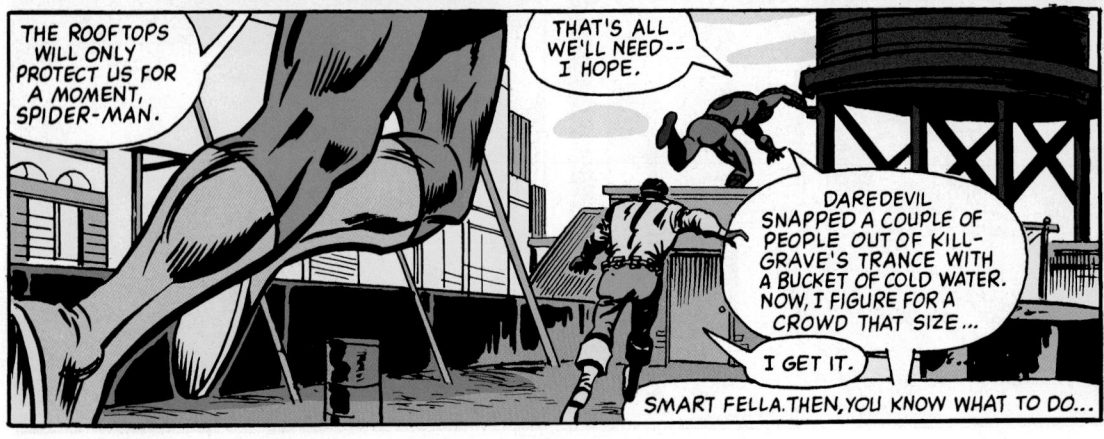

THE ROOFTOPS WILL ONLY PROTECT US FOR A MOMENT, SPIDER-MAN.

THAT'S ALL WE'LL NEED-- I HOPE.

DAREDEVIL SNAPPED A COUPLE OF PEOPLE OUT OF KILLGRAVE'S TRANCE WITH A BUCKET OF COLD WATER. NOW, I FIGURE FOR A CROWD THAT SIZE...

I GET IT.

SMART FELLA. THEN, YOU KNOW WHAT TO DO...

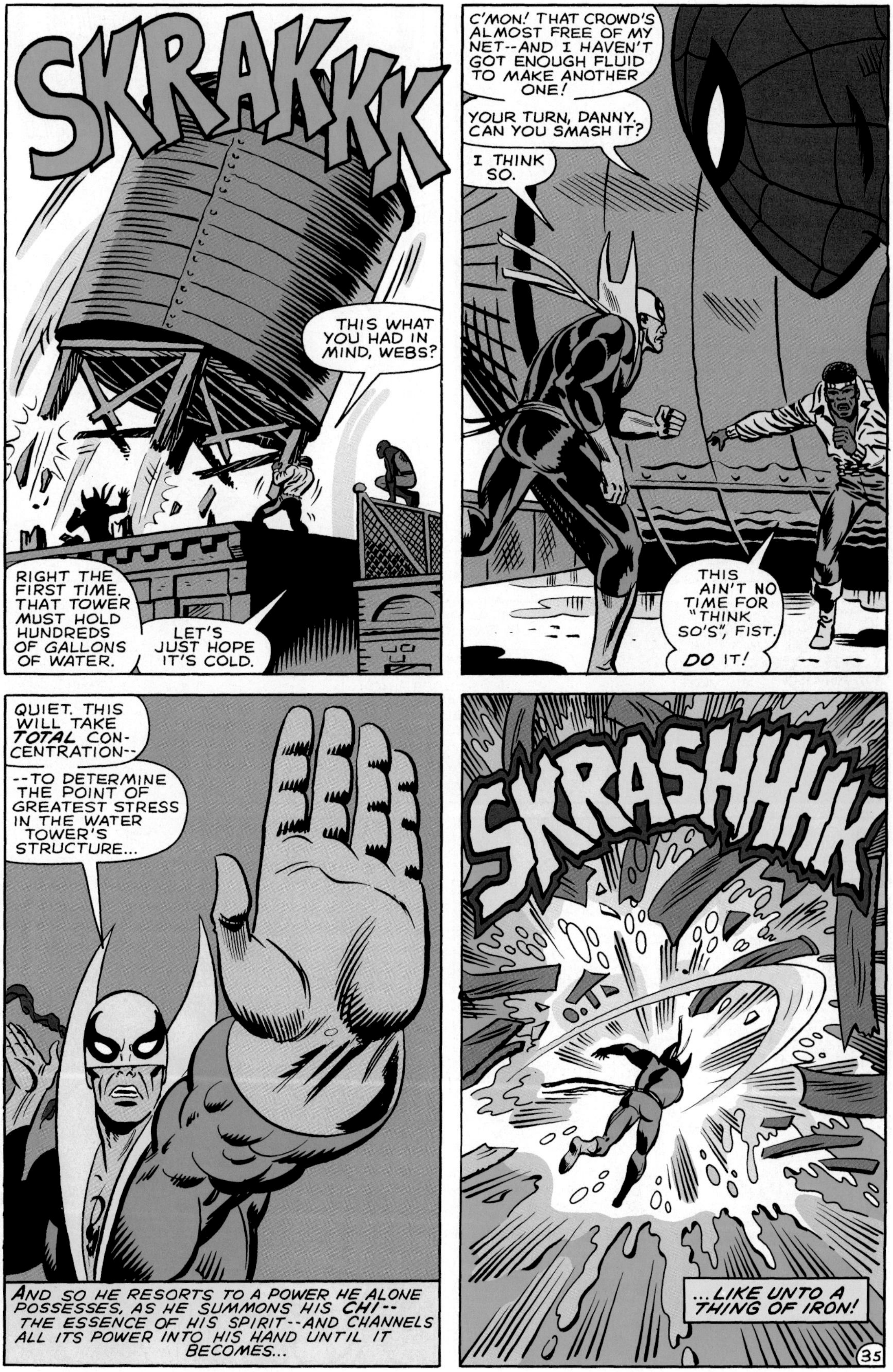
SKRAKKK
THIS WHAT YOU HAD IN MIND, WEBS?
RIGHT THE FIRST TIME. THAT TOWER MUST HOLD HUNDREDS OF GALLONS OF WATER.
LET'S JUST HOPE IT'S COLD.
C'MON! THAT CROWD'S ALMOST FREE OF MY NET--AND I HAVEN'T GOT ENOUGH FLUID TO MAKE ANOTHER ONE!
YOUR TURN, DANNY. CAN YOU SMASH IT?
I THINK SO.
THIS AIN'T NO TIME FOR "THINK SO'S", FIST.
DO IT!
QUIET. THIS WILL TAKE TOTAL CONCENTRATION--
--TO DETERMINE THE POINT OF GREATEST STRESS IN THE WATER TOWER'S STRUCTURE...
AND SO HE RESORTS TO A POWER HE ALONE POSSESSES, AS HE SUMMONS HIS CHI -- THE ESSENCE OF HIS SPIRIT--AND CHANNELS ALL ITS POWER INTO HIS HAND UNTIL IT BECOMES...
SKRASHHHK
...LIKE UNTO A THING OF IRON!
35

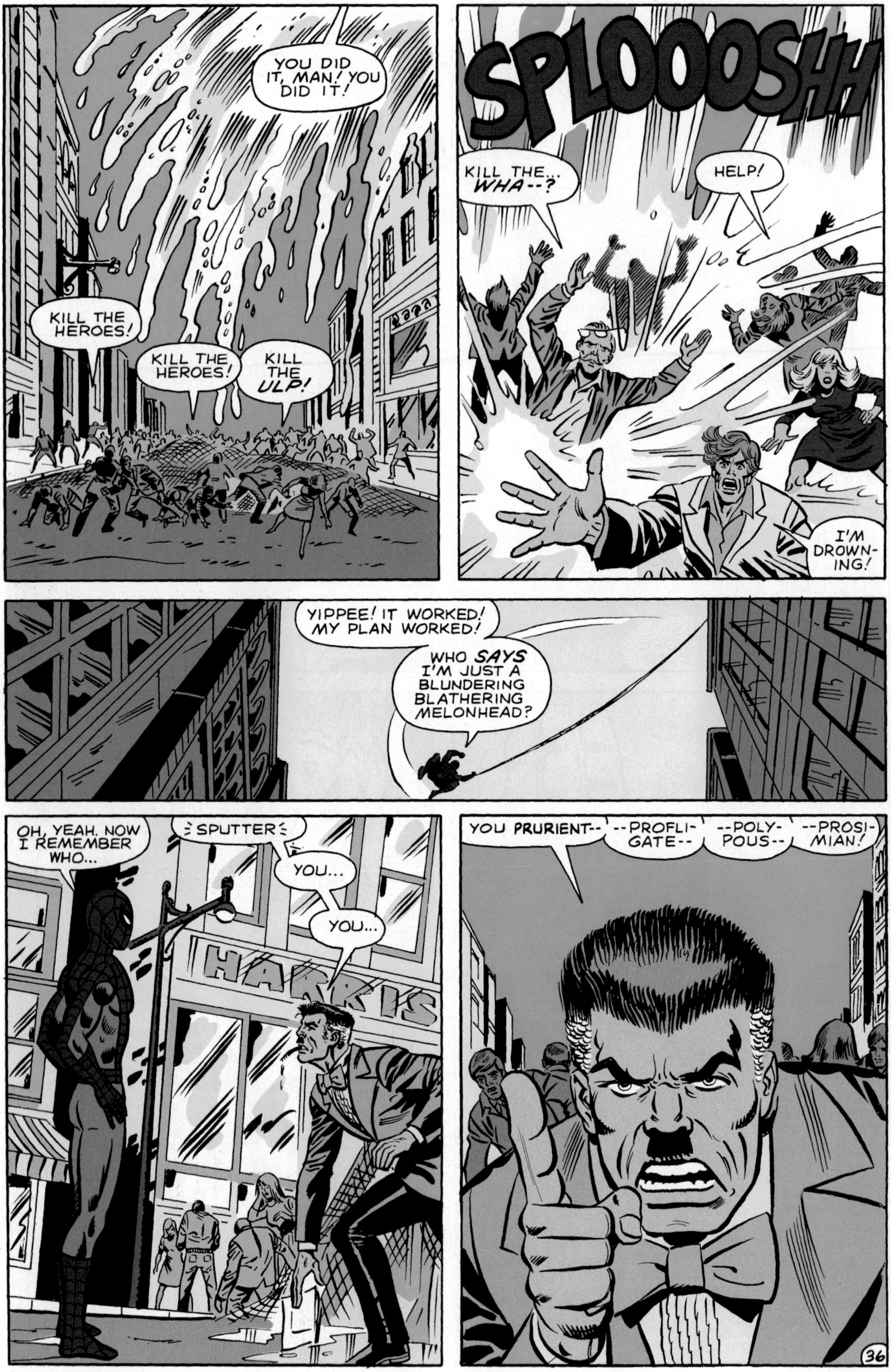
YOU DID IT, MAN! YOU DID IT!
KILL THE HEROES!
KILL THE HEROES!
KILL THE ULP!
SPLOOOSHH
KILL THE... WHA--?
HELP!
I'M DROWNING!
YIPPEE! IT WORKED! MY PLAN WORKED!
WHO SAYS I'M JUST A BLUNDERING BLATHERING MELONHEAD?
OH, YEAH. NOW I REMEMBER WHO...
SPUTTER
YOU...
YOU...
HARRIS
YOU PRURIENT--
--PROFLIGATE--
--POLYPOUS--
--PROSIMIAN!
36

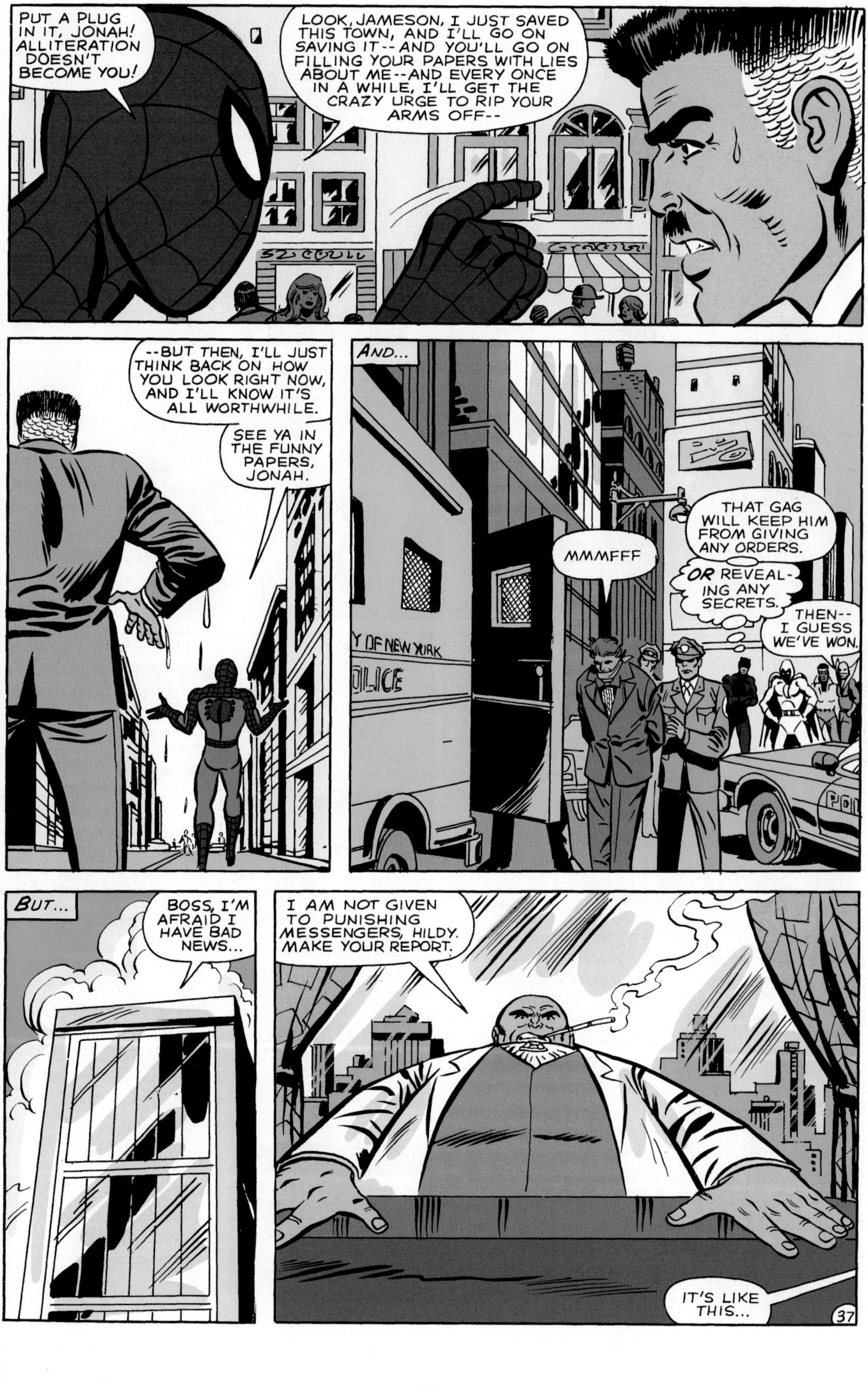
PUT A PLUG IN IT, JONAH! ALLITERATION DOESN'T BECOME YOU!
LOOK, JAMESON, I JUST SAVED THIS TOWN, AND I'LL GO ON SAVING IT-- AND YOU'LL GO ON FILLING YOUR PAPERS WITH LIES ABOUT ME--AND EVERY ONCE IN A WHILE, I'LL GET THE CRAZY URGE TO RIP YOUR ARMS OFF--
--BUT THEN, I'LL JUST THINK BACK ON HOW YOU LOOK RIGHT NOW, AND I'LL KNOW IT'S ALL WORTHWHILE.
SEE YA IN THE FUNNY PAPERS, JONAH.
AND...
MMMFFF
THAT GAG WILL KEEP HIM FROM GIVING ANY ORDERS.
OR REVEAL-ING ANY SECRETS.
THEN-- I GUESS WE'VE WON.
BUT...
BOSS, I'M AFRAID I HAVE BAD NEWS...
I AM NOT GIVEN TO PUNISHING MESSENGERS, HILDY. MAKE YOUR REPORT.
IT'S LIKE THIS...
37

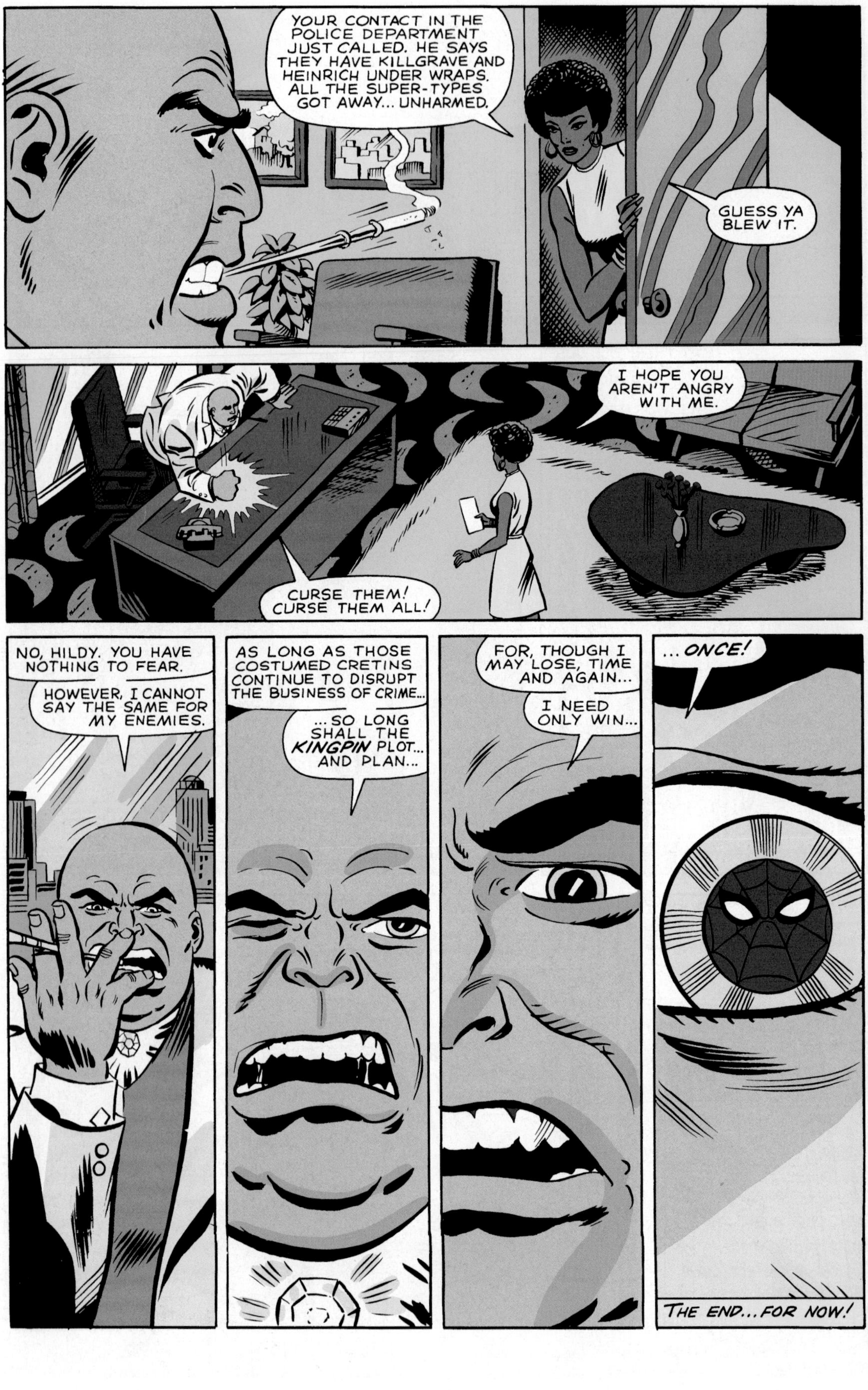

YOUR CONTACT IN THE POLICE DEPARTMENT JUST CALLED. HE SAYS THEY HAVE KILLGRAVE AND HEINRICH UNDER WRAPS. ALL THE SUPER-TYPES GOT AWAY... UNHARMED.
GUESS YA BLEW IT.
I HOPE YOU AREN'T ANGRY WITH ME.
CURSE THEM! CURSE THEM ALL!
NO, HILDY. YOU HAVE NOTHING TO FEAR.
HOWEVER, I CANNOT SAY THE SAME FOR MY ENEMIES.
AS LONG AS THOSE COSTUMED CRETINS CONTINUE TO DISRUPT THE BUSINESS OF CRIME...
...SO LONG SHALL THE KINGPIN PLOT... AND PLAN...
FOR, THOUGH I MAY LOSE, TIME AND AGAIN...
I NEED ONLY WIN...
...ONCE!
THE END... FOR NOW!

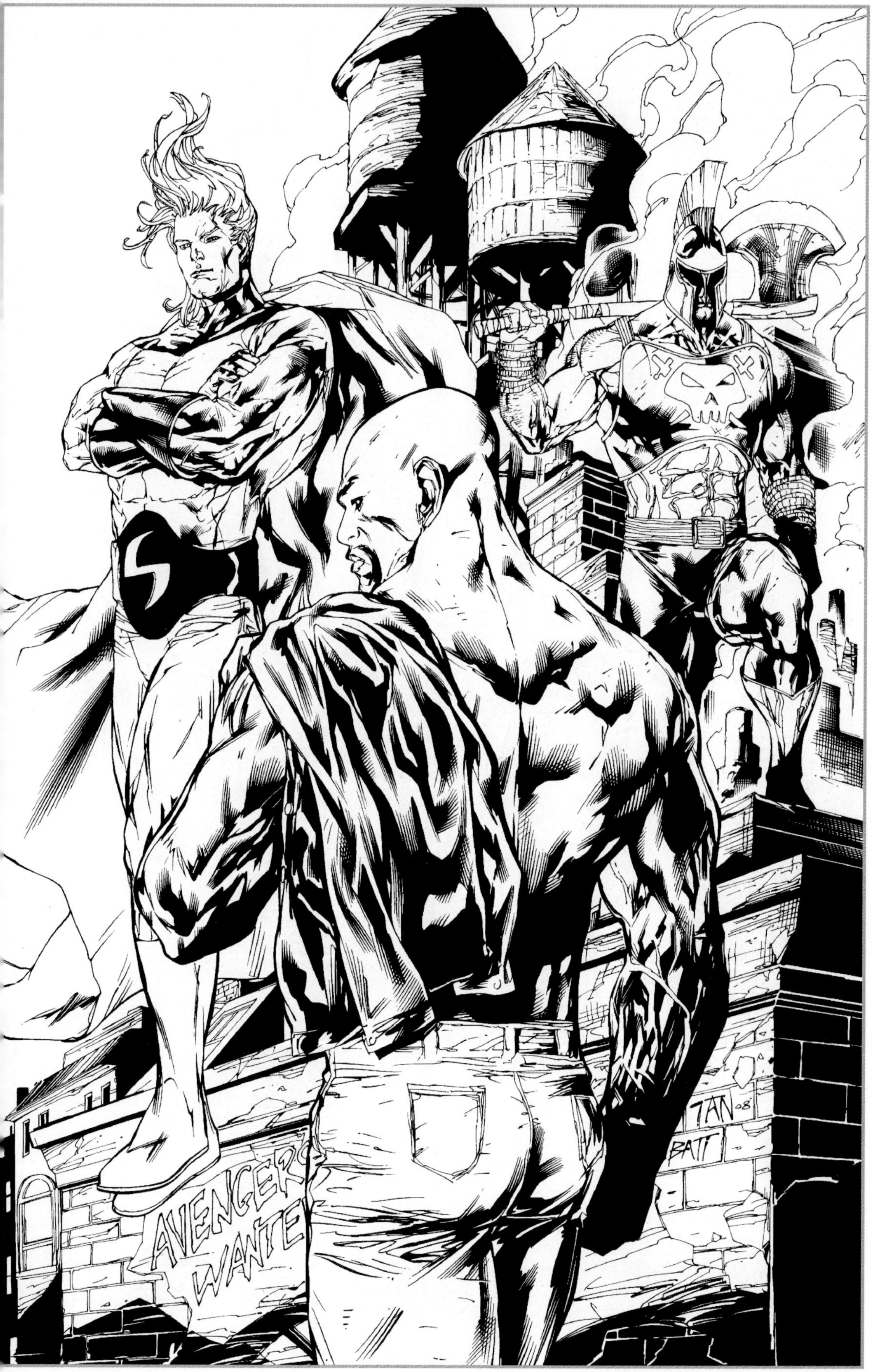
AVENGERS
WANTE
TAN '08
BATT

BILLY TAN & BATT

NEW AVENGERS #49 2ND-PRINTING B&W VARIANT

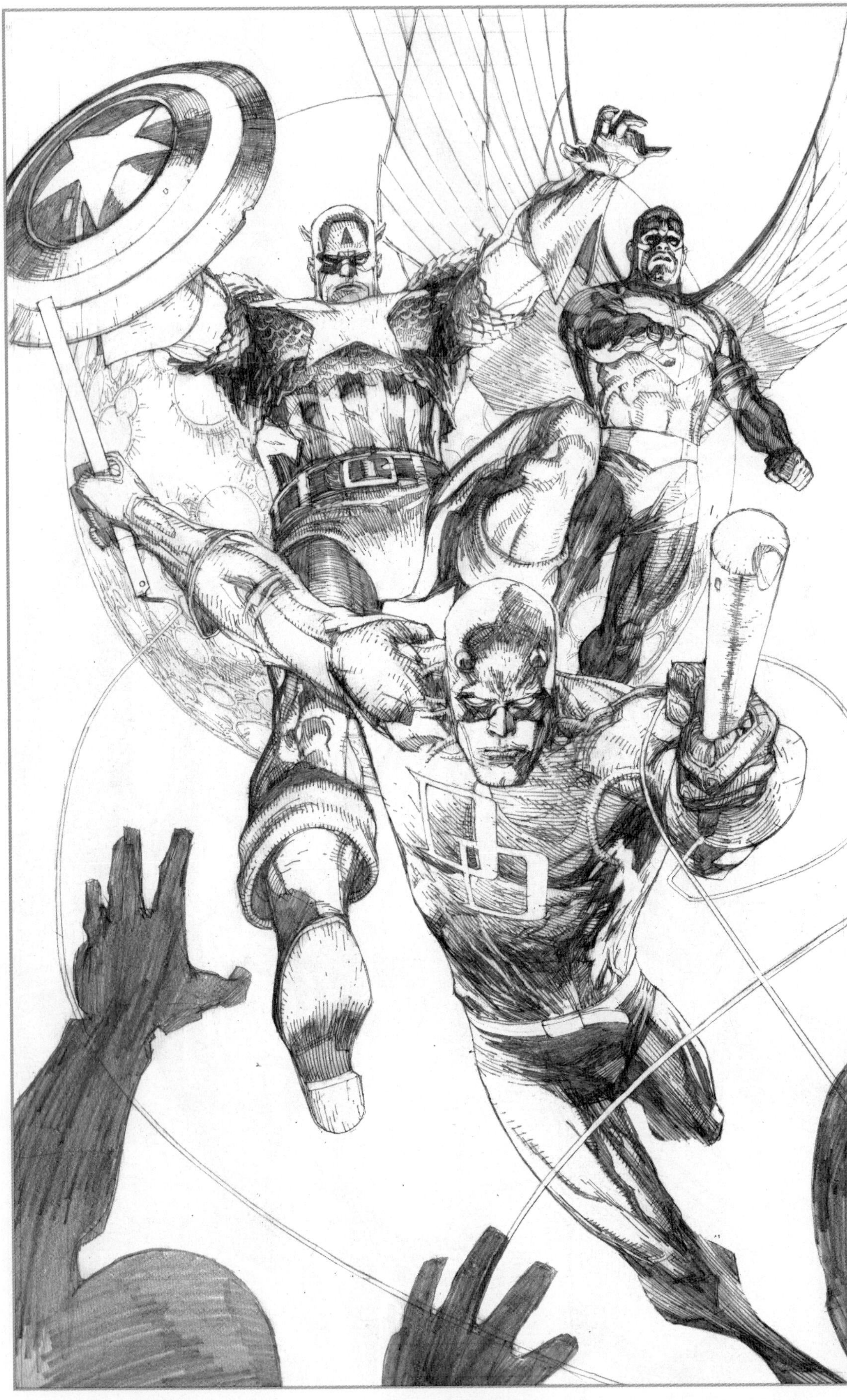

LEINIL FRANCIS YU

NEW AVENGERS #22, PAGE 17 PENCILS

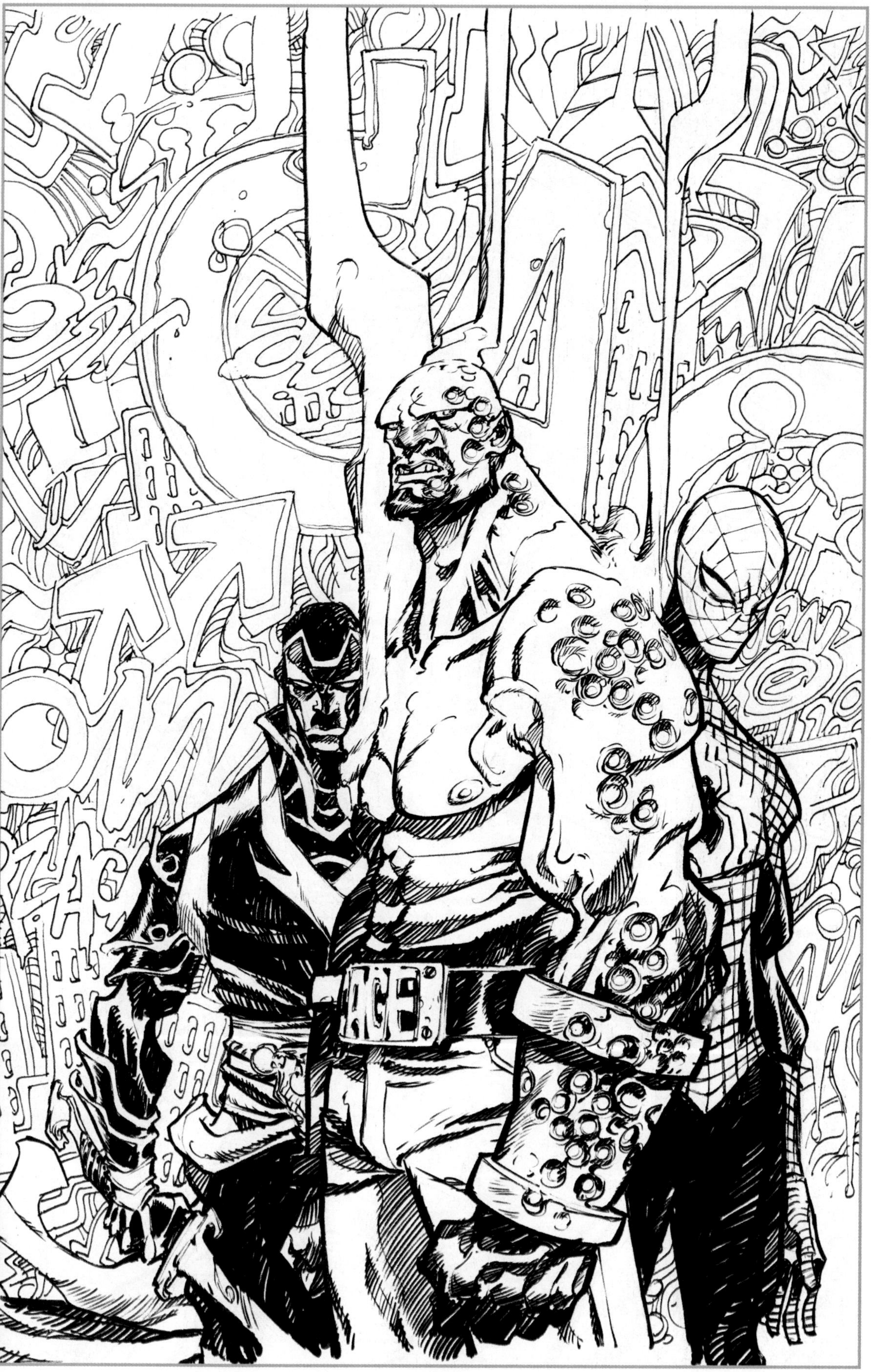

ERIC CANETE

NEW AVENGERS: LUKE CAGE #1 COVER INKS

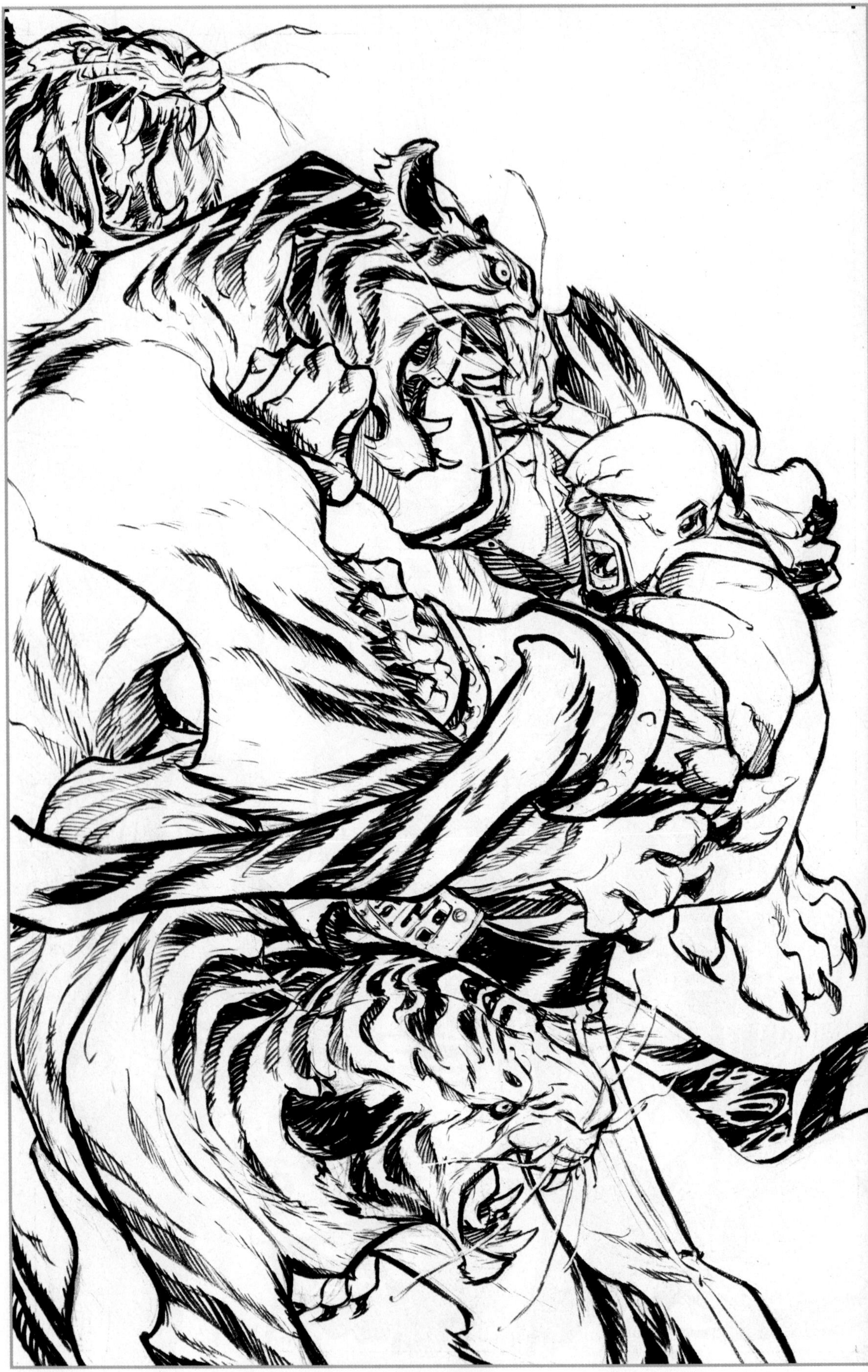

ERIC CANETE

NEW AVENGERS: LUKE CAGE #2 COVER INKS

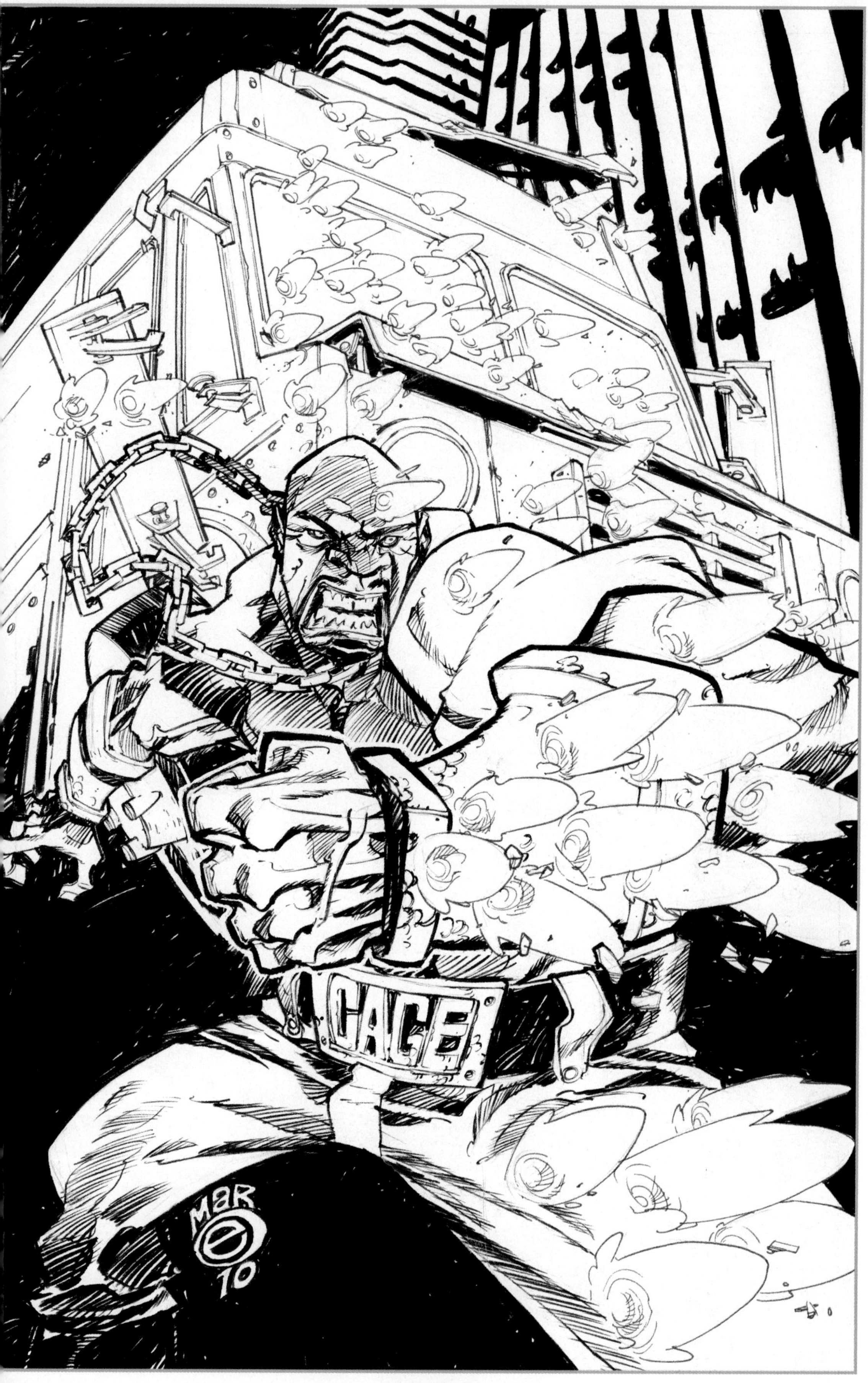
CAGE
MAR
10

ERIC CANETE

NEW AVENGERS: LUKE CAGE #3 COVER INKS

AVENGERS EXTRA!

by Jess Harrold

Before he united with long-time partner Iron Fist, before he became a team player with the New Avengers, before he became a leader of men in the pages of Thunderbolts, Luke Cage was a solo hero to the people on the streets of Harlem. Now, in a series set in the last days of Norman Osborn's Dark Reign, writer John Arcudi and artist Eric Canete take him back to his roots, in tone if not geographically, in the pages of *New Avengers: Luke Cage.*

Describing the series, John says: "Luke takes a closer look at his 'Hero for Hire' days through the eyes of an old friend, or rather the son of a friend. And what he sees takes him back to street- level crime (and punishment). This is where he came from; a world where super heroes usually didn't exercise much influence. However, since Harlem has seen another renaissance of sorts, the setting is the seedier streets of North Philadelphia. The story takes place right before the Heroic Age. Luke is still classified as an outlaw and this status complicates his mission somewhat. He can't quite do business as he would like, and he can't involve law enforcement authorities without getting tangled up himself. But the funny thing about that is that he learns a new way to achieve justice. Not the usual vigilante type either. It's kinda neat."

No less neat is the work of series artist Eric Canete. "Eric's work is dynamic and graceful all at once," John says. "There is a brutal fight scene in the first issue and Eric doesn't flinch in his depiction. The impact of each blow is right there on the page, but then he can make a slum look gorgeous with all this detail. And his tigers are awesome! (Oops, did I say tigers?)"

John's unleashing tigers on an urban jungle, and as far as the writer is concerned, that's where Luke Cage works best – making a difference on the streets. "It seems to me Luke has grown more as a man than as a hero," John says. "He's in a committed relationship with a woman and with a child and he's making it work. How many other Marvel Universe characters can you say that about? He's mature in the most meaningful sense of the word. But isn't there still some part of him that chafes at his role as an Avenger? He does what he's supposed to, he's responsible to the team, but he's not really a cheerleader, and his language and demeanor reflect that."

As a result, he says that Luke's teammates won't feature too prominently in the story: "This is more or less a solo project that Luke takes on, one he probably couldn't convince the other Avengers to take an interest in anyway. They make brief appearances in the first and third issues, but this is really all about Luke and who he is."

As for that wife and child he mentions, John says that Jessica Jones and baby Danielle don't appear on panel very much in *New Avengers: Luke Cage*. However, he says: "Luke's family life is a large part of what makes the story so pressing. Their presence is felt in every issue by Luke, and he comes away at the end of the series with a finer appreciation for his home life and how far he's come."

> **"He's in a committed relationship with a woman and with a child and he's making it work."**
>
> *– New Avengers: Luke Cage* writer John Arcudi

Luke will also come away with his fair share of bruises if the series antagonist has anything to say about it – a certain flat-topped gangster more used to clashing heads with Luke's Avengers pal, Spider-Man. "If I wanted this to be 'street level' sort of story, I needed to dig up a less-than-world-devouring villain who was still tough enough to give Luke a good fight. Hammerhead in his suit and tie seemed perfect. And since this story is concerned with elements of organized crime, again, who better than Hammerhead?"

Who better indeed?

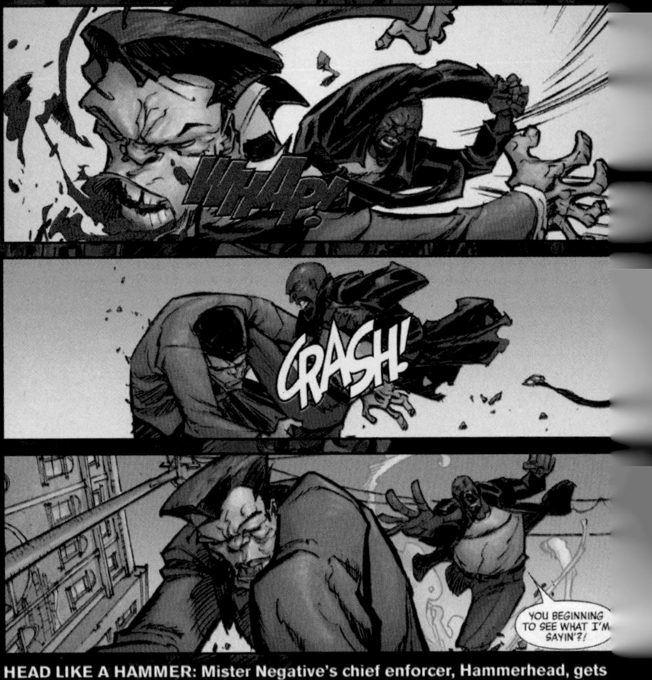
CRASH!
YOU BEGINNING TO SEE WHAT I'M SAYIN'?!

HEAD LIKE A HAMMER: Mister Negative's chief enforcer, Hammerhead, gets told off by Luke Cage. (Art from *NA:LC* #1 by Canete.)

ARTICLE EXCERPT FROM *AVENGERS SPOTLIGHT* (2010)

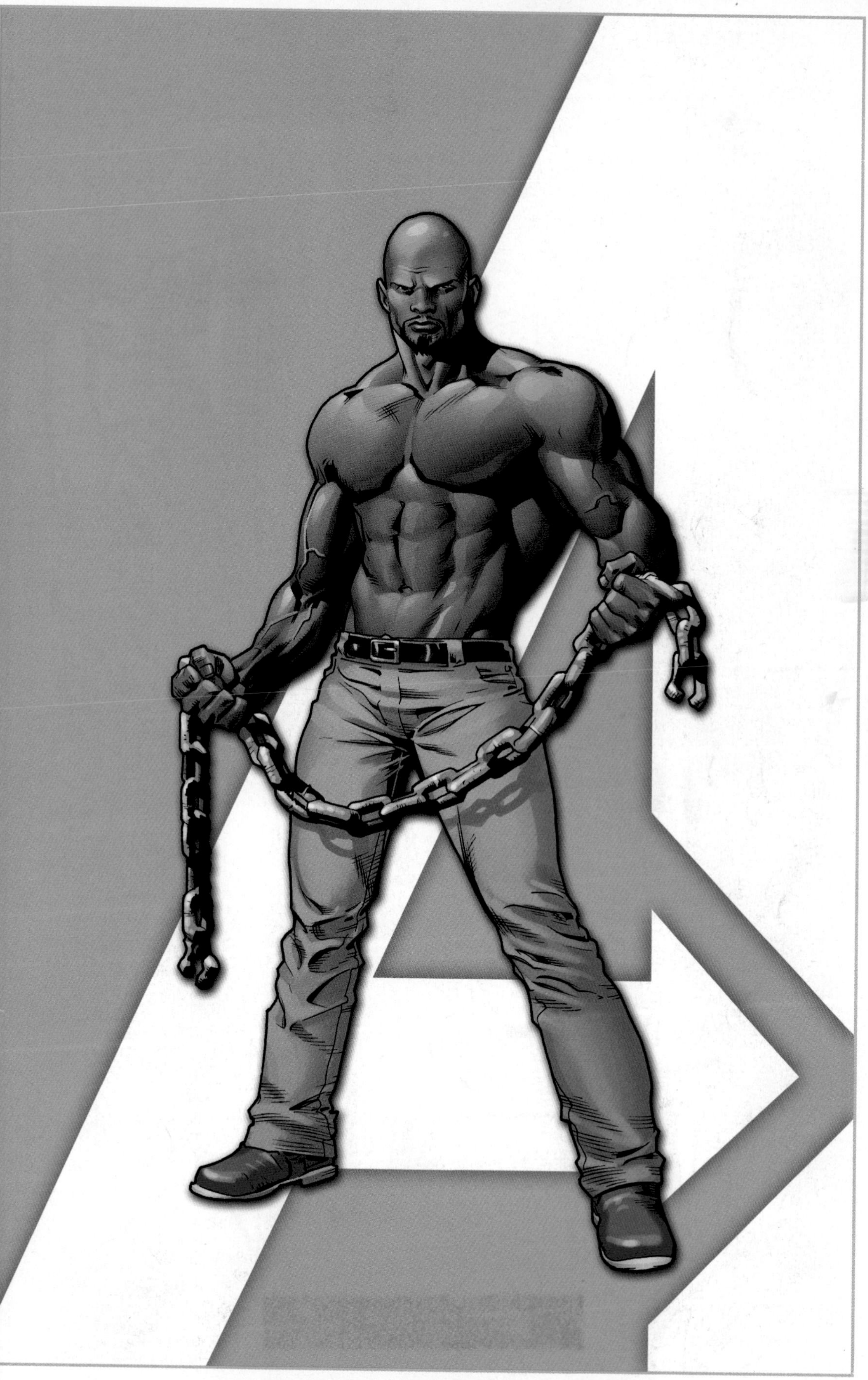

STUART IMMONEN, WADE VON GRAWBADGER & LAURA MARTIN

NEW AVENGERS (2010) #1 VARIANT

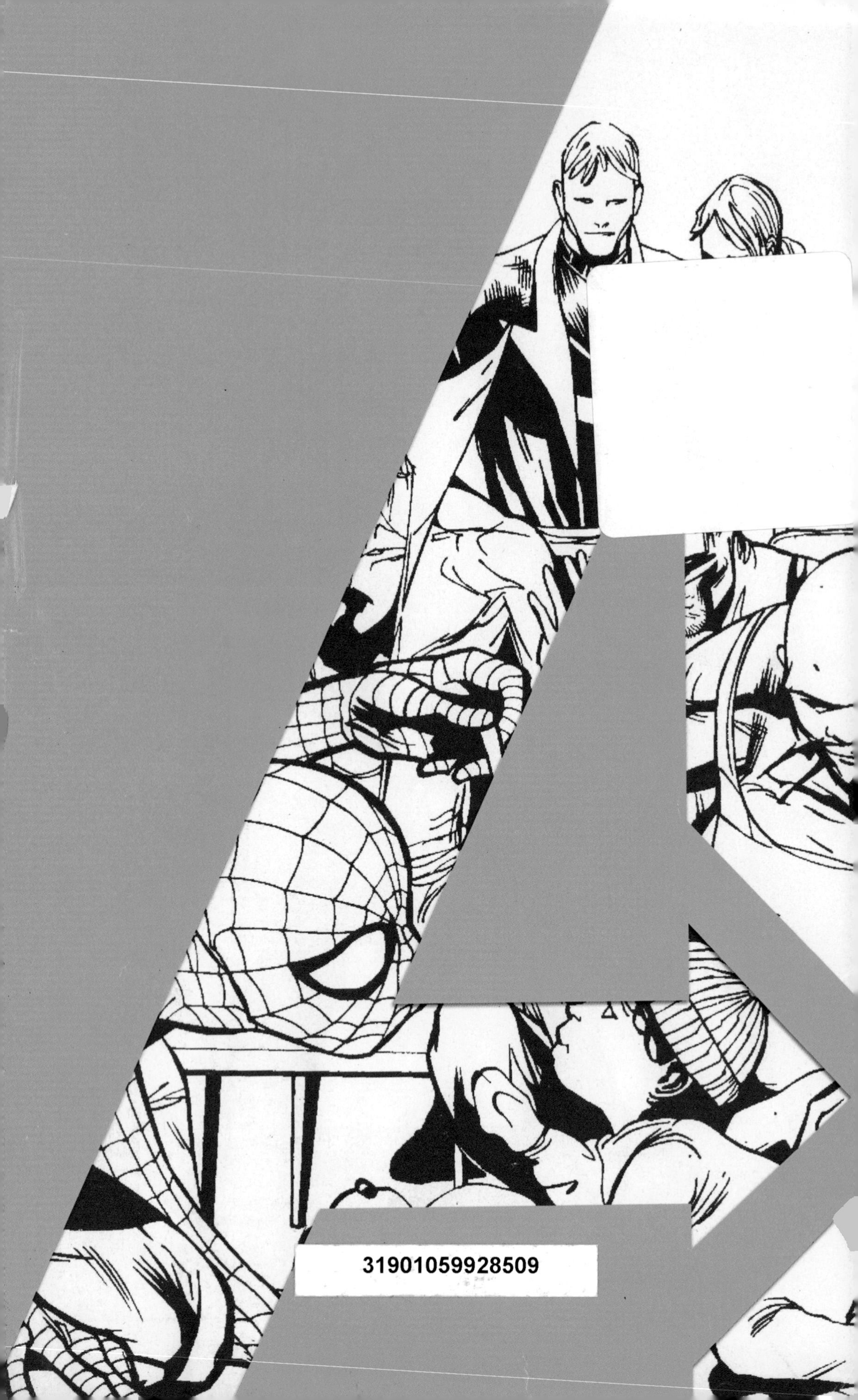